W9-AZT-303

THE FIRST WORLD WAR IN

100

OBJECTS

A FIREFLY BOOK

Published by Firefly Books Ltd. 2014

Copyright © 2014 Octopus Publishing Group Ltd
Text copyright © 2014 John Hughes-Wilson
Object text copyright © 2014 Imperial War
Museums

All rights reserved. No part of this publication
may be reproduced, stored in a retrieval system,
or transmitted in any form or by any means,
electronic, mechanical, photocopying, recording or
otherwise, without the prior written permission of
the Publisher.

First printing

Publisher Cataloging-in-Publication Data (U.S.)

A CIP record for this title is available from the
Library of Congress

**Library and Archives Canada Cataloguing in
Publication**

A CIP record for this title is available from Library
and Archives Canada

Published in the United States by
Firefly Books (U.S.) Inc.
P.O. Box 1338, Ellicott Station
Buffalo, New York 14205

Published in Canada by
Firefly Books Ltd.
50 Staples Avenue, Unit 1
Richmond Hill, Ontario L4B 0A7

Printed and bound in China

This book is dedicated to the memory
of Professor and Brigadier Richard
Holmes, CBE, TD; scholar, gentleman
and soldier patron and founder of the
Guild of Battlefield Guides

Conceived, designed, and produced by
by Cassell, an imprint of
Octopus Publishing Group Ltd,
Endeavour House,
189 Shaftesbury Avenue,
London, WC2H 8JY
www.octopusbooks.co.uk

For Cassell:
Group Publishing Director: Denise Bates
Senior Managing Editor: Clare Churly
Managing Editor: Mark Hawkins-Dady
Art Director: Jonathan Christie
Designer: David Rowley
Map illustrations: Nick Rowland
Picture Researcher: Jennifer Veall
Assistant Production Manager: Caroline Alberti

THE FIRST WORLD WAR IN
100
OBJECTS

John Hughes-Wilson

IWM Consultant, Nigel Steel
Editor, Mark Hawkins-Dady

FIREFLY BOOKS

INTRODUCTION 8

PART 1

**IMPERIALISM, NATIONALISM
& THE ROAD TO WAR** 10

01 KING GEORGE'S IMPERIAL CROWN 12
The Heyday of the British Empire

02 THE PEN THAT SIGNED THE
ULSTER COVENANT 16
British Troubles & Irish Tensions

03 A PRUSSIAN *PICKELHAUBE* 20
Prussian Militarism & Germany's Rise

04 SERGEANT MILLER'S RECRUITMENT SIGN 24
Anglo-German Naval Rivalry

05 A MAP OF EUROPEAN RIVALRY 28
Europe's Alliances & Animosities

06 THE ARCHDUKE'S BLOODSTAINED
TUNIC 32
Assassination & the Road to War

PART 2

THE SHOCK OF THE NEW 38

07 THE NEW PAPER MONEY 40
British War Measures & "DORA"

08 "YOUR COUNTRY NEEDS YOU" 44
Lord Kitchener & the Recruitment Drive

09 THE NEWCASTLE COMMERCIALS' DRUM 48
Pals Battalions

10 HMS *LANCE*'S 4-INCH GUN 50
The Opening of Naval Hostilities

11 GERMAN JACKBOOTS 54
The Schlieffen Plan & German Invasion

12 *PANTALONS ROUGES* –
"A NATIONAL AFFAIR!" 58
The Battle of the Frontiers

13 AN ATROCITY POSTER 62
German Atrocities & Schrecklichkeit

14 PATTERN 1908 WEB EQUIPMENT 66
The British Expeditionary Force Joins Battle

15 B43 – A LONDON BUS AT THE FRONT 70
The BEF & the First Battle of Ypres

16 AN IRON CROSS FOR "BABY-KILLERS" 74
German Bombardment & the Battle of Dogger Bank

17 ERIC ROWDEN'S CHRISTMAS BUTTON 78
The Christmas Truce

18 AUSTRIAN COMMEMORATIVE RIBBONS 80
Tannenberg & the Eastern Front

19 BARNARDISTON'S SAMURAI SWORD 86
Japan Enters the War

20 THE IMPERIAL EAGLE IN AFRICA 88
The War in Africa

21 ADMIRAL SOUCHON'S MEDALS 92
The Ottoman Empire Enters the War

PART 3
THEATRES OF WAR 96

22 A PIG CALLED TIRPITZ 98
War in the Pacific & South Atlantic

23 MAJOR ANDERSON'S STICK 102
The Mesopotamian Campaign

24 AN AUSTRALIAN BATTALION'S FLAG 106
The Gallipoli Campaign

25 AN ITALIAN TRENCH HELMET 112
Italy in the First World War

26 THE HIGHLANDERS' BULGARIAN MAXIM 118
Salonika & the Balkan Front

27 A *LUSITANIA* SURVIVOR'S CAMISOLE 122
Unrestricted Submarine Warfare

28 A ZEPPELIN'S AMMUNITION BOX 126
The Aerial Bombing of Britain

29 A TICKET COLLECTOR'S HAT 130
Women's Work in Wartime Britain

30 THE MUNITIONETTES' FIRST
HEAVY SHELL 134
The Struggle to Produce Munitions

31 KAISER BILL TOILET ROLL 138
Propaganda in the War

32 NURSE CAVELL'S SECRET DIARY 142
The Creation of an Icon

33 CAPTAIN FRYATT'S WATCH 144
Defying the U-Boats

34 WILLIAM HARRISON'S NO-CONSCRIPTION
FELLOWSHIP CARD 146
Enlistment to Conscription

35 THE "MOTHER" OF GUNS 150
Artillery in the First World War

36 THE VICKERS MACHINE GUN 154
Machine Guns on the Western Front

37 A MESSAGE STREAMER 158
The Early Air War

38 A TRENCH SHOVEL 162
War in the Trenches

39 A PETRIFIED GLOVE 166
Gas Warfare & the Second Battle of Ypres

40 CONWAY JACKSON'S PRAYER BOOK 170
The Battle of Loos

41 THE FULLERPHONE 174
Communications in the War

42 A DECEPTIVE TREE 178
Camouflage in the War

43 THE GEOPHONE 180
Military Mining in the War

44 CAPTAIN SHAW'S ESCAPE AIDS 184
Prisoners of War

45 "WAR DOG 180" 188
Animals on the Frontline

46 MAIRI CHISHOLM'S DECORATIONS 192
Military Medals

CONTENTS

PART 4
MUD & BLOOD 196

47 PRIVATE BÉRENGER'S *ADRIAN* HELMET 198
Helmets for the Troops

48 WILLIAM SHORT'S BRODIE HELMET 202
The Road to the Somme

49 HAROLD STARTIN'S TRENCH CLUB 206
Trenches – a Day in the Life

50 THE *SOIXANTE-QUINZE* FIELD GUN 210
Assault on Verdun

51 POSTCARD FROM THE EASTERN FRONT 216
The Brusilov Offensive

52 BILLIE NEVILL'S FOOTBALL 220
The First Day of the Somme

53 HAROLD COPE'S JACKET 224
Continuation of the Somme Campaign

54 A FILM PROGRAMME 228
Tanks & the End of the Somme

55 ARMY RATIONS 232
Food in the Trenches

56 A DUMMY CALLED "DOUGLAS" 234
Relaxation at the Front

57 A FRENCH PHRASE BOOK 238
The British Soldier Abroad

58 TUBBY CLAYTON'S CHALICE 240
Consolation & Human Contact

59 A BODY DENSITY MAP 244
Casualties on the Western Front

60 A BAIRNSFATHER CARTOON 248
Soldiers on Leave

61 LAST REMAINS OF HMS *INDEFATIGABLE* 252
The Battle of Jutland

62 A U-BOAT'S WIRELESS RECEIVER 258
Submarine Warfare After Jutland

63 EDWARD THOMAS'S LAST WORDS 262
A "Lost Generation"?

64 THE EASTER REBELS' SURRENDER 266
Ireland's Easter Rising

65 MODEL PRIME MINISTERS 270
A Change of Leadership

66 THE STARS & STRIPES 274
America Enters the War

67 A BOLSHEVIK BANNER 278
Russia in Turmoil

68 CULLEY'S SOPWITH CAMEL 282
The Battle for the Skies

69 A TRENCH MORTAR FROM VIMY 286
The Battle of Arras & Nivelle's Offensive

70 A TOY SOLDIER 292
Mutinies in the French Army

71 A GERMAN OFFICER'S CAP 294
The Third Battle of Ypres – "Passchendaele"

72 GORDON HASSELL'S TANK MASK 300
The Battle of Cambrai

73 A SIMPLEX TRENCH LOCOMOTIVE 304
Logistics in the War

74 THE "C TYPE" AERIAL CAMERA 308
British Intelligence During the War

75 PRIVATE HIGHGATE'S CHARGE SHEET 312
Military Discipline & Deserters

76 SIEGFRIED SASSOON'S REVOLVER 316
Writers at War

77 JOHN SINGER SARGENT'S *GASSED* 320
Artists' Responses to the War

78 A HANUKKAH LAMP FROM JERUSALEM 326
The Palestine Campaign

79 LAWRENCE OF ARABIA'S RIFLE 330
T.E. Lawrence & the Arab Revolt

PART 5
FROM NEAR-DEFEAT TO VICTORY 334

80 *THE FOOD QUEUE* 336
Shortages & Rationing In Britain

81 A RATION OF EGGS 340
Germany under the Blockade

82 THE PRESIDENT'S FOURTEEN POINTS 342
US Peace Feelers & Russian Exit

83 DAZZLE CAMOUFLAGE FOR SHIPS 346
Convoys & "Q" Ships

84 FIELD MARSHAL HAIG'S
SPECIAL ORDER 350
The German Spring Offensives – Kaiserschlacht

85 A TOBY JUG FOR THE FIELD MARSHAL 356
Generalship in the War

86 THE RED BARON'S BROKEN ENGINE 360
Fighter Aces & the Later Air War

87 A BRITISH MARK V TANK 364
The Black Day of the German Army

88 CAPTURED GERMAN
SHOULDER STRAPS 368
The Last Hundred Days

89 A WREATH FOR SALADIN 374
The End of the Palestine Campaign

90 AN *ERSATZ* NIGHTDRESS 378
The Collapse of the Central Powers

91 QUEEN MARY'S UNION JACK 384
The Armistice

92 "HANG THE KAISER" 388
The Khaki Election

PART 6
A NEW EUROPEAN LANDSCAPE 390

93 SIR WILLIAM ORPEN'S *UNKNOWN
BRITISH SOLDIER* 392
The Paris Peace Conference

94 A GUN TO SHOOT SEAGULLS 398
The End of the High Seas Fleet

95 A NEW STAMP FOR A NEW COUNTRY 402
The Birth of the League of Nations

96 THE OLD KAISER'S CROWN 406
Germany in Turmoil

97 AUGUSTUS AGAR'S BOAT 410
The Allies Versus the Bolsheviks

98 THE FAMOUS NÉRY GUN 414
The Creation of the Imperial War Museum

99 GUNNER MILLER'S CROSS 418
War Graves & Remembrance

100 A SKETCH FOR THE CENOTAPH 424
Enduring Symbols of the Great War

MAPS 428

FURTHER READING 440

INDEX 441

OBJECT SOURCE REFERENCES 447

ACKNOWLEDGEMENTS 448

CONTENTS

Without a doubt, the First World War changed everything. The years 1914–18 stand as a Rubicon over which all those who were involved in the war, directly and indirectly, were forced to cross. What seemed a gilded way of life of the late Edwardian era, imbued with wealth and empire and majesty, was lost as irretrievably as if a giant pair of iron gates had slammed shut across it.

Moreover, the seeds of so much discontent were sown in the war's immediate aftermath that they bore poisoned fruit over succeeding decades. The disillusionment that set in during the late 1920s led to appeasement in the face of aggressive dictators in the 1930s, and to yet another world war in the 1940s as – in the view of many – the First World War's unfinished business exploded again. Later, Communist Russia, born in the chaos of 1917, provided one side in a Cold War that framed world events from the 1950s to the 1980s, and which saw proxy "hot" wars in the Middle East, Africa and Asia. In the 1990s and 2000s even renewed worries about Germany's power and the outbreak of Balkan violence returned, so familiar from 1914. In short, so much of what defines us and our world in the early 21st century can be traced back to "The Great War for Civilization".

The story of that war has been told many times, but this book offers a fresh approach. As its starting point it takes the material legacy of the war. Thousands of different objects and artefacts dating back to 1914–18 survive, ranging from the mundane to the extraordinary, from the terrifying to the humorous. Each has its own story to tell. Here, 100 of these micro-stories form a spine around which has been woven a comprehensive narrative relating what happened in the run up to the war, during the war itself and in its immediate aftermath.

As a result, this book offers a multi-track approach. For a straightforward, full narrative, readers can start at the beginning and move forward, following developments on a broadly chronological basis. They can trace events as they played out over several continents – events which led to the demise of four empires (German, Austro-Hungarian, Russian and Ottoman) and casualties in their millions, confirming that it was truly a war like no other ever experienced before.

Alternatively, readers can take a more thematic approach and, via the chapter headings and cross-references, pursue particular strands – for example, the Western Front year by year, or changes in the way of life for civilians back home; the arrival of aerial warfare, or the development of submarine warfare; the advent of poison gas and the tank, or the emergence of modern propaganda.

At the heart of the book lies the fundamental relationship between the "big picture" and the intimate insights offered by the 100 objects, the majority taken from the unparalleled collections of Britain's Imperial War Museum – an institution itself inaugurated in 1917 as a direct response to the war. Looking at history via objects is not a new idea. But rather than 100 purely generic or symbolic objects, those chosen here invariably have particular stories to tell – of their makers, of their users and of how they were discovered or preserved. By appreciating these dimensions, we are brought more starkly face to face with the human angle – the individuals connected with the objects. To really understand the First World War, it is as important to listen to the thoughts of an individual Tommy about his rations, or his wife's disgruntlement at food queues back home, as it is to grasp the grand strategy of battles or the horrifying statistics of casualties.

We live daily with the consequences of the First World War. Truly, it still shapes the world in which we live. Its bloody history sounds out as a warning to us all, and each one of these 100 objects echoes like a bell across the intervening passage of time.

John Hughes-Wilson
Nigel Steel

Warships of the Imperial German Navy's 2nd Battle Squadron make a stately progress into the North Sea, prior to 1914. The most visible flexing of German military muscle in the years before the war was the expansion of her navy. To British eyes it suggested that German ambitions went well beyond continental Europe, threatening the British Empire itself. The stage was being set for a global war, fought on land, at sea and in the air.

INTRODUCTION

IMPERIALISM, NATIONALISM & THE ROAD TO WAR

01

KING GEORGE'S IMPERIAL CROWN
THE HEYDAY OF THE BRITISH EMPIRE

BEFORE 1914

In the early years of the 20th century, the British Empire was arguably at its zenith. Britain did not just rule the waves, but also administered vast swathes of land – accounting for a quarter of the globe. It was a situation that, as the great Victorian statesman Lord Salisbury observed, encouraged the sentiment that "the sun never sets on our Empire".

Such an empire was not achieved by brute force and bayonets – which is not to say that force had not played a part in the building and policing of empire. From Henry Morgan's first piratical looting of the Spanish West Indies in the late 1600s to the annexation of the gold and diamonds of South Africa in 1899, Britons had never flinched from using arms to seize valuable assets. And when the future Earl Kitchener of Khartoum marched into the Sudan in 1898 he brought with him a modern army and several Maxim machine guns, both of which proved extremely efficient in slaughtering the native opposition.

However, Kitchener illustrates the counterbalancing dimension, too. He – and Britons generally – saw his imperial mission not as crude conquest but as enlightening liberation, in this case to crush the Islamic fundamentalism of the day. From a Victorian perspective, the British Empire brought the benefits of civilization, law, commerce and Christianity to less-favoured peoples; it was a kind of duty, in Kipling's poetic phrase the "White man's burden". In a post-imperial age it is unacceptable to espouse such ideas and values. But by the standards of the time they were a reflection of noble ideals, and for Britons of all classes – from the great aristocratic houses to

> "THE SUN NEVER SETS ON OUR EMPIRE."
>
> *Lord Salisbury*

> "THAT'S BECAUSE GOD DOES NOT TRUST THE BRITISH IN THE DARK!"
>
> *Colvin R. De Silva*

> British imperial majesty was encapsulated in the Imperial Crown of India. It was created by royal jewellers Garrard & Co. in 1911, to be worn by George V at the spectacle of the Delhi Durbar to mark his accession as "King Emperor". The combined weight of its emeralds, rubies, sapphires and 6,100 diamonds prompted him to note: "Rather tired after wearing the Crown for 3 ½ hours, it hurt my head, as it is pretty heavy." The band at its base is set with 16 jewelled clusters of emeralds, sapphires and diamonds, and above this four cross-*pattées*, containing rubies, alternate with four fleurs-de-lys containing emeralds. Out of each of these a half-arch rises up to the *monde* (or globe), topped by another emerald set in a cross-*pattée*. Not actually part of the Crown Jewels, the Imperial Crown is nevertheless today kept with them in the Tower of London. No Durbars were held for the accessions of Edward VIII and George VI, so the Delhi Durbar of December 1911 represented the only occasion on which this majestic symbol was used.

the grimiest slums – the empire represented something solid, something proud and a force for good. Its showcase was the (generally efficient and honest) administration of what was long regarded as the empire's "jewel in the crown", India, by a mere 1,000 civil servants.

The truth is that the rationale of the British Empire was complex and many-faceted. It was part global commerce, economics and trade; part military and naval bases worldwide to protect those interests; and part the bringing of civilization, "true religion" and progress.

There were, of course, critics of empire even then. In southern Africa, the Anglo-Boer War (1899–1902) was a defining moment, seen by British radicals as little more than a greedy war of conquest. The herding of Boer wives and children into "concentration camps" and their subsequent deaths from poor sanitation and disease created an outcry that rattled many of the Victorian Establishment's complacent certainties. In the House of Commons, the Welsh MP David Lloyd George denounced what he called a "naked war of annexation" in ringing terms as one in which "the savagery which must necessarily follow will stain the name of this country". Anti-imperialist thinkers also saw – quite correctly – that Britain's armed forces served overseas primarily to protect the flow of money back to London. They also observed – equally correctly – that this money did not go to benefit the British taxpayer, who had subsidized those armed forces, nor to Britons in general, but to a tiny handful of plutocrats, bankers and speculators such as Cecil Rhodes, with his grandiose dream of a British railway from the Cape to Cairo, and the great banking houses like Rothschilds. Well might J.A. Hobson argue, in his 1902 study *Imperialism*, that "Finance is the governor of the Imperial engine, directing the energy and determining the work." Many politicians, including the former prime ministers Gladstone and Disraeli, had made large sums from imperial finance. While riches appeared to accrue to the few, the costs of maintaining and defending the empire, and the drain of some of the best brains to run it, arguably constituted an enormous burden on the motherland.

To the man or woman in the street none of this was apparent. They saw only the shop-front glories of empire: the Diamond Jubilee of the old Queen in 1897 or the ever-spreading tide of red across the map of the world. To even the poorest members of society this demonstration of Britain's imperial pomp and reach was living proof that the British were somehow a superior race, that Britain's achievements were unsurpassed and that Britain really was a great power.

One exotic occasion, captured on early film, says it all. In December 1911, British imperial majesty demonstrated its potency on the dusty plains outside Delhi. There, "King Emperor" George V received his Indian subjects' homage in a magnificent traditional ceremony known as a Durbar, combining pomp, demonstrations of allegiance and opulence. Hundreds of thousands of visitors flocked to the Durbar, with a great tented city built to house them. Foremost were more than 560 Indian princes and rulers, each of whom was to pledge allegiance and bow three times before the king emperor and queen empress as they sat on silver thrones beneath the rich canopy of the Royal Pavilion. Although the Durbar marked George's accession, it was not a coronation; nevertheless, a crown was needed to complete the ceremony. Yet, as the Old Royal Law of Britain forbade the Crown Jewels from being taken abroad, a new one was needed. There could scarcely have been a more dazzling embodiment of the empire's glory in the years leading up to 1914 than the Imperial Crown of India,

its thousands of gemstones set within a frame of silver, laminated with gold. It cost £60,000, a princely sum paid for by the exchequers of India.

Such a spirit of imperial self-confidence and cohesion stretched well beyond India, too, and ensured that the "British lion's cubs" of the great White Dominions also lined up behind British interests. In 1914, the British government regarded Canada, Australia, New Zealand and South Africa as virtual extensions of metropolitan Britain herself. Fortunately, so did the Dominions. If the empire was a hidden burden to Britain in peacetime, in war it would suddenly become a major asset.

Thus, when Britain did declare war in August 1914, the government automatically committed the colonies and Dominions, who gave solid military, financial and material support over the next four years. Over 2.5 million men would serve in the Dominions' armies, as well as many volunteers from the Crown Colonies, including hundreds of thousands from India. In 1917 this contribution was recognized by Lloyd George, by then British prime minister, when he invited the Dominions' prime ministers to join the Imperial War Cabinet and help coordinate Britain's global policy.

The British Empire survived the war, of course, and even expanded in its aftermath. But it is salutary to remember that in 1914 imperial glory and maritime reach were no guarantees of victory in a scenario that Britain had managed to avoid for a century: full-scale conflict with the massed armies of powerful European rivals.

King Emperor George V and Queen Empress Mary glance towards the camera during the affirmation of Britain's imperial control over India that was the Delhi Durbar (12 December 1911). In the war of empires that followed in 1914, Indian troops would play a full part, on the Western Front, in Mesopotamia, in East Africa, in Palestine and at Gallipoli.

02

THE PEN THAT SIGNED THE ULSTER COVENANT
BRITISH TROUBLES & IRISH TENSIONS

1909 TO 1914

There is a view that the high summer of 1914 represented a brief golden age, when the country bathed in its imperial glow and the British Isles stood strong, prosperous and united. Pride in empire there was, but as for the domestic situation nothing could be further from the truth. From the time that Herbert Asquith became prime minister in April 1908 until the outbreak of war in August 1914, Britain was rocked by crises and spasms of increasingly violent confrontation. Industry, already being economically outstripped by foreign rivals, was beset with strikes; the government battled with the House of Lords in a constitutional crisis; and there was an increasingly militant movement to win votes for women.

By far the greatest threat was of Irish civil war. The prospect of granting Home Rule for Ireland, with a Parliament in Dublin, provoked the threat of a violent backlash from Protestants in Ulster – and even mutiny in the British Army. Nothing offers a clearer window onto the troubled times than the pages of the popular magazine *Punch*. Its headline cartoon for 1 July 1914 portrayed Britannia gazing nervously from her ramparts across the Irish Sea to the dark clouds on the horizon, where a storm whips up the words "civil war".

> "THE ARMY WILL HEAR NOTHING OF POLITICS FROM ME, AND IN RETURN I EXPECT TO HEAR NOTHING OF POLITICS FROM THE ARMY."
>
> *Prime Minister Herbert Asquith*

This pen was used by Colonel Fred Crawford at the signing – reputedly in blood – of the Ulster Covenant, one of the totemic occasions of modern Irish history. A leader of the Protestant resistance to the introduction of Irish Home Rule, it was Crawford who organized the illegal landing, in April 1914, of rifles and ammunition for use by the new paramilitary Ulster Volunteer Force. Eighteen months earlier, on 28 September 1912, he used this pen to put his name to the Ulster Covenant, the solemn pledge eventually signed by more than 470,000 men and women in Ulster stating their loyalty to the United Kingdom and their determination to resist the establishment of an independent Irish Parliament. The tradition that Crawford signed in blood persisted, but a forensic analysis of the bright red signature in 2012 revealed no residual traces of blood. It appears more likely that the claim was simply part of the heightened emotions of this pivotal day. The pen is now kept in the Ulster Museum.

The years 1909–14 witnessed widespread industrial unrest, as many working people experienced rising prices and stagnant incomes. Wage cuts, poor working conditions and steady inflation left many of the lower paid increasingly disgruntled and militant. Trades union membership rose by half, and organized labour began to flex its muscles with greater confidence, resulting in strikes, some of them violent. Troops were sent to reinforce police at Tonypandy in South Wales in November 1910, when striking miners rioted through the streets, and to Liverpool in the following, hot, summer, when dock strikes fuelled months of virtual anarchy. The army shot two rioters, the Cabinet ordered a battleship to the Mersey, and Liverpool's lord mayor even warned that "a revolution was in progress".

Inevitably, productivity was affected. In 1913, over 11 million days were lost to strikes and related actions. By 1914 the nation that had proudly proclaimed herself the "Workshop of the World" at the Great Exhibition of 1851 was beginning to lag behind. Manufacturing enterprises built up half a century before were

being challenged by the more modern processes of the United States and, more seriously, Germany.

In politics, the Liberal government's welfare reforms – non-contributory old age pensions and a national insurance scheme – drove up taxes, as did the naval expansion to counter German ambitions (*see* Chapter 4). The House of Lords voted down the budget, and a constitutional crisis was only avoided by the king threatening to create enough new Liberal peers to curtail the power of the Lords as the government pushed through a new Parliament Act (1911).

All this was taking place against a vociferous and highly visible campaign of direct action by Emmeline Pankhurst's "Suffragettes", the Women's Social and Political Union, who represented the more radical element of the suffragist campaign for women's voting rights. The Suffragettes recognized the oxygen of publicity that a spell in jail generated and moved from chaining themselves to railings to violent protest. From 1912 an arson campaign began, artworks were slashed and golf courses sprayed with acid. While their actions at no time imperilled the state, they contributed to a national mood of instability.

Amid this sea of troubles, it was in Ireland, though, that Britain faced her most acute crisis. Since 1801, Ireland had been constitutionally part of the United Kingdom, and a vociferous and determined Protestant minority in the northern counties ("Ulster") had seen off previous attempts to reach a Home Rule settlement, fearing Catholic domination.

When, in April 1912, Asquith introduced a third Parliamentary Bill that offered Ireland a separate Parliament and limited self-government, many of Ireland's Protestants were outraged. They were supported at Westminster by other Unionists, including the bulk of the Conservative Party Opposition. The previous September, Sir Edward Carson, leader of the Ulster Unionist Party, had told a rally outside Belfast that Unionists might soon have to form their *own* government in Ulster if Home Rule were granted, and he ordered a draft constitution be drawn up for it. A week after the introduction of Asquith's Bill, Carson addressed another massed rally, at which his supporters agreed to sign a solemn pledge of unwavering opposition to Home Rule.

Thus, on 28 September 1912 – Ulster Day – in a well-organized ceremony combining religious fervour with political defiance, 80,000 people gathered in Belfast to sign the Ulster Covenant. After attending church, Carson headed a march to Belfast City Hall, guarded by 2,500 men armed with wooden staves and commanded by Fred Crawford. Using a special silver pen, Carson was the first to sign the Covenant, on a table draped with the Union flag.

Protestant resistance now moved up a gear with the establishment of the paramilitary Ulster Volunteer Force (UVF), many of its members Covenant-signers. In the south the Catholic nationalists, too, were beginning to mobilize, by way of the Irish Volunteers. They lacked the organization of the UVF, but they contributed to the overall sense of an inexorable slide towards direct confrontation.

As the Home Rule Bill progressed through Parliament, tensions continued to rise and now began to permeate the army. In March 1914, the army commander in Ireland, Lieutenant General Sir Arthur Paget, was warned to prepare for the securing of key buildings. But he was concerned that many of his officers came from Ulster families and faced divided loyalties. His advice from the War Office was that "officers whose homes are actually in the province of Ulster ... may apply for permission to be absent from duty during the period of operations, and will be 'allowed to disappear'

"A LIFE OF SECURITY; A LIFE OF SEDENTARY OCCUPATION; A LIFE OF RESPECTABILITY: THESE THREE QUALITIES GIVE THE KEY TO [ENGLAND'S] SPECIAL CHARACTERISTICS ... AND ASPIRATIONS."

C.F.G. Masterman, The Condition of England, *1909*

from Ireland". But those without this close connection, and who simply found the prospect of firing on other British citizens distasteful, would "at once be dismissed from the service". Many of his officers regarded it as an ultimatum.

Matters reached a head when, at the Curragh barracks in central Ireland, Brigadier General Hubert Gough, whose home was in Ulster, warned that 57 of his 70 officers would resign on the spot rather than enforce Home Rule. The government was shocked by the so-called "Curragh Mutiny" and the realization that the army could not be relied on. In the end, Gough was given a Cabinet guarantee that his troops "would not be called upon" to enforce Home Rule.

Despite every effort to find a political solution, there appeared to be no way out of the deadlock. The paramilitaries were openly arming and preparing for a bloody confrontation. At the end of April 1914, the UVF landed a shipment of 30,000 foreign rifles and 3 million rounds of ammunition in Ulster and swiftly spirited them into hiding. At the beginning of July, the Irish Volunteers landed its own cache of arms in the south. This time British soldiers blocked the way, but the guns got through nonetheless. Across Ireland, two armed militia were now drilling and preparing for a civil war. Meanwhile, far away in the Balkans an international crisis of ever greater proportions was forcing Whitehall's attention onto mainland Europe.

Irish Home Rule *did* come into effect a few weeks after the outbreak of the First World War, but it was then suspended for the duration of the conflict. Yet it is worth remembering that in July 1914 the shooting war expected by many Britons looked more likely to begin on their own doorsteps than in some far-off foreign field.

Workers gather to hear speeches outside the Woolwich Arsenal, London, during their strike of July 1914. Around 8,000 of them downed tools following a dispute over the use of non-union labour, which the Spectator *described as "one of the very gravest incidents in the recent history of labour unrest". In summer 1914, the British Isles was a volatile place.*

Because most officer appointments were restricted to the nobility and landowners, this meant that many *Junkers* were simultaneously army captain and landlord over their serf-conscripts. Military discipline reinforced feudal jurisdiction and frequently encroached into strictly civil affairs. Thus, if a man wanted to leave the country without permission, he could be charged with desertion – for every man was either a trained soldier or a potential recruit. It is not for nothing that the French thinker and politician Mirabeau observed, following the exploits of Frederick the Great (1712–86), that: "Prussia is not a state with an army, but an army with a state." The serfs were emancipated in 1807, but the country remained essentially a "military-agrarian complex", controlled by the interlocking interests of the monarchy, the army and a feudal aristocracy.

The combination of Prussia's stunning victories and Minister-President Prince Otto von Bismarck's considerable diplomatic skills proved powerful arguments for persuading Berlin's neighbours to unite under Prussia. However, despite recognizing the practical advantages of unification, they remained wary of an inevitable Prussian dominance and its potential dangers. For one thing, the appointment of the imperial chancellor – Bismarck – lay in the hands of the new Kaiser, and as such effectively became a Prussian choice. Not directly linked to the elected Parliament (*Reichstag*), the German chancellor was nevertheless responsible for devising and instituting national policy. With the appointment in his gift, the Kaiser was able to exert a much stronger degree of direct political control over his chancellor than, for example, the British monarch could do over his prime minister, particularly in areas such as defence and foreign policy.

Between 1871 and 1914, the united Germany underwent a massive transformation. Socially and politically, there remained tensions between Prussia and the other regions, between the aristocratic landowning elite and the emerging middle classes, whose prosperity was linked to rising urban industries, and above all between liberal civilians and the military cabal that lay at the heart of the state. The liberals steadily sought to limit the power of the military and win control over the army, but failed.

Possibly the greatest change in Germany's first 40 years was her emergence as a major global economic power. With great dynamism, she set about introducing the latest, most efficient industrial practices. The result was a rapid increase in manufacturing capability. In 1870 British industry dominated the world, meeting almost one-third of the world's industrial demands. By 1910, Britain's share of the global manufacturing market had fallen to less than 15 per cent, now supplanted by the United States which had over one-third. But the real surprise lay in the upstart Germany, now – albeit narrowly – besting Britain with a market share of almost 16 per cent. Not only in specialist areas, such as chemicals and optics, was Britain falling behind, but her capacity even lagged in traditional materials like steel. British output may have almost doubled in two decades to reach 6.4 million tons by 1910, but in the same period, German output more than quintupled to reach 13.5 million tons.

This rapid rise unsurprisingly worried many of Germany's neighbours. Initially, Bismarck pursued the diplomacy of peaceful coexistence, while projecting the new Germany as a mature and responsible nation. But in June 1888 this situation was radically altered by the accession of a thrusting new Kaiser, Wilhelm II, who harboured ambitions for Germany's growing political strength to be more widely recognized across the world. Dismissing Bismarck within two years, Wilhelm began to lead Germany on a "new course", most notably in international affairs.

As the balance of power now shifted, Germany deepened ties with her cultural and linguistic compatriots in Austria-Hungary. But relations with the powers that flanked Germany to east and west – Russia and France – deteriorated, and in 1894 a Franco-Russian *entente* was signed. It was intended to provide both countries with mutual support, but it contributed to a German sense of containment and encirclement. Increasingly feeling herself under threat, Germany's overconfident military now became a political factor. The Prussian-dominated General Staff in Berlin was determined to avoid a war on two fronts. Its head, Count Alfred von Schlieffen, outlined a plan that would come to bear his name, by which Germany could strike a swift knockout blow to eliminate France from any war and then tackle Russia. Through its close links to the Kaiser, and with little concern for the feelings of the *Reichstag*, the General Staff effectively became a political force in its own right, encouraging and even setting the nation's European foreign policy agenda. Guided by the rigid parameters of the railway timetables that would need to be followed in the event of mobilization, the army began to set in train – literally – operational plans as precise as a jeweller's watch movement that were effectively outside civil political control and diplomatic restraints.

The army thus played a powerful role in Germany in the years leading up to the First World War, and German society became increasingly dominated by what was seen by many observers as rampant militarism. But while the army may have been *the* dominating influence, it was not the only service flexing its muscles. At the very end of the 1890s the Imperial German Navy began to emerge from the shadow of the army. While the navy's influence in society as a whole may have been slight, its hold over the imagination of the Kaiser was great and, through this, its impact on Germany's fate between 1900 and 1914 eclipsed even that of the army.

A display of Pickelhauben *and other headgear, as a confident Kaiser Wilhelm II of Germany* (foreground, left), *flanked by his six sons, leads a parade through Berlin in 1913. It was a year that witnessed patriotic celebrations of the centenary of Prussia's Wars of Liberation against Napoleonic France, as well as the Kaiser's 25th year on the throne.*

04

SERGEANT MILLER'S RECRUITMENT SIGN ANGLO-GERMAN NAVAL RIVALRY

1898 TO 1914

For over 100 years following Nelson's victory at Trafalgar (1805), Britain's Royal Navy had undisputed command of the world's oceans. This situation was a natural adjunct to protecting maritime commerce and projecting imperial power. Periodically waves ruffled the waters, such as when the French launched the world's first ironclad battleship, *La Gloire*, in 1859. But by 1861 Britain had her own iron-hulled battleship, HMS *Warrior,* prompting Lord Palmerston's satisfied observation that it looked like "a black snake among rabbits". Supremacy bred a certain complacency. Yet, as the century closed, Britain still possessed more battleships in service than the combined strength of Germany, France, Russia, the United States and Japan.

The picture was beginning to change, however, most acutely through the emergence of the new German *Kaiserliche Marine* (Imperial Navy), aggressively expanded from 1898 under Kaiser Wilhelm II and his naval secretary of state, Admiral Alfred von Tirpitz. The consequences for European security would be immense, as Berlin's naval ambitions ratcheted up tensions, reconfigured diplomatic relations and strained resources.

> The reign of Edward VII (1901–10) marked a period of resurgence for Britain's Royal Navy. A renewed vigour imbued its ranks in response to the alarming German efforts, from 1898, to create their own world-class navy. From 1904, Admiral Sir John ("Jackie") Fisher introduced sweeping changes and the frenetic Anglo-German naval arms race was turned on its head. As a vast shipbuilding programme progressed, recruitment continued to deliver the sailors and Marines to man the vessels. This unembellished, enamelled Edwardian recruitment sign was posted by Sergeant Major John Miller, Royal Marines, outside his house in Norwich. The "Admiralty recruiting office" was, in this case, his own front room. In King Edward's name, Sergeant Major Miller invited men to join the world's greatest navy and carry the essence of the British way of life across the empire. In a few years they would be doing considerably more than that.

The new Kaiser's ambitions reflected his personal admiration – and resentment – of the history, power and prestige of the Royal Navy. Germany possessed a small coastal fleet, mostly based in the Baltic, and had no real need for a wider "blue water" navy. But the Kaiser increasingly saw the size and strength of his fleet as a determinant of German aspirations and a symbol of Germany's right to a "place in the sun". Capricious and impulsive, Wilhelm wanted a navy big enough to challenge Britain's, and in Tirpitz he found an only too-willing partner. Both men absorbed US Captain

> "THE NAVY IS THE MOST IMPORTANT DEFENCE OF THE COUNTRY, IN WHICH EVERY SUBJECT OF THE QUEEN HAS AN INTEREST OF THE DEEPEST CHARACTER."
>
> *Justice Willes, Henwood versus Harrison (1872)*

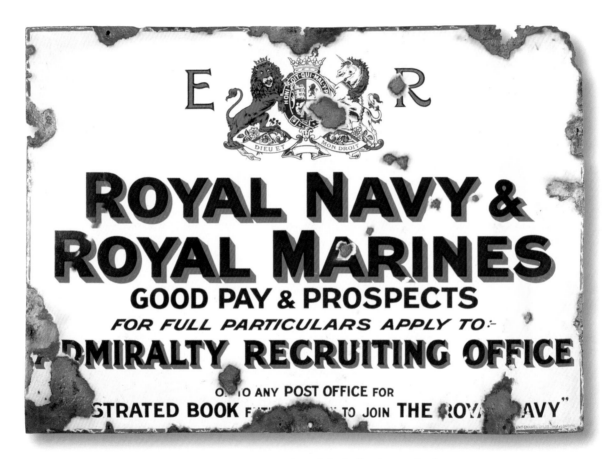

Alfred Mahan's *Influence of Sea Power Upon History* (1890), including its emphasis on maritime control to encourage and protect commerce, and they thought that by building a navy to challenge British dominance they might convert the German *Reich* from a land-based *Grossmacht* into a global *Weltmacht* – from a great power into a world power.

They were well aware how provocative this move could be, and they also realized they could not create a larger fleet than the Royal Navy. But had not Mahan written that even an inferior fleet, simply through its existence, could influence the policy and actions of a larger one by maintaining the threat of a "fleet in being"? With sufficient strength, Tirpitz believed, they could inflict enough damage in a confrontation to eliminate Britain's fleet as a *world* power. In fact, he believed that to avert such a risk Britain would avoid battle, in which case her navy would be emasculated anyway. Moreover, such was the extent of the Royal Navy's global responsibilities that Tirpitz did not believe Britain would be able to concentrate enough ships in the waters around Germany to fight with the full weight of her theoretical power.

Tirpitz called this his *Risikogedanke*, or "risk theory", and risky it certainly was. The problem was that it cut both ways: Britain might back away, fearing potentially catastrophic losses, or she might rise to the challenge, solidifying British hostility to Germany. Thus, Tirpitz initially favoured a stealthy "brick by brick" approach, and his navy bills of 1898, 1900 and 1906 were designed to *discreetly* transform German naval might.

It was a dire miscalculation. Both Tirpitz and Wilhelm failed to appreciate just how sensitive the British were to any naval challenge, however disguised. The incipient German threat was a major factor in forcing Britain to re-examine strategic priorities, and effectively signalled the end of the century-long *Pax Britannica* and Britain's years of "splendid isolation". In 1902, an alliance was signed with Japan, which allowed Britain to reduce the strength of her fleet in the Far East (*see* Chapter 19). Two years later, with earlier colonial squabbles neatly shelved, Britain and her traditional rival France signed the Entente Cordiale. Among other things, this began a long process of redistributing Britain's naval strength from the Mediterranean to its home waters in the North Sea and the Channel. In exchange, the French navy began to take responsibility for the Mediterranean. By 1907 Britain had concluded a second *entente*, with Russia. Ironically, Germany's provocative naval expansion had actually precipitated an increased sense of German encirclement and helped create the Triple Entente in Europe against which it would fight in 1914.

Within the Royal Navy, profound changes were also at work. In October 1904, Admiral Sir John Fisher was appointed First Sea Lord, the navy's professional head. Eccentric and energetic, he was exactly the man to revitalize the Senior Service. He organized a major overhaul, scrapping old ships held in dockyard reserves ("a miser's hoard of useless junk" was his description of obsolescent cruisers) and embarking on a new strategy based on a large fleet concentrated in home waters – yet again, calling Tirpitz's bluff. Most importantly, he began a major shipbuilding programme based on an innovative design of battleship, HMS *Dreadnought*, which stunned the world at her launch in February 1906. She was the first all big-gun battleship, clad with heavy armour, boasting 12-inch guns and propelled by powerful steam turbines. She was a fast, formidable – and expensive – addition to the Royal Navy. At a stroke Fisher made all other battleships obsolete, including his own.

Tirpitz responded by openly demanding funds from a compliant *Reichstag* "to meet the British challenge". What followed was a naval arms race to rival the later Cold War in its relative cost and intensity. Between 1906 and 1912 Britain launched 29 capital ships (battleships and battlecruisers) compared to Germany's 17; Germany's naval budget doubled and Britain's shot up by 40 per cent. As costs heated up, relations between the two countries cooled.

By 1909 it was clear that Germany was building warships on an unprecedented scale. The Royal Navy's slender margin of superiority risked falling to just four dreadnoughts, and something like panic ensued. The "great naval scare" mobilized

British people and politicians into throwing funds behind a rapid construction programme: as politicians debated over whether to build four or six more dreadnoughts, in the end, as Winston Churchill wittily put it in 1909, "we compromised on eight". In fact, the government was responding to popular pressure under the slogan "We want eight, and we won't wait!" It made all the difference, when war came. By 1912 the Royal Navy's battle fleet had mushroomed to over 30 capital ships, consolidating what was now a solid margin over Germany.

The wisdom, albeit expensively bought, of ploughing money into Britain's strategic naval defence was demonstrated by the so-called Agadir Incident of 1911, concerning colonial rivalry in Morocco. France unilaterally sent troops, ostensibly to help put down a revolt against the sultan, but in the process defying an earlier agreement with Germany. So the Kaiser ordered the German gunboat SMS *Panther* to the coastal city of Agadir, on the pretext of protecting German citizens and business interests. It was a naked act of gunboat diplomacy and generated a crisis defused only by intense diplomacy and a run against German banks. It also demonstrated two realities: that German naval power was now a major factor in international disputes; and that relations between Berlin and the Entente allies were highly volatile.

By 1913, while the British continued to build battleships and battlecruisers as fast as they could, Germany discreetly switched to a policy of launching submarines. For both countries, the naval arms race was a massive drain on resources and fuelled pre-war suspicions. For Britain, it was, at least, a logical move to protect her security, her commerce and her empire. In 1918, as in 1914, Britannia still ruled the waves. As for the Kaiser, he suffered the indignity that, in 1918, sailors of his precious High Seas Fleet were in the forefront of the revolution that overthrew him.

A drawing, based on a photograph, of HMS Dreadnought after her launch by King Edward VII at Portsmouth (17 February 1906). This warship, the world's most powerful, lent her name to a whole new class of battleship, and Germany and Britain vied with each other to build more of them. In the subsequent war, both sides took great care to protect such naval assets.

05

A MAP OF EUROPEAN RIVALRY
EUROPE'S ALLIANCES & ANIMOSITIES

1870 TO 1914

The radical changes that swept through the Royal Navy in the decade before 1914 responded to the particular challenge of Germany's growing naval strength. But they also reflected Britain's more pragmatic strategic repositioning in an increasingly polarized world, as old rivals formed new pacts and dangerous threats emerged, creating a complex and – ultimately – too fragile Europe.

Perhaps the starting point for this European realignment was the bitter Franco-Prussian War of 1870–71, in which Prussian success spurred the unification of the German nation on the back of French defeat and humiliation. Indeed, it was on French soil, at Versailles, that German unity was proclaimed on 18 January 1871, and a month later the Prussian army marched through the Arc de Triomphe and down the Champs Elysées to underscore the sense of triumph. The concurrent loss of the French territories of Alsace and Lorraine to Germany fed an enduring French national desire for *la Revanche*: "revenge".

As a consequence, it could be said that France both expected and indeed wanted another war. And if renewed war was going to be inevitable, France needed allies when it came. Initially, Britain stood aloof, while Russia was kept sweet by Germany's Bismarck – at least until the new Kaiser, Wilhelm II, ditched his wily chancellor and abandoned this pragmatic friendship. Thus, when France and Russia signed a formal alliance in January 1894, Germany found herself sandwiched between them. The balance of power seemed to be shifting.

The polarization of Europe in 1914 is clearly reflected by this British poster, originally printed in London a few weeks after war began with a sardonic English caption. Each country is represented by national stereotypes, with the main belligerents as "Dogs of War" now let "loose in Europe". To the northwest stands a British bulldog, protected by a stocky Jack Tar restraining warships on leads. Aligned alongside a French poodle, the bulldog bites the nose of a German dachshund "thought to have gone mad". The dachshund is yoked to an "Austrian Mongrel" intent on bullying little Serbia. But Serbia is being protected by a Russian bear, exactly as the dachshund had hoped as this should allow it to "steal a bone or two through the fighting". Beyond the Balkans, a crouching Turk with a fez-wearing dachshund stretches out one hand to close the Dardanelles, while in the other he holds two German warships on a leash in the Black Sea. This clear piece of anti-German propaganda was actually reprinted in Hamburg and sold for 50 pfennigs, with the English title and text translated to lay the blame for war on aggressive, untrustworthy Britain. This is one of those German copies.

> "IF EVER THERE IS ANOTHER WAR IN EUROPE, IT WILL COME OUT OF SOME DAMNED SILLY THING IN THE BALKANS!"
>
> *Attributed to Chancellor Prince Otto von Bismarck*

35060

The new scenario increased the importance of Germany's already deepening relationship with Austria-Hungary. Prussia had fought and defeated Austria in 1866, and usurped from Austria the moral leadership of Europe's ethnic Germans. But Bismarck had been careful to nurture relations, and the two powers moved closer together in the years that followed. This process was fortunate for the Habsburg monarchs of Austria, as it disguised a steady decline in power for their multilingual, multinational patchwork empire of ethnic Germans, Magyars, Slavs, Czechs, Poles, Slovaks, Serbians and Italians. In 1867, recognition of the special position of the Magyars of Hungary created the Dual Monarchy, in which the Emperor of Austria became simultaneously King of Hungary.

Closer links produced a formal alliance (1879) between Germany and Austria-Hungary, which became a Triple Alliance when joined by Italy in 1882. Austria-Hungary, though, remained most threatened by the turbulent region of the Balkans. Here, as the Ottoman Empire contracted towards the edge of mainland Europe, local and nationalist rivalries filled the vacuum. In 1878, three new independent countries emerged – Serbia, Montenegro and Romania – and Bulgaria and Greece grew larger. These were dynamic nation-states, whose ethnic groups overlapped with those of Austria-Hungary's southern provinces.

Of particular concern, the emergence of Serbia created a new nation of Slavs. Vienna looked on, alarmed, at growing Serbian ambitions to unite all of the region's Slavs. Moreover, the changes in the political complexion of the Balkans exacerbated Austro-Hungarian tensions with Russia, who saw herself as protector of all the Balkans' Slavs. Conscious that such tensions could precipitate war, the two powers signed a ten-year pact (1897) agreeing not to intervene directly in the affairs of the Balkan nations. However, in 1908, Austria-Hungary stoked Balkan tensions when the old Ottoman region of Bosnia-Herzegovina declared unilateral independence. Instead Austria, given responsibility for Bosnia-Herzegovina at the Congress of Vienna that year, seized the opportunity to formally annex it, but in doing so, the empire acquired a million more Slavs, most of whom had no desire to fall under Habsburg rule.

Neither the Russian nor Austro-Hungarian empires were directly involved, though, in the vicious Balkan Wars of 1912 and 1913. In the First Balkan War, Bulgaria, Greece, Montenegro and Serbia united and successfully fought the Ottoman Empire for her residual territory in Europe. In the internecine Second Balkan War, Bulgaria fought Greece and Serbia over some of the spoils (Macedonia), with the Ottoman forces (and Romania) taking the opportunity to attack Bulgaria and regain territory. Almost 230,000 casualties died from the fighting or from disease.

Austria-Hungary itched to use the First Balkan War to resolve the issues that had long threatened her own internal stability, but fear of Russia's response kept her out. In Berlin's eyes, however, the war was perceived as one fought *by* Russia at arm's length, and Chancellor Theobold von Bethmann Hollweg made it clear that Germany would fully support Austria-Hungary if the fighting spilled out of the Balkans and Russia became involved. In return, London signalled that if a German attack on Russia pulled in the French, under the terms of the Franco-Russian alliance, then Britain would not be prepared to see the French defeated. These uncompromising diplomatic statements provided a chilling preview of the scenario that would play out only 18 months later.

By now, Britain's repositioning from her years of "splendid isolation" was complete. Indeed, the 1904 Entente Cordiale with France, underscored by the charm of Edward VII, had the effect of turning the politics of Europe upside down. It was a fact most clearly highlighted by the Agadir crisis in 1911 (*see* Chapter 4), where German hopes that Britain would criticize French actions came to nought – and, in fact, Germany's gunboat diplomacy simply moved the British and French closer together. After Agadir, the Franco-British redeployment of ships to protect the Mediterranean and the northern waters around the Channel was completed, and secret military discussions laid down clear plans for the despatch of an expeditionary force to France in the event of war.

Britain's deepening friendship with France was mirrored by her relationship with Russia. Never quite as close, it nevertheless moderated strategic threats to the security of the British Empire. Russia no longer cast quite such a shadow over India, or over Britain's position in the Middle East, allowing the British to reconsider the risks they faced and see ever more clearly where the primary threat lay – in Germany's increasingly aggressive policies.

In truth, the emergence of a new, enlarged and unified Germany – complete with a booming economy, a growing population of 68 million by 1914 and a large and efficient army – was always likely to destabilize the balance of power in Europe. For nearly 20 years this threat had been kept at bay by Bismarck's

THE BOILING POINT.

The Balkan pot threatens to boil over in this 1912 Punch *cartoon by Leonard Raven-Hill. Attempting to keep a lid on the simmering tensions are some familiar national stereotypes of the Great Powers: Britain's John Bull and a French general* (back row) *along with a bearded Russian, a Pickelhaube-wearing Prussian and an amply moustached Austro-Hungarian* (perhaps the emperor).

pragmatic diplomacy, but after his dismissal by Wilhelm II there is little doubt that Germany became a bellicose and ambitious state, whose world-power aspirations were ill-concealed. In October 1908, the Kaiser gave an alarming interview to the London *Daily Telegraph*, in which he boasted that his General Staff had planned British strategy during the Anglo-Boer War, warned that the majority of Germans were openly hostile to Britain and stated that "the legitimate ambition of patriotic Germans refuses to assign any bounds". British popular sentiment reflected Germany's challenge, with children cheekily claiming that the German product trademark "DRGM" really stood for "Dirty Rotten German Make".

With hindsight, it is clear that by the summer of 1914 the European nations stood on the verge of a geo-strategic earthquake. Like the subterranean shifts of vast tectonic plates, the European balance of power had changed in such a way that dangerous fault lines had built up, storing up enormous pressures. Whole nations, as well as individual citizens, stood waiting for an eruption. Both Germany and France were expecting and preparing for a showdown. But no-one knew when that would be or where it would occur.

In the end, it was to be in the Balkan city of Sarajevo in June 1914.

06

THE ARCHDUKE'S BLOODSTAINED TUNIC
ASSASSINATION & THE ROAD TO WAR

SUMMER 1914

The original "shot heard 'round the world" was poet Walt Whitman's description of the opening salvo that led to American independence. But the phrase found a truly global context in the single shot that ended the life of the heir-presumptive to the Austro-Hungarian throne on 28 June 1914. The conspirators who set out to murder Archduke Franz Ferdinand had no clue that they would spark a cataclysm. They calculated that the worst that might happen would be another localized Balkan war, from which a Greater Serbia could emerge having "liberated" the remaining Serbs of the Austro-Hungarian Empire. Their miscalculation, soon to be compounded by the mis-steps of political and military leaders, meant that within six weeks the power blocs of Europe were lined up against one another in war across the continent. The archduke's cut and bloodstained military tunic remains as mute testimony to a deed that would result in the deaths of an estimated 16 million people.

Franz Ferdinand and his wife Sophie met their end in Sarajevo. This was the capital of the former Ottoman province of Bosnia-Herzegovina, whose annexation by Austria-Hungary in 1908 caused alarm in neighbouring Serbia. Serbia's military successes in the two Balkan Wars of 1912 and 1913 had emboldened elements within her army, and government, to stir up Serb nationalism within Austria's Balkan territories, including among the many ethnic Serbs of Bosnia.

> **"THE LIGHTS ARE GOING OUT ALL OVER EUROPE; WE WILL NOT SEE THEM LIT AGAIN IN OUR LIFETIME."**
>
> *British Foreign Secretary Sir Edward Grey, 1914*

Unusually for Archduke Franz Ferdinand, on his visit to Sarajevo he was accompanied by his wife, Duchess Sophie of Hohenberg. It was rare for the couple to be seen together in public. The duchess was not of royal birth, and the marriage was considered to be "morganatic" – she could never have the same status as her husband, nor could her children inherit the Austro-Hungarian throne. On that day she shared her husband's fate, though, when one of the assassin's bullets hit her in the stomach; she collapsed onto the floor of their car, dying soon afterwards. The other bullet hit the archduke in the neck, and blood instantly spurted across the front of his blue high-collared ceremonial tunic, where the dark stains remain today. The archduke's aides tried to undo the jacket, but soon realized it would be quicker to cut through it. These cuts are also still clearly visible. Franz Ferdinand's tunic has traditionally been displayed in Vienna's *Heeresgeschichtliches Museum* (Military History Museum), in its Sarajevo Gallery, alongside the Graf & Stift car in which the royal couple were travelling, the gun used by killer Gavrilo Prinćip – and even the sofa on which the archduke died back at the town hall. The macabre, blood-spattered garment provides a visceral link with one of the most momentous events of the 20th century.

On Sunday 28 June 1914, the archduke and his wife were driven together into the Bosnian capital. His presence in Bosnia was officially as Inspector General of the Army; more symbolically, his presence demonstrated Austrian sway over the province. Unbeknown to him and his entourage, distributed along the route were six assassins from the Young Bosnia nationalist movement. They were sponsored by the Black Hand, a secret Serb society, and ultimately directed by the chief of Serbian military intelligence, Colonel Dragutin Dimitrjević, known as "Apis". Many Black Hand members held important Serbian army and government positions. The organization trained guerrillas and saboteurs, and had been responsible for a range of political murders (and attempted murders) and atrocities since the Balkan Wars. The Serbian Prime Minister Nikola Pašić may have known about some Black Hand operations, but seems to have been afraid at this stage to intervene with its operations. On 28 June, though, it was less the murderous professionalism of the Black Hand's proxies that delivered Franz Ferdinand to his fate, and more a series of bungles and confusions, by all parties.

At Sarajevo station, the royal couple were greeted by a motorcade of open-topped cars. From the start there was a security blunder as three local police officers got into the first security car and sped off, leaving the archduke's special security detail behind. Franz Ferdinand, Duchess Sophie, the local governor and the archduke's military aide got into the third car and followed on to inspect a local barracks.

At shortly after 10 a.m. the motorcade passed two of the would-be assassins on the route, but they seem to have frozen when they had a chance, and ten minutes later it was left to a third, Nedeljko Cabrinović, to throw a bomb, which bounced off the folded roof of the archduke's car to explode under the vehicle behind, seriously wounding its passengers. Cabrinović's own attempt at instant martyrdom failed when he vomited up his suicide pill and was unable to drown himself in the shallow River Miljacka. Dragged out by the police, he was beaten by an enraged crowd before being led off under arrest. The motorcade sped off at high speed to its destination, the town hall, giving other conspirators no chance to get at the archduke.

A shaken Franz Ferdinand read out his planned speech from bloodstained notes – the papers had been in the damaged car – before discussing changes to the planned programme. Finally it was decided to visit the wounded in hospital. At about 10.45 a.m. the royal visitors boarded the third car in the motorcade and drove off. Unfortunately, no-one had advised the driver of the new route, and he took a wrong turning, bringing his royal passengers directly outside a delicatessen where one assassin had retreated from the fray, convinced the plot had failed. As the car attempted to back out, and stalled, Gavrilo Prinćip took his unexpected opportunity: two 0.38-calibre shots, at point-blank range hit home, mortally wounding the couple. The archduke's jugular was severed, and in his last words to his wife he supposedly begged her to live for the sake of their children. In the event, her death, from a stomach wound, preceded his as she slumped to the floor of the car. The archduke was rushed back to the town hall where he reportedly said of his wound "it is nothing", before expiring.

Prinćip was arrested on the spot and anti-Serbian rioting broke out in Sarajevo. Indeed, all the conspirators were rounded up and put on trial: several were hanged, but both Prinćip and Cabrinović, being underage, were imprisoned – to die of tuberculosis in 1918 and 1916 respectively. A year later, Serbia clamped down on

Black Hand members, and Apis and two of his associates were charged over different allegations and executed by firing squad. On his way to execution he admitted his guilt and acknowledged that he'd become a political embarrassment: "I am to be killed today by Serbian rifles solely because I organized the outrage at Sarajevo."

By then, of course, the tensions that had been brought to a height by the intelligence chief's squalid Balkan conspiracy had set Europe ablaze – with incalculable consequences. In the immediate aftermath, as news of the assassination spread, a wave of revulsion swept the chancelleries of Europe. Clearly, some sort of confrontation appeared imminent between Serbia and Austria-Hungary and a third Balkan war seemed inevitable. Less clear was how the crisis would propel the wider geo-politics of alliances towards catastrophe. In the face-offs that now ensued, behind Austria-Hungary stood Germany, while behind Serbia stood Russia – and behind Russia stood France, technically committed to aid Russia in the event of war. But the polarized alliances of Europe needed some further ingredients before the peace would catastrophically fail.

In Germany, the General Staff's operational plans had come to dominate any planning for transition to war at the expense of flexible diplomacy. That Germany's military elite, and Kaiser Wilhelm too, was hot for war is no great secret. Chief of the General Staff Helmuth von Moltke had recorded in 1913 that the chance for a showdown and a war with Russia had been missed; a few days after Franz Ferdinand's fatal day, the Kaiser convened a secret war council on 5 July at Potsdam, bringing together politicians, generals, diplomats, industrialists and bankers, asking them if they were ready for war. Only the bankers demurred, explaining that they needed at least two weeks to convert their stocks into cash.

A photograph, partially retouched, captures the moment when assassin Gavrilo Prinćip is taken out of the reach of the baying crowds and into custody at Sarajevo's police headquarters, on 28 June 1914. His assassination of Archduke Franz Ferdinand well and truly made the Balkan pot boil over.

THE SHOCK OF THE NEW

Beyond such monetary measures, Whitehall moved swiftly to control a large swathe of national life, much of it in an unprecedented way, clamping down to censor communications, muzzle dissent, seize property, control labour and direct vital industries and transport mechanisms for the duration of the war.

The key instrument was the Defence of the Realm Act (DORA), which was rushed through Parliament and became law on 8 August 1914. The Act – extended on 28 August and 27 November, and supplemented in 1915 and 1916 (and indeed throughout the war) – was to influence British life long after the First World War. The original Act was unusually short, but that belied its potency, for it started with a blanket preamble that gave great power not only to the government but also to many other authorities: "His Majesty in Council has power during the continuance of the present war to issue regulations as to the powers and duties of the Admiralty and Army Council, and of the members of His Majesty's forces, and other persons acting on His behalf, for securing the public safety and the defence of the realm."

Security fears were uppermost, and the original Act threatened court martial for any soldier and, tellingly, any civilian who communicated information to the enemy that would jeopardize "the success of the operations of any of His Majesty's forces or the forces of his allies or to assist the enemy".

As the Act was revised and supplemented, its reach extended across the nation's communications and industrial base. By November 1914 all factories linked to army and navy needs had to be placed at official disposal, giving government control over such industries as shell production and shipbuilding. The government took control of coal mines, and though it did not nationalize the railway companies they had to be run as the authorities ordained. Whitehall now effectively directed labour, while the production of coal and the movement of trains could be prioritized for the war effort. From 1915, engineering firms could be commanded to produce only the products the government ordered.

Security, communications and war *matériel* were obvious targets. But the laws went into other areas of life, and explicitly removed age-old British liberties in the name of wartime security. The population relied on the printed word for information, and now newspapers were censored (and self-censored), with access to military information controlled by the authorities; indeed, initially no war correspondents were allowed anywhere near the frontlines.

It can be argued that such measures were merely prudent precautions, but other sacrificial lambs of pre-1914 British life were quietly led to the slaughter. In an age when Temperance movements flourished but beer flowed freely, DORA now allowed publicans to dilute beer and began to force pubs to tighten their opening hours under the new licensing laws, until by late spring 1915 most were limited to two daily sessions, from noon to 2.40 p.m. and 6.30 p.m. to 9.30 p.m. The theory was that the enforced abstinence would make workers in the vital industries fitter for their tasks. It also became illegal to buy a round for anyone.

Although the precise hours would change, like the paper money the licensing of alcohol sales was one very long-lasting legacy of the "temporary" wartime measures. But perhaps the most enduring piece of national engineering introduced under the umbrella of DORA was the adoption, from May 1916, of British Summer Time (BST). In ordering clocks to move forward by an hour in the summer, the government ensured that factories, especially, had maximum daylight and could work for longer.

DEFENCE OF THE REALM ACT, 1914.

Evacuation Orders.

Section VIII.   GREEN SECTION.

Sub-Section _____   Sub-Marshal   Mr E H Budds

                                    Address   20 Penshurst Rd

Place of Assembly: DUMPTON PARK.
Alarm Signal will be TWO MAROONS.

On the Alarm Signal take Two Days' Provisions, Lock-up your House
and proceed to the Place of Assembly. All Special Constables for
your Section will wear a Green Scarf round their Left Arm and you
must Obey their Orders.

TAKE NO HOUSEHOLD GOODS WITH YOU.
The Police will look after your House.

NOTE.—There is no immediate likelihood of any attack, but precautions must be taken for
such an event in time of war.

                    BY ORDER OF THE MAYOR,
                    For the Naval and Military Authorities.

A proliferation of paperwork was one result of the Defence of the Realm Act. This Evacuation Order (c.1914) gives instructions on where to assemble and what to take in case of an emergency such as invasion, and optimistically reassures civilians that the police will take care of their houses. Emerging threats such as aerial bombardment would change the nature of the domestic threats, too.

Public clocks themselves were banned from chiming during the day – indeed, a whole raft of measures stipulated times when things could, or could not, be done. Theatres and other entertainment venues had to close by 10.30 p.m., and from August 1916 woe betides anyone whistling for a taxi after 10 p.m. As the war progressed, more and more regulation was introduced under the blanket of DORA. The ones that would make the biggest difference to ordinary people's lives would be the gradual introduction of food rationing, from January 1918 (*see* Chapter 80), and the extension of income tax to lower-middle and lower class earners.

Inevitably, there was some opposition to the successive Acts, which intensified with the introduction of conscription in 1916 (*see* Chapter 34). Pre-war Britain had experienced considerable industrial unrest, and the industrial needs of war now bolstered workers' bargaining power – to the worry of managers and government alike. The imposition of controls on labour were seized on by some trade union activists as a pretext for strikes. In March 1915, the Treasury reached pay agreements with 35 unions, but pockets of militancy remained, a prime example being at the shipyards on Clydeside. In official eyes, a small group of near-revolutionaries was openly fomenting dissent and looking for a confrontation. After the Clyde Workers' Committee journal, *The Worker*, was prosecuted for an article criticizing the war, leading agitators Willie Gallacher and John Muir were convicted and imprisoned under the provisions of DORA. Other left-wing activists were dealt with similarly. A better-remembered victim of DORA is the philosopher Bertrand Russell, kicked out of his Cambridge college for his pacifist activities and finally jailed in 1918 for six months.

DORA undoubtedly succeeded in giving the British government immense power over the population during the war. Overall, the Acts were significant for three main reasons: they made Britain better equipped to wage a long and industrial-scale war; they pushed government control into areas that had hitherto never been considered as the business of the state; and, just as the £1 note endured, Whitehall would continue to cling to some of those powers long after their original purpose was long forgotten.

08

"YOUR COUNTRY NEEDS YOU"
LORD KITCHENER & THE RECRUITMENT DRIVE

1914 TO 1915

The adjective "iconic", outside its strict religious context, refers to an image that is instantly recognizable and appears to encapsulate an era, a brand, an idea – or even a nation. If ever there was an iconic figure of the British war effort it was the imperial celebrity Kitchener – or, more fully, Horatio Herbert, Earl Kitchener of Khartoum. It is Kitchener's sternly commanding face and implacably stabbing finger that has come to symbolize the uniquely British recruiting campaign of 1914–15, and which left an image that was much replicated and adapted, imitated and subverted, to become one of the most familiar and influential of the 20th century.

Since the resignation of the Secretary of State for War following the Curragh Mutiny earlier in 1914 (*see* Chapter 2), the War Office had been run by the prime minister, Herbert Asquith. On the outbreak of war, he realized a new military figurehead was essential and, responding to public demand, hoisted Kitchener into the Cabinet as the new secretary of state.

> The 1914 poster in which Lord Kitchener summoned Britons to military service achieved subsequent fame as *the* graphic image of the First World War. It is even falsely claimed that the poster alone inspired a million men to join up. The real story, though, is more complex. For a start, the now famous poster was only published on a very small scale, and almost certainly not outside London. It never formed part of the official recruiting campaign orchestrated by the Parliamentary Recruiting Committee, and so few were printed that today the only known surviving poster is in the Imperial War Museum (and was acquired only in the 1950s). The original version, which is shown here, was not even drawn as a poster, but rather for the cover of the 5 September edition of the magazine *London Opinion*. Cartoonist Alfred Leete created it. In the subsequent poster versions, reprinted some weeks later, a revised wording was adopted, while the original design found itself on another locally produced poster, surrounded by the flags of Britain's Allies. It is one of the great ironies of the First World War that, through the sheer strength of Kitchener's personality and his intimate connection with the uniquely British voluntary recruiting programme of 1914–15, a simple magazine cover has come to be remembered as one of the most influential posters of the 20th century.

Kitchener's career as imperial warrior and administrator seemed entirely fitting for his new role. Born in 1850, he was a classically Victorian figure of a soldier: sober, serious and heavily moustached. Towering over his contemporaries in every way – he

"WELL, IF KITCHENER WAS NOT A GREAT MAN, HE WAS, AT LEAST, A GREAT POSTER."

Attributed to Margot Asquith or her daughter

was 6 feet 2 inches in height – he struck an imposing figure from the start and enjoyed a remarkable career. By 1892 he was *Sirdar*, or Commander, of the British-controlled Egyptian army. While there he led the British expedition up the Nile to the Sudan to defeat the Khalifah's Dervish army at the Battle of Omdurman (1898) and went on to rule the Sudan as an enlightened and reforming governor-general, by the standards of the day.

By contrast, as commander-in-chief in South Africa during the latter part of the Second Anglo-Boer War (1899–1902), Kitchener's methods were not pretty. Farms were burned, and Boer women and children rounded up into concentration camps where bad sanitation and lack of care killed one-third of them and caused a public outcry in Britain. This was the ruthless, hard-headed soldier who became the face of Britain's early contribution to the First World War.

Purely by chance, in the summer of 1914 Kitchener was on leave in Britain, thus prompting Asquith's unexpected offer. He immediately issued a stark warning to his fellow ministers that this would be a long and bloody war lasting at least three years, and that the effort to defeat Germany would need huge new armies, requiring Britain's manpower "to the last million". His Cabinet colleagues looked at one another in disbelief.

But Kitchener was right. He had only to look at the German army – with its 98 mobilizable divisions, 850,000 soldiers and 2.9 million reservists – to realize that this was going to be no lightning war. By contrast, on 4 August 1914, the British Army, consisting of the Regular Army, the Reserves and Special Reserves, and the newly formed part-time Territorial Force, could muster immediately just 235,000 professional soldiers, of whom about half were serving overseas, mainly in India. Unlike its continental neighbours, Britain had always eschewed national service or conscription, and traditionally relied on volunteers. The British Expeditionary Force that crossed the Channel in the first weeks of war was a mere 150,000 strong. So the need to build up a bigger army was obvious, and on 6 August the Cabinet agreed to Kitchener's request to recruit half a million more men.

Kitchener's aim, to be precise, was to raise and equip a completely *new* force, separate from the existing organization within the War Office (such as the Territorial Force, which he distrusted), to become what was effectively a New Model Army of citizens. On 11 August, he initiated a massive recruiting campaign. At first the poster appeals were very plain, using only printed words. But, with the formation of the Parliamentary Recruiting Committee (PRC) later that month, they became more sophisticated in their emotional reach. Gradually the PRC took on responsibility for maintaining the momentum of recruitment and continued this relentlessly into 1915. As a result hundreds of thousands of young men flocked to volunteer for the colours every week: 462,000 in September and more than a million by Christmas 1914. Recruiting offices were swamped with men impelled by patriotism, by a sense of adventure and, very often, by a desire to escape – from the drudgery of mill, mine, factory, field or office, from a domestic difficulty or even a pregnant girlfriend.

To say that the army and the War Office's slender resources were overwhelmed by the speed and enthusiasm of the Kitchener recruits is an understatement. Britain lacked the uniforms, weapons, tents and trainers to administer this new horde of recruits, certainly in the early months. With an intake of more men in a weekend than a regimental depot might normally take in a year, the system was jammed. As a result many would-be soldiers spent the autumn and winter of 1914 in their civilian clothes,

"Your King and Country Need You" proclaims the notice at the back of the Marylebone Recruiting Office, as two men undergo medical checks after answering Kitchener's call for *"an addition of 100,000 men"* for the British war effort. There would be further calls for more hundred-thousands to feed the war's insatiable appetite for manpower.

drilling with broom handles and living in lodgings. They were often trained by "dug outs" from the Anglo-Boer War, elderly NCOs and, very occasionally, a lightly wounded survivor returned from the trenches.

By the spring of 1915 things had improved. Uniforms, rifles, newly built camps – even field guns – had begun to equip Kitchener's "New Armies". Each normally consisted of six divisions, drawn from all over the country, and the "First Hundred Thousand" (K1) was soon followed by a Second (K2), Third (K3) and even a Fourth (K4). In all, nearly 2 million men would respond to Kitchener's call to arms. More men volunteered between August and November 1914 (900,000) than were in the entire army at the outbreak of war. It was a stunning achievement, for which Maurice Hankey, War Cabinet Secretary from 1916, gave due credit: "He had conceived and brought into being, ... a national army capable of holding its own against the armies of the greatest military power the world had ever seen."

Kitchener's star waned subsequently. In 1915, the inability to produce enough shells – the great "shell scandal" – was laid at his door (rather than at the failings of British industry), and he was implicated in the failure of that year's Gallipoli campaign. Autocratic and secretive by nature, and growing ever more weary of the gossip and intrigues of his Cabinet colleagues, he withdrew further into himself. There was relief in the Cabinet when it was decided that Kitchener should make a diplomatic mission to Russia, and so it was that on 5 June 1916 he sailed from Scapa Flow aboard HMS *Hampshire*. Battling against a Force 9 gale off the Orkney Islands, the cruiser struck a German mine laid just the week before. Kitchener died of exposure with over 600 others in the freezing, mountainous seas, his body never to be recovered.

News of Kitchener's death produced mixed emotions. The verdict recorded by Asquith's wife, the acid-tongued Lady Margot Asquith, was reputedly that "if Kitchener was not a great man, he was, at least, a great poster". The judgement did not reflect his achievements; but it did sum up his popular image for later generations.

10

HMS *LANCE*'S 4-INCH GUN
THE OPENING OF NAVAL HOSTILITIES

AUGUST AND SEPTEMBER 1914

Given the intense naval rivalry preceding the war, it was appropriate that the first actual Anglo-German hostilities occurred at sea.

Mid-July 1914 had heralded a long-planned royal review of Britain's vast fleet off Portsmouth. When the Austrian rejection of Serbia's reply to her ultimatum became known, the First Sea Lord (Admiral Prince Louis of Battenberg) suspended the review and ordered full mobilization, approved by Churchill. On 28 July, as the European crisis worsened, the lion's share of the fleet was ordered to its secure war station at Scapa Flow in the Orkney Islands, there to be renamed the "Grand Fleet". An 18-mile-long column of warships, without lights, steamed through the narrow Straits of Dover and headed north. Other ships were directed to Portland to guard the exits from the Channel into the Atlantic, and to Harwich to watch over the southern reaches of the North Sea. Whatever happened, the Royal Navy was prepared for war – which came soon enough. Only hours after Britain entered the war the destroyer HMS *Lance* fired the very first British shot.

Early on 5 August 1914, with the reality of war sinking in, the Royal Navy's 3rd Flotilla, based at Harwich, left to patrol the Thames Estuary. Its ships received reports of a strange vessel dropping objects overboard, and two destroyers, HMS *Lance* and HMS *Landrail*, went to investigate. They found a ship that appeared to be a Great Eastern Railway North Sea ferry, but it suspiciously raced off as they approached. Another destroyer signalled by lamp that the ship appeared to be laying mines. HMS *Lance* opened fire with this weapon, one of its 4-inch Quick-Firing Mark IV Guns. It was the first British shell fired in the war – but it missed. *Landrail* now also started to fire, along with the flotilla leader, the light cruiser HMS *Amphion*. Their target turned out to be a disguised German auxiliary minelayer, SMS *Königin Luise*. Under heavy fire, the ship sank shortly after midday – the first German naval casualty. Nevertheless, the German minelayer had a posthumous revenge. As the British returned to Harwich next day, HMS *Amphion* hit one of *Königin Luise*'s mines and it, too, sank, to create another "first" of the war – the first British naval casualty. Three years later, the Royal Navy was determined to match the British Army in securing powerful objects for the nation's new war museum, and the Director of Naval Ordnance suggested "the first gun that was fired after the commencement of hostilities". It was presented to the Imperial War Museum in 1919 and remains a constant reminder of the first of millions of shots fired in anger by British forces over the next four years.

"WEDNESDAY
WE GOT A WIRE.
'WAR IMMINENT.
STAND BY TO
MOBILISE.'
THERE WAS
TREMENDOUS
EXCITEMENT
OF COURSE"

*Naval Cadet Herbert Williams,
writing to his mother, 1 August
1914*

The previous day the Grand Fleet had been rocked by a change of leadership. Its ageing commander-in-chief, Admiral Sir George Callaghan, was nearing retirement but nevertheless was peremptorily relieved of command to be replaced by a reluctant Admiral Sir John Jellicoe, who protested to Churchill: "You court disaster ... Fleet is imbued with loyalty for C-in-C." Jellicoe had other reasons to be worried. He was only too well aware of the modern dangers from mines and torpedoes, and the submarine threat to Scapa Flow soon became clear. On 15 August, HMS *Birmingham*

11

GERMAN JACKBOOTS
THE SCHLIEFFEN PLAN & GERMAN INVASION

AUGUST 1914

That the First World War developed into a titanic four-year-long struggle could well be blamed on the failure of the German General Staff's audacious opening gambit. A plan conceived as a means to knock out France within six weeks, allowing Germany then to turn unhindered on Russia, became one of the biggest politico-military mistakes in history.

The plan in question has become known as the Schlieffen plan, having originally been formulated by Count Alfred von Schlieffen, Chief of the General Staff of the German army between 1891 and 1906. Once France and Russia became allies in 1894, the dangers of a two-front war were obvious to Berlin, and Schlieffen sought to tackle this problem – but as a purely military challenge. This Prussian military technocrat appears to have totally ignored the political implications of his proposed solution, and his political contemporaries were too weak to overrule him.

German thinking was governed by three main factors. First, since her defeat in the Franco-Prussian War, France had constructed strong lines of defensive forts along her border with Germany. Second, while France was expected to mobilize within a month, the conventional wisdom was that Russian mobilization would be much slower. Last, thanks to Belgium's neutrality, the Franco-Belgian border was wide open and unfortified. For Schlieffen, this last point made the solution obvious: invade France quickly, with a huge sweep through Holland and Belgium.

> The German plan for 1914 depended on speed. But there would come a point when the soldiers would have to rely on the oldest means of movement – on foot. In the first month of the war the Germans on the right wing of their attack marched over 300 miles and were soon over 60 miles beyond their nearest railhead. Since the Prussian victory over Austria in 1866, one of the key components in the Prussian uniform had been a pair of tough, knee-length field boots. With only minor changes, what were formally known as the M1866 *Marschstiefel* ("marching boots") remained one of the iconic symbols of German soldiers thereafter. Often referred to as "jackboots" because of their similarity to the much taller, strongly reinforced (or "jacked") cavalry riding boots, in 1914 *Marschstiefel* were made in natural light brown leather, and they were unpolished, with the rough side facing out – as the pair depicted here. It was only in 1915 that orders were issued for the boots to be blackened and polished. To make the boots more durable their soles were embedded with around 40 hobnails and the heels with curved strips of iron. Such well-made and rugged boots equipped the Germans soldiers well for the rigours ahead.

"YOU WILL BE HOME BEFORE THE LEAVES HAVE FALLEN FROM THE TREES."

Kaiser Wilhelm II, to his troops, August 1914

12

PANTALONS ROUGES – "A NATIONAL AFFAIR!" THE BATTLE OF THE FRONTIERS

AUGUST 1914

An observer in a balloon looking down on France's eastern border in mid-August 1914 may have seen an unusual line of red rolling towards Germany. He would have glimpsed the massed ranks of the French infantry as they launched their long-cherished bid to regain Alsace and Lorraine from Germany. These men were still kitted out in their traditional 19th-century uniforms, including the famous *pantalons rouges*, or red trousers, considered by traditionalists as representing the "martial soul of France".

Once war in the West began, there was little doubt as to exactly where France would mount her offensive against Germany. Regaining the territories of Alsace and Lorraine, lost almost half a century before to Prussia, drew the French like moths to a candle flame and represented the overriding aim of the French General Staff's planners. Accordingly, over the years they had built up a fortified zone from Verdun south to Toul and Nancy, and they planned to use this as the springboard for mass attacks further south. As a result, by 1914 this stretch of Franco-German border appeared too well defended for any German offensive.

To the north of Verdun, France's defence relied on the difficult terrain of the central Ardennes forest, with its lack of good roads, and the promise of Belgian neutrality beyond (not to mention the circuitousness of any German attack through Belgium). It also seemed logical to the French that any major German attack in the north would have to sap German defences elsewhere, to French benefit.

> A desire to restore a sense of French martial glory fuelled the French national psyche on the eve of war. It partially explains the French military emphasis on personal courage and will power, virtues summed up in the idea of "*élan*". And the intensity of this belief was reflected in the deep, rich red of the *pantalons rouges*. In the Franco-Prussian War, French infantrymen had marched to war effectively wearing the colours of their national flag: red trousers, white gaiters and a long blue coat. By the end of the 19th century, the red trousers and blue coat still formed the standard French infantry uniform. As other armies modernized their field dress, adopting neutral, less conspicuous colours, French politicians resisted all attempts to update theirs, rejecting the recommendations of the French military. The *pantalons rouges* in particular were seen as sacrosanct, French parliamentarian Étienne Clémentel declaring them resolutely in 1911 to be "a national affair!" The result was that in 1914, when the French armies charged across the frontiers into Germany they were dressed much as they had been over 40 years before – and were highly visible targets against the landscape.

"ABOLISH RED TROUSERS? NEVER! RED TROUSERS ARE FRANCE."

Eugène Étienne, French politician

The key to what became collectively known as the Battle of the Frontiers lay in the most recent French operational plan, known as Plan XVII. It reflected the fact that the French General Staff had begun to emphasize offensive operations as the only real battle-winning option. Lieutenant General Ferdinand Foch, one of France's most influential military thinkers, had, when he was a lecturer at the French Staff College, pointed out that defensive battles would be unable to bring about a decisive result, and final victory would always require decisive, offensive action. But some disciples had promoted Foch's doctrine as *"attaque à l'outrance"* – attack to excess – and promulgated the idea that the best method involved troops hurling themselves at the enemy and relying on *élan*, raw courage and the power of the bayonet to sweep the enemy away. In an age when tactics and technology were bolstering the effectiveness of the defence, these were dangerous thoughts. Plan XVII was to spawn the most costly French campaign of the whole war.

However, its concept was simple enough. On completion of French mobilization (which turned out to be 14 August), France attacked straight across the frontier into Lorraine, with the First Army heading towards Sarrebourg and the Second Army towards Morhange. Opposing them was the army of Crown Prince Rupprecht of Bavaria, with strict orders from the German High Command to make a fighting retreat and suck the French into a trap. The victorious French obligingly surged ever deeper into the occupied territories. Foch's XX Corps reached the outskirts of Morhange on 17 August and General Auguste Dubail's army entered Sarrebourg in triumph the next day, marking the high water mark of Plan XVII.

The problem was that 200 miles to the north, a worried General Charles Lanrezac, tasked with covering the French left flank with his Fifth Army, was examining reports of huge German forces massing to his north, advancing through Belgium and threatening to outflank him. He begged the French commander-in-chief, General Joseph Joffre, to allow him to realign his forces accordingly.

Joffre reluctantly agreed to some minor adjustments. But he, too, had reasons to be worried. To the south, Rupprecht's army had turned the tables at Sarrebourg and Morhange and shot the impetuous French attacks to ribbons. On 20 August, the Germans were counterattacking, sending the French reeling back to the fortifications of the Grande Couronné around Nancy. It was a major French defeat. To the north, against the inexorable German progression through Belgium, Lanrezac was hastily repositioning around Charleroi, aiming to hold bridges over the Meuse and Sambre – as he faced the numerically far superior German Second and Third armies.

Despite all this, Joffre remained intent that the French should continue with the second phase of Plan XVII – their own offensive, eastwards, into the Ardennes. He was not alone in supposing that if the Germans were strong in the north and south, they must logically be weak in the centre. Thus, from Verdun north to Neufchâteau, the French Third and Fourth armies advanced into the misty hills and forests of the Ardennes. Expecting weaker forces, they instead collided with two German armies advancing west with orders to act as a hinge for the main German attacks to the north and the south. The resulting encounter battles, between 21 and 22 August, were every bit as catastrophic for the French as the defeats at Morhange and Sarrebourg, as the infantry yet again hurled themselves forwards in the attack to be mown down by machine guns and well-directed artillery fire. A future French president, Charles de Gaulle, then a young lieutenant in the French 33rd Regiment, wrote movingly of the futility and carnage of the scene:

"IN THE NORTH, OUR ARMY ... APPEARS TO HAVE SUFFERED CHECKS OF WHICH I STILL DO NOT KNOW THE FULL EXTENT, BUT WHICH HAVE FORCED IT TO RETIRE ... ONE MUST FACE FACTS ... OUR ARMY CORPS HAVE NOT SHOWN ON THE BATTLEFIELD THOSE OFFENSIVE QUALITIES FOR WHICH WE HAD HOPED."

General Joseph Joffre, 24 August 1914

Suddenly the enemy's fire became precise and concentrated. Second by second the hail of bullets and the thunder of the shells grew stronger. Those who survived lay flat on the ground, amid the screaming wounded and the humble corpses. With affected calm, the officers let themselves be killed standing upright, some obstinate platoons stuck their bayonets in their rifles, bugles sounded the charge, isolated heroes made fantastic leaps, but all to no purpose. In an instant it had become clear that all the courage in the world could not withstand this fire.

In 1914, French North African regiments of Zouaves normally wore summer uniforms of white trousers and blue tunics, but for the rest of the year they too donned the patriotic pantalons rouges. *Here, Zouaves go on the attack in Lorraine during the Battle of the Frontiers.*

By 23 August Plan XVII lay in ruins. The idea that moral courage and an attacking spirit alone could prevail over modern firepower had been exposed as a massive error. Despite it being only three weeks since the start of the war, France had already suffered 140,000 casualties, including over 4,000 officers – 10 per cent of her officer corps – and everywhere the French armies were in retreat. In the north, only the arrival of the British Expeditionary Force at Mons had saved Lanrezac's Fifth Army from being completely outflanked to the west.

Joffre gradually became aware of the magnitude of the defeat. As his battered armies began to pull back he took two decisive steps. First, he blamed his subordinates ("grand shortcomings on the part of commanders"), sacking dozens of them and replacing them with younger, more dynamic men. And on 25 August he ordered a great retreat and the formation of a new army to counterattack on the River Marne. These were difficult decisions, but they stabilized and restored balance to the French position.

The first month of the war cost the French a staggering 260,000 casualties, including 75,000 dead, 27,000 of whom were killed on 22 August alone – a third more than the numbers of British killed on the first day of the Somme in 1916. Despite the undoubted bravery of the ordinary French soldiers – the *poilus* – everywhere *pantalons rouges* now carpeted the fields and forests of eastern France, sometimes literally stacked up; those men who had survived were shuffling back, exhausted.

The Battle of the Frontiers was over. It had been, quite literally, a bloody disaster for the French.

13

AN ATROCITY POSTER
GERMAN ATROCITIES & *SCHRECKLICHKEIT*

FROM AUGUST 1914

As the invading German forces marched through Belgium in August 1914, stories of atrocities against civilians quickly began to spread. They were to be seized on and exaggerated by Allied propaganda, but they had clear roots in the acts that were summed up in the word *Schrecklichkeit* – "frightfulness" or "terror".

To make matters worse, many of these actions were not the kind of casual brutalities committed against a conquered population by an ill-disciplined soldiery. They were deliberate operations ordered by the General Staff. The aim was to cow the civilian population and to prevent them from attacking the occupying troops – while punishing those who did. Clausewitz, the high priest of German military theory and doctrine, had written that "terror" could shorten wars. But more than that the German army was drawing on memories of an earlier war.

During the Franco-Prussian War, the Prussians had been harassed in France by civilian snipers known as *franc-tireurs* (literally "free shooters"), who then faded back into the population. The morale of the invaders was sapped by this often unseen enemy, and the Prussians regarded such acts as cowardly, unethical and against the laws and customs of war. Thus, in 1914 the Germans were almost pathologically determined to contain, even extinguish, any acts of civilian resistance from the outset. With the policy of *Schrecklichkeit*, they visited instant reprisals on the occupied population, as well as shelling and burning buildings.

This vibrant poster was produced in Dublin in May 1915, and it exploited a general sense of moral outrage at German killing and destruction beyond the battlefields of Belgium and northern France. It formed part of an ongoing programme to reinvigorate Irish enlistment, which, after initial enthusiasm, was waning. Over the rousing exhortation "Irishmen Do your Duty!", it highlighted one of the last, but most infamous, instances of German *Schrecklichkeit*: the burning of Rheims cathedral. This historic building – where in earlier times French kings were crowned – was intermittently shelled by German artillery for ten days from 20 September 1914. The Germans claimed it was a legitimate target, because the tower was being used for observation and French guns were positioned nearby, but the French denied it and the world believed them. Images of flames engulfing this architectural masterpiece proved deeply damaging to Germany's reputation and did much to sway international opinion against her, compounding the earlier reports of Belgian atrocities. This poster was also able to appeal to a sense of shared Catholic outrage at religious "desecration". Here, in plain sight, was the very essence of what everyone was fighting against.

"THE GERMANS SENTENCED LOUVAIN ON WEDNESDAY TO BECOME A WILDERNESS AND WITH THE GERMAN SYSTEM AND LOVE OF THOROUGHNESS THEY LEFT LOUVAIN AN EMPTY AND BLACKENED SHELL."

Richard Harding Davis, New York Tribune, *31 August 1914*

Belgian women make their way gingerly through rubble, passing German guards, outside what is left of the Hôtel de Ville (town hall) of Louvain, Belgium (August 1914). The result of retribution, rather than of battle, the destruction of this centre of culture outraged neutral opinion and simplified the Allies' propaganda battle.

Executions of Belgian civilians began as early as 4 August. From the first week of the German invasion, reports gained currency of potshots being taken at the invading army, and the Belgian newspapers boasted of the fact. Soon the occupied areas began to pay a terrible price, with stories of massacres and mass killings appearing in the international press. By 21 August rumours were circulating that the little town of Andenne on the Meuse had been sacked. Two days later, General Karl von Bülow's Second Army posted notices warning the civilian population of the recently captured Liège that "the general commanding these troops has burned the town [Andenne] to ashes and has had 110 persons shot". As the Germans advanced further into Belgium and the policy of retribution deepened, the list of atrocities lengthened. At Seilles 50 civilians were executed; at Tamines more than 380 died, with many herded into the town square and systematically shot and bayoneted. The epitaph on their gravestones says it all: "*1914 – Fusillée par les Allemands*".

Visé was said to have been sacked completely, with hundreds of inhabitants shot. The survivors fled over the border into Holland carrying their tales of horror. When the US Minister to Belgium and Holland later visited the town he reported it completely empty and described it as "a vista of ruins that might have been Pompei". German *Kultur* (culture), which embraced the glories of Beethoven and Goethe, was beginning to be seen as something rather different by a shocked world.

At Dinant, also on the Meuse, German troops from Saxony appear to have run amok. They herded several hundred civilians into the square, including the congregation of a church, and lined them up against the sides. They then marched two firing squads into the middle and opened fire. Six hundred and thirty-two men, women and children were murdered, including little Felix Fivet, five weeks old. Astonishingly, but tellingly, the German commander, General von Hausen, insisted that the real responsibility for the killings lay not with his soldiers but with the Belgian government, as it had "approved this perfidious street fighting contrary to international law".

Disbelief that Belgians had the temerity to oppose the German invasion was one factor stoking such retribution; the genuine fear that civilians might start a guerrilla campaign, egged on by the Belgian government, was another. Belgian posters warning civilians *not* to snipe at Germans were even regarded by some German commanders as a cunning means to implant the idea of attacking the invaders.

Major General Erich Ludendorff, who before the war had been Chief of Operations to Moltke, the Chief of the German General Staff, had led the successful assault on Liège. He believed that the Belgian government had "systematically organized civilian warfare" and expressed his personal disgust at the methods of the alleged *franc-tireurs*. Ordinary German soldiers, too, appear to have been genuinely terrified of falling out on the march, one recording that "the thought of falling into the hands of the Walloons was worse than sore feet". To keep them alert, German propaganda made ludicrous claims about Belgian priests leading armed bands of civilians against isolated German sentries and cutting up their bodies. Back in Berlin, Princess Blücher, an English-born aristocrat and diarist, recorded her belief that there were 30 German officers lying in Aachen hospital with their eyes put out by Belgian women. It was simply not true.

In contrast with such wild allegations, the most notorious German atrocity of all was well documented and witnessed by hundreds. It began on 25 August, when German forces moved into the ancient Belgian university city of Louvain. At first the nervous townsfolk went about their business, with their invaders paying for souvenirs and even having their boots shined and hair cut. Things began to go wrong the next day. When stories began to circulate of a German soldier shot in the leg by a Belgian civilian, the *Burgomaster* (mayor) and his staff were arrested as hostages. That night, a riderless horse bolted through the town square, overturning wagons and panicking the German soldiers, who later claimed that they had been fired on by civilians. The citizens said that the Germans had fired on each other in the dark.

The next morning, the Germans decided to act. General von Lüttwitz, the new military governor of Brussels, solemnly told the astonished US and Spanish representatives that the Germans proposed to destroy Louvain because, he (mistakenly) claimed, "our general has been shot by the son of the Burgomaster", and that "the population has fired on our troops". True to their word, the Germans set fire to the city and started killing its inhabitants and looting. American journalists confirmed the stories, reporting flames rising from burning rows of houses and drunken German soldiers on the rampage.

Louvain University's world-renowned library of medieval books and manuscripts, housed in the Clothworkers Hall, was deliberately set alight: 230,000 books and an irreplaceable collection of tapestries were destroyed. Across the square in the church of St Pierre were priceless medieval painted altar panels and statues. In a six-day orgy of destruction, the occupying forces burned the lot. Louvain was comprehensively sacked, its stories of death and destruction disseminated by the thousands of distraught refugees fleeing from the city.

A storm of international protest burst over the Germans, but to little avail. To make sure that there was no misunderstanding, Berlin announced that its "reprisals" were deliberate and measured and that war on non-combatants was a policy designed to punish those who dared to oppose the occupying German army.

The atrocities, real or alleged, merely united opinion around the world in the belief that the German forces were akin to a new barbarian horde and added weight to a growing feeling that the defeat of Germany was a truly just cause. This sense of shared outrage soon cemented the Allies' relations and encouraged them to issue a declaration in September, promising that none of them would agree a separate peace with Germany. And *Schrecklichkeit* delivered an enduring propaganda tool to the Allies, to be exploited throughout the war (*see* Chapter 31).

14

PATTERN 1908 WEB EQUIPMENT
THE BRITISH EXPEDITIONARY FORCE
JOINS BATTLE

AUGUST TO SEPTEMBER 1914

In August 1914, the British Army began its own contribution to the land war across the English Channel. The British Expeditionary Force (BEF) that crossed to the Continent eventually consisted of six infantry divisions and five brigades of cavalry; at just over 150,000 men, all professionals, they were a tiny force compared to the mass conscript armies of France and Germany.

Despite the deficiency in size, the BEF was arguably the best-trained and best-equipped army Britain had ever fielded. It was shaped under two main influences: the impact of the Boer farmers, who had inflicted embarrassing defeats and serious casualties on Britain's Imperial Forces in South Africa at the turn of the century; and the reforms introduced by Richard Haldane, Secretary of State for War (until 1912), which had modernized and revitalized the service. The results were striking. New organizations, new tactics and new training had all placed the army on a fresh footing, and a new General Staff ensured that when war came the BEF could be efficiently run. The BEF that set out to France in 1914 truly was a well-trained, highly mobile and tightly knit "band of brothers", confident of victory.

An infantryman must carry all he needs – food, tools and ammunition – as comfortably as possible. During the Anglo-Boer War, British soldiers still wore their traditional white leather equipment, but its colour and gleaming brass buckles picked them out on the veldt. Ammunition sweated in the equipment's pouches and easily fell out, and something new was clearly needed. In 1908, an innovative new set of personal equipment was introduced, made of flexible, woven cotton webbing. Put together from more than 12 individual pieces, it formed a single unit that could be taken on and off by undoing just one buckle on the main belt. Attached to the shoulder straps was a large pack, containing a change of clothes and a sewing kit. Strapped to the belt was a smaller haversack holding rations, a knife and fork and the means to clean the owner's rifle. Fixing the shoulder straps to the main belt were two sets of ammunition pouches, holding a total of 150 bullets in strips of 5 for easy loading. A 17-inch sword bayonet hung at the back, along with a water bottle and the components to make an entrenching tool. Despite its complexity, the equipment was carefully balanced and comfortable to wear, and in 1914 it outclassed the comparable equipment of other armies in the field. Indeed, this "Pattern 1908 Web Equipment" – as it was formally known – proved so popular that it changed little over the next 30 years.

> **"THE ANGEL OF THE LORD, ON THE TRADITIONAL WHITE HORSE AND CLAD ALL IN WHITE WITH A FLAMING SWORD, FACED THE ADVANCING GERMANS AT MONS AND FORBADE THEIR FURTHER PROGRESS."**
>
> *Brigadier John Charteris, describing the mythical "Angel of Mons" that troops claimed to see, 1914*

After landing in France early in August, the BEF moved to the left of the French General Lanrezac's Fifth Army, at Maubeuge on the River Sambre, before marching over the Belgian border. Neither the British nor the rapidly advancing German First Army, under General Alexander von Kluck, knew of the other's presence until they collided, at Mons, on 23 August. For the first time since Waterloo, the British Army was fighting in continental Europe. When the news of the Kaiser's instruction to "exterminate" this "contemptibly small army" reached the regiments of the BEF they adopted the insult proudly, responding in kind in their marching songs – not always "It's a Long Way to Tipperary" and more likely to be "Oh we don't give a f***, For old von Kluck, And all his barmy army" (to the tune of "The Girl I Left Behind Me").

15

B43 – A LONDON BUS AT THE FRONT
THE B.E.F. & THE FIRST BATTLE OF YPRES

OCTOBER TO NOVEMBER 1914

In mid-September 1914, as the weary British survivors of Mons, Le Cateau and the Marne threw themselves against the first German trenches along the River Aisne, it became clear that frontal assaults were unlikely to succeed. The BEF had now suffered three weeks of steady casualties, and it needed to regroup, re-equip and absorb new drafts.

With overextended supply lines and communications, it made strategic and logistic sense for the BEF to shorten its links to the Channel ports. During the last two weeks of September, with minimum fuss, the BEF moved north in stages, returning to its original position on the left flank of the French armies. In fact, with stalemate on the Aisne, *both* sides began manoeuvring to the north, looking to turn the other's flank in what became known as "the race to the sea". It ended when the Belgian army opened the sluice gates to flood the low-lying plains by the coast, and neither side could go any further. Opposing lines of trenches started to spread, reaching down as far as the Swiss border.

One of the key problems exposed by the frenetic pace of events in these weeks had been transport. Large troop movements could be carried out by the French rail network, but as the fighting slowed and began to coalesce around smaller areas of intense confrontation, the shifting of men between these places proved more difficult and required a different solution. It was provided, in part, by the introduction of London buses.

Bus B43 was one of the first batch (1910) of B-type vehicles built for the London General Omnibus Company. Before the war it worked routes 8 (Willesden–Old Ford) and 25 (Victoria–Seven Kings), and it carried up to 34 passengers. But in October 1914 it became one of the first buses requisitioned for service at the Front, seeing service during the First Battle of Ypres. It survived the conflict, returning to its civilian role, and in 1920 it was selected to parade with a group of veteran drivers before King George V at Buckingham Palace – said to be the only time the king ever boarded a bus.

Bus B43 was withdrawn from service in 1924 and given to the drivers' Old Comrades' Association. Decorated with a brass radiator cap in the image of Bruce Bairnsfather's famous wartime cartoon character "Old Bill", it became a feature of special events, parades and even old comrades' funerals, until on 30 April 1970 members of the Association handed it over to the Imperial War Museum for safekeeping. Bus B43 remains a unique object – a pioneering piece of mechanical engineering, unexpectedly drawn into the turmoil of war.

16

AN IRON CROSS FOR "BABY-KILLERS"
GERMAN BOMBARDMENT & THE BATTLE
OF DOGGER BANK

DECEMBER 1914 TO JANUARY 1915

By October 1914, British naval strategy had consolidated around conducting a "distant" blockade against Germany, converting the North Sea into a watery no-man's land. With an inferior number of capital ships – battleships and battlecruisers – the Imperial German Navy could only respond by attempting to lure small groups of Royal Navy warships into a chase and then onto freshly laid minefields or the guns of its main High Seas Fleet. This was the thinking behind Admiral Franz von Hipper's audacious bombardment of Great Yarmouth on the Norfolk coast on 3 November 1914. Little damage was done, but it demonstrated that the British northeast coast was open and vulnerable to attack. Encouraged by that success (and the realization that two of Britain's most modern warships were far away, off the Falkland Islands: *see* Chapter 22), Hipper's "Scouting Group" of battlecruisers mounted another, more ambitious operation. Emerging from the mist, at dawn on 16 December 1914, they opened fire on the coastal towns of Old (East) Hartlepool, West Hartlepool, Whitby and Scarborough.

West Hartlepool was, it could be argued, a legitimate military target. It was the base of the 9th Destroyer Flotilla, had three munitions factories and was defended by a battery of three guns. But Scarborough and Whitby were different; they were not military targets, and thus specifically excluded from attack by the terms of the Geneva and Hague Conventions.

For the Germans, the attack on Britain's northeast coast may have had the clear strategic purpose of drawing out the British ships, but to the British public the bombardment represented nothing more than a brutal, unprovoked attack on innocent civilians in their own homes – another German atrocity. That widespread view was clearly, and sardonically, expressed through the production and sale of this rough copy of a Prussian Iron Cross. Embossed on the front were the names HARTLEPOOLS (reflecting the distinct East and West Hartlepool, which were only combined into one decades later), SCARBORO' and WHITBY, with the date 1914. On the back were three more names, from France and Belgium: RHEIMS, LOUVAIN and AMIENS. The implication of this twinning was clear: that the Germans were now meting out the same kind of *Schrecklichkeit*, or "terror", on British civilians as they had visited on those continental cities.

From the earliest days of the war, a specialist intelligence unit in the Admiralty, known as Room 40, had been able to read German naval wireless signals. Using

"THREE QUIET, PEACEFUL TOWNS HAVE FELT THE RAIN OF SHELLS; ALMOST FIVE SCORE NON-COMBATANTS, MEN, WOMEN CHILDREN, HAVE MET DEATH FROM THE HURTLING MISSILES. THIS IS NOT WARFARE – IT IS MURDER."

The Independent *(New York)*, *28 December 1914*

a series of captured enemy codebooks, Room 40 could now provide advance warning of many intended German operations, and in mid-December the Admiralty was made aware of Hipper's planned raid. But it did not know that the main High Seas Fleet intended to shadow Hipper's battlecruisers across the North Sea.

A squadron of battlecruisers and destroyers under Vice-Admiral Beatty had set out from Cromarty on 15 December to rendezvous with the 2nd Battle Squadron (of dreadnought-type battleships) from Scapa Flow, under Vice-Admiral Sir George Warrender, and the combined group headed south.

At 07.55 the German battlecruisers *Derfflinger* and *Von der Tann* appeared off Scarborough and opened fire with their 11-inch guns. Seventeen civilians were killed and several hundred wounded. Further north, at Hartlepool, the battlecruisers *Seydlitz*, *Moltke* and *Blücher* began to bombard the town. Although there were Royal Navy ships (and a submarine) in harbour at Hartlepool, a lack of steam and other factors prevented any effective response from them. In all, the Germans fired 1,150 rounds leaving 102 killed and 467 wounded – including 424 civilians. They did not have it entirely their own way, though; the Heugh Coastal Defence Battery returned 123 rounds and damaged *Blücher*'s upper works and turrets.

At sea, the outlying ships of both fleets met and a running battle began. Afraid that the full might of the Grand Fleet might be bearing down upon it, the High Seas Fleet turned tail and headed for home – losing an opportunity to destroy Beatty's battlecruisers. The British now searched for Hipper's battlecruisers as the latter pulled away from the northeast coast, but they were hampered by, among other things, bad weather, poor visibility and confused communications. Hipper's ships were able to evade interception and return successfully to port.

The attacks were hailed as a triumph in Germany, which justified the targets by describing them as "fortified towns". The Kaiser even awarded (a reluctant) Hipper the Iron Cross and German newspapers crowed over the "heroism of our sailors". In Britain there was universal denunciation of "the baby-killers of Scarborough", as Winston Churchill described the raiders. Indeed, the most important effect of the raids on the larger British war effort was in galvanizing public support, as outraged British men, rallied by the cry "Remember Scarborough!", rushed to the colours.

As for the Royal Navy, Jellicoe now began to deploy elements of his Grand Fleet further south, moving Beatty and his battlecruisers to Rosyth. For Hipper, the ease with which his ships had eluded any British pursuit emboldened him, as 1915 opened, into planning a sweep into the shallow waters of Dogger Bank to investigate British trawlers suspected of relaying intelligence to London. However, the British advantage of access to German signals and intentions paid off again, and the tables were turned. Beatty's battlecruisers sailed to intercept. In this engagement it was the Germans who were ambushed, at dawn on 24 January 1915, and who had to flee. Despite serious mistakes – by both sides – the battle was a definite British victory. Ironically, its legacy was good for the Germans but disastrous for the Royal Navy.

It was a clear day and the faster British ships gradually overhauled the strung-out, fleeing German squadron. In the rapid long-range exchange of gunfire two notable events were to alter the course of the battle. SMS *Seydlitz* was hit by a 13.5-inch shell, which penetrated a gun turret. The explosion caused a flash fire in the ready-use ammunition, which set fire to the magazine. A brave sailor opened the red hot valves with his bare hands and flooded the magazine, saving the ship.

The damaged German cruiser SMS Blücher *lists dramatically during the Battle of Dogger Bank, her crew clinging desperately to the side – or already in the water. Owing to a Royal Naval signalling mix-up, British warships concentrated on finishing her off rather than pursuing other enemy ships. As many as 1,000 of* Blücher's *crew met a watery end.*

The second event was the 14 hits on Beatty's flagship, HMS *Lion*, which slowed her to half speed. Beatty could only fume impotently as his battlecruisers began to disappear ahead of him. As he transferred his flag to a destroyer he attempted to keep his ships in pursuit of Hipper by way of two simultaneous flag signals – "steer northeast" and "engage the enemy's rear" – on the same flag hoist. They were misunderstood. The curse of over-tight Victorian Royal Navy discipline then struck as, schooled to obey senior officers' orders or be court-martialled, the British ships left the fleeing German battlecruisers and turned northeast to concentrate instead on the already damaged heavy cruiser SMS *Blücher*. Under a hail of fire, *Blücher* rolled over and sank. Beatty attempted to correct the mix-up with a new flag signal, but by now the distance between him and the other ships was too great. Meanwhile, the battered German battle squadron made good its escape.

In terms of what it might have achieved, Dogger Bank was, for the Royal Navy, a classic case of a golden opportunity lost. But British public opinion celebrated a victory, and the Germans rightly regarded the battle as a major reverse. SMS *Seydlitz* remained in dry dock for four months, while a worried Kaiser once again ordered that no risks were to be taken by his High Seas Fleet and replaced Friedrich von Ingenohl as its commander-in-chief with Hugo von Pohl.

As with all early battles in any war, Dogger Bank provided some vital lessons. It highlighted the need for safer ammunition handling, better communications, well-practised damage-control drills and tighter control of the distribution of fire to targets. But while the chastened Germans learned those lessons, the victorious British did not. At Jutland in 1916 they would learn them the hard way (*see* Chapter 61).

17

ERIC ROWDEN'S CHRISTMAS BUTTON
THE CHRISTMAS TRUCE

DECEMBER 1914

War is one of humanity's oldest social activities, and soldiers have always found ways and pretexts to fraternize with the enemy. The Christmas Truce of 25 December 1914 is the best known among many "live and let live" instances that, perhaps surprisingly, pervaded trench warfare. Informal truces and agreed ceasefires to rescue wounded men were not uncommon, and trench routine appears to have included a tacit early morning truce, as the cold and tired soldiers on both sides got on with cooking their breakfasts. But Christmas 1914 was something different in scale.

On 24 December, Germans put out small Christmas trees on their parapet and sang carols. British soldiers joined in, and then shouted conversations began where the lines were close. As Christmas Day dawned, the sense of goodwill spread. Private Frank Richards of the 2nd Battalion, Royal Welsh Fusiliers, recorded that both sides put up boards saying "Merry Christmas", and then a few brave souls walked, with their hands up, towards the Germans, who responded in kind, met and shook hands. Richards' company commander tried to stop it all, but was too late.

Elsewhere, Captain Sir Edward Hulse of the Scots Guards agreed a truce with a German officer. What followed was an exchange of gifts, as German beer, sausages and spiked helmets were swapped for bully beef, biscuits, tunic buttons and regimental badges. Someone even organized an impromptu hare coursing.

On Christmas Day 1914, Eric Rowden was a 19-year-old corporal with the Queen's Westminster Rifles (1/16th Battalion, London Regiment). It was one of the first Territorial battalions to go to France, arriving on 1 November 1914, and some weeks later, on 23 December, it entered the trenches east of Armentières for its second tour in the frontline. The next day was Christmas Eve, and Rowden and his fellow soldiers could hear the Germans opposite begin singing. That night not a shot was fired. Christmas Day itself began frostily and with a heavy mist. There was some contact with the Germans but it was not until after Christmas lunch, when the mist had cleared, that large numbers of the "enemy" were seen standing in no-man's land. In his diary, Rowden noted: "I went out and found a German who spoke English a little and we exchanged buttons and cigarettes and I had 2 or 3 cigars given me and we laughed and joked together, having forgotten war altogether." He got the soldier with whom he exchanged buttons to write down his name, "Werner Keil", and added his regiment, "179th Saxon", on a postcard. The button still remains firmly attached to the same postcard a hundred years on, a testament to that extraordinary day.

"SHOOT 'IM? WHY SIR? 'E AIN'T DONE NO 'ARM TO ME!"

British frontline sentry, as quoted in the diary of a brigadier general

In Richards' sector, the Germans brought two barrels of beer, and further afield an informal football match took place, one of several. The cartoonist Bruce Bairnsfather even recorded one of his machine gunners cutting a German's "unnaturally long hair". In fact, all nine British divisions reported verbally arranged truces on Christmas Day. It was not an exclusively Anglo-German phenomenon either; in the villages of the Vosges, for example, French and Germans exchanged presents in disused trench tunnels.

Newspapers printed stories and photographs of German and British soldiers celebrating Christmas together in no-man's land, and soldiers wrote home about their extraordinary experiences. But "Authority" took a dim view. An angry General Smith-Dorrien ordered an investigation and insisted that the spontaneous truce not be repeated. To make sure, it was bombardments, rather than carols, that accompanied Christmas the following year.

On 20 August, the Russian First Army pushed the Germans back from the German–Russian border at the Battle of Gumbinnen, and a worried Prittwitz ordered a retreat, with half his force falling back to the north to defend Königsberg. The rest of his Eighth Army was ordered to make a general retreat behind the line of the River Vistula, 140 miles to the west, thus abandoning most of East Prussia to the advancing Russians. Prittwitz was promptly sacked for his troubles.

Berlin replaced him with General Paul von Hindenburg, together with Erich Ludendorff as his chief of staff, who was fresh from his early conquest of the Belgian fortress complex at Liège. On arrival at their new HQ they were met by the Chief of Eighth Army's Operations Branch, Colonel Max Hoffmann. The intelligent and articulate Hoffmann was the General Staff's Russian expert: he spoke the language, he had served in Russia and, most important of all, he had produced a plan. Rather than concede East Prussia to the Russians, Hoffmann advocated attacking the Russian Second Army in the south while leaving Königsberg to defend itself in the north.

This was risky, but Hoffmann had a trump card up his sleeve. The Germans were able to read all the Russian signals. The poorly educated Russian signallers seemed unable to master codes and ciphers, and to avoid delays they were often transmitting "in clear" – verbatim. The result was a windfall of intelligence: Russian troop strengths, movement schedules and operational orders were now an open book, and messages between the First and Second armies showed how poorly the two Russian generals were cooperating: General Paul von Rennenkampf, commander of the First Army, and General Alexander Samsonov of the Second had allegedly even come to blows a decade before, after the Russian defeat by the Japanese in 1905.

Rennenkampf refused to move south and assist the Second Army, signalling that he needed at least three days before his men could march. His units had outrun their supplies. Another signals intercept provided a complete order of battle of Samsonov's dispositions as well as his army's planned route of attack. Faced with this gift of opportunity, Hindenburg and Ludendorff agreed Hoffmann's plan and promptly authorized the immediate movement of one army corps to the south via the excellent East Prussian railway system. The German dispositions were completed with the march south of two further corps to face Samsonov's right flank, while a fourth was moved by rail over 100 miles against the Russian left flank.

On 27 August, General Hermann von Francois's I Corps commenced battle by attacking Samsonov's exposed left flank. Samsonov attempted to push through in the centre, but thereby exacerbated the vulnerability of his flanks. German signallers began to intercept desperate pleas for assistance from Samsonov. But they knew from intercepted orders from the Russian High Command, *Stavka*, that Rennenkampf's First Army was to continue northwest towards Königsberg and thus even further away from the embattled Second Army. Aerial reconnaissance confirmed that a huge gap was opening up between the two Russian armies. By 29 August the Germans had completed their encirclement. As the pincers closed and Samsonov's army collapsed, the general and his staff fled through the forests in the dark. Somewhere in the fastness of the night Samsonov blew his brains out.

By contrast, Hindenburg became a national hero overnight and Germany's saviour. He took up Hoffmann's idea to name the battle "Tannenberg" to redress the defeat, in 1410, of the Teutonic knights, from whom he claimed descent. The contribution of Colonel Hoffmann – the originator and coordinator of the brilliant

plan – was overlooked in the euphoria of victory. Of the 150,000 Russian soldiers who fought at Tannenberg, about 50,000 were killed or wounded and around 95,000 captured. The Germans had destroyed a complete Russian army, captured more than 500 guns and gained an historic victory.

Tannenberg stands as one of the most decisive battles of the First World War. It was to have two related and enduring effects: first, the defeat demoralized the Russians to such an extent that many Russian generals thereafter acquired a serious inferiority complex and never really believed that they could beat the German army; second, it brought the "Duo" – Hindenburg and Ludendorff – to national prominence and power as Germany's virtual warlords.

More immediately, Hindenburg and Ludendorff, once reinforced by the two corps transferred from the Western Front, quickly moved north against the Russian First Army around the Masurian Lakes. Rennenkampf was lucky to escape being surrounded and pulled back hastily to the border. That second German victory, in the second week of September 1914, effectively destroyed Russia's capacity for carrying out offensive operations against northeastern Germany.

However, the advantages of this strategic victory for the Central Powers were threatened by the defeat of the Austro-Hungarian armies far to the south, along the Carpathian Mountains, where Russian fortunes were better and quantities of troops much more numerous. The grand strategy favoured by Franz Conrad von Hötzendorf, the Austrian chief of staff, had been for a pincer movement with German forces to swallow much of Russian Poland. But, in a confused mobilization, Austria-Hungary had split her forces ineptly across two fronts, south against Serbia and northeast against Russia. Initial success in the latter had dissipated, and now Russian armies had advanced deep into the Austro-Hungarian province of Galicia and up to the Carpathian Mountains, while also threatening, to the west, the vital industries of German Silesia. The Russians had scored major victories, isolating the massive

Some of the nearly 100,000 Russian PoWs from the ill-fated Second Army (30 August 1914), after the comprehensive German victory at the Battle of Tannenberg. At this stage, Germany was both an invading power and an invaded nation, but victories at Tannenberg and, shortly afterwards, the Masurian Lakes pushed the fighting back over her borders.

19

BARNARDISTON'S SAMURAI SWORD
JAPAN ENTERS THE WAR

AUGUST TO DECEMBER 1914

It was the entry of Japan into the war, on 23 August 1914, that turned the conflict from a clash of European powers into a war of global belligerents. In 1902, Japan, a burgeoning sea power, had entered into an alliance with the world's greatest maritime power, Britain. The outbreak of European war now gave competing factions in Japanese politics – the army, the navy and ambitious imperialist politicians – an opportunity to build an imperial presence in the Pacific and to make inroads into China.

When Germany declared war on France, Tokyo – encouraged by London – issued a warning to the German Empire to withdraw German troops from Tsingtao (Qingdao), the German navy's East Asia Squadron base in China. (This was the base that German troops had seized in 1897, after which China had formally ceded it to Germany.) Berlin did not respond. Now, with a British request for help in hunting down any German armed merchantmen at sea providing a welcome catalyst for Japanese ambitions, Japan declared war.

The German East Asia Squadron was commanded by Admiral Maximilian Graf von Spee, and it consisted of the heavy armoured cruisers *Scharnhorst* and *Gneisenau* together with escorting light cruisers. They could have posed a serious threat to the Royal Navy's warships based at Hong Kong and merchantmen all over the South Seas. Spee, mindful of orders that his ships "retain their freedom of movement for as long as possible", had no intention of waiting to be trapped in port and he set sail immediately from Tsingtao. Maintaining radio silence, the German squadron headed into the central Pacific, avoiding the more powerful ships of the Imperial Japanese Navy, notably the British-built *Kongō* – possibly the finest warship of the age.

The North China Field Force was hastily assembled for the siege of Tsingtao under Brigadier General Nathaniel Barnardiston, a widely experienced officer. He successfully kept his small British and Indian contingent at the forefront of operations alongside the much larger Japanese force. When Tsingtao was finally seized, Barnardiston was showered with letters and telegrams of congratulation from towns and cities across Japan; some municipalities went further, and the Mayor of Yokohama sent a gift in the form of a *katana*, a samurai sword. He explained that this particular sword had been "made some three hundred and fifty years ago by Fijiwara Shigetaka, a famous artist". Given the symbolic resonance of such swords within Japan, this was indeed an impressive way for the mayor to express his appreciation of, as he put it, British "co-operation with our army in the capture of the German stronghold in the Far East".

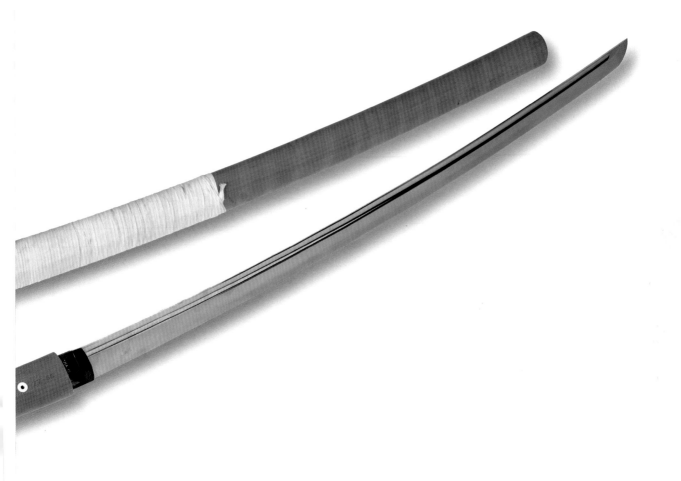

Kongō and her sister ships did not pursue the Germans as they slipped away and instead laid siege to Tsingtao in support of 60,000 Japanese troops, who were aided by two British-led battalions of the North China Field Force. When Tsingtao finally surrendered on 7 November, the Japanese fleet sailed on to seize German island possessions in the western Pacific, in an agreed division of spoils with Britain and her Dominions. (British, Australian and New Zealand landing parties had already scooped up other former German Pacific islands.)

By Christmas 1914 Japan's brief war was effectively over, and victorious soldiers and sailors paraded to celebrate their victory. It had allowed Tokyo to create a mini-empire at virtually no cost; it bolstered Japanese demands for commercial and military rights in China of the kind that European powers enjoyed; and it guaranteed Japan a seat at the top table in any peace conference. For the Far East, Japan's brief involvement in the First World War would cast a long shadow.

instead, on Austria-Hungary's Croatian coast, he risked being bottled up in the Adriatic for the duration of the war, which was unthinkable. Thus, fully coaled, Souchon took up the challenge and ordered his ships to head full steam eastwards across the Mediterranean for the Dardanelles, boldly running the British gauntlet. For Souchon and the world, it was to prove a fateful decision.

British ships spotted the *Goeben* immediately. The cruiser *Gloucester* followed, but at a safe distance, as the German battlecruiser's heavy guns raised shell splashes around her, to the amazement of the passengers on a passing Italian cruise ship. Belatedly, a British squadron of four elderly cruisers tried to chase the fleeing German vessels but could only watch them disappear into the Aegean. *Goeben* had escaped. The British thought that Souchon was now trapped, since by international treaty the Dardanelles were closed to the ships of belligerent nations; they did not know that Souchon had been told to sail right through. Greeted by a Turkish destroyer that appeared flying the signal "Follow Me", the Germans ships were eventually led through the minefields to Chanak. Souchon was determined to make a decisive contribution to Ottoman–German relations and, in his later words, "to force the Turks, even against their will, to spread the war to ... Russia".

For years the Ottoman Empire had sought the support of one or more of Europe's leading powers. But Russia had been its fiercest rival for almost 100 years, while the French (and British) held ambitions of one day taking control of the Levant, particularly Syria, and the British were otherwise lukewarm, despite sending a naval mission in 1908 to help rebuild the Ottoman navy. By contrast, Germany had assiduously courted the Ottoman Empire for many years, and its bankers and engineers had invested time and technology in what became known as the Berlin-to-Baghdad Railway. The young and conceited Kaiser Wilhelm II had visited Constantinople twice as the guest of the sultan, the second time (1898) bringing gifts of weapons, travelling to Jerusalem and Damascus, praising Islam and even decorating Saladin's tomb (*see* Chapter 89) – all giving rise to the myth of 'Hajji Wilhelm', the supposedly Muslim Kaiser of Germany. Now, the prospect of levering Constantinople into war on Russia and fostering *Jihad*, a Muslim rebellion in British India and Egypt, were tempting goals.

Outwardly, the Ottoman Empire remained neutral. However, a secret Ottoman–German treaty signed on 2 August 1914 in theory pledged the Empire to support the Austro-German cause against Russia. Chief among the "pro-war" faction were Enver Pasha, Djemal Pasha and Talaat Pasha, the Ottoman ministers of War, the Navy and the Interior respectively. They led the nationalist Young Turk movement, with sufficient power to shape events.

At the same time, Britain's stock with Ottoman opinion fell sharply. Prior to the war two dreadnought-type battleships had been under construction for the Ottomans in British shipyards but, with war imminent, the First Lord of the Admiralty, Winston Churchill, had cancelled the contracts and – quite legally – on 28 July, seized both ships for the Royal Navy, with a paltry offer of compensation. The more than £6 million cost of commissioning the two ships, the *Sultan Osman I* and the *Reshadieh*, had been raised from millions of individual donations throughout Ottoman territories. Turkish pride was outraged and nationalist sentiment was stoked.

In Constantinople, the German ambassador sensed an exploitable opportunity. For two days *Goeben* and *Breslau* waited just inside the Dardanelles Straits. Souchon sailed to Constantinople on his own and persuaded the Ottoman government that the time had come. On 15 August, he returned to his ships and next day led them

"THOSE WARSHIPS' ACTIONS BROUGHT MORE SLAUGHTER, MORE MISERY AND MORE RUIN THAN HAS EVER BEFORE BEEN BORNE WITHIN THE COMPASS OF A SHIP."

Winston Churchill, referring to Goeben *and* Breslau

German–Ottoman closeness is reaffirmed, as Enver Pasha, the pro-German Minister of War in the Ottoman government, salutes Kaiser Wilhelm II aboard SMS Goeben, *now renamed* Yavuz Sultan Selim *(October 1917). The Kaiser was visiting Constantinople and touring the former Gallipoli battlefields.*

in line across the Sea of Marmara to Constantinople, where they won a rapturous welcome. The German ambassador promptly offered both ships to the Ottoman navy, lock, stock and barrel, in recompense for the two battleships that had been – in Turkish eyes – "stolen" by the British. The offer was accepted, and *Goeben* and *Breslau* were renamed *Yavuz Sultan Selim* and *Midilli*, though they retained their German crews. Admiral Souchon was even proclaimed the new commander-in-chief of the Ottoman navy. To ram the point home, he and his men were photographed sporting the naval-issue Ottoman fez instead of the German naval cap.

It was a masterstroke of diplomatic opportunism, which suited Enver Pasha and the other pro-war leaders. Although the Ottoman Empire remained *technically* neutral, its sympathies were forced into the open. For several months all was quiet, as the *Goeben* and *Breslau* sat at anchor and Souchon worked up the rest of the Ottoman fleet. But in late October, and despite the misgivings of many ministers, Enver Pasha despatched the two German ships into the Black Sea where they bombarded the Russian ports of Odessa and Sebastopol. This was an open act of war, and, on 4 November 1914, Russia declared war on the Ottoman Empire, to be followed by British and French declarations a day later.

Constantinople was now irrevocably locked into the war as Berlin's ally. Eventually, a different Middle East would emerge – but not before the Ottoman Empire had suffered humiliating defeat, disintegration, millions of dead and economic ruin.

THEATRES OF WAR

22

A PIG CALLED TIRPITZ
WAR IN THE PACIFIC & SOUTH ATLANTIC

AUGUST 1914 TO MARCH 1915

When Japan (with British help) moved against Tsingtao (*see* Chapter 19), the German East Asia Squadron under Admiral von Spee was left without a home port and base. The question now arose: should he disperse his ships and cause mayhem on the high seas for as long as he could, or should he keep his little fleet together? The principles of cruiser warfare dictated that he should split his forces and harry enemy shipping wherever he could, and for as long as possible, while trying to avoid full-scale battle. One of his captains, Karl Friedrich Max von Müller of the SMS *Emden*, argued forcefully for just such a plan. Spee detached *Emden* to act as a single independent raider in the Indian Ocean, but kept the rest of his ships together.

Müller fully justified Spee's decision. During a two-month rampage, he sank a Russian cruiser, raided and bombarded Madras and Penang, and captured or sank around 30 merchant vessels. His exploits disrupted British shipping and diverted no less than 60 warships to hunt him down. It was a bravura performance, but such success could not continue indefinitely.

> By March 1915, only one of Spee's squadron remained: SMS *Dresden*. She was short of ammunition and fuel, and arranged to rendezvous with a German collier off the Chilean island of Más a Tierra (now Robinson Crusoe Island). But the signal was intercepted by the British light cruiser HMS *Glasgow*, which, together with HMS *Kent*, surprised *Dresden* on 14 March. The German ship sought to parley, but during negotiations its crew scuttled her. Amid the floating debris, *Glasgow*'s sailors noticed something unusual: a large pig swimming as fast as its trotters would allow. One man jumped in, was nearly drowned by the struggling animal, but managed to haul it back to the ship – where it was christened "Dennis, the pig PoW". In 1916, *Glasgow* returned to Britain, and Dennis – by now renamed "Tirpitz" (in "honour" of Germany's naval supremo) – was sent to Whale Island gunnery school in Portsmouth. The following year, Tirpitz was sold at the first of three charity auctions, on each occasion being bought by the Duke of Portland, whose payments totalled £1,785 (roughly £68,000 today). Tirpitz's death in 1919 was not the final chapter in the porcine saga. His head, seen here, was stuffed and mounted in Piccadilly and his trotters became the handles of a carving set – an enduring, unusual legacy of the East Asia Squadron's dramatic exploits across two oceans.

On 9 November, *Emden*'s luck ran out. She was finally caught by the Australian cruiser HMAS *Sydney* as Müller was raiding the radio station in the Cocos Islands.

"I AM QUITE HOMELESS. I CANNOT REACH GERMANY. WE POSSESS NO OTHER SECURE HARBOUR. I MUST PLOUGH THE SEAS OF THE WORLD, DOING AS MUCH MISCHIEF AS I CAN UNTIL MY AMMUNITION IS EXHAUSTED, OR A FOE FAR SUPERIOR IN POWER CATCHES ME."

Admiral von Spee

Emden was trapped while her landing party was ashore, and outgunned in a hopeless contest. With over 130 of his crew dead, his guns out of action and his ship on fire, Müller beached *Emden* and hauled down his flag. His enemies were generous in victory, and Müller was hailed as a hero by the British press. The *Daily Telegraph* wrote: "von Muller has been enterprising, cool and daring in making war on our shipping, and has revealed a nice sense of humour. He has moreover shown every consideration to the crews of his prizes. There is not a survivor who does not speak well of him."

While *Emden* was creating havoc off India, Spee sailed his squadron east across the Pacific towards Chile, which was neutral but traditionally friendly to Germany. Here he hoped to collect intelligence and coal prior to a hazardous dash around Cape Horn to reach Germany and safety. But he stopped to bombard the French island of Papeete on 22 September, thus broadcasting his location to the world. The British Admiralty correctly deduced that Spee must be heading for South America and thence Cape Horn, and Rear Admiral Sir Christopher Cradock's Western Atlantic Squadron was ordered to deploy south to intercept.

This put Cradock, now in the Falkland Islands, in a quandary. His only big-gun ship was the obsolescent battleship HMS *Canopus*. She had been sent to join his regular squadron, but Cradock was told (incorrectly) that she could only manage 12 knots. So he decided to leave *Canopus* behind and split his force into two squadrons for the Pacific and Atlantic coasts of South America. He sailed west around the Horn into the Pacific, heading towards German radio signals at Coronel, off the coast of Chile, and meeting the German squadron on 1 November 1914. Cradock's squadron consisted of the outdated armoured cruisers HMS *Monmouth* and his flagship HMS *Good Hope*, plus some escorting light cruisers. They were substantially outgunned and outmatched by Spee's squadron, added to which *Good Hope*'s reservist crew had only performed one main armament practice shoot in three months.

As the battle lines closed at the Battle of Coronel, the British initially had the advantage of the setting sun behind them, which dazzled their opponents. But the 8.2-inch guns of the German armoured cruisers *Scharnhorst* and *Gneisenau* outranged the elderly British cruisers and as the sun sank below the horizon the British ships were silhouetted against the afterglow. Cradock's flagship was hit before she could even open fire and within half an hour was pounded into a blazing ruin by accurate German fire from the winners of the Kaiser's prize for fleet gunnery. Within an hour *Good Hope* sank with all hands, including Cradock. *Monmouth* was badly hit too. An hour later the German light cruiser *Leipzig* found the stricken cruiser in the dark, listing and on fire, with gun turrets blown away. Opening fire at 1,000 yards – effectively point-blank range – she blew *Monmouth* apart. Heavy seas prevented any attempt at rescue, and there were no survivors.

Spee's victory was a shattering defeat for the Royal Navy, which, since Nelson's day, had an expectation of nothing less than victory. The words of a German commentator, claiming that "Germany had dealt the most severe blow that British prestige had suffered in a century", stung the Admiralty into action. Vice-Admiral Sir Doveton Sturdee with two of the Grand Fleet's fast battlecruisers was sent to the South Atlantic. Spee remained all too aware of his true vulnerability, alone in a hostile ocean with dwindling ammunition. Two days later he reached Chile and put in to Valparaiso Roads to coal and gather up-to-date intelligence. A friendly Chilean lady pressed a bouquet of flowers into his hand. "They will do nicely for my grave", he responded.

The following month, after Spee had rounded Cape Horn into the South Atlantic, the British finally got their revenge. On 8 December 1914, Spee decided to bombard the Falkland Islands; its capital, Port Stanley, was the main British coaling base and wireless relay station covering Cape Horn. He was surprised to discover two battlecruisers in the harbour that could both outrun and outgun him, for Sturdee had already arrived there to refuel. The German squadron fled, but by mid-afternoon was overhauled by the British and brought under fire by the battlecruisers' 12-inch guns. Realizing that he could not hope to outpace the faster British ships, Spee decided to engage them with his two armoured cruisers alone, to give his light cruisers a chance to escape.

The result was inevitable. *Scharnhorst* and *Gneisenau* were both battered into submission and sunk: 2,200 German sailors were killed or drowned in the freezing South Atlantic, including Spee and his two sons. The British mopped up the other fleeing German light cruisers, and only *Dresden* escaped, to survive for another three months.

Admiral Lord Fisher, the First Sea Lord, who had despatched the two battlecruisers to the South Atlantic, recognized the significance of the Battle of the Falkland Islands immediately. He wrote to Churchill: "The consequences ... have affected our position in every part of the globe." Not only was the morale and prestige of the Royal Navy restored, but now no German warship threat remained beyond the North Sea to threaten British merchant shipping and its imperial communications. The elimination of Spee's cruisers allowed dozens of British warships from around the world to return to home waters – one carrying a captured pig.

Admiral von Spee's flagship SMS Scharnhorst, *pictured in November 1914, during the time when it was taking on coal and supplies off the Chilean coast. Just a few days earlier, the* Scharnhorst's *guns had helped despatch Rear Admiral Cradock's HMS* Good Hope *and HMS* Monmouth. *A month later, Spee and his ship would also go to the bottom.*

23

MAJOR ANDERSON'S STICK
THE MESOPOTAMIAN CAMPAIGN

NOVEMBER 1914 TO NOVEMBER 1918

In cultivating the Ottoman Empire's entry into war (*see* Chapter 21), Germany, and especially the Kaiser, had ambitions to unleash the furies of Islam against the British, including fomenting rebellion in India and Egypt. German diplomatic pressure culminated in the Ottoman *Fatwa* of 14 November 1914, when the sultan, as "Caliph of all Islam", proclaimed *Jihad* (holy war) against infidels – excepting, of course, Germans, Austro-Hungarians or neutral Americans.

In the event, nothing like a mass rising of India's 100 million Muslims took place. And by then, Britain had already taken action to secure her regional interests. Forces moved immediately on the outbreak of war to protect the Suez Canal, and an Indian Army Expeditionary Force (IEF "D") went to Ottoman Mesopotamia (modern Iraq) to secure the partly British-owned oilfields at Abadan in neighbouring Persia. The government of India, and particularly the Viceroy, Lord Hardinge, had long wanted to establish British control over southern Mesopotamia and to bring a region only loosely ruled by the Ottomans under Anglo-Indian influence. A three-year campaign would witness early success, and eventual victory. But it also saw misery – not least from the often appalling conditions of temperature extremes, flies, disease (and inept medical arrangements) and, for some, the ravages of forced marches into captivity.

In August 1914, Alexander Anderson was managing the Bombay Burmah Trading Corporation Ltd in Rangoon. Following the outbreak of war, the government of India appealed for recruits, and in Rangoon a company of gunners was mustered to join a larger Volunteer Artillery Battery in Bombay. Anderson led just under 50 men to Bombay where, to their surprise, they were immediately sent to Basra in Mesopotamia. From there, he followed earlier Indian Army contingents, leading his men up the Tigris to Amarah and (by November 1915) to Kut. The next month, Anderson's guns were in the thick of the action as Kut was besieged by Ottoman forces, and by April 1916 things were looking grim. When the garrison finally surrendered, he noted in his diary: "So ended the long period of fighting, waiting and hoping, suspense and anxiety, and starving. The impossible and unthinkable had happened and one felt stunned." With as much dignity as their tired, emaciated frames allowed, the men marched out of Kut. But after the squalor and deprivation of the siege, worse awaited them in captivity. Anderson took only this gnarled, knotted wooden walking stick. He had it in Kut, he carried it throughout the terrible march to the camps, and he kept it with him for the next two years in Turkey. It was, like Anderson himself, a great survivor.

"THERE IS A DRY WIND BLOWING THROUGH THE EAST, AND THE PARCHED GRASSES WAIT THE SPARK. AND THAT WIND IS BLOWING TOWARDS THE INDIAN BORDER. WHENCE COMES THAT WIND, THINK YOU?"

John Buchan, in his 1916 novel of Ottoman intrigue, Greenmantle

As Anglo-Indian troops had been ready for some days, the Mesopotamian campaign began on 6 November 1914, the day war was declared. A naval bombardment of Ottoman forts at the Shatt el Arab, where the Tigris and Euphrates run into the Persian Gulf, was followed by the IEF's landing and seizure of Basra. Ottoman forces fled north, while the British quickly secured the pipeline at Abadan and consolidated their position around the Gulf. For imperial planners, wider horizons now beckoned.

By April 1915 the IEF had moved slowly northwards from Basra with apparent ease, but temptations lured the victorious British into biting off more than they could chew. GHQ in Delhi now regarded the security of the Abadan pipeline as secondary to a successful advance up the Tigris, ultimately all the way to Baghdad. However, back in London British ministers were divided between, on the one hand, guarding the pipeline and limiting the deployment of more British forces to the region and, on the other, encouraging the push to Baghdad, if only for propaganda reasons. A compromise was agreed. The ambitious new IEF commander, Lieutenant General Sir John Nixon, would make a limited upriver advance as far as Kut-al-Amara, about 120 miles south of Baghdad. But in the muddle of divided command, conflicting orders and slow communications, Nixon tried to do *everything*. He split his force, moving to secure the pipeline with 9,000 men and ordered Major General Sir Charles Townsend to advance up the Tigris with a division and drive the Turks back.

Townsend was successful – at first. In a series of sharp actions, supported by gunboats on the river, he drove the enemy back to Kut by September. There, after further debate in London and Delhi, he was ordered on to Baghdad. Less than 20 miles short of his goal, Townsend reached the ancient city of Ctesiphon, where his increasingly overstretched forces were halted in a tactically indecisive battle on 22 November 1915. Townsend pulled his exhausted division back to Kut, where he entrenched in early December and waited for reinforcements. But Kut was isolated. It could be defended, but it could not be resupplied. The Ottomans encircled the defences and sent fresh forces downriver to prevent any British relief. Townsend's offers to break out were initially rejected by Nixon, who eventually did send a relief force, but its three attempts to break the siege failed. Come spring 1916, Townsend's men were still hopelessly trapped. By 21 April all normal rations had gone. With food supplies running low and disease rife, Townsend surrendered on 29 April 1916. Over 13,000 soldiers became Ottoman prisoners, and about 4,000 of those would perish,

Fascinated locals look on, while others help a British gunnery team, kitted out in solar topees, as they haul a 6-inch howitzer up a Baghdad slope (1917). The terrain and climate of Mesopotamia, and the nature of its logistical problems, made the campaign a punishing experience for all those who took part.

many on the forced march north into Anatolia. Townsend, though, was housed comfortably on an island in the Bosphorus for the duration of the war.

Knives were sharpened in Whitehall and India at what was seen as a humiliating reverse. Townsend and Nixon were inevitably the principal scapegoats, but, if nothing else, the disaster forced a complete reorganization of the force in Mesopotamia. Defeat brought the very reinforcements and improvements that should have been committed earlier, and responsibility for the campaign passed from the Indian government to London. There, the War Committee authorized a renewed offensive under a new commander, Lieutenant General Sir Stanley Maude. Logistics remained a problem: at first, supplies were mostly loaded up at Basra and sent north in special shallow-draught steamers along the Tigris. Over the next year thousands of lorries were sent out and a road was built north to Baghdad, along with a light railway. From May to November 1916, as these vital logistic issues were being addressed, four new British divisions arrived to beef up the existing force.

British fortunes now improved greatly. When Russian troops moved into northern Persia towards the end of 1916 and threatened any retreat by the Ottomans (and their German advisors), Maude also struck in Mesopotamia, advancing methodically up both banks of the Tigris, bypassing the enemy at Kut and sweeping around to Baghdad, where he defeated a weakened Turkish defence. On 11 March 1917, the IEF finally entered Baghdad to be greeted as liberators. Both sides then paused the fighting during the intense seasonal heat, which allowed British supplies and reinforcements to catch up, and the battered remnants of the Ottoman Sixth Army to withdrew north to Mosul, to regroup.

Beginning again in early autumn 1917, Maude's forces resumed their advance. But on 18 November, Maude died of cholera in Baghdad. He was replaced by Lieutenant General Sir William Marshall, and though operations continued they were on a reduced scale. British and Russian forces advancing from the north and east were closing in on the Ottomans by the spring of 1918. But, after the 1918 hot season, Marshall slackened his pace: he was constrained by the demands from other Ottoman theatres (*see* chapters 78 and 89) and the need to support the mobile "Dunsterforce" campaign being carried out by Major General Lionel Dunsterville in Persia and Azerbaijan. One later critic, historian Cyril Falls, was less understanding, describing Marshall as "astonishingly inactive, not only in the hot season but through most of the cold".

By October 1918, as an armistice with the Ottoman forces began to look a real possibility, Marshall was directed by Whitehall that "every effort was to be made to score as heavily as possible on the Tigris before the whistle blew". A British force from Baghdad advanced a remarkable 80 miles in two days to the Little Zab River, where it defeated the Ottoman Sixth Army at the Battle of Sharqut. The Ottoman commander İsmail Hakkı Bey knew of the concurrent peace talks, and to spare his men unnecessary losses he surrendered on 30 October, as the Armistice of Mudros was signed.

The Mesopotamian campaign was over. It left some sobering statistics for the IEF: 11,012 killed, 3,985 dead from wounds, 12,678 dead from sickness, 13,492 missing and prisoners, and 51,836 wounded. There was also a final act. In blatant contravention of the Armistice, the British continued their advance north to seize the oilfields of Mosul on 2 November. Control and the ownership of them would become an internationally contentious issue for years to come.

"OUR ARMIES DO NOT COME INTO YOUR CITIES AND LANDS AS CONQUERORS OR ENEMIES, BUT AS LIBERATORS."

General Sir Stanley Maude, in the "Proclamation of Baghdad", March 1917

24

AN AUSTRALIAN BATTALION'S FLAG
THE GALLIPOLI CAMPAIGN

FEBRUARY 1915 TO JANUARY 1916

The Gallipoli campaign of 1915 was a major geo-strategic defeat for the Allies and a disastrous reverse for Britain. By contrast, it reinvigorated the Ottoman Empire, spreading a sense of national pride that continues to this day. For Australia and New Zealand, too, the skill and tenacity of the Australian and New Zealand Army Corps – the ANZACs – stoked an emerging sense of nationhood. All together the campaign killed and maimed hundreds of thousands of men and consumed scarce resources. For Britain, it changed the face of domestic politics in the middle of an increasingly intensive war, while globally it helped condemn Tsarist Russia to ultimate defeat and revolution. Without any doubt, Gallipoli and its consequences were one of the key episodes of the war.

"WHATEVER MAY BE THOUGHT OF HIS INTELLIGENCE AND SKILL, THE TURKISH SOLDIER IS AT LEAST NO COWARD."

The War Illustrated,
13 March 1915

The first Australians to land at Gallipoli on 25 April 1915 did not come from the more developed, earlier colonized New South Wales or Victoria, but the less-populated outer states of Queensland, South Australia, Tasmania and Western Australia. Together, the men formed the 3rd Brigade of the 1st Australian Division. This careworn flag belonged to the 12th Battalion, which went ashore on the beaches around the headland of Ari Burnu in the first assault. Apparently extemporized during the months of training in Egypt, it is made of coarse cloth with crudely sewn details ("12 Bn" on top, "III Bde" underneath). It was essentially a giant version of the battalion's colour patch – the unique coloured identification symbol worn by every Australian unit. The 12th Battalion's patch was a rectangle of white above an identical one of light blue, exactly like the flag before it faded with age. Landing part of the 12th Battalion from his destroyer HMS *Ribble*, Lieutenant Commander Ralph Wilkinson RN told his wife: "The Australians were fine. I felt proud that I was a Briton. They pulled in singing a song, 'Australia will be there!' and I could see them scaling the cliffs waving their sword bayonets, and hear them 'cooeeing' like mad." The Gallipoli landing now stands at the heart of Australian and New Zealand national identity. The qualities of endurance, initiative and "mateship" that the ANZACs showed throughout the campaign are now held to epitomize the pioneering roots of both nations – strengths somehow engrained in this rudimentary flag.

In August 1914, the First Lord of the Admiralty, Winston Churchill, resurrected a long-standing idea for an attack on the Dardanelles to strike at the Ottoman capital of Constantinople; he proposed it again in November – but was rebuffed on both occasions. What added new impetus to this idea was an urgent Russian appeal on

Further south, two hours after dawn the 29th Division stormed ashore on five separate beaches surrounding Cape Helles. Because of the strong current flowing out of the Dardanelles, many of the boats were late and the naval bombardment, intended to compensate for landing in full daylight, lifted before they reached the shore. At "W" Beach, immediately north of Helles, the Lancashire Fusiliers met withering fire from the Turkish trenches. But, despite appalling losses, they made it ashore and began to assault the cliffs, an achievement that led to the celebrated award of "six VCs before breakfast".

South of Helles, at "V" Beach, men were to be landed from an old collier called the *River Clyde*, converted with gangplanks and doors cut in the side to put men directly on the beach. But heavy Turkish rifle and machine gun fire mowed down the first two companies as they surged onto the gangplanks. One company commander recorded in his diary: "We got it like anything. Man after man behind me was shot down but they never wavered. I think no finer episode could be found of the men's bravery and discipline than this ... to go to what was practically certain death." It was not until the next day that the men were finally able to fight their way off the beach and join hands with the men from W Beach.

The landings were now locked in rough beachheads, a long way from the high ground inland, and faced increasingly effective Turkish defences. Hamilton tried to break out, both at Anzac and at Helles, but little was achieved and as spring turned to summer the beachheads degenerated into the troglodyte trench conditions already so familiar on the Western Front. In the first five weeks of the campaign the Imperial troops suffered nearly 40,000 casualties, the French a further 20,000.

Gallipoli had become a bloody failure. On 15 May 1915, the First Sea Lord, Admiral Lord ("Jackie") Fisher, resigned over Churchill's handling of the naval side of the campaign; but even at the time Fisher's own petulant and arbitrary behaviour attracted much criticism. Combined with the uproar surrounding the British shortage of shells on the Western Front (*see* Chapters 30 and 40) the political fallout forced Asquith to form a Coalition government with the Conservatives. Their price was Churchill's sacking. Meanwhile, at Gallipoli the campaign stagnated as the summer heat built up. Flies, disease and lack of water and sanitation became the real enemy in the blistering heat of a Mediterranean summer.

In August, the promise of new troops encouraged Hamilton to launch a renewed attack from Anzac Cove. An ANZAC force would break out, sweep north and assault the ridge of hills that dominated the whole area. It would link up with two new British divisions simultaneously coming ashore at Suvla Bay. In the hope of drawing off Turkish reserves, diversionary attacks would also be made from existing positions at Helles opposite Krithia and Anzac Cove at Lone Pine. They all failed. By the end of August it was clear that nothing had been gained except a longer line winding through the same three beleaguered beachheads – Helles, Anzac Cove and now also Suvla Bay. Hamilton refused to contemplate withdrawal, and in October was summarily replaced by General Sir Charles Monro, fresh from the Western Front. Within days Monro had recommended evacuation. As Churchill quipped, "He came, he saw, he capitulated."

But Monro had a point: there was nothing further to be gained at Gallipoli. Whitehall dithered, and Lord Kitchener himself came out to see what conditions were like. He instantly realized that the campaign had to be shut down. A dreadful run of weather at the end of November confirmed his conclusion. First a gale struck,

An Australian soldier carries a wounded comrade to a medical aid post for treatment, on the ANZAC beachhead. Turkish machine guns were deadly enough; but dysentery and other diseases in the fly-infested summer heat, compounded by inadequate water supplies, made even greater demands on the medical facilities.

then there was torrential rain. "Lightning and thunder absolutely incessant for two hours and rain indescribable since the Flood. It simply dropped in lumps, whole chunks of it," wrote one officer at Suvla. Both sides were forced to evacuate their flooded trenches and take shelter, and they huddled on the open ground in an undeclared silent truce of mutual misery. There followed a bitter frost, and immediately afterwards a blizzard, both causing widespread frostbite. At least 30 British sentries froze to death. And then the sun came out.

Evacuation was finally ordered on 8 December, but only for Anzac Cove and Suvla Bay. Between 10 and 20 December the troops extricated themselves from under the very noses of the Turks with great skill, without the loss of a single soldier. In a bow to the inevitable, the evacuation of Helles was also ordered on 24 December. Just before dawn on 13 January 1916, the last Allied soldier left the Gallipoli Peninsula, in a withdrawal as smooth as the earlier one. Indeed, the evacuation was easily the most successful element of the entire campaign – though it did not feel like a success. Leaving Helles in one of the final boats, Joe Murray, who had served there with the RND continuously since May, remembered: "We were so packed we couldn't move at all. We left there like a lot of cattle, being dumped into a lighter and just pushed out to sea, and nobody gave a tinker's cuss whether we lived or died."

As Churchill later observed of Dunkirk, "wars are not won by evacuations". Gallipoli had proved, in Hamilton's phrase, "an unlucky show" indeed.

Triple Alliance Treaty did not apply, because neither Austria-Hungary nor Germany had been attacked – rather, they had gone on the offensive. Many Italians could see little advantage in joining their "allies" in war, and there was fear that Italy, as a peninsular nation, was much more exposed to attack by Britain's powerful Royal Navy.

A loose opposition coalition advocated strict neutrality. However, many Italian nationalists saw the war as a chance to seize the "Italian" territories from Austria-Hungary. Faced with these conflicting voices, the government remained neutral, to the ire of the Central Powers. Italy sat on the fence to see which way the war was going, while being wooed by both sides and maintaining secret links with both sides.

As New Year 1915 dawned it was the Allies who tipped the balance. France saw Italian participation as a way of forcing Germany to divert forces away from the Western Front. The Allies dangled promises of Italy taking over Austro-Hungarian territory. The Central Powers could not match such territorial bribes, as Austria was unlikely to surrender voluntarily her own territory in return for Italian support. A Bank of England £50 million loan to finance any Italian war finally clinched the deal, and in the secret Treaty of London (26 April 1915) Italy agreed to enter the war as one of the Allies.

It was a controversial move: an outraged Italian Chamber of Deputies brought a vote of no confidence in Salandra and forced him to resign. It reckoned without the palace, for King Victor Emmanuel III exerted considerable political influence. He refused to accept Salandra's resignation and personally made the decision to declare war on Italy's erstwhile Triple Alliance partner Austria-Hungary on 23 May 1915, invoking Italy's "*Sacro Egoismo*" (sacred self-interest).

Italy was, however, ill-prepared for major European war. In 1914, she was a poor country, the weakest of the warring partners, and her centuries of internal divisions were still palpable. A more advanced, industrializing north contrasted with a south that was primarily agrarian, the latter chiefly populated by peasants whose lives were often little better than feudal serfdom. Southerners were, however, the primary pool of manpower for massive conscription. One-third of them were illiterate. Deficiencies in human resources were matched technically: the Italian army could only muster 120 heavy or medium artillery pieces and about 700 machine guns.

Nonetheless, the fighting started surprisingly quickly. The Italian Chief of the General Staff, General Luigi Cadorna, assembled 25 infantry and 4 cavalry divisions on the Austrian border, and on 23 June launched a major offensive northeast across the River Isonzo towards what is nowadays Slovenia. The river was prone to heavy flooding and was overlooked by steep mountains to the north. Cadorna's strategic objective was the city of Trieste, 150 miles to the southeast: it was vital to the mostly landlocked Austro-Hungarians, because it was their major commercial port.

For their part the Austrians were well prepared in the region and had built a system of trench defences rivalling anything seen on the Western Front. Although the Italians outnumbered the defenders by two to one, their offensive quickly ran out of steam because they were launching frontal attacks uphill against well-dug-in troops and uncut barbed wire. In the two weeks of the First Battle of the Isonzo, the Italians suffered 60,000 casualties. On 7 July 1915, Cadorna called off the attack.

This was only a respite. On 18 July, the assault was renewed using the same tactics but with a heavier bombardment. Although in places the fighting was savage, and even hand-to-hand, the Italians were repulsed with heavy casualties. The battle ended on 3 August when both sides appear to have run out of artillery ammunition. On 18 October, Cadorna tried again, launching a major offensive with over 1,300 guns massed against the whole line of Austrian positions overlooking the river; it was as unsuccessful as its predecessors, and by 3 November had run out of steam. Astonishingly, a week later Cadorna continued the offensive in the Fourth Battle of the Isonzo, hurling another 370 battalions mainly against the fortress town of Gorizia, although the fighting was spread all along the 60-mile river front. Yet again the attack collapsed. An unofficial "live and let live" truce was agreed between the weary combatants as the first serious snows of winter reduced both sides to trying to survive, and operations were halted through lack of supplies.

By the end of 1915 the Italians had lost 300,000 men, mainly through artillery fire, which was even more devastating in mountainous terrain than on the Western Front: it could send deadly razor-sharp splinters of rock flying into its victims. Yet the gain was less than 10 miles of Austrian territory. Cadorna's brutal head-butting offensives appeared to have achieved little. However, they had at least succeeded in alarming the Austro-Hungarian High Command, whose forces had also suffered seriously. Worried by the persistent Italian attacks, Vienna formally requested assistance and reinforcements from Berlin. But Italy and Germany were not yet at war with one another, and for now the Germans resisted the requests.

Specialist Italian mountain troops clamber up Monte Nero, on the limestone Karst Plateau, during the Second Battle of the Isonzo (July 1915). It was a radically different sort of terrain compared to that which the BEF confronted in Flanders or on the Somme, though often as deadly.

Cadorna launched seven more costly offensives on the Isonzo over the next two years. In May 1916, a concerted Austro-Hungarian push in the Trentino was contained by an Italian counterattack, and in the subsequent Sixth Battle of the Isonzo (6–17 August 1916) Cadorna's men finally did succeed in capturing Gorizia. But it was only a relative Italian success. By September 1917, and despite some territorial advances in the Eleventh Battle of the Isonzo, the shattered Italian army was suffering mutiny and disaffection.

The Austro-Hungarians were equally worn down. But things were about to change. In August 1916, Italy had declared war on Germany, and now – with the failure of the last Russian offensive on the Eastern Front – Germany was able to transfer troops to the Italian theatre. Thus the Twelfth Battle of the Isonzo – better known as Caporetto – saw one of the great *German* victories of the war. A new Fourteenth Army under General Otto von Below, with seven German and five Austrian divisions, secretly massed 1,000 guns each with 1,000 rounds in the mountains to the north. On 24 October 1917, a surprise bombardment of mixed gas and High Explosive eliminated the Italian batteries and headquarters as stormtroopers infiltrated the frontlines. Mountain troops seized the mountain defences and the main assault fell down on the Italians in the plain below, routing

An Italian soldier prepares to hurl a grenade, from beneath his protective corrugated canopy on the Monte Grappa massif, in the Venetian Alps (1918). He wears the Italian version of the French Adrian helmet. The Italian Front saw trenches, too, but rather than holes in the ground they were often perches carved into the mountainsides.

them and causing havoc as they fell back more than 60 miles in disarray. Italian gas masks didn't work and Cadorna's men fled in panic as the Germans surged forward, capturing whole units miles behind the lines. Many bewildered soldiers just ran away; key generals went into hiding. The offensive only stopped when the attackers ran out of supplies two weeks later.

The Battle of Caporetto ranks as one of the most comprehensive victories of the war: it resulted in the capture of half the Italian army's artillery and inflicted 600,000 casualties on the hapless Italians – the vast majority surrendering or deserting.

There was one silver lining. Despite the threats of revolution in a weakened Italy, the new frontline, on the River Piave, was now on Italian territory and the war had become a defensive one, a war for survival, which concentrated minds. Moreover, the new line was now only half as long and could be held – just. The Italians begged for help and the British and French rushed forces to stabilize the situation – but only on condition that Cadorna was sacked. His tactical stubbornness had been matched by a ruthlessness meted out on his own troops. As Hew Strachan has noted, almost 6 per cent of Italian soldiers faced a disciplinary charge, and "about 750 of them were executed, the highest number of any army in the war". Cadorna had even brought back "decimation" – the Roman practice of executing every tenth man in units deemed to be underperforming – *pour encourager les autres.*

The uneasy stabilization of the line in the winter of 1917–18 gave both the demoralized Italians and their overstretched attackers a breathing space. But in the spring the Germans withdrew most of their troops to support the offensives of March to June on the Western Front. In its turn, the Austro-Hungarian High Command decided to attack along the whole line, with the aim of knocking out what it saw as an enfeebled Italy once and for all.

However, the Italians had learned from their mistakes and their new Chief of the General Staff, General Armando Diaz, had reorganized his battered army. Behind new defences in depth, and with an operational reserve of 13 lorry-borne divisions ready to be rushed to any critical point, the Italians were this time prepared. Good intelligence had alerted Diaz that the attack would start at 03.00 on 15 June 1918, and so he ordered a massed bombardment of the packed Austrian forming-up trenches at 02.30, catching the attackers by surprise and causing serious casualties. The offensive did eventually break in for 5 miles over a 15-mile front along the River Piave, but then stalled as the swollen river tore bridges away and cut off many advanced Austrian units. By 19 June the Italians were counterattacking and up to 20,000 Austro-Hungarians are thought to have drowned as they tried to flee. By 26 June it was all over. The Italians had recaptured all the Austrian gains and had inflicted over 175,000 casualties in the process.

The Battle of the Piave was Italy's first real victory and had decisive repercussions. At the same time Germany's great offensive in the West was running out of steam, and Piave contributed to Ludendorff's growing sense of crisis. It finally dashed any hopes in Vienna that military victory was possible. It also served to accelerate the disintegration of the Austro-Hungarian army, whose destruction was completed by the Italians at the Battle of Vittorio Veneto – but not immediately. Ignoring Allied pleas urging him to press a counterattack, Diaz stopped to regroup and resupply between July and October 1918. Then, on 24 October, the anniversary of Caporetto, Diaz launched his main offensive, pitting his now reinforced and re-equipped 60 divisions against the same number of weak and demoralized Austro-Hungarians. The flooded river plain slowed progress in the centre, but near the river's mouth into the Adriatic at Papadopoli Island on 27 October, Allied troops broke through and crossed the river. Ominously, the enemy units ordered to counterattack by Field Marshal Svetozar von Bojna refused to move and mutinied. In Ludendorff's later opinion: "In Vittorio Veneto, Austria did not lose a battle, but lose the war and itself, dragging Germany in its fall. Without the destructive battle of Vittorio Veneto, we would have been able, in a military union with the Austro-Hungarian monarchy, to continue the desperate resistance through the whole winter, in order to obtain a less harsh peace, because the Allies were very fatigued."

From then on, the Austrian Front collapsed as soldiers voted with their feet, surrendering in droves to the advancing Italian forces who were now threatening to cut off any retreat to the Trieste plain. The retreat turned into a rout as the Austrian divisions fled east. The political consequences of the disaster rippled outwards: on 28 October, the Czechs withdrew from Vienna's stricken empire, to be followed by Hungary herself in November. The Austro-Hungarian Empire fell apart.

By this time, an Austrian Armistice Commission was already in discussions with the Italians, and on 3 November the Armistice of Villa Giusti was agreed. It came into effect the following day. Italy had won her war, and to the victor the spoils of the Trentino/Alto-Adigo and South Tyrol, Istria (including Trieste) and portions of the north Dalmatian coast and islands, all as agreed secretly with the Allies in 1915. Many Italians considered this the final act of Italy's long drawn out Risorgimento and reunification.

Yet Italy's victory had cost her over 650,000 dead and a million wounded, and other Italian ambitions (including for colonies) were rebuffed during the subsequent Versailles peace negotiations. An impression grew among many Italians of a "mutilated victory", helping to drive growing political instability after the war – and ultimately the rise of Mussolini and the *Fascisti*.

26

THE HIGHLANDERS' BULGARIAN MAXIM
SALONIKA & THE BALKAN FRONT

1915 TO 1918

Salonika is very much the forgotten theatre of the war. This is a serious oversight as it saw over 600,000 Allied soldiers of half a dozen nationalities deployed to "the Balkan Front" and was – eventually – one of the Allied victories that brought the Central Powers crashing down.

The First World War's opening shots were Austria-Hungary's bombardment of the Serbian capital, Belgrade. Yet Serbia had managed to hold off the Austro-Hungarian armies until the spring of 1915. German involvement and Bulgaria's entry into the war in October 1915 changed all that. With powerful German and Austrian armies to the north and now a major Bulgarian threat from the east, Serbia faced annihilation.

In 1915, British and French plans for a Balkan campaign were driven by three main factors: first, to persuade other Balkan countries – particularly Greece – to join the Allies; second, as part of the reassessment of grand strategy, since the Western Front seemed a stalemate; and lastly as a way of propping up the hard-pressed Serbian army. In the event, the Greek port of Salonika would pay host to a large encampment of Allied soldiers for almost three years. The British became the junior partners in a French-led theatre, where they occasionally battled the enemy, but mostly battled boredom and disease.

Summer was always the worst time at Salonika. In the river valleys life was unsupportable amid malarial mosquitos, forcing the British to fall back to the nearby foothills. In 1917, when the weather cooled in September, the British prepared to re-establish their forward line along the Struma valley – but to cover this move they needed temporarily to recapture the village of Homondos. So, on the night of 13/14 October, a tricky attack attempted to take the village from behind. As D Company, 2nd Battalion, the Cameron Highlanders, moved forward, the Bulgarian defenders rallied around a strongpoint, at the heart of which stood a machine gun. Lieutenant Robert MacIntyre gathered a group of men and charged the gun, killing or capturing all the Bulgars in an action that won him the Military Cross. "Homondos II", as it was called, secured the village and the British line could be rebuilt along the Struma's left bank. MacIntyre's gun, one of three captured by his battalion, was this MG09 Maxim made in Berlin in 1916 for the Bulgarian army. General Headquarters at Salonika took hold of the gun and immediately sent it back to London. Before the end of the year, it was lodged in the (Imperial) War Museum as exhibit number 742. Battle-scarred and still highly prized, it remains on display proudly bearing the defiant message: "CAPTURED BY 2D CAMERON HDRS HOMONDOS 14TH OCT 1917."

"IT WOULD BE VALUABLE IF YOU WOULD KINDLY EXPLAIN
TO THE PRIME MINISTER ... WHAT THE NATURE OF THE BALKAN
COUNTRY IS ... HE SEEMS TO THINK THAT THERE IS A SINGLE
RANGE OF HILLS ... WHEREAS THE WHOLE COUNTRY IS A
MASS OF MOUNTAINS ... IN WHICH A SMALL ARMY WOULD
BE MURDERED AND A LARGE ARMY WILL STARVE."

*Chief of the Imperial General Staff, Field Marshal Sir William Robertson, to Lord President of the Council,
Lord Curzon, July 1917*

Greece was neutral when Prime Minster Eleftherios Venizelos called for intervention in September 1915 – which the Allies were happy to regard as a legal invitation. Venizelos was soon sacked by King Constantine, who was anxious to preserve Greek neutrality; but there was little the king could do to prevent the landings of French and British troops, which began on 5 October.

The following day, combined German and Austro-Hungarian forces under Field Marshal von Mackensen promptly invaded Serbia. Bulgaria declared war on 14 October and within 24 hours attacked Serbia from the east, before successfully turning back the Allied forces advancing north into Serbia from Salonika. The Serbs now faced two choices: surrender or retreat. By an extraordinary feat of endurance, of the 140,000 men of the Serbian army and refugees who escaped westwards over the snow-covered mountains to Montenegro and neutral Albania, 125,000 survived to take ship and escape to Corfu. The hardy Serbs would themselves arrive in Salonika in May 1916.

The Central Powers' total victory over Serbia opened up the railway from Berlin to Constantinople and ensured that German supplies could reinforce their Ottoman allies. For Bulgaria there was the prize of Serbian Macedonia, a major war aim. British politicians and generals now faced the difficult question of what to do next. The recent débâcle in Gallipoli (*see* Chapter 24) made most of them sceptical of new fronts. But French internal politics demanded a continuation of a Balkan Front, to be run by the general favoured in left-wing quarters, Maurice Sarrail; there was strong support, too, from Italy, Russia – and of course the Serbs themselves. Thus, the four divisions (three French, one British) that were pushed out of Serbia in December 1915 now fell back to Salonika, there to be reinforced. In vain did King Constantine protest he "would not be treated like some native chieftain" at this ignoring of Greece's neutrality.

The Allies dug themselves into a vast military encampment packed with men and huge stockpiles of war equipment. The whole was surrounded by dense thickets of barbed wire and was known irreverently as "the Birdcage". Eventually, a multinational force under French command held a line that ran from the Adriatic through Macedonia to the Aegean. French, Serbs and others manned the western portions of the line and two British corps held the east. The mystified Bulgarians looked on in amazement, and after a couple of tentative probes left the Allies alone. The force posed no threat to the Ottoman Empire, Austria-Hungary or Germany and was tying up hundreds of thousands of Allied troops to no end. A German journalist sardonically called the Salonika Front "the greatest internment camp in the world": it was.

It was also very unhealthy. Disease was rife, mosquitoes were plentiful and malaria was endemic. Along with boredom, poor food and little action, the conditions sapped the strength and morale of an already badly supplied army, now effectively beached in northern Greece.

The stalemate was interrupted, though, in August 1916, when Romania finally threw in her lot with the Allies, a move helped by extravagant promises of Austrian territory. A Franco-British sortie into Macedonia, to distract the Bulgarians and thereby help Romania, achieved surprise and made progress until November snows halted it. The gain of some territory and the "liberation" of the Serbian town of Monastir provided a morale boost for the Allied effort. Romania was less fortunate. German, Austro-Hungarian, Ottoman and Bulgarian armies swiftly moved to crush Bucharest for its temerity. By December 1916, and after losing 310,000 men, Romania was effectively out of the war, reduced to an isolated rump of an army huddling in the wintry protection of the Russian lines in far-off Moldova.

British military dugouts and bivouacs monopolize a terraced hillside near Salonika (1916). The defensive line around Salonika created the massive encampment dubbed "the Birdcage"; contemporary newspapers criticized its apparent inactivity and failure to take the fight to the enemy.

The forces at Salonika went back to holding the line and waiting. Greece, meanwhile, had fractured into two competing governments when the Allies supported a regional coup by Venizelos; now some Greek forces loyal to his cause joined the Allied force. In April 1917, action resumed, as three British divisions launched an attack in the hills around Doiran as a diversion from a larger Franco-Serb attack west of the River Vardar. Both attacks failed with heavy losses, the offensive was called off and the stalemate returned. But Greece now made up her mind. In June 1917, King Constantine abdicated in favour of his son Alexander, who, under pressure from Venizelos, finally issued the nation's declaration of war.

By early 1918, the force around Salonika – now including Italians, Russians and the Greek army, too – was preparing a major offensive intended to end the war in the Balkans. On 15 September, the new French commander, General Louis Franchet d'Espèrey ("Desperate Frankie" as the British called him), unleashed the main Franco-Serb thrust, and three days later the British once again attacked the well-fortified hills of the Lake Doiran area – only to be repulsed, as before with major losses. However, in the west the French and Serbs finally broke through at Gradsko, then took Skopje, forcing the Bulgarian army into a general retreat as it was harried by the pursuing Allies on the ground and by the Royal Air Force from above. Bulgarian discipline collapsed, and the retreat became a rout. This time no help was forthcoming from the exhausted Germans, already under severe pressure on the Western Front. Faced with faithless allies, a disintegrating army and unrest at home, Bulgaria was finished and signed an armistice on 29 September 1918.

The political effects of this surrender went far beyond the Balkans. The supply route from Germany to Constantinople was finally severed, and the whole Central Powers' southeastern front was now vulnerable. D'Espèrey, forgetting the logistical problems, wrote excitedly on 2 October: "I can with 200,000 men cross Hungary and Austria … and march immediately on Dresden."

He didn't, and elsewhere the war still had time to run. But there was no doubt that he had struck the Central Powers a decisive blow, albeit at heavy cost. For the British, the battle casualties of less than 20,000 were dwarfed by the 480,000 cases of disease, principally malaria; accusations that the whole thing was a drain on resources lingered long after. Yet, after three years of monotony, sickness and misery, the Salonika Front had delivered a decisive Allied victory and kicked away one of Germany's props, and to that end had finally vindicated itself and helped to end the war.

27

A *LUSITANIA* SURVIVOR'S CAMISOLE
UNRESTRICTED SUBMARINE WARFARE

1915 TO 1916

By spring 1915, although Germany's High Seas Fleet was bottled up at its Wilhelmshaven base, her U-boats were beginning to flex their muscles in increasing numbers. The Royal Navy's senior leadership was acutely aware of how vulnerable even their largest warships were to underwater attack. But it was gradually becoming apparent that the *really* exposed targets were the vessels of the British Merchant Navy, and by attacking these ships German submarines had the potential to threaten a counter-blockade of Britain. In May 1915, all these issues exploded into an international incident with the sinking by torpedo of the Cunard passenger liner RMS *Lusitania*.

> On board the *Lusitania* in May 1915, a young British couple, the Reverend Herbert and Mrs Margaret Gwyer, were returning from Canada, where they had recently married. When the ship was struck, they made it into a lifeboat and seemed to be escaping – but their boat lacked oars and remained perilously close to the sinking ship. As the wreck of the *Lusitania* rose in the water before plunging to the bottom, it looked as if it would crush the Gwyers' boat. Margaret never remembered why, but, unnoticed by her husband, she leapt into the water and fainted, coming to in the darkness of one of the liner's funnels. All she could see was a distant light. Suddenly there was a massive explosion as the boilers burst, shooting her clear of the ship as it went down. Margaret, though blackened by oil and smoke, was picked up and deposited safely in Ireland, to be reunited with her frantic husband some hours later. The Gwyers were taken to London, where Margaret tried to get the black stains off her face by washing it "twice with Vim", before she faced the daunting prospect of meeting her husband's parents for the first time. For the rest of her life she carefully preserved the stained camisole she had been wearing on 7 May – a reminder of her miraculous escape.

In 1914, the reappointed First Sea Lord, Lord Fisher, had warned of the threat to merchant shipping; however, the prime minister had pointed to the pre-war international agreements (to which Germany was a signatory), which laid down the accepted rules governing "cruiser warfare": passenger ships were off-limits and enemy merchant ships could only be sunk without warning if they resisted or failed to stop. If neither of these was the case, the ships could only be sunk after the crew had been evacuated. As Germany's scattered cruisers were hunted down worldwide, the German navy pressed the Kaiser to use the growing number of U-boats to attack merchant shipping – including that of neutral countries trading with Britain. German

"IT IS STARVATION, NOT INVASION WE HAVE TO FEAR."

First Sea Lord, Admiral Lord Fisher

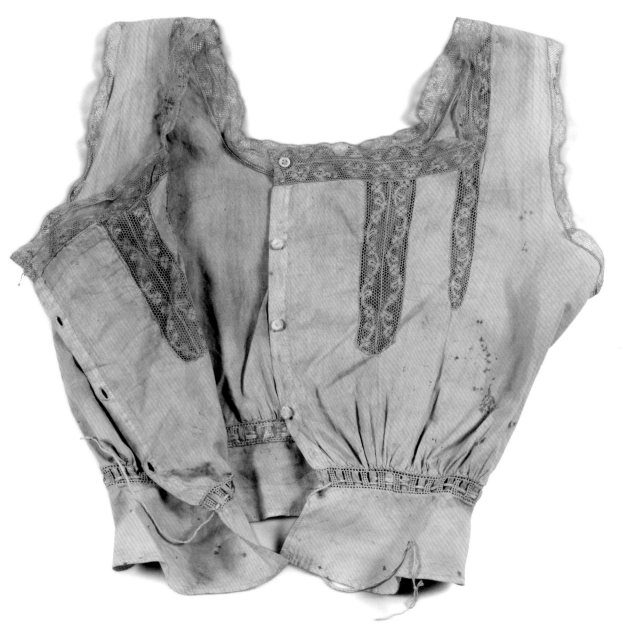

politicians and diplomats warned of the political dangers. Nevertheless, on 4 February 1915 Berlin declared that from 18 February the waters around Britain would be treated as a "war zone", that all British merchant vessels would be considered fair game, and in a deliberate ploy to scare off Britain's trading partners warned them that "their becoming victims of attack against enemy ships cannot always be avoided".

Neutral powers inevitably reacted angrily, but they continued trading, for there appeared little *tangible* risk to their ships from a few submarines. In 1915, unlike today's nuclear deep-sea boats, submarines were primarily surface ships that submerged only when necessary. Their *modus operandi*, in line with the agreed rules, would be to overhaul a merchant ship, order her to stop and then determine her identity. British-flagged ships were legitimate targets, and the crew would be ordered to the lifeboats and the vessel sunk either by a boarding party or more usually by gunfire rather than wasting one of the submarine's few and expensive torpedoes (of which a U-boat in 1915 carried a maximum of six).

The problem for a U-boat was that while on the surface she was at risk. Even merchant ships could ram a submarine – and some did (*see* Chapter 33). For self-preservation, it made more sense to attack without warning. In January 1915, Captain Otto Dröscher of *U-20* torpedoed and sank three merchant ships without warning, in the English Channel, before going on to damage the fully illuminated hospital ship *Asturias* off Le Havre. During March, *U-28* sank five British merchant ships without warning, including the 5,000-ton *Falaba* and even the passenger liner *Aguila*. By mid-April 1915 the U-boats had made 57 torpedo attacks on merchant ships, of which 38 had been successful. Another 90 ships had been attacked by gunfire.

During May the U-boats also turned their attention to the North Sea, where Scandinavian neutrals suffered most. However, in the waters to the west of Ireland and in the Irish Sea, where shipping had to concentrate to make landfall, U-boats found a target-rich environment. It was here, on 7 May 1915, that the new captain of *U-20*, Walther Schwieger, confronted the 45,000-ton *Lusitania*.

The *Lusitania* had sailed from New York on 1 May 1915, under command of the experienced Captain Bill Turner, with 2,000 passengers and crew on board and a small cargo of ammunition – rifle cartridges, empty shell-casings, non-explosive fuses, but no explosives. All aboard were aware of a warning posted by the German Embassy that passengers travelling on British-flagged ships "did so at their own risk".

During the first week of May, *U-20* had already been busy off the coast of County Cork, attacking six ships and prompting the Admiralty on 6 May to warn shipping of U-boat activity off southern Ireland. On the morning of 7 May, the liner entered what was known as the "Danger Zone", increased her speed to 18 knots, closed all watertight doors, posted double lookouts and swung out all lifeboats "just in case".

At 14.10 Schwieger ordered one torpedo fired at a range of 700 metres. It struck *Lusitania*'s starboard side just below the bridge and was followed by a second explosion – probably the rupturing of high-pressure steam boilers, accompanied by clouds of coal dust from the ship's bunkers. The stricken vessel continued for another 2 miles, settling with a 15-degree list to starboard as water flooded in. Electric power failed and bulkhead doors could not be reopened. Captain Turner gave the order to abandon ship. It took ten minutes for *Lusitania* to slow down and start lowering her boats in the water. But on the starboard side the listing meant they were swinging out too far for people to step aboard, while on the port side several boats crashed down the sloping hull, spilling their occupants into the cold water below. A mere handful out of the almost 50 boats eventually proved usable.

Eighteen minutes after the torpedo struck, *Lusitania* sank, just over 11 miles offshore. By the time help arrived, many of those in the water had died of hypothermia. The final death toll for the disaster shocked the world: of the 1,959 passengers and crew, 1,195 had been lost. The bodies of 885 victims were never recovered.

Most of the reaction swiftly and unequivocally condemned Germany and Captain Schwieger. President Woodrow Wilson had already made plain his view that "no warning that an unlawful and inhumane act will be committed" would be accepted

A German U-boat of the UC-1 type surfaces, and her crew appreciate some fresh air. This particular class of submarine was used mainly for mine-laying, carrying up to 12 mines at a time. Together with their cousins, the attack submarines, U-boats alarmed Allied politicians, the public and traditional naval men alike.

as a legitimate excuse for that act. Of the 139 US citizens aboard *Lusitania*, 128 had been killed. *The Nation* newspaper called the sinking "a deed for which a Hun would blush, a Turk be ashamed, and a Barbary pirate apologise". There was even loose talk of an American declaration of war on Germany.

The furore had an impact in Berlin. Realizing that many Americans were now calling for war, the German High Command bowed to political pressure and imposed strict limitations on U-boat activity. The British continued to lose about 150 merchant vessels a month to the U-boats over the summer, but high-profile attacks on passenger liners were banned. Despite this, on 19 August 1915 the debate exploded once again when *U-24* mistook the liner *Arabic* for a troop transport and sent her to the bottom with a single torpedo. The liner sank in ten minutes with 44 dead, including 3 Americans, and Washington began to make another round of strong protests with a serious undertone of threats. The sinking of an unarmed French-registered passenger ferry, the *Sussex*, in March 1916 again prompted an American threat to sever diplomatic relations with Germany.

In May, the German offensive was called off, in what was known as the "*Sussex* pledge"; it was not worth the risk of US intervention on the Allied side. For the moment, the U-boat war would be confined to the North Sea and to the Mediterranean, where there was an abundance of targets – and few Americans to complain. But submarine warfare was here to stay.

29

A TICKET COLLECTOR'S HAT
WOMEN'S WORK IN WARTIME BRITAIN

1914 TO 1918

Looking back from a hundred years on, it seems inevitable that the huge demands on manpower exerted by the war would be most sharply reflected in the changing role of women. Women's position in British society had already been the subject of heated debate before 1914. But the outbreak of war split the campaign for the vote: Mrs Emmeline Pankhurst and many militant Suffragette followers called a "ceasefire" out of patriotism, as did most other less strident groups, although some radicals continued to agitate. But the demands of a "total war" economy pushed women's roles and rights higher up the political agenda, and transformed the working options for women.

"WORK GIRLS WORK / MAKE THE SHOT AND SHELL / WORK GIRLS WORK / BLOW THE HUNS TO HELL"

Slogan on wartime ephemera

From leading figures like the pioneering doctor Elsie Inglis – who overcame male hostility to establish hospitals that treated thousands of wounded – to ordinary mothers, sisters and daughters across the country, women stepped out of the shadows during the war to challenge convention in the range and accomplishment of their contribution. Wartime transport was one key area. From 1915 increasing numbers of women began to work on trams, buses and the railways, so that by 1918 there were 117,000 women transport workers – a 650 per cent increase from the start of the war and the highest proportional rise in any sector. This straw hat was part of the summer uniform of a ticket collector on the Lancashire and Yorkshire Railway (LYR), which carried passengers and freight across the Pennines. By November 1918 the LYR employed 4,459 women, three-quarters of whom undertook jobs previously carried out by men. Their uniforms, badges, photographs and statistics were just part of what, as early as April 1917, a specialist War Museum sub-committee of visionary women was starting to gather, to make sure that the full range of women's work in 1914–18 was remembered.

In 1911, the census recorded about one-third of women doing some paid work, but autumn 1914 saw a shake-up. Textile employment fell 43 per cent in the first five months of the war, and many women were laid off. However, as hundreds of thousands of men enlisted in the armed forces a general shortage of employees began to emerge. At first, working women began moving from one major traditional employment – domestic service – into the more obviously "respectable" new jobs such as typing and clerical posts. Other women, mainly from the more leisured classes, rushed to do voluntary work, such as helping with Belgian refugees or setting up, or nursing in, private hospitals.

However, during 1915 women began to move across the workforce in larger numbers and in different ways, stimulating a year-long debate about what jobs were suitable for women. One Suffragette wrote: "There are some jobs for which women are 'naturally suited' such as clerks or teachers", and the burgeoning Civil Service attracted large numbers of women, helping to release men for the Front. Many of these jobs attracted younger, unmarried women, because dismissal or retirement on marriage was still considered normal. In the view of one journalist, "The extremist feminist in her wildest moments would not advocate dock-labouring, mining or road-digging as suitable employment for women." But women's work continued to diversify – over 60,000 were in the banking sector in the later stages of the war, and nearly twice that number in transport, whose numbers were in turn dwarfed by those in local government.

The biggest change, though, in women's work came in factories manufacturing material for the war effort. A government poster showing a woman donning overalls, "doing her bit" as the slogan ran, emphasized that working in a factory was *real* war service. After the advent of the Ministry of Munitions in May 1915 (*see* Chapter 30), women found plenty of jobs as "munitionettes" in the new factories and created the most enduring image of the wartime woman worker. Explosives work generally went to married women, who were considered to be more sensible and "steady"; but single women were often preferred for working with certain explosives, such as TNT, because of their suspected gynaecological hazards. The work could be long, arduous and dangerous. Over a hundred women died from TNT poisoning, and several factories witnessed deadly explosions.

For the trade unions the arrival of women in large numbers was greeted with suspicion and obstruction. Their main concern was "dilution", the threat to wage levels from the replacement of highly paid skilled men with semi-skilled or unskilled workers – which usually meant women. Most new female employees in wartime industry were eventually regarded by the unions as "substitutes", despite the fact that in many cases they were actually extra workers. Women's representatives were not consulted in the discussions over pay, because theoretically the agreements were for the men they had "replaced". Nevertheless, by 1918 women's membership of trade unions had grown threefold, to over 1.2 million.

Some women were concerned that they were producing objects to kill and maim. One wrote in a factory magazine: "The fact that I am using my life's energy to destroy human souls gets on my nerves. Yet on the other hand, I'm doing what I can to bring this horrible affair to an end. But once the war is over, never in creation will I do the same thing again." For many women, work on the factory floor was a liberating – if exhausting – experience. The welfare on offer mattered, and canteens were popular, of which hundreds were established. For particularly older women from the poorer districts, it was the first full meal they could sit down to and eat regularly. On almost 40 munitions sites, government housing was provided, too. It was common later to recall war work as a happy time because of the camaraderie, better wages and jokes with friends, as well as factory-run social activities such as plays, concerts, football matches, and even hair competitions. Many factories had crèches, too, as a way of attracting and keeping workers.

Number Seven Filling Factory at Hayes in Middlesex may be considered typical. It employed 10,000 women, aged 18 upwards, on relatively good wages. Safety and discipline were tight; to set foot in a hazardous area without protective clothing was

Women workers somewhat self-consciously pose for the camera as they fill trays with bullets at Cartridge Factory 5, part of the huge Royal Arsenal complex at Woolwich. The great expansion in munitions production represented the most overtly war-related work that women undertook, though the range of occupations that opened up to women was diverse.

an offence punishable by a fine or dismissal. Production workers worked shifts of a 9½-hour day and a 10-hour night. Workers' facilities included cycle sheds, changing rooms, bathing facilities with plentiful supplies of hot water and canteens capable of feeding several hundred at a time. There was also a medical centre with a resident doctor and dispenser. The morale and spirit of the workforce were high; in the crisis that followed the German attacks of March 1918 workers volunteered to work over the Easter Holiday, many without pay.

Inequalities in wages remained, of course, and it was normal for women to earn less than men, including for doing the same job. Although women formed the majority of the workforce in manufacturing fuses and cartridges, they were still forced to rely on male skilled-engineer tool-setters, to whom they had to pass on some of their wages. Earnings averaged 30 shillings (£1.50) a week – much better than the pre-war average of 11 shillings and sixpence, but still only half the men's wages.

July 1916 saw the largest number of additional women entering the workplace, and during the 12 months from July 1916 to June 1917 women comprised a full half of the workforce. The female contribution to the economy grew still further in March 1917, when the Women's Land Army was set up; perhaps as many as 250,000 women were working the land in 1918. Beyond the Home Front, it should also be remembered that women joined the armed forces in non-combatant roles. By the end of the war, 80,000 women were performing auxiliary roles such as nursing, driving and cooking in new services like the Women's Army Auxiliary Corps.

The trend started to reverse even before the Armistice. There is little doubt that many working women would have welcomed a chance to continue their occupations, and they had demonstrated prowess in hitherto untried tasks from tram driving to forging heavy metal. But the roles began disappearing, or were taken up again by the returning men. Some women went back to domestic service, but far fewer returned to live or work in the great households.

Britain's women had made a significant contribution to the war effort, one that could not now be ignored by politicians. With the passing of the Representation of the People Act in 1918, women aged over 30 finally won the vote. As for the wartime experience itself, many women were very conscious of their efforts and spoke proudly of their contribution. For many individual women, just as for the men, the First World War was a unique defining experience and a radical force for social change.

expected to mobilize industry as quickly as possible, regardless of expense. In the panic of war hasty contracts were issued to the existing domestic arms manufacturers and to American companies. Unfortunately, most of the early ammunition contracts were for shrapnel shells, which had given good service in the open veldt of South Africa but which proved useless for cutting barbed wire or for blowing up enemy dugouts on the Western Front. The War Office ordered millions of them.

Three key factors now hampered a rapid expansion of the British armaments industry: a shortage of key raw materials, including chemicals; a paucity of the specialist armaments factories, which were already at full capacity; and a fragmented railway distribution network of over a hundred competing companies (which had at least been placed under overall government direction by September 1914).

The result was that the British Expeditionary Force was seriously short of shells in spring 1915. The BEF's Sir John French was bitter. After the disappointment of Neuve Chapelle on 10 March and especially the failure at Aubers Ridge on 9 May (*see* Chapter 40), French briefed Lieutenant Colonel Charles Repington, military correspondent of the *Times*, in detail. He even showed him confidential military documents. The *Times* described the BEF's shortage of shells in graphic detail: "We had not sufficient high explosives to lower the enemy's parapets to the ground ... The want of an unlimited supply of high explosives was a fatal bar to our success." Ironically, the brief "hurricane" bombardment necessitated by the shell shortage had contributed to the preliminary success of Neuve Chapelle. But it was one thing to make a positive tactical choice, and quite another to be in a position of having no alternative.

Thus, a "shell scandal" broke out as an angry public demanded action. This crisis, compounded by the failure of the Gallipoli landing (*see* Chapter 24), effectively brought down Asquith's Liberal government. David Lloyd George – a vociferous critic of alleged War Office profligacy in peacetime – now berated the Ordnance Department for its "dilatoriness and sloth". Under pressure, Asquith formed a new Coalition government, and the War Office lost responsibility for munitions as Lloyd George was appointed to head the new Ministry of Munitions in May 1915. He soon found out the truth. British industry lacked the high-quality modern machine tools and the specialist semi-automatic forging machines needed for shell manufacture, had no chemical industry big enough for the mass manufacture of explosives, and possessed few companies able to manufacture precision fuses. He addressed these with his characteristic energy, helped by the passage of the Munitions of War Act in July 1915, which brought munitions production under state control.

Lloyd George recognized that Britain's whole economy needed to be geared for war. The state now took over direction, with munitions the key industrial priority. An Imperial Munitions Board was set up to ensure that supplies and factories in Britain and Canada were organized to provide adequate shells and other war material for the duration. A huge munitions plant, officially named "His Majesty's Factory", was built near Gretna, on the English–Scottish border outside Carlisle, and by mid-1916 was in production. A large bureaucracy developed to administer the vast state effort. For months to come the shells supplied still reflected orders placed by the old War Office, but during the latter part of 1916 the speed and volume of manufacture was transformed by these changes.

The Ministry of Munitions was staffed by experienced businessmen able to coordinate the needs of big business with those of the state and reach a compromise on price and profit. Government agents bought essential supplies from abroad and

then controlled their distribution in order to prevent speculative price rises and profiteering. The government controlled all dealings in metals as well as coal. All over the country factories were converted to munitions production, and machines and skills were adapted to military use. In Birmingham's jewellery quarter skilled craftsmen turned to making hand grenades; pen manufacturers found themselves producing cartridge clips.

The efficient production of munitions required a consistent, ample and stable workforce. "Treasury agreements" had been reached with 35 unions, which, among other things, sought to prohibit strikes and lockouts, created means for arbitrating disputes and allowed for the so-called "dilution" of labour – the replacement of "skilled" men who had enlisted with "semi-skilled" or "unskilled" men and (even!) with women. These measures were then incorporated into the Munitions of War Act, along with restrictions on the movement of labour, which made it hard for workers in vital industries to change jobs.

The government's centralization of control was thus paralleled in the enhanced status of trades unions and their leaderships, who now carried a raft of responsibilities as partners in the war economy. They were initially opposed to the introduction of women workers, whose wages never reached parity with men's, but the facts spoke for themselves. By mid-1917, women dominated fuse production, overcoming a backlog of 25 million fuses. But the general shortage of labour also gave unions considerable muscle, as the law of supply and demand drove wages up to unprecedented levels. Skilled machine operators could command £3 and 10 shillings a week at a time when a private soldier's basic pay was 7 shillings a week. Unsurprisingly, trades union membership doubled during the war, reaching 4.5 million in 1918.

Rising food prices, rising rents and other factors provided reasons for disgruntlement and fuel for militancy, and (the laws notwithstanding) Britain lost 27 million days in strikes – more than four times the number in Germany. By the end of the war, though, it was clear that the overriding need for munitions had been met. At war's end, the Ministry of Munitions had a staff nationwide of 65,000, employing some 3 million workers in over 20,000 factories, including 250 government-controlled ones (143 of them state-owned).

In 1914, British factories produced 300 machine guns; in 1918, they made over 120,000. In 1917, the 76 million shells produced that year was over 150 times the quantity made in 1914. And by the end, many thousands of the new war machines – tanks and aircraft – had rolled off the production lines. As the Germans ruefully acknowledged, they had lost the *Materialschlacht*.

Shells stretch as far as the eye can see at the National Filling Factory at Chilwell, Nottinghamshire. The plant was responsible for packing explosives into many of the shells eventually fired by British forces, but disaster struck on 1 July 1918, when more than 130 workers were killed and a large part of the factory destroyed by an accidental explosion.

31

KAISER BILL TOILET ROLL
PROPAGANDA IN THE WAR

1914 TO 1918

The First World War was the first conflict to witness the full exploitation of the mass media (including film) for propaganda purposes. From the start, the populations of the belligerent nations were flooded with exhortations and emotional appeals, along with demonizations of the enemy and uplifting political assurances such as "This is the war to end war." Governments targeted their own populations to maintain the war effort and motivate the will to fight. But they also wanted to influence neutral, international opinion and, where possible, undermine the enemy – though in an era before broadcast radio, there was relatively little that they could do to *directly* influence the enemy's citizens, beyond dropping leaflets behind the lines.

In Britain, as early as August 1914 the War Propaganda Bureau was established under Charles Masterman to coordinate propaganda at home and abroad, which it did until 1917. It was better known as Wellington House, after its London HQ. Masterman discreetly recruited famous writers such as Arthur Conan Doyle, John Masefield, G.K. Chesterton, Rudyard Kipling, John Buchan and H.G. Wells to draft articles, pamphlets and books supporting the government's line.

> The phrase "a scrap of paper" became notorious after German Chancellor Theobald von Bethmann Hollweg used it, on 4 August 1914, to convey his dismissive astonishment that Britain might declare war merely on account of a 75-year-old treaty regarding Belgian neutrality. What he saw as Britain's inflated sense of honour and obligation was, by contrast, regarded in Whitehall as an absolute moral guarantee. Over the coming months, British propaganda seized on Bethmann Hollweg's words to vindicate the very values that he had dismissed, as the words "scrap of paper" appeared on posters and handbills and quickly entered popular culture. Fragmented and tatty, this roll of 1914 toilet paper reflected the essence of Britain's total defiance of Germany's perceived conceit and arrogance. Each sheet showed a picture of Kaiser Wilhelm and offered the opportunity to any British man, woman or child to express his or her contempt in an unambiguous way. Wilhelm's moral bankruptcy was headlined by Bethmann Hollweg's famous phrase. Topping the lot, there was the bold claim: "SCENTED". In a classic piece of bawdy British humour, the toilet roll sardonically suggested that in a crisis any scrap of paper would do.

The official efforts were greatly helped by the impact of the principal mass medium of the day, the daily newspaper. It was less than 20 years since the *Daily Mail* had first appeared, the first truly mass-market daily. To a highly literate public,

"PROPAGANDA ... DRAWS NOURISHMENT FROM THE SINS OF THE ENEMY. IF THERE ARE NO SINS, INVENT THEM! THE AIM IS TO MAKE THE ENEMY SO GREAT A MONSTER THAT HE FORFEITS THE RIGHTS OF A HUMAN BEING."

General Sir Ian Hamilton

newspapers were an important tool for war information, aided by posters, magazines, pamphlets and other ephemera. The press – at first not allowed anywhere near the Western Front – tended to fall into line through self-censorship, and anyway had to rely on a government Press Bureau for information about the actual fighting. Indeed, the government–press closeness became explicit later in the war, when Lord Beaverbrook, owner of the *Daily Express*, headed up a new Ministry of Information and Lord Northcliffe, owner of both the *Daily Mail* and the *Times*, was put in charge of an Enemy Propaganda Department.

Allied propagandists were helped early on in the task of demonizing the enemy by the allegations of German brutalities against Belgian civilians (*see* Chapter 13), which came to acquire a life of their own. Starved of real news from the Front, editors relied on uncorroborated tales to sell newspapers. In an enduring visual and verbal vocabulary, German soldiers were depicted as sadistic, bestial violaters and murderers of defenceless women and children and, after the sack of Louvain and the bombardment of Rheims cathedral, as vandals and destroyers of civilization and culture. While German forces may indeed have killed women and children in their reprisals, there is no evidence that they went about cutting off hands, bayoneting women and babies, and crucifying captured soldiers, as some of the propaganda claimed. Despite this, a wave of anti-German propaganda swept Britain, justifying intervention to save "gallant little Belgium". The Kaiser was especially singled out as a fanatical, bloodthirsty tyrant bent on world domination. In 1915, documentary credence was lent to the whole picture when the Bryce Committee Report on atrocities in Belgium appeared. It was mostly rooted in facts as they were understood and based on 1,200 sworn witness depositions. Translated into 30 languages, it had a significant impact, making front-page headlines in major newspapers in Allied and neutral countries, and it was actively promoted by Wellington House.

French propagandists had an even easier task. It was *les sales Boches* who had invaded the sacred soil of France and so obviously had to be driven back, and especially after Verdun a theme of "they shall not pass" emerged (*see* Chapter 50). But they, too, were quick to mine the rich seam of atrocity stories. Even the Americans, recruiting for the war three years later, could fruitfully exploit images of *Pickelhaube*-wearing apes and burning cathedrals to whip up anti-German feeling.

As the war progressed, individual incidents were seized on for propaganda value, especially if they bolstered the "atrocity" theme. The execution of British nurse Edith Cavell in October 1915 (*see* Chapter 32) provided a focus for countless articles, pamphlets, images and books publicizing her shocking end. The torpedoing of RMS *Lusitania* in May 1915 presented, amid its tragedy, another sort of propaganda opportunity, this time with a high international value on account of the 128 American victims (*see* Chapter 27). And the continuing German air campaign over England maintained British outrage (*see* Chapter 28).

Germany's own propaganda apparatus combined a War Press Office and Supreme Censorship Office. But the overall effort lacked focus, and often failed to comprehend how German actions and policies came across abroad – as the ruthlessness in Belgium testified. With her forces on foreign soil, Germany could not very plausibly claim defence against aggression. German propaganda appears to have favoured relatively simple slogans, such as "*Gott strafe England*" ("God smite England"), which was widely distributed on memorabilia. Also popular was the poem *Hassgesang gegen England* ("Hate Song Against England", better known as the "Hymn of Hate"), written by Ernst Lissauer. It was hugely popular, and Crown Prince Rupprecht of Bavaria ordered copies distributed to his soldiers.

For much of the war, German domestic propaganda concentrated on boosting the image of Hindenburg, initially following his victory over the Russians at Tannenberg, and later as the *de facto* leader of Germany's war effort, alongside Ludendorff. But the subordination of political leadership to military men produced its own problems of a relatively inflexible message that risked looking increasingly threadbare, as the population was urged to greater sacrifices with phrases such as "The times are hard, but victory is assured."

As the war ground on, the need to supply it with men, money and machines created the dominant propaganda across the home fronts. In Britain, having first appealed to individuals' patriotism – and before conscription decided the issue – recruitment posters increasingly exploited shame and guilt, asking "Daddy, what did <u>YOU</u> do in the Great War?" or shouting "Women of Britain say 'GO!'". Appeals to people on the Home Front urged them to "Save Wheat and Help the Fleet", to "crush the Germans" by lending the government money, and women were summoned to "enrol at once" for munitions work.

After America entered the war in 1917, as well as being presented with the "brutal Hun", Americans were told that they were fighting for abstract concepts like liberty, democracy and a new postwar world. A long-running campaign to sell "Liberty Bonds" (war bonds), using the powerful symbol of the Statue of Liberty, raised around $17 billion for the war effort, or about $170 per citizen – a huge sum at the time.

Perhaps the most audacious piece of Allied negative propaganda was the German "Corpse Factory", which has been described as the "master hoax" of the war. It originated in some disinformation planted by Wellington House in a Chinese newspaper, to take advantage of presumed Chinese horror at the desecration of the dead and so tilt Chinese opinion towards the Allies. But it was supported by the *Times*, which lifted a German newspaper description of a "corpse exploitation establishment" but omitted one important fact: that the corpses being processed for oils and animal feed were of *animals*, not dead German soldiers. The story mushroomed, was taken up all over the world and was helpfully reinforced by later accounts of a misrouted freight wagon full of dead Germans and "confirmations" of the story by interrogated Germans. The outright lie was not officially repudiated by Britain until 1925.

Propaganda, spread through mass media, seemed to work. But as war gave way to peace, a reaction set in. Frank admissions of wholesale lying on the part of trusted governments, especially in Britain and America, were not soon forgotten – and they fundamentally shaped how propaganda would be conducted in the next war.

Even in 1917 the "atrocity" theme was potent propaganda, as this US Army recruitment poster shows. Adapting a British design, it combines the familiar indicators of German bestiality, brutality and cruelty. In the background is the much-used landscape of a shattered Louvain or Rheims; in the foreground, the Pickelhaube-*wearing monster threatens "America" herself.*

32

NURSE CAVELL'S SECRET DIARY
THE CREATION OF AN ICON

1915

The story of British nurse Edith Cavell evokes the values of an earlier era. Here was a woman steeped in religion, duty, care for others, with an unflinching sense of right and wrong, and imbued with a sincere patriotism; qualities that, allied to her unbending character, led to her execution at the hands of a German firing squad.

Cavell was born in 1865, the daughter of a rural Norfolk vicar. Reared to share what she had with the poor of the parish, and to respect rules, it was perhaps inevitable that she was drawn to the disciplined and caring world of nursing. Her skill, leadership and strength of character led to her becoming matron at a new nursing school in Brussels, and by 1911 she was training Belgian nurses for hospitals, schools and kindergartens.

Cavell was on holiday in Norfolk when war broke out, and she promptly returned to Brussels. The expected flood of wounded failed to materialize – the war had moved on – but in the harsh winter of 1914–15 Cavell and her nurses began to harbour Allied soldiers caught in occupied Belgium and secretly trying to get to neutral Holland. She became part of a network, in which escapees, equipped with identity documents, were sheltered in Cavell's clinic before being led to the Dutch frontier.

But Cavell was betrayed. On 5 August 1915, she and Sister Elizabeth Wilkins were arrested. Wilkins denied all the charges, but Cavell, characteristically, refused to lie and admitted everything. After two months in a solitary cell she was charged with "conducting soldiers to the enemy" and treason – a capital offence. Despite pleas for clemency from the US and Spanish representatives, on 12 October 1915, Cavell, dressed in her matron's uniform, was shot.

The repercussions were immediate. Newspapers worldwide proclaimed Cavell's death as further proof of German barbarism, with comparisons to the burning of Louvain and the sinking of *Lusitania*. Her steadfast character, womanly status and her caring profession combined to create a lasting propaganda figure for the Allies.

> In solitary confinement in St Gilles Prison, Brussels, Cavell wrote these fragments, recording her feelings and many acts of assistance to escaping soldiers. But they only revealed their secrets decades later. Following Cavell's death, and the return of her personal belongings, her sister Edith received a cushion, which was hard and lumpy. She passed it on to another woman, whose husband later opened it up – to reveal a tightly bound roll of paper. It was only in the late 1960s that the handwriting was identified as Cavell's and the words deciphered. They revealed a secret prison diary and cast new light on one of the war's most remarkable, yet elusive, women.

"PATRIOTISM IS NOT ENOUGH. I MUST HAVE NO HATRED OR BITTERNESS TOWARDS ANYONE"

Cavell's reputed last words, inscribed on the Cavell Monument (1920), London

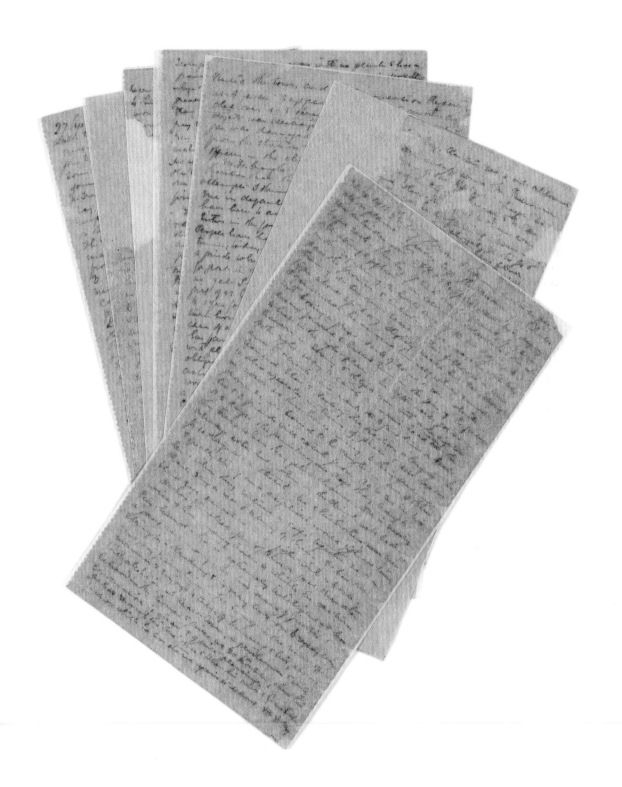

33

CAPTAIN FRYATT'S WATCH
DEFYING THE U-BOATS

1915 TO 1916

A year after the execution of Edith Cavell, Germany earned British and international opprobrium again with the execution of another civilian. This time it was a captain in the Merchant Navy.

In 1914, Charles Fryatt captained a regular ferry on the Rotterdam–Harwich route, and he continued operating across the North Sea once war broke out, in spite of the hazards of unlit coasts, mines, enemy submarines, aircraft and warships. Unfortunately, ferries became particular targets once Germany, in February 1915, commenced unrestricted submarine warfare (*see* Chapter 27). At least three attacks were made on railway company ferries, and Captain Fryatt was in command on two occasions.

On 2 March 1915, the SS *Wrexham*, sailing to Rotterdam in neutral Holland, was intercepted and challenged by a U-boat. Fryatt ignored the signal to stop and turned away at high speed, steaming for the Dutch coast. The submarine gave chase but the *Wrexham* gradually drew away, travelling at 16 knots, her funnels on fire. After 40 miles the U-boat gave up. Fryatt was hailed as a hero. Within the month, on 28 March, he had another narrow escape, as submarine *U-33* ordered the SS *Brussels* to stop. Instead, Fryatt commanded "full steam ahead" and proceeded to try to ram the U-boat, which was forced to dive to avoid being hit.

A year later Fryatt paid the price, when the Germans deliberately hunted him down. Five destroyers intercepted the *Brussels* and she was taken into Zeebrugge, in occupied Belgium. On 27 July 1916, Fryatt was charged with attempting to ram *U-33* illegally because he was "not a member of a combatant force", and he was court-martialled at Bruges. Predictably, he was found guilty of "acting like a *franc-tireur*" and condemned to death, a sentence officially described by Germany as a "merited expiation" for his "nefarious" behaviour. His execution, by firing squad, came within 48 hours.

On both occasions when Captain Fryatt outwitted his U-boat attackers, he was rewarded with gold watches. After the first incident, his employers, the Great Eastern Railway Company, gave him this elegant piece, a half-hunter with a small glass cover, to mark "their appreciation of his courage and skilful seamanship". It was only three weeks later that Fryatt turned the SS *Brussels* on *U-33*. To the Germans, his actions were seen as an illegal act of war. By, contrast, the British Admiralty lauded the skipper's feistiness and gave him another gold watch "in recognition of the example" that he had set. For Britons, Fryatt's actions were seen as a fine act of British pluck.

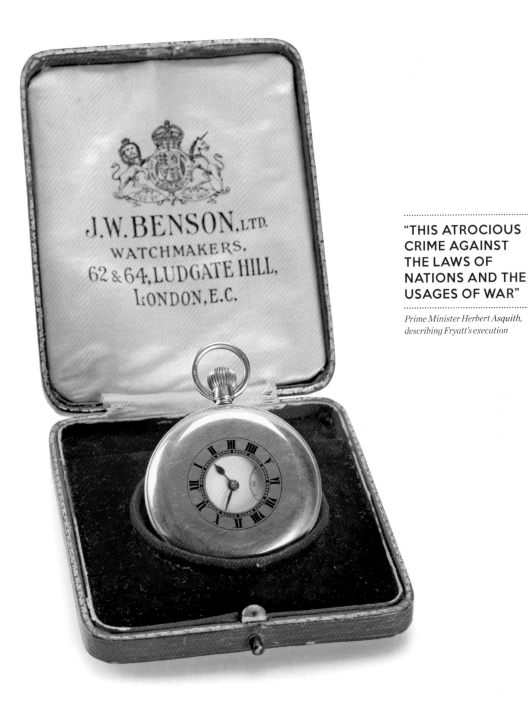

J.W. BENSON, LTD.
WATCHMAKERS,
62 & 64, LUDGATE HILL,
LONDON, E.C.

"THIS ATROCIOUS CRIME AGAINST THE LAWS OF NATIONS AND THE USAGES OF WAR"

Prime Minister Herbert Asquith, describing Fryatt's execution

International outcry followed. Neutral Holland and the United States were particularly outraged, describing U-boat attacks as "piracy" and pointing out that a merchant ship's captain had every legal right to defend his passengers and crew. Yet again, German actions translated into a brutal overreaction that alienated world opinion.

34

WILLIAM HARRISON'S NO-CONSCRIPTION FELLOWSHIP CARD
ENLISTMENT TO CONSCRIPTION

1915 TO 1918

Conscription was a vexed topic long before 1914. The distinguished former Commander-in-Chief Field Marshal Lord Roberts VC had eyed the mass enlisted armies of the continental powers and – backed by some of the press, the Conservative Party and the National Service League – argued powerfully for conscription. He was opposed by Asquith's Liberal government and the wider Labour movement, who felt that the compulsion of freeborn Britons was an infringement of their liberty, and by many ordinary professional soldiers.

When war did come, Lord Kitchener's call for voluntary enlistment (*see* Chapter 8) was resolutely answered and took the pressure off any moves to compel men to serve. But the supply slowly dried up during 1915. In the following year, two new concepts in British life became realities: conscription and conscientious objection.

> William Harrison was a man of deep-seated principle: a lifelong vegetarian, teetotaller and pacifist. He immediately joined the No-Conscription Fellowship when it was established in 1914, as testified by this membership card. When claiming exemption from the army on the grounds of conscience, he explained to his local Military Service Tribunal in July 1916: "War inevitably means that the nations involved degenerate and become like brutes. This contention is supported by the facts of the present day. Love, mercy, pity, tenderness and forgiveness, things which our Master Jesus bids us practise, are all gone. I love my country too dearly to assist it in coming to such a deplorable state." Despite letters testifying to the sincerity and longevity of his views, Harrison's appeal was rejected. In May 1917 he was arrested, court-martialled and began a sentence of hard labour in Wormwood Scrubs Prison. Released a week after the Armistice, Harrison was arrested again and, still refusing to take any part in the military system, went back to prison, this time in Newcastle. He was not finally freed until April 1919. Throughout his experience, he was sustained by a deep religious faith, which enabled him to emerge from prison free of bitterness and to even see the lighter side. At his first trial, it was reported that the magistrate deducted £2 from his pay as a soldier. Fifty years later, Harrison wondered where that money went: "I never had any pay and have always wondered what happened about the £2!"

The first recognition that something more than voluntary enlistment might be needed came in August 1915, when a mandatory National Register of able-bodied

"CONSCRIPTION ... INVOLVES THE SUBORDINATION OF CIVIL LIBERTIES TO MILITARY DICTATION; IT IMPERILS THE FREEDOM OF INDIVIDUAL CONSCIENCE AND ... DIVIDES THE PEOPLES OF ALL NATIONS."

The No-Conscription Fellowship, response to the Military Service Act, 1916

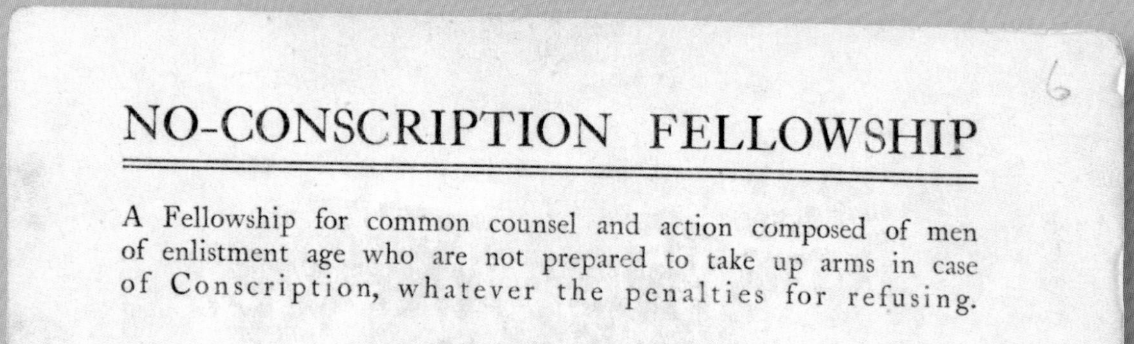

NO-CONSCRIPTION FELLOWSHIP

A Fellowship for common counsel and action composed of men of enlistment age who are not prepared to take up arms in case of Conscription, whatever the penalties for refusing.

MEMBERSHIP CARD

Mr. *W. Harrison,* 58, Bonn Road

Address ~~67, Hyde Grove~~ *Heaton*

~~Plymouth Grove, Manchester~~ *Bradford*

is hereby certified a Member of the above.

_____ *Bradford* _____ Group

Office : 8 Merton House
Salisbury Court, E.C.

_____ Local Sec.

6

men was announced. It was primarily aimed at the labour market, and was a natural consequence of the new Ministry of Munitions' need to ensure labour was being used efficiently. But it laid the groundwork for later conscription by identifying those who might be eligible for military service.

It became clear towards the end of 1915 that volunteers would no longer be able to sustain any long-term military effort. The Secretary of State for War, Lord Kitchener, approached Lord Derby, now Director General of Recruiting, asking him to devise a scheme by which all men of fighting age on the Register would be invited to formally "attest" their willingness to serve, but would not have to honour this promise until absolutely necessary. The "Derby Scheme" promised that married men would not be called up until *all* single men had been enlisted. But only just over half the eligible single men signed up, leaving thousands of married men liable to be called forward before those non-signing men. Lord Derby anxiously observed: "It will not be possible to hold married men to their attestation unless and until the services of single men have been obtained by other means." Seen in hindsight, the Derby Scheme was a rather clever piece of political coercion: either sufficient numbers attested, or the case for conscription would become hard to resist.

The Coalition government was split. Liberal sentiment was still strongly opposed to compulsion, but in early January 1916 Asquith proposed the Military Service Bill, whereby single men aged 18–41 would be deemed eligible for military call-up. One Liberal minister resigned over "compulsion", the Labour Party was against it and the Trades Union Congress overwhelmingly condemned it – for one thing, they were fearful of conscription spreading to industry. But behind the scenes the Labour leadership accepted the inevitable, and the Bill became the Military Service Act, coming into force in March.

That was not the end of it. On 25 April a *universal* conscription bill was howled down in the Commons after a bitter debate; but the demands of the trenches, and the army, could no longer be ignored. In May, the Second Military Service Act was enacted, extending conscription to married men.

There were practical obstacles. Politicians, soldiers and industrialists were well aware that a modern war could not be fought if thousands of skilled men were removed from the workplace. The Reserved Occupations Committee, set up under the Derby Scheme, grew into a Manpower Board in late 1916, with the power to identify and direct that certain functions were "reserved occupations".

There were other objections, too. With the new legislation, the former Derby Scheme tribunals were recast as Military Service Tribunals, which heard appeals for exemption – usually on grounds of infirmity, an existing occupation or training (such as religious ministry), or vital domestic or economic responsibilities. More contentious were the appeals on the grounds of morality and principle. The No-Conscription Fellowship (NCF) had been formed by determined pacifists in December 1914, and it had evolved into an active pressure group. Via sympathetic MPs it persuaded the government to extend the tribunals to take into account "conscientious objection to the undertaking of combatant service". The idea of the "conscientious objector" was born.

Pacifism was, for society then and later, a difficult concept, cherished by some, derided by others. A rejection of *all* violence could, arguably, mean either having to live with highly disagreeable consequences or a reliance on non-pacifists to defend those conscientious freedoms. For many pacifists, the principles remained clear.

But the 16,000 recognized conscientious objectors in the war reacted in different ways. About 7,000 did serve in the army, in ways that did not require them to carry weapons: mostly as stretcher bearers and in the Non-Combatant Corps, in which roles they were much respected by their arms-bearing colleagues. Another 3,000 were allowed to do work considered of national importance, such as on farms, or were Quakers who had volunteered for the independent Friends Ambulance Units in France. That left a hard core of 6,000 men who chose to go to prison rather than submit to the state's demands. Of these many later accepted places in work camps under a Home Office scheme, leaving a rump of about 1,500 "absolutists" who remained in the conventional prison system.

The treatment of those arrested reflected the tenor of the times; at least 41 were illegally sent to France and placed under military discipline, court-martialled and sentenced to "Field Punishment Number One" – tying a man to a wagon wheel for two hours a day – and even to death. Asquith's government intervened hastily and remitted them to civilian custody in Britain.

In 1917, Dartmoor Prison was emptied of its regular convicts and renamed "Princetown Work Centre". It was used to house conscientious objectors on the Home Office scheme, eventually numbering 1,100, ranging from anarchists to Bible Students (Jehovah's Witnesses). There they were treated by the prison staff – many of whom had lost relatives in France – with all the prejudice and rigour of the day. Most work was outdoors, and many were subjected to hard physical labour, such as quarrying, and suffered accordingly. Campaigning by women members of the NCF did improve conditions, and even stoked accusations that "conchies" were living soft lives.

The NCF's chairman, Clifford Allen, was one of the "absolutists": he was arrested and imprisoned three times and became seriously ill before the Home Office eventually released him. But some 70 conscientious objectors *did* die in prison or work centres. And even war's conclusion did not end the punishment. Conscientious objectors were banned from voting for a period of five years.

The crisis in manpower that conscription addressed in 1916 was real. And conscription delivered almost 400,000 men to the armed forces that year, dwarfing 1916's crop of volunteers. But it was a watershed in British history, a break with centuries of tradition in response to the exigencies of war, which divided old Whig-Liberal notions of liberty and the small state from the modern fact of an all-powerful state bureaucracy. Conscription drew men away from their workplaces, requiring women to take over millions of jobs. The war compelled almost a third of the male population into uniform and then to undergo the horrors of modern war. Both those who had volunteered and those who were called up never forgot the experience. In a very real sense, conscription changed British society.

Members of the "London and Home Counties Workers' and Soldiers' Council" are ejected from a pacifist meeting at London's Brotherhood Chapel. As revolutionary fervour rippled outwards from Russia's turmoil in 1917, Britain was not immune; but anti-war politics did not necessarily sit easily with the conscientious objection of those spurred by religious principle or moral scruple.

35

THE "MOTHER" OF GUNS
ARTILLERY IN THE FIRST WORLD WAR

1914 TO 1918

The greatest inducer of fear in the First World War was artillery. Shellfire terrified everybody. From the steel flail of a barrage to just the sheer chance of the odd shell – and whether from a long-barrelled cannon or a snub-nosed howitzer with its steeper, plunging fire – "the guns" reduced strong men to nervous wrecks. One who experienced them, Guy Chapman, "could never stand shell fire. I got into a thoroughly neurotic state". He was not alone. Another wrote of "cowering in abject terror, praying that it would stop". Even the Australians, supposedly the toughest of soldiers, were recorded "shaking like leaves and weeping" on receiving their baptism of fire on the Western Front at Pozières.

Such were its technological advances that a weapon which accounted for only 2.5 per cent of casualties in the 1877–8 Russo-Turkish War became one that killed almost 60 per cent of the BEF's dead in 1914–18, and perhaps as many as 80 per cent of German dead in 1917–18. Not for nothing did Stalin, in a later conflict, call artillery "the God of War".

While the war was mobile, heavy guns played only a limited role. But once positions became fixed, these bigger, heavier weapons came into their own. By 1913 the Coventry Ordnance Works had developed this mighty 9.2-inch howitzer – so big it had to be dismantled into three loads for transport, weighing over 41 tons. Its missing ballast box needed 14 tons of earth to be shovelled in before it could be brought into action. The 9.2 was tested by the Royal Garrison Artillery at its range in South Wales in July 1914 and quickly approved, so that by the end of the year more than 30 were in production. As the trench network spread across France and Belgium, the 9.2-inch howitzer became one of the main British weapons for destroying Germany artillery, and around 450 were eventually used, firing more than 3 million shells. This, that very first one, became known as "Mother", parent to a new generation of heavy artillery. It was sent into action with the 8th Siege Battery, RGA, on 31 October 1914, and the following year, now with the 10th Siege Battery, it fought at Neuve Chapelle and Festubert, before being returned to Britain where the barrel was eventually relined. It saw action in France again in 1918.

The transformation in artillery's deadly capabilities came through developments in four key areas during the late 19th century.

First, new nitro-cellulose propellants were three times as powerful as gunpowder or "black powder", weight for weight, and left little residue to foul the gun's barrel. They also produced little of the smoke that had obscured the battlefields of earlier eras and which had given away the position of the guns to the enemy.

"MOTHER"

36

THE VICKERS MACHINE GUN
MACHINE GUNS ON THE WESTERN FRONT

1914 TO 1918

Artillery may have wrought the most destruction in the First World War, but there seemed something very contemporary and uniquely malevolent about the machine gun, which scythed down men in no-man's land.

The Maxim-Vickers (and its international variants) is the device that caused so much of the slaughter. Its earliest forerunner was the American Gatling gun, designed in 1862, ironically to "show how futile war is". But, like the French Mitrailleuse, as used in the Franco-Prussian War, it still relied on a handle being cranked to rotate the barrels. The Maxim, by contrast, was the first true automatic-firing machine gun. Its inventor, the American Hiram Maxim, claimed he was told: "Hell, if you want to make a pile of money, invent something that will help the Europeans to cut each other's throats more efficiently." The Maxim used the recoil power of the fired bullet to reload a new bullet into the breech: as long as the trigger was pressed, the gun kept firing. He demonstrated his patented mechanism in 1884, and from then on the Maxim – and later its British version, the Vickers – was used by the British Army. The patent was eventually exported to many other European countries, including Germany for its efficient MG08, which killed so many Allied soldiers.

The machine gun emerged as the most infamous weapon of the war. Machine guns were directly aimed by men who consciously pulled the triggers, whereas artillery seemed more remote and its casualties more random. The Vickers .303-inch (7.7mm) Machine Gun became the British Army's standard automatic weapon in November 1912. It was a direct adaptation of the Maxim. Vickers literally turned Maxim's design upside down, making it more compact, efficient and lighter. One of its most distinctive changes was the replacement of Maxim's original brass jacket with the lighter corrugated steel jacket, seen here. This contained water to keep the barrel cool during firing. As the water gradually heated, it was siphoned off as steam and condensed into a reservoir to be reused. The standard .303-inch cartridges were fed into the gun on cloth belts of 250. Technically, the Vickers could fire between 450 and 600 rounds per minute, but gunners rarely fired continuously in that way; more commonly they worked in shorter bursts. As the war progressed, machine gun fire became increasingly sophisticated, with guns working in batteries for increased firepower, and unseen, distant targets attacked by firing against specific map references. Such was the success of the Vickers gun that it remained in use by the British Army little changed until 1968, when its retirement from active service was marked by a feature on the front page of the *Times*.

"THE BLUE CROWD OF FRENCH
SOLDIERS SLID ABOVE THE GRASS ...
'TO THE SLAUGHTERHOUSE!' CRIED
LA POULE. RIGHT ON THE HORIZON,
AT THE POINT WHERE THE SKY MERGES
INTO THE LAND, MACHINE GUNS
BEGAN TO SIZZLE AND SPIT, LIKE OIL
IN A FRYING PAN."

Jean Giono, 100th Regiment of Infantry

37

A MESSAGE STREAMER
THE EARLY AIR WAR

1914 TO 1915

Use of the skies was nothing new to battlefield warfare in 1914. The French had occasionally employed air observation balloons during the Napoleonic era, and both the Union and Confederate armies used balloons during the American Civil War. Some nations before 1914 even attempted to drop bombs from balloons: it was banned by the 1899 Hague Convention, but military reality was already outstripping diplomatic ideals. In 1914–18, the air became integral to the conduct of war as never before.

While the public's imagination, then and now, came to be captured by the stories and images of gladiatorial fighter aces and their dogfights, it was the more mundane but crucial work of reconnaissance and observation that provided the real *raison d'être* for the first air war. It began with fragile constructions of canvas, wood and wire, such as the Maurice Farman Longhorn, which accompanied the BEF in August 1914. With its underpowered, unreliable engine and large wings it could wobble through the sky at just over 50 miles per hour on a calm day carrying a pilot-observer. But this apparently flimsy aircraft and its companions would revolutionize warfare.

Throughout the war, aircraft provided armies with their eyes in the sky. In the opening days, pilots collected and sent back vital intelligence as troops moved across Belgium and northern France. They included Euan Rabagliati, a newly qualified pilot with the Royal Flying Corps. Observing beyond Mons just before hostilities began, he was astonished by what was revealed below him: "Instead of seeing a few odd German troops I saw the whole area covered with hordes of field grey uniforms – advancing infantry, cavalry, transport and guns. In fact it looked as though the place was alive with the Germans." But to pass on this information, Rabagliati had to land. He was then driven direct to GHQ and reported to Sir John French in person. For the first few months of the war, RFC aircraft were not fitted with wireless radio sets. Even when they were, communications remained unreliable, so the only alternative while still in the air was to drop messages, either in weighted bags or on coloured streamers. This blue, yellow and red cloth streamer landed near 3rd Division headquarters during the Battle of the Marne in 1914. It was retrieved by the division's senior staff officer, Lieutenant Colonel (later Major General Sir) Frederick Maurice, who donated it to the Imperial War Museum in 1933, of which he was then a Trustee.

After the Wright brothers' first successful manned flight in 1903, aircraft development was fast, and some soon saw its military potential. In September 1910,

a young captain called Bertram Dickson took off in a private Bristol Boxkite to locate the "Blue Force" during the annual British Army manoeuvres on Salisbury Plain. Once he had found them, he landed and reported back to "Red Force" HQ by telephone. The next day another aviator, actor Robert Loraine, successfully transmitted a Morse Code signal through a primitive on-board wireless. In 1911, Dickson submitted a paper to Britain's Committee of Imperial Defence, in which he predicted:

> In case of a European war, between two countries, both sides would be equipped with large corps of aeroplanes, each trying to obtain information on the other ... the efforts which each would exert in order to hinder or prevent the enemy from obtaining information ... would lead to the inevitable result of a war in the air, for the supremacy of the air, by armed aeroplanes against each other. This fight for the supremacy of the air in future wars will be of the greatest importance ... .

His prescient submission informed the Committee's recommendation to form a Royal Flying Corps for the army in 1912, while the Royal Navy set up its own Air Service. By 1914 Britain had nearly 100 military aeroplanes and, on 13 August, despatched 4 squadrons to France, when 60 machines flew from Dover to Boulogne.

So it came as no surprise when the armies finally clashed in August 1914 that the aeroplane was the obvious reconnaissance tool to supplement the cavalry's traditional role. The *Official History of the War in the Air* is unequivocal: "The single use in war for which the machines of the Military Wing of the RFC were designed and the men trained ... was reconnaissance." It was near Mons on 22 August 1914 that Captain Charlton and Lieutenant Wadham observed the Germans outflanking and outnumbering the BEF as it advanced into Belgium. Doubtful at first, over the following days GHQ became convinced, and aerial reconnaissance played an important part in allowing the BEF to retreat from Mons in line with the French, and enabling it to fight another day.

And it was French aerial reconnaissance that identified the move that finally derailed the Germans' Schlieffen plan. Aircraft designer Louis Breguet observed General von Kluck's First Army swinging down towards the east of Paris. Joseph Gallieni, the military governor of Paris – and a great pre-war advocate of aviation – seized his chance, ordering the newly formed French Sixth Army to advance due east and drive into the Germans' exposed flank. With the BEF and the French advancing from the south, the resulting rebuff of the Germans that was the "Miracle of the Marne" owed a great deal to the "eyes in the sky".

The Eastern Front was no different. There, in late August 1914, it was German aerial reconnaissance that confirmed intelligence reports of the two invading Russian armies failing to coordinate, and of a huge gap opening between them. The intelligence enabled the Germans to surround and annihilate the Russians at the battles of Tannenberg and later at the Masurian Lakes (*see* Chapter 18).

Once the war had settled into static lines of defensive trenches, aerial reconnaissance became an essential tool for seeing what was happening on what the Duke of Wellington had described as "the other side of the hill". Unarmed aeroplanes flew over enemy lines, reporting the location of gun batteries, supply dumps, the movement of troops and the subsequent location of enemy soldiers.

The efficacy of aerial reconnaissance depended on the ability not only to see, but also to report what was observed in an accurate and timely fashion. But one of the greatest difficulties – as in all areas of command and control in the First World War – was communications. In the very early days, air-to-ground communication had to be a matter of dropping notes (e.g. with bags or streamers), which was not always reliable. Waiting until a flight landed so the pilot could report in person wasted valuable time. By December 1914 developments in Morse wireless transmitters enabled the first reliable sets to be installed in British aeroplanes, finally allowing them to communicate directly to artillery batteries so they could adjust their fire.

Soon, aircraft roles expanded. Cameras were routinely installed to photograph enemy lines (*see* Chapter 74). And aerial reconnaissance spawned the attempt, by both sides, to put out the other's "eyes in the sky". Airmen who, early on, had been exchanging cheery waves with the other side's flyers were now quick to fire at enemy aeroplanes with rifles and pistols. In December 1914, French aviation pioneer Roland Garros noted development work on metal deflector wedges attached to propeller

"THE VICTOR IN THAT AERIAL STRUGGLE WILL TOWER WITH PITILESS WATCHFUL EYES OVER HIS ADVERSARY, WILL CONCENTRATE HIS GUNS AND ALL HIS STRENGTH UNOBSERVED ... EVERYWHERE THE VICTOR WILL SOAR."

H.G. Wells, Anticipations of the Reaction of Mechanical and Scientific Progress upon Human Life and Thought, *1901*

blades, and asked for them to be attached to his Morane-Saulnier aircraft. With this crude installation, on 1 April 1915, he achieved the first ever shooting-down of an aircraft by a machine gun that fired directly through the propeller. On 15 and 18 April 1915, he shot down two more German aircraft. However, on his last sortie he crash-landed and was captured by the Germans who examined the wreck of his plane with some interest.

They promptly devised their own much more efficient system, using an interrupter mechanism that only allowed the machine gun to fire when no propeller blade was in front of it. The Dutch aircraft designer Anthony Fokker quickly fitted this to his new E1 monoplane. With its 7-cylinder, 99-horsepower rotary engine, its single MG14 machine gun and top speed of 80 miles per hour, the Fokker Eindecker went on to become the world's first fighter plane. It was fast, light and well armed, and in the hands of a trained pilot a deadly threat to the slow, awkward two-seaters, already weighed down with their heavy wireless equipment. By the autumn of 1915 the Eindecker had shot down hundreds of Allied aircraft and become the scourge of the skies.

The battle for control of the air had begun, and life for the airmen was becoming highly hazardous.

An almost unimaginably fragile-looking Maurice Farman Longhorn S.7, a two-seater reconnaissance plane, which was also used for training. It was with aircraft like these that the BEF first attempted to monitor the battlefield from the air. Such aircraft were rapidly superseded by more sophisticated machines in the fast-paced innovations of 1914–18.

38

A TRENCH SHOVEL
WAR IN THE TRENCHES

1914 TO 1918

In some ways, trenches should have come as no surprise to the men of 1914. "Digging in" to avoid enemy fire has always been a natural reaction in warfare. For centuries, those besieging fixed positions have sought to push themselves towards enemy strongholds under cover, while building up for a final assault. The somewhat different *battlefield* use of trenches emerged during the American Civil War. In 1863, General Ulysses Grant wrote to a friend in words that could almost come from 1915: "We have our trenches pulled up so close to the enemy that we can throw hand grenades over into their forts. The enemy do not dare show their heads above the parapet at any time, so close and so watchful are our sharpshooters." At Sebastopol during the Crimean War, facing Paris in the Franco-Prussian War and confronting entrenched Boers across the South African veldt – trench warfare taught sharp lessons to all involved.

The Russo-Japanese War (1904–05) witnessed scenes that would, a decade later, become tragically familiar. Over several months, dug-in Russians armed with rapid rifle and machine gun fire repelled massed Japanese bayonet charges. Combined with modern firepower, trenches underlined the growing dominance of defensive capability over attack. The First World War cemented that reality in a way that was unparalleled in duration, and in scale, as trenches sprouted across France and Belgium, the Austro-Italian border, Gallipoli and beyond.

In the dying minutes of 25 April 1915, the commanders of the ANZAC landing at Gallipoli sent a note to General Sir Ian Hamilton asking if they should re-embark their troops after the setbacks of the day. Hamilton knew this was impossible and immediately signalled his response, concluding: "You have got through the difficult business, now you have only to dig, dig, dig until you are safe." It was testament to the fact that throughout the war, in so many theatres, the spade was the soldier's salvation, wherever men went to ground to seek protection from bullets and shellfire. British soldiers carried a small entrenching tool, but this was only for digging shallow scrapes and shelters. For more extensive work – including trenches, dugouts and gun emplacements – a more suitable tool was required. The professional "sappers" of the Royal Engineers, who were trained to dig, used the large, broad-bladed "Shovel, R.E". For wider use there was the "Shovel, G.S." (i.e. General Service), lighter in weight and with a smaller blade. Anyone could use it. This one was found more than 80 years after the war in an excavated Flanders dugout. The thumbs of successive diggers have buffed it smooth, each man no doubt hoping that if he dug, dug, dug he would be safe.

> "ENTRENCHMENTS ARE ONLY TO BE USED WHEN, OWING TO FURTHER ADVANCE BEING IMPOSSIBLE, THE EFFORTS OF THE ATTACKING FORCES MUST BE LIMITED TEMPORARILY TO HOLDING GROUND ALREADY WON."
>
> Infantry Training 1914, *a British War Office manual*

40

CONWAY JACKSON'S PRAYER BOOK
THE BATTLE OF LOOS

25 SEPTEMBER TO 14 OCTOBER 1915

The Battle of Loos, fought in autumn 1915, was the first large-scale offensive in which the British attempted to overcome the problems of trench warfare. But it was fought on the wrong ground, to a weak operational plan, and was marked on the British side by some suicidal tactics, bad staff work, poor communications, weak artillery support and uncoordinated control. It degenerated into a hopeless muddle, at the cost of 61,700 casualties, of whom at least 8,000 died.

There was, though, no reason in the autumn of 1915 to suppose that a great breakthrough was *impossible*. Britain's first independent operation at Neuve Chapelle on 10 March had made – at first – a clear breach in the German lines. Following a hurricane bombardment of only 35 minutes (because of the shortage of shells), British and Indian troops had swept the surprised first-line German defenders away. The British then lost the initiative and were unable to exploit their brief success as German reserves rushed to seal the breach. But, despite 12,000 casualties, Neuve Chapelle proved that at least making a breach was *possible*. It was exploiting it that was the issue. Unfortunately, two problems then arose: the French under Joffre insisted on a major attack from the BEF, which was now a mixture of half-trained volunteers and the survivors of the old Regular army, and an unsuitable battlefield, the slag heaps of Loos.

Two days before the Battle of Loos, Conway Jackson of the 6th Battalion, King's Own Scottish Borderers, wrote to his mother. It was to be his last letter. "How many things I have to thank you and Daddy for. I know I have always been an anxiety to you both, as I am afraid I am very headstrong." He had been reading the *Daily Light* prayer book his mother gave him and drew strength from the text for 26 September: "If we be dead with Christ, we believe that we shall also live with him." On 25 September 1915, Jackson attacked northwest of the Hohenzollern Redoubt, but his battalion suffered over 350 casualties. Later, the eyes of a German officer moving among the dead "were attracted by the peaceful face of a young officer, the features of which seemed to be transfigured in death. My servant handed me a little book, which lied beside of [sic] his body. I took it in my possession, intending to send it to his mother after the war." In June 1919, Captain E. Wynne Jones was billeted in Cologne with the Army of Occupation. He received a request, from a relative of his landlord, to help with returning a prayer book found by her brother on the body of a young British officer in 1915. Through the War Office, Captain Jones sent Conway's *Daily Light* back to Mrs Jackson, adding: "I feel sure you will derive comfort in days to come from this positive proof that your loving son died as you had taught him to live."

"MY NEW FRONT AT LOOS IS AS FLAT AS THE PALM OF MY HAND ... IT WILL COST US DEARLY AND WE SHALL NOT GET VERY FAR"

General Sir Henry Rawlinson, commanding IV Corps, to Joffre

41

THE FULLERPHONE
COMMUNICATIONS IN THE WAR

1914 TO 1918

Good communications have always been vital in war. As the Second World War US General Omar Bradley put it, so succinctly, "Congress makes a man a general, but communications make him a commander." But in the trench warfare of 1914–18, generals invariably lost control of their units once battle was joined, because military communication reflected the technology of the time – and that technology was both primitive and vulnerable, its deficiencies highlighted by contrast with the deadly effectiveness of the latest artillery and machine guns.

Over centuries of warfare, flags and semaphore had replaced horns and trumpets. Two developments revolutionized communications, including military, in the late 19th century: the electric telegraph and the telephone. The former spurred the first ever professional Signals Corps, founded by the US Congress in 1863, during the Civil War. By 1908 the British Army had formed the Royal Engineers Signal Service, which provided communications such as field telephones, despatch riders on motorbikes and crude wireless sets. Field and trench telephones were common in 1914, but their use was limited, and their lines liable to be disrupted by enemy action.

One of the greatest challenges facing British Army communications during the early years of the war was in making them secure. Most field telephones and "buzzer" telegraphs used only a single wire, with the return circuit being achieved by connecting the device to the earth. As a result, British conversations with the frontline could be intercepted by specially designed German "tapping" devices, often installed in dugouts or tunnels. Many perplexed British units wondered how the Germans knew who they were, and exactly what they were planning. The answer was simple: they were using the earth in order to listen. In 1915, this problem was solved by a technically advanced, but relatively simple, invention. It became known as the "Fullerphone" after its designer, the Royal Engineer signals officer Captain A.C. Fuller. He devised a portable Morse telegraph that sent a Direct Current signal through a single wire, but incorporated what was in effect a primitive scrambler. Electrical chopping mechanisms and filters produced a sound in the headphones that was only audible if the devices and circuits at each end were synchronized. Although the signal still passed through the earth, it could no longer be intercepted and understood by the enemy, and it was therefore fully secure. At first, the device was used only for Morse signals, but in time voice communication also became possible. (The model shown here, made in 1917, includes both facilities.) By the end of the war the Fullerphone was the standard way to send secure messages up and down the line.

"WITH A BASKETFUL OF MOBILE GSM TELEPHONES YOU COULD HAVE BROKEN THROUGH ON THE WESTERN FRONT IN A WEEK!"

Military historian Richard Holmes, CBE

42

A DECEPTIVE TREE
CAMOUFLAGE IN THE WAR

1914 TO 1918

By tradition, military forces marched conspicuously into battle, behind brightly coloured flags, flaunting their presence. Armed forces only slowly came to learn the importance of camouflage when the range and accuracy of weapons improved.

Irregular troops tended to provide lessons. In revolutionary America, riflemen adopted the hunting colours of green and brown, in striking contrast to the bright scarlet of the British Army. In the late 19th century, regular armies also began to blend in with the environment, beginning when army units in British India began to dye their uniforms pale brown, or *khaki*, the Hindi for "earth-coloured".

Other nations followed. The United States adopted khaki by 1902 and in Germany the traditional Prussian blue uniforms were replaced with *Feldgrau* ("field grey") in 1910. And so in 1914 the BEF went off to war in khaki; the French, however, fought the devastating Battle of the Frontiers clad in their traditional blue coats and red trousers – and paid the price accordingly (*see* Chapter 12). By early 1915 they, too, had conformed and were in lighter, horizon blue.

Aerial reconnaissance, and static trench lines, meant that anything rendering units less detectable mattered. First attempts were usually painted tarpaulins hastily thrown over the top of artillery batteries. In 1915, though, a full-time French *Service de Camouflage* was set up, employing artists, designers and architects, whose talents ranged from repainting buildings, hangars and guns to contriving false landscapes and pop-up figures of soldiers to draw sniper fire. "Camouflage" was also coming to mean "deception". The BEF set up its own camouflage section, too, a specialist group of Royal Engineers. By 1918 camouflage had become an integral part of war, from earth-coloured aircraft to painted steel helmets, to the "Dazzle" painting on ships (*see* Chapter 83) that made it harder for U-boats to see them.

The intimacy and claustrophobia of trench warfare made it difficult to hide. Using new wartime skills in the art of camouflage, artificial positions were created, where possible, to overlook the frontlines. In March 1918, the Imperial War Museum acquired this camouflaged observation post that had stood in no-man's land between the lines. Made from thin metal to resemble the battle-worn trunk of a pollarded willow, it is hollow, with irregular-shaped holes cut into the sides for observation. To render them, and the observer, invisible, the holes were covered with painted metal gauze. The trunk contains a thick steel lining to protect the occupant, the necessity of such protection being underlined by the shrapnel and bullet marks peppering the outer shell. Amid the desolate landscape of the battlefield, the tree – and its secret occupant – would probably have passed unnoticed.

"... 'FEAR NOT, TILL BIRNAM WOOD / DO COME TO DUNSINANE!' AND NOW A WOOD / COMES TOWARD DUNSINANE."

Shakespeare's Macbeth, *as the witches' prophecy appears to be coming true – in reality, his enemies were using camouflage as deception*

It was as beasts of burden, rather than glamorous cavalry chargers, that horses played a fundamental role on the frontlines in France and Flanders. Here, a horse belonging to the 1st ANZAC Corps is loaded up with a Vickers machine gun and ammunition, for an official photograph (August 1917).

and rail took everything, and everyone, most of the way; but horses were vital thereafter. It was inevitable, therefore, that as the armies marched off to war they took with them horses, *millions* of them. Every artillery gun, save for the very heaviest, was pulled by teams of horses, and it is estimated that over 20 million horses took part in the First World War – and that as many as 8 million of them died during it. The British Expeditionary Force alone had upwards of 368,000 horses in 1917. Maintaining the stock, and treating ill and wounded horses, therefore became a mammoth exercise. It is estimated that around 2.5 million horses passed through British veterinary hospitals, of which four-fifths were returned to duty. The horse was so important, so necessary, that it was ubiquitous. Although, as the BEF quickly discovered, more mechanized transport was needed to ferry troops around (*see* Chapter 15), the horse remained vital, along with mules, for most armies in the war. Feeding and watering these millions was, inevitably, a huge logistical effort – though a different sort of challenge than the upkeep of a large fleet of lorries.

On the Eastern Front things were different, though. The wide spaces there allowed cavalry to roam in the gaps, and at the Battle of Tannenberg in August 1914 and a host of other engagements cavalry proved their usefulness – but only as mobile troops, not through traditional cavalry charges using their weight and power. Mounted troops of the British, Antipodean and Indian contingents also came into their own in Palestine and Sinai, seeing many deployments and culminating in a classic example of cavalry exploitation in the breakthrough at Megiddo in September 1918.

Horses were initially the prime means of reconnaissance, at least until the trenches sank into their seemingly immovable shapes on the Western Front. Cavalry warfare was soon highly problematic. The BEF cavalry was undoubtedly the best-trained and equipped at the Front, and the experience of the Anglo-Boer War a decade earlier had taught the British how to use cavalry as mobile infantry. Yet, after a few frustrating charges in the opening weeks of the war, the cavalry was sent to the rear to await the great breakthrough. Apart from a few incidents late in the war at Cambrai and during the open warfare of the last "Hundred Days" (*see* Chapter 88), cavalry remained impotent against the machine gun and barbed wire.

On the Eastern Front things were different, though. The wide spaces there allowed cavalry to roam in the gaps, and at the Battle of Tannenberg in August 1914 and a host of other engagements cavalry proved their usefulness – but only as mobile troops, not through traditional cavalry charges using their weight and power. Mounted troops of the British, Antipodean and Indian contingents also came into their own in Palestine and Sinai, seeing many deployments and culminating in a classic example of cavalry exploitation in the breakthrough at Megiddo in September 1918.

Soldiers of all armies became very attached to their horses. It is perhaps summed up in the words of one Royal Artillery officer, who wrote of one horse: "He (Sailor) would work for 24 hours a day. He was quiet as a lamb and as clever as a thoroughbred, but he looked like nothing on earth, so we lost him. The whole artillery battery kissed him goodbye and the drivers and gunners who fed him nearly cried."

As a beast of burden, the horse was supplemented by the mule, that curious half-horse, half-donkey, highly valued since Ancient Greece. Considered less obstinate, faster and more intelligent than donkeys, mules also offered the advantage of being able to cope with difficult terrain because of their harder hooves. They were also considered easier to train than a horse, and could cover 50 miles in a day with only a few hours of sleep. All sides looked to the mule when the going got tough, and by the end of the war the British Army owned over 230,000 of them. But mules knew when they had had enough. Henry Williamson worked with them as a member of the Machine Gun Corps and noted how: "When a mule lowered both ears, it had given up. It stood awhile in dejection, nosebag and net of hay unwanted. In the black night it sank down, its eyes in the morning were glazed." In situations like that, the mule would normally be put out of its misery.

The different theatres of war demanded different animals. The British formed an Imperial Camel Corps (ICC) in 1916 in Egypt to fight mostly in Sinai and Palestine, making use of the "ship of the desert's" unrivalled ability to endure long distances in the blazing heat. The unit fought dismounted as a multinational infantry brigade and included its own light artillery. Its Australian component had a particularly tough reputation, because unit commanders had used it as a repository for some of their more difficult characters. By 1918 the British Army had 47,000 camels.

In their contribution on the Western Front, dogs played a small but useful role as messengers, and also sometimes in locating wounded men. They presented less of a target to a sniper and could travel over any terrain. One dog is recorded as running nearly 3 miles in less than 60 minutes with an important message to a brigade's headquarters. Perhaps inevitably, soldiers (including a young Adolf Hitler) also adopted dogs as pets, which sometimes prevented the dogs being sent on dangerous missions.

A usually more reliable messenger was the homing pigeon, which saw service on all the battle fronts. They played a vital part in the war, especially when more modern means of communication broke down, as they frequently did. Signallers carried them forward into action to report progress – or lack of it – in special baskets strapped to their backs, and pigeons were also used to send messages from ships at sea. When the French advanced at the Marne in 1914, they took 72 mobile lofts with them, to which, incredibly, all the pigeons returned despite the changes of location. Over 100,000 British pigeons were recorded as flying in action, with an astonishing success rate of 95 per cent in getting the message back. Several birds were even decorated for their exploits (*see* Chapter 41).

All animals had their vulnerabilities in war, as the poignant images of horses sinking into the treacherous Flanders mud in 1917 testify. Occasionally, too, the bond between human and animal broke down. One Australian divisional commander was recorded waiting impatiently for news of an attack when a pigeon from the frontline fluttered back to its loft. The orderly recovered the message and handed it to the general. It read: "I am absolutely fed up with carrying this bloody bird around France!"

50

THE *SOIXANTE-QUINZE* FIELD GUN
ASSAULT ON VERDUN

FEBRUARY TO DECEMBER 1916

It was barely more than two months after the Allies agreed, in December 1915, to coordinate future offensives (*see* Chapter 48) that the Germans delivered a shock of their own – a massive attack on the fortress complex of Verdun. It would signal the start of the biggest, bloodiest and longest battle on the Western Front.

Verdun was supposedly chosen as the target because it was the place that France would *have* to defend to the end, thereby expending valuable French lives and resources. After the war, Chief of the German General Staff Erich von Falkenhayn claimed that he wrote a memorandum to this effect for the Kaiser over Christmas 1915, outlining his attritional plan to "bleed France white", saying: "the French will be compelled to throw in every man they have. If they do so the forces of France will bleed to death."

Whether he really did intend such a bloody, grinding battle, Falkenhayn's decision set in train a titanic Franco-German struggle that has become synonymous with mass slaughter and which resonates to this day. By the time the field guns, including the French "75s" and their heavier equivalents, had finished pounding one another, around three-quarters of a million French and Germans had been killed, wounded or were missing.

The French M1897 75mm Field Gun revolutionized the way wars were fought. It used a combination of liquids and gas in a recuperator to absorb the energy of each shell. While the barrel shot back nearly 4 feet on the carriage, nothing else moved. The wheels remained in place and, once the barrel had returned to its starting position, the gun could be fired again and again at the same target. It was its speed and accuracy that made the "75" so effective. The Germans tried to copy the gun's technology for their own M1896 77mm Field Gun, as did the British for their 18-pounder. But the French kept the 75's details secret and it arguably remained the supreme field gun for much of the war. Fully aware of this, in September 1919 the Imperial War Museum asked the French for a 75 with a good war history. This particular gun fought throughout the war with the 2nd Battery, 61st Field Artillery Regiment – playing key roles on the Marne and north of Ypres (1914), in the Argonne and in Champagne (1915), at Verdun (including the battles for Fleury Ravine and the hill of *Le Mort Homme*) and the Somme (1916), on the Aisne (1917), and again on the Somme and the Argonne (1918). Since it was first displayed in 1920, it has provided an enduring reminder of both the heroic efforts of the French army and the close bond that existed between Britain and France during the war.

"DEAFENED BY THE NOISE, DIZZY WITH SMOKE, SUFFOCATING WITH GAS, THEY ARE THROWN AGAINST THE GROUND OR HURLED AGAINST EACH OTHER IN THE BLASTS. PIECES OF SHRAPNEL WHISTLE PAST THEIR EARS. THE SOIL, THE STONES, THE RIFLES, THE BEAMS OF THE SHELTERS AND THE EQUIPMENT ALL SPRING OUT AND THEN FALL DOWN AROUND THEM."

Sub-Lieutenant Jacques Péricard, reservist and journalist, author of Ceux des Verdun *(1917) and other works on the battle*

An apocalyptic profusion of fire, shattered earth, smoke and leaden skies fill Georges Paul Leroux's painting L'Enfer – "Hell" (1921). This eloquent depiction of battle's comprehensive destructiveness – a scene devoid of human life, except for two cowering poilus in a shell hole – was based on sketches drawn by Leroux immediately after a reconnaissance patrol at Verdun.

Pétain set up his headquarters in the south at Souilly, arriving on 25 February just in time to learn of the devastating loss of Fort Douaumont that day. As the French infantry retreated, a small garrison had remained there, but it took to the lower levels to escape the shelling. Eventually, it took just one enterprising German, Pioneer-Sergeant Kunze of the 24th Brandenburgers, to put the fort out of action: he broke in through a shell hole and single-handedly captured the small gun crew. He was followed by two captains of his regiment with their sections, Hans-Joachim Haupt and Cordt von Brandeis, who rounded up the rest of the garrison without a shot. German children were given a day's school holiday to mark the occasion and both officers were awarded Germany's highest military decoration, the *Pour le Mérite*. Sergeant Kunze was ignored.

For the French, Douaumont's fall was a public disaster. It commanded the whole northeastern approach to Verdun itself and had huge symbolic value. As the French consolidated on the last line of hills only 3.5 miles north of the city, the situation was looking desperate for the French – and now for Pétain himself. The 60-year-old had contracted pneumonia in the freezing winter weather. Yet, wrapped in blankets, he proceeded to fight the battle by telephone from his bed and his desk. His early decisions and orders were unequivocal: "hold on", "re-man the forts" and, most famously, "They shall not pass!" (*"Ils ne passeront pas!"*). The French artillery now began to disrupt fresh German attacks, and the Germans found it difficult to drag their heavy guns forward across the shell-cratered battlefield. Their advance slowed.

Another Pétain decision was to set up a permanent supply line to the beleaguered town through a narrow road corridor from Bar le Duc in the southwest. This became known after the war as *"La Voie Sacrée"*. Nearly 80 per cent of men and materials involved in the defence came along this route, with the residue arriving on a narrow-gauge railway line. Over 220 French divisions rotated along the 45 miles of the *Voie* during the ten months of the battle, and 23 million shells passed along it. The road was maintained by a small army of 10,000 troops, and patrolled from the air. One calculation is that a truck passed along it every 15 seconds, night and day.

The battle itself, fed by enormous resources on both sides, developed into a vast artillery mincing machine. The successful German advances on the eastern side of the Meuse had, though, exposed their right flank to bombardment from the French positions on the west bank. The Germans had not counted on such a withering barrage from these superb, massed French "75s". More and more batteries of these quick-firing guns blasted the German attacks as they sought to struggle forwards, forcing Falkenhayn to tackle the problem head-on and widen his front. On 6 March, the Germans attacked the west bank of the Meuse to push the French back. Instead, they became embroiled for months in a battle of attrition for two west-bank hills, *Côte 304* and, nearer the river, the ominously named *Le Mort Homme*.

As spring arrived, on both sides of the Meuse the battle deteriorated into the familiar pattern of trench warfare, with endlessly mounting casualties. This was a different scenario to the desperate defence in February, and by May Joffre promoted the defensive-minded Pétain away to be commander of the Army Group Centre and put the more aggressively-minded General Robert Nivelle in charge at Verdun. Meanwhile, on the east bank, the Germans slowly pushed further south. On 7 June, after bitter fighting deep underground, the Germans captured Fort Vaux and pressed closer to the city itself.

Everything changed on 1 July, when the British and French launched their Somme offensive to the north. Along with recent Russian resurgence in the shape of Brusilov's offensive on the Eastern Front (*see* Chapter 51), Falkenhayn was so alarmed, by 12 July, that he ordered the attacks around Verdun to be stopped in order to move vital reserves to counter these new threats. The Germans had lost the initiative and were now on the defensive. But the mutual shelling continued all summer long. Gradually, things were turning to the French advantage. Air superiority over the battlefield was regained and finally, in October, Nivelle began a slow and bloody counteroffensive to retake the forts, culminating in the recapture of Fort Douaumont on 24 October. Fort Vaux was retaken, too, on 2 November.

By December 1916 the battle was finally over as the Germans found themselves back on the attack lines from which they had set out on 21 February. At Verdun, France and Germany had fought themselves to a standstill. It had been one of the longest, most indecisive, greediest battles (in terms of human life) in history. There has been dispute about casualties, but however viewed they are horrific: French official numbers are 377,231, including 162,308 dead, while German estimates are 337,000, including at least 100,000 dead.

The landscape bears the scars of battle a century later. Whole villages are represented only by a sign and a rolling series of grassed-over silent shell holes in the woods. The battle appeared to teach lessons. For one French sergeant called André Maginot, who was wounded near Verdun in 1914, the stubborn durability of the fort complex suggested it was still the way to protect France. In the 1920s, when Minister of War, his proposed "Maginot Line" was supposed to stop German aggression once and for all. Fifty years later, in the very different atmosphere of 1984, Verdun was the place where German Chancellor Helmut Kohl and French President François Mitterrand held each other's hands for a public act of joint remembrance, beneath the shadow of the towering monument and the massive Douaumont cemetery (*see* Chapter 99).

54

A FILM PROGRAMME
TANKS & THE END OF THE SOMME

SEPTEMBER TO NOVEMBER 1916

By September 1916 the British high hopes of June for breakthrough on the Somme had turned into a grim determination to keep up the wear and tear on a tenacious enemy. One prospect, though, of transforming the nature of the battle lay in the novel and highly secret weapon that the British had been developing: the tank. General Haig now planned to unleash it in a new offensive timed for 15 September, where the British would fight on a 1.5-mile front between Courcelette and Flers supported by the French to the south.

Of the film *The Battle of the Somme* (*see* Chapter 53), civilian Frederick Robinson had noted in his diary: "Londoners cannot go to the front to see the war, but the war has been brought to London for Londoners to see." He was one of the estimated 20 million Britons who saw that film, Britain's biggest-ever box-office hit. It recorded the battle's opening phase and, in the way that would come to typify the film industry, its success prompted a sequel. Thus *The Battle of the Ancre and The Advance of the Tanks* filmed the closing stages of the Somme campaign and highlighted the extraordinary phenomenon of the tank. The film was released in London on 15 January 1917, and this programme accompanied one of the first West End showings. The public were again captivated by the sight of genuine soldiers, the men they knew, fighting a real war. But this time there was the added excitement of seeing the new secret weapon. The films were, Robinson felt, totally absorbing: "You see in an hour more than you could see at the front itself in a month and all this is compressed into sixty strenuously exciting minutes. No wonder after the ordeal you come away both mentally and physically exhausted."

Notions of an armoured vehicle had existed before 1914. But it was the harsh realities of artillery, machine gun and trench warfare that supplied the impetus for action. As early as 24 August 1914, the French Colonel Jean Baptiste Estienne expressed the view that "Victory in this war will belong to the belligerent who is the first to put a cannon on a vehicle capable of moving on all kinds of terrain."

In November 1914, Major Ernest Swinton, later commissioned in the British Royal Engineers, suggested the idea of an armoured tracked vehicle to the War Office. The project was taken up, perhaps surprisingly, by the Admiralty in early 1915. Winston Churchill, as First Lord of the Admiralty, formed a "Landships Committee" charged with the design and construction. The first "landships" were built in conditions of great secrecy and called "tanks" to disguise the true purpose of the large

"I HEAR THAT OUR NEW FORM OF ARMOURED CAR WAS MENTIONED IN THE COMMUNIQUÉ YESTERDAY. THEY ARE A WONDERFUL CONTRIVANCE AND ARE EXACTLY LIKE A CREATION OF H.G. WELLS, OR JULES VERNE. THEY ARE ON THE CATERPILLAR PRINCIPLE, AND CAN GO OVER AND THROUGH ANYTHING."

Captain Arthur Gibbs, Prince of Wales Company, Welsh Guards, in a letter to his mother, 18 September 1916

THE BATTLE OF THE ANCRE AND THE
ADVANCE OF THE TANKS.

PART III.

At 6.20 a.m. the attack is launched. The men climb "over the bags" and stream across the rugged waste of "No Man's Land." The Scottish troops stand to arms, eager for the signal. A "Tank," impressive in its power, surges forward over wire, hillocks, and craters. Another "Tank" is far away, well on to the enemy's lines.

As the attack progresses, waves of men are seen pouring into the German positions. The first prisoners arrive from "No Man's Land," their faces expressing great relief. As our reserves watch the progress of the battle the brave stretcher-bearers can be seen at work under a heavy shrapnel fire.

Of this Phase Sir Douglas Haig Remarks in his Despatch :—

"Our assault . . . . met with success altogether remarkable for rapidity of execution and lightness of cost. . . . At 9 a.m. the number of prisoners was actually greater than the attacking force."

PART IV.

The wounded are carried in as the action continues, a Padre assisting a disabled Tommy with the devotion that has been so characteristic of "the cloth" in every battle. Scenes in the dressing station show how friend and foe receive the same attention. A large column of prisoners is assembled for removal to the compounds. Hot tea and sandwiches are given to the wounded, the lesser injured being sent to hospital in motor char-a-bancs.

Batteries of the R.H.A. move off to follow the advance.

Among the prisoners one observes a Hun colonel and his staff, captured in Beaumont Hamel. Our anti-aircraft guns are actively at work preventing the German scouts from reporting on the fight. At the close of the battle the mail arrives and the weary lads are gladdened by the latest news from home.

The Royal Naval Division assembles after seizing Beaucourt. The troops march back to rest laden with mud and glory. German helmets of two varieties—both the traditional Pickelhaube and its later relative the shrapnel headguard—appear to have been taken in profusion.

PART V.

At the close of the battle, the weary lads await the char-a-bancs that carry them back to billets. The West Yorks and the Worcesters are seen returning.

The shattered trail of war is seen in the condition of Beaumont Hamel and Martinpuich as they appeared on the British entry. Scottish troops are seen resting in the former. Australian gunners discourage their musician as they rest around a campfire. A view of the Ancre from the elevated bank, shows the inundated valley and the wire entanglements half hidden in the flood. Our men stormed through these obstacles and drove the Germans out.

The "Tanks" return triumphant, with an escort of cheering Tommies. The victors enjoy a meal in the captured German lines.

The return of the Cameron men. Irish heroes enjoy a well earned rest. The boys clean arms in readiness for the next attack, while a stern bombardment is maintained throughout the night.

And all that night, in a long drawn twilight, the shadowy forms of men and transport move forward to continue the Fight for Freedom.

GOD SAVE THE KING.

COPYRIGHT.   IMPERIAL WAR MUSEUM   ALL RIGHTS RESERVED.

Pollit Ltd., 62, Pitfield Street, London, N.   'Phone London Wall 1377.

Programme
OF THE

Official Pictures of the British Army in France

Presented by

The War Office Cinematograph Committee.

The Battle of the Ancre
AND
The Advance of the Tanks

PRESENTED AT . . .
CINEMA HOUSE,
225, Oxford Street, W.
MONDAY, January 15th, 1917
And Throughout the Week.

metal objects being transported by rail. Ostensibly, they were water tanks for Mesopotamia and for the Russians.

In December 1915, the first real prototype, "Little Willie", proved that the concept was feasible and demonstrated its basic features: an armoured box to protect the crew, sitting upon caterpillar tracks to get across muddy fields. Two questions remained: how to cross trenches, and what type of armament should it could carry.

In January 1916, a new design was trialled, called "Mother", with a distinctive rhomboid-shaped frame over which the tracks extended. It could easily cross gaps of 9 feet, and its guns – normally two Hotchkiss 6-pounders (in a "male" tank) or four Vickers machine guns (in a female) – were mounted in two "sponsons" protruding from the sides, intended to sweep enemy trenches. The War Office ordered its first 100 machines into production, with a new Heavy Section of the Machine Gun Corps designated to operate them.

During August 1916 over 50 of the new Mark 1 tanks were shipped to France, and Haig agreed that they should be trialled during his upcoming offensive. On 4 September, the French Tenth Army began attacking the wider southern flank, below the Somme. Then, on 15 September, the British went into action, and Captain H.W. Mortimore achieved a historic first as he took his tank, *D-1*, into Delville Wood. But of the 49 tanks committed that day, only 32 made it to the start line, and only 21 of those actually advanced. They proved too easily prone to breakdown and mechanical failure, and too easily trapped in the pulverized, rain-swelled mud.

One tank, *D-17*, commanded by Lieutenant Stuart Hastie, was more successful than most on 15 September, smashing through the barbed wire protecting Flers. The sudden appearance of this mechanical monster shocked the Germans as it crunched through their trenches before driving through the village, blasting the defenders in the houses on either side. One overexcited reporter wrote of a tank "walking up the High Street of Flers with the British Army cheering behind". Overall, though, there weren't enough tanks and they didn't work very well. So their first attack – and many of the tanks themselves – petered out, leaving the infantry still to take the strain.

At Morval, later in September, General Rawlinson's Fourth Army did just that, demonstrating how well his men were learning their trade. Under cover of a tightly controlled creeping barrage, attackers of the 55th Division literally walked into German frontline trenches before the terrified defenders could emerge from their dugouts. And finally Thiepval fell on 28 September, with the 18th Division of Gough's Reserve Army showing once again that good training, limited objectives and tightly controlled artillery were the keys to success in trench warfare.

Throughout October Haig kept the pressure on, but only in the face of growing opposition from his own officers. The men were exhausted and conditions in the field were terrible. A series of attacks in the autumnal rain and chalky mud yielded few gains. Quite why Haig persisted remains a puzzle, but it can probably be attributed to French pressure. The fact that a major Allied strategy conference was scheduled for 15–16 November would also have made him aware of the need to try and secure a success to bring to the conference table.

It was against these realities that Haig ordered a final push on the northern flank of the line, against Serre and Beaumont-Hamel – both uncaptured strongpoints from 1 July – and up the River Ancre towards Beaucourt. The assault went in on 13 November and, in spite of yet another failure against Serre, was largely successful. The 51st (Highland) Division seized Beaumont-Hamel, taking thousands of

....

"AND WE SAW THESE TANKS COMING OVER FOR THE FIRST TIME; THEY'D NEVER BEEN USED BEFORE. IT WAS A FUNNY SENSATION TO SEE A DOZEN TANKS COMING OVER SHELL HOLES, NO STOPPING. DIDN'T MATTER WHAT THEY CAME OVER, THEY GOT OVER IT ALRIGHT, AND IT WAS HORRIFYING."

....

Gunner Sidney Taylor, 250th Brigade, Royal Field Artillery, recalling the sight of tanks near Flers, 15 September 1916

Tank C-19, Clan Leslie – a "male" type – rumbles along the curiously named Chimpanzee Valley on the Somme in September 1916. Visible are its grenade screens and rear steering wheels. It was commanded by Captain Archie Holford-Walker and intended for the debut of tank warfare on 15 September. Unfortunately, damaged axles en route to the starting line prevented its committal to battle – which was not a unique story.

prisoners. On its right, the 63rd (Royal Naval) Division, a curious hybrid of Marines, naval reservists and wartime volunteers organized as infantry, surprised the German defenders of Beaucourt, where the high morale of the "Navy's soldiers", inspiring leadership, and a fierce but brief artillery barrage swiftly smashed through the Germans' frontline. This Battle of Ancre was also another outing for the tanks of the (now renamed) Heavy Branch MGC. Once more, the deficiencies of these early machines limited their tactical usefulness; however, their sheer presence induced enough fear to make some Germans simply give up and surrender.

By 19 November, as thin snow covered the corpses and litter of the battlefield, the main fighting on the Somme was over. The British and French had gained a maximum depth of territory of around 7 miles. Was it worth it? In the six months between build-up and November at least 128,000 British and Imperial troops were killed, an average of nearly 900 men a day. Frustration at the campaign fed a political crisis (*see* Chapter 65) that brought in Lloyd George as prime minister. Despite all this, the national mood remained remarkably resilient. But it was different. From the press, from the films and from troops on leave, the British public was becoming only too well aware of the sacrifices being made. Lloyd George may have been shocked at the casualty figures, but he could come up with no alternative solution. A grim determination to see it through now became the prevailing British mood.

On the German side, though, the outcome of the Somme was greeted with something akin to horror. Ludendorff admitted that "the Army has been fought to a standstill and was utterly worn out". Over 100,000 irreplaceable regular NCOs, the backbone of the German military structure, had fallen. Moreover, the probability of worse to come in 1917 weighed heavily on German strategic planners, and would underpin the decision that year to fall back to the formidable defences of their new Hindenburg Line, now being constructed.

For the British Army, the Somme was merciless. But the BEF was now much better trained to fight a modern war. Operational and battle staffs acquired hard-won experience, new weapons and tactics had been forged, and it is no exaggeration to say that the battle-hardened BEF that went into battle from 1917 was a very different force to the hopeful amateurs that attacked on 1 July 1916.

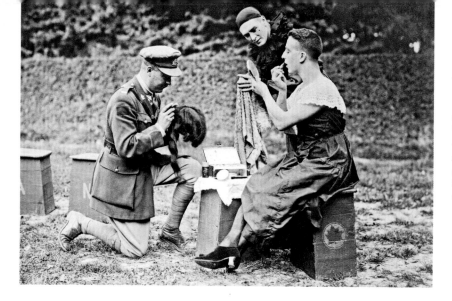

A female impersonator from the Canadian Concert Party "The Maple Leaves" makes up and prepares to don his wig, which is being combed by the kneeling officer. Theatrical productions were always popular behind the lines, and most concert parties could boast at least one drag artist.

The future prime minister, Harold Macmillan, wrote of the job as being his most valuable experience of the war as it "gave him knowledge of the poorer classes".

After having reassured the folks back home that he was still fine ("in the pink" was a favourite phrase), many a Tommy looked for diversion. This often took the form of cards or gambling games. A popular game was the North Country miners' "Pitch and Toss", where pennies were thrown at a line and the nearest scooped the pool – after the table had taken its cut, naturally. Others were "Over and Under" and "House" or Bingo. Authority tolerated these but not the most popular of all, "Crown and Anchor", in which men threw special dice – marked with the four playing-card suits, a crown and an anchor – in an effort to match their stake on a board of the same symbols. The "board" was usually a blanket, for quick concealment. The game was invariably run by a well-practised syndicate of three: a patter merchant; a money man; and a lookout, watching for any sign of approaching authority. One Tommy, Frank Richards, wrote ruefully of losing all his backpay during a long evening's gambling on the day the Armistice was signed.

A more active diversion, and antidote to cramped trench life, was football – played everywhere, at any opportunity, and by almost everybody. Officers marvelled at their soldiers' energy and willingness to play "footy" every moment they could. "However tired the rascals may be for parades, they always have enough energy for football!" observed one general. When troops were on rest, inter-platoon, inter-company and inter-battalion soccer matches were commonplace.

Organized sports extended far beyond football. Officers at rest or stationed behind the lines carried on their field sports as if back home in the country. The Northamptonshire Yeomanry kept a pack of hounds and when possible hunted fox and hare. Some officers kept dogs – the Earl of Feversham and his deerhound were killed and buried together on the Somme. Shooting game was common, mainly of the fat, over-fed partridges that would whirr out of cover at dusk heading for the loose grain and oats where the horses lined up. The chalk streams of the Somme were a dream for the dedicated angler. One reported taking 70 trout while at Blangy, saying "it was the best moment in my war service". His bait was, it seems, processed cheese.

Once the sun had gone down, off-duty soldiers would head for the canteen, "wet" or "dry". In those days, before the NAAFI was set up to organize such things, canteens were often run by charitable organizations such as the Salvation Army or the YMCA, where men could get a cup of tea and a bun. Many preferred the wet canteen with its beer, and even more soldiers would head out of camp looking for local hospitality at an *estaminet* (small café) with its invariable omelette and chips, *vin blanc* (often mixed with grenadine, as many soldiers craved sweetness) and the company of other men – and women. Indeed, every base camp attracted the attentions of local entrepreneurs. Cafés, bars and brothels quickly sprang up to service the off-duty soldier's needs and to relieve him of his money. In towns, business boomed for the *restaurateurs*. At Montreuil, well behind the lines and home of GHQ, the establishments in town were strictly segregated: "for Senior Officers", "Officers Only" and even "NCOs Only".

The three liveliest towns – magnets for soldiers on a very brief holiday from the horrors of the trenches – were Poperinghe (just 8 miles behind the Ypres Salient), Armentières near the Belgian border, and Amiens on the Somme. Here, an off-duty soldier could find almost anything he wanted, provided he paid. For the officers at Poperinghe, champagne was available at a popular club presided over by Madame Beutin and nicknamed "Skindles" after a similar hotel in Maidenhead, Buckinghamshire.

Sex was much in demand, and many soldiers lost their virginity in France. Young unmarried officers, often straight from public school, found much to excite their curiosity, and many soldiers had serious relationships with French and Belgian women – some going on to marry them. But for most men, the overriding aim was more transitory – to sleep with a woman before death or injury knocked on the door. Decorum could slip away – one soldier on the way up to Ypres remembered seeing a Highlander, kilt up, quite openly making love to a local girl. Later in the war, the stream of British nurses and WAAC drivers meant there were more women intermingling with the men, on duty and off, a proximity that contributed to an unwarranted reputation for "availability".

Other kinds of off-duty entertainment were organized by officialdom. Out of the line, Christmas dinner or regimental days were usually, as in peacetime, a sumptuous regimental feast served by officers to the men, washed down with lashings of drink. Perhaps the most amusing memories for many BEF men were the various semi-official concert parties playing to packed houses behind the lines. The 4th Division's "Follies" were in existence as early as December 1914, and by 1918 a whole series of well-organized official concert parties shadowed the popular music hall back home, putting on reviews and making fun of the Army, the General Staff, officers, NCOs and stingy quartermasters in a mix of ribald humour and sentimental songs and sketches, many performed by young men in drag.

On the last day before having to go back into the line, many companies and battalions organized "smokers" for the men: a day of more contemplative relaxation – drinking beer, perhaps listening to a talented member of the regiment singing or an officer playing a borrowed piano, while swapping cigarettes and talking with chums, all the while knowing that the next day the war would reassert its rigours and regime of fear. After a round of singing together, often ending with sentimental favourites like "There's a long, long trail a'winding, into the land of my dreams" or "Keep the home fires burning", all ranks would disperse to their billets, wondering just what tomorrow might bring – and just how many of them would be at the next smoker … .

"IN SPITE OF – INDEED PERHAPS *BECAUSE* OF – THE IMMINENCE OF DANGER, CONCERTS AND FILM SHOWS (WHICH WERE EQUALLY POPULAR) WERE OFTEN HILARIOUS AFFAIRS … EVERYBODY IS READY TO LAUGH AT EVERYTHING & MIRTH IS THE PREDOMINANT FEATURE OF THE WHOLE PERFORMANCE."

2nd Lieutenant E.W. Jacot,
14th Battalion, Royal
Warwickshire Regiment

A FRENCH PHRASE BOOK
THE BRITISH SOLDIER ABROAD

1914 TO 1918

In 1914, many regular soldiers of the British Army had already had experience of service abroad, or had heard stories from those who had served somewhere in Britain's Empire. But for the hundreds of thousands of volunteers and conscripts that followed in their wake, the shock of modern warfare was accompanied by the strangeness of living amid foreign places, people and cultures.

For most British soldiers in the First World War, little was familiar, from the brutal, dehumanizing nature of fighting to the alien environments in which they found themselves living. In Palestine, men who had grown up in houses with a family bible now found themselves walking through the ancient Holy Land where ploughs were still pulled by an ox and an ass. Battles were fought within sight of the Plains of Troy or close to Agincourt. Yet for the ordinary Tommy perhaps the most troublesome feature of life was language. All the natives spoke funny. Places had strange, unpronounceable names and it is no wonder that Ypres became "Wipers" and Auchonvillers "Ocean Villas". To help with this, handbooks were published like this one, the *Familiar French* pocket guide to French conversation and slang, or a *Soldier's Language Manual*, giving useful tips on how to be understood. With goodwill and a cocky smile, a little bit of "Franglais" went a long way to bridging the cultural divide.

On the Western Front, locals and their uninvited guests came to terms with their coexistence, and a relationship flourished that was based on supply and demand. Small towns, many packed with refugees, were swamped by foreign troops with money in their pockets and – never knowing if the next shell was for them – eager to spend it on the better things of life.

In the trenches, soldiers lived in sealed worlds, cut-off from the wider environment. But they became different creatures once out of the line and at rest. In towns and villages they were billeted on locals (who were well paid for the disturbance to their lives) or, more likely, were dropped off on a large farm with barns and a farmhouse, and left to their own devices for three or four days to rest and recuperate.

Relations with the locals continued, for the most part, according to a mutual suspicion balanced by a desire for mutually satisfactory commerce. Interaction, so far as it went given language barriers, was often about trading, whether it was buying wine at an improvised *estaminet* or, higher class, a restaurant, or even purchasing some female company at one of the officers' brothels in Poperinghe (*see* Chapter 56). Relations could be strained if the balance was put in jeopardy by some

"MY MAN BOBETT NEARLY MAKES ME DIE WITH LAUGHING SOMETIMES AS HE GESTICULATES TO THE PEASANTS FOR EGGS: SQUATTING DOWN, FLAPPING HIS ARMS AND SQUAWKING. HE THEN GRUNTS AND MAKES AS IF HE WERE SLICING BACON. FOR MILK HE SAYS 'MOO, MOO', BUT YOU SHOULD SEE HIM TRYING TO GET BOOT POLISH."

2nd Lieutenant Cyril Rawlins, 1st Battalion, Welch Regiment, June 1915

of the heartier soldiers' behaviour (stealing wood, milk, chickens and fruit; getting roaring drunk; seducing farmers' daughters), and none of the French locals were anxious to share the soldiers' lice. For their part, the soldiery was not impressed by entrepreneurial locals attempting to overcharge their captive market.

But commerce wasn't everything. Some soldiers came away as married men. And for many soldiers, the locals offered the possibility of domesticity. When they were hosted by kind, hospitable civilians, with children or pets, sentimental soldiers often broke down, such was the contrast with the frontline. Such relationships reminded them of the things the soldier dreamed of above all others: freedom from fear; comfort; love; and hearth and home.

Others managed better, and a remarkable stoicism and endurance was often witnessed. Frank Richards, of the Royal Welsh Fusiliers, recorded numerous incidents when the survivors of a bloody attack or a ferocious bombardment would settle down to drink and gamble, shrugging off the horrors of the day. "San Fairy Anne" *(Ça ne faire rien)* seems to have been the old soldiers' universal sentiment – "it doesn't matter". Such fatalism was perhaps the only way of coping with the arbitrary nature of enemy shells or the chance of getting killed by a bullet.

The main support came from a man's friends. Soldiers didn't fight and endure for King and Country; they stuck it as part of a mutual support system with their chums in the trenches. Shared talk, shared hardship and shared fears helped many a man to cope with the horrors.

Officers and NCOs seem to have coped better because of the burdens of responsibility. When an officer led his men down a communication trench under fire, pretending to be as cool as a cucumber, or "hopped the bags", going over the top, he was keenly aware that his men were watching him closely for a lead and example. For an officer to run away screaming in terror was deemed unthinkable. (The struggle to stay in control later featured in R.C. Sherriff's play *Journey's End*.) Regimental pride and loyalty became extraordinarily powerful if intangible influences.

In an age when religion mattered, there were many who found comfort in their faith (*see* Chapter 40). The role of the chaplain or padre changed dramatically in war and the various incumbents reacted to it in different ways. Church parades were impossible in the trenches and only seem to have been held in reserve or rest billets. Increasingly, padres found themselves talking to the wounded at dressing stations, or even going round the line distributing chocolate or – as in the case of the Reverend Geoffrey Studdert Kennedy, nicknamed "Woodbine Willie" – giving out cigarettes to frightened soldiers; and, of course, burying the dead. Actual observance varied. To give but two contrasting examples, the Catholic Connaught Rangers held a well-attended Mass before going over the top at the Somme on 1 July 1916, but, despite the strong Welsh Chapel influence, the 2nd Battalion, Royal Welsh Fusiliers, seems to have delighted in substituting obscene words in the hymns at compulsory church parades.

Nevertheless, religion undoubtedly had a close hold on many in the line between 1914 and 1918, and it is no surprise that the Reverend Tubby Clayton's "Toc H" retreat in Poperinghe became a magnet for all ranks, offering an oasis of normality and an opportunity for spiritual contemplation. It went on, after the war, to become the centre of an international Christian movement.

Superstition, too, remained ever present. If someone casually said "touch wood" it was taken deadly seriously. Many men carried lucky mascots, or had bibles or letters from home in their breast pockets (*see* Chapter 40). Others carried their superstition to more practical levels. Major Buckley of the Northumberland Fusiliers recorded a premature explosion of a rifle grenade that scored his steel helmet: "After that I would never part with that helmet, though newer ones were issued later." Another soldier, Charles Edmonds, admitted an obsession with omens and fetishes as a way to grapple with the randomness of shellfire and "the absurdity of dark, overpowering fatalism".

An extraordinary example was Private Dann of the Royal Welsh Fusiliers. At Hulluch in 1915, he was suddenly confronted by "the biggest black rat I have ever seen". Dann decided it was an omen, and told his comrades that "when I go west [die] that

"GOD HEARD THE EMBATTLED NATIONS SING AND SHOUT / 'GOTT STRAFE ENGLAND' AND 'GOD SAVE THE KING!' / GOD THIS, GOD THAT, AND GOD THE OTHER THING – / 'GOOD GOD!' SAID GOD, 'I'VE GOT MY WORK CUT OUT!'"

J.C. Squire, satirical verse in his Epigrams, *1916*

rat will be close by". His mates told him not to be daft. Two months later Dann was sniped through the neck, and as he died he pointed to a huge black rat watching on the parapet. The next moment, an explosion killed the rat, which lay dead at his side.

Alcohol helped. For many, of all ranks, the constant danger and fear of the trenches could be dulled by copious libations of drink, which lent a particular importance to the morning half-gill rum ration, ceremonially dished out in an officer's presence. Indeed, when Authority interfered with sacred matters like the rum ration – as when a teetotal quartermaster thought pea-soup powder would make a more edifying beverage – morale slumped and soldiers became resentful. Alcohol in its many forms became the universal panacea. It relaxed tortured nerves, and encouraged blissful sleep and a few hours forgetfulness of ever-present dangers.

Beyond the community of the men, and such human comforts as the local French inhabitants could provide, there was the bond with home maintained through letters – millions of them – and parcels. By mid-war the BEF's well-oiled postal service ensured that no letter took longer than four days to reach a soldier, even in a frontline trench, and parcels with their creature comforts would be waiting when the battalion went into reserve. Soldiers treasured this link with a different, safe, *normal* world, and would endlessly reread the letters. All ranks agreed that this reminder of the outside world was one of the most powerful and important props to keep a soldier content. And if, at post call, a soldier turned away disappointed, a luckier friend might even say, "Here, d'you want to read mine?" It was a close-knit world.

Like Santa at Christmas, a cheerful artilleryman near Aveluy, on the Somme, bears gifts of parcels and packets for his battery (July 1916). Any small and practical comfort or comestible sent from home was highly prized. The British Army understood the value for morale and put considerable effort into ensuring an efficient postal and distribution service.

Over half a million British and Imperial soldiers on the Western Front were killed – almost 60 per cent of them the victims of artillery. The possibility of death was always with soldiers in the line, and the dead were much in evidence. After a battle, no-man's land was littered with bodies. Most soldiers were revolted by the sight at first, but slowly became inured to it. On the Somme, Corporal Joe Hoyles of the Rifle Brigade witnessed a staff officer's first sight of death. Staring across at the bodies of the slain, the officer exclaimed: "Good God! I didn't know we were using Colonial troops." He was wrong. A week in the blazing sun had turned the dead men's bodies black.

With the accumulation of bodies came the unenviable task of collecting and burying them. Hoyles describes it well: "There was a terrific smell. It was so awful it nearly poisoned you. The old German front line was covered with bodies – seven or eight deep and they had all gone black. Our job was to put the bodies on [stretchers] and with a man at each end we threw them into that crater. I'll never forget that sight." Because British battle dead were buried close to where they had fallen, the sites – as later documented by the Graves Registration Commission and its successors – in themselves mapped the fighting.

Wounds were the subjects of mixed feelings – mostly feared, but sometimes welcomed. The technology of the day meant that when a shell exploded its fragments could be of any size, and chunks of red hot steel whizzing around could – and frequently did – slice off arms and legs, rip stomachs and chests open and cut off faces. Most men had seen the horrific effects of shellfire on the bodies of their friends. One shell exploded near Lance Corporal William Moon of the Cheshires in 1915, blowing his friend's head off and splattering Moon with his blood and brains – an experience that shook him so much he refused to go into the line, for which he was eventually executed. The bullet wound most dreaded was being shot in the stomach – it was frequently fatal. Despite the ravages of wounds, however inflicted, over 80 per cent of British wounded returned to active service.

The wound most wanted, by contrast, was a coveted "Blighty one" – the wound that didn't cripple or disable, but which took the victim away from the horrors of the frontline with his self-respect intact, perhaps even back across the Channel. The future writer Stuart Cloete was a Coldstream Guards officer in August 1916 when he was shot while tackling the enemy: "As I ran at him he fired. I spun round and sat down. I felt no pain. I felt as if someone had hit me in the shoulder with a great wooden mallet with such force as to knock me over ... Now I had my blighty one".

"Blighty ones" were not always unexpected, though. Frank Richards recalled that soldiers would actively court a nice clean bullet wound. In the winter of 1914–15 he remembered bailing out the flooded trenches, and "a man called Davies had his thumb shot off whilst bailing. Every one of us volunteered to take his place, but one man got the bucket first. He deliberately invited a bullet through his hands by exposing them a little longer than necessary; but the bucket got riddled instead."

When a soldier was hit in no-man's land many heroic acts were performed in getting the him back. Unarmed stretcher bearers risked their lives on countless occasions: it is no coincidence that the most decorated British non-commissioned soldier of the war was a stretcher bearer – Sergeant William Coltman VC DCM and Bar MM and Bar. Once a wounded man was back at the Regimental Aid Post, the wound was cleaned and, if possible, stabilized and then he would be passed back to a Field Ambulance behind the lines or a Casualty Clearing Station (CCS), where

major surgery could be carried out. The "walking wounded" would make their own way back. A badly wounded man would then either be moved to a Base or General Hospital, which had all the facilities of a normal civilian hospital, or sent to Étaples, Boulogne or Rouen before transit back to England on hospital ships.

Once in the casualty evacuation system most wounded men felt relief and an immediate loss of any sense of personal responsibility, after they had surrendered their bodies to the great, and increasingly well-organized, medical machine. After crossing the Channel they would be met by trains and dispersed to a network of voluntary and military hospitals across the country. Wounded soldiers were provided with a special blue uniform and were a common sight in provincial towns. Britain's *Official History* of the war states that while 36,879 men died in hospital, 169,842 returned to duty after treatment.

The final – and, perhaps surprisingly, the biggest – source of casualties between 1914 and 1918 was disease. Indeed, it was not until the Second World War that combat deaths came to outstrip deaths from disease. In Africa, Mesopotamia, Palestine, Gallipoli and Salonika soldiers sickened and frequently died from malaria, dysentery, typhoid and typhus. On the Western Front few soldiers died of trench foot or venereal disease, but both incapacitated large numbers of men – as did "trench fever", which was passed on by the ever-present lice. This infection, of which the BEF reported 800,000 cases, was rarely fatal, but it required a hospital stay and was totally incapacitating with its combination of fever, severe headache, pains in the muscles of the trunk and characteristic shin pains. Among the British Imperial forces, over 5,688,000 men were hospitalized from some form of disease during the war. That is nearly twice as many as the official total of battle casualties, 2,937,600.

After four years of war, the number of British and Imperial dead alone – from whatever cause – was well over a million, half of them "missing". And these losses were the least among the original belligerents. Nothing had prepared the warring nations for such numbers.

In a haunting image, a wounded man is wheeled on a stretcher along the road somewhere between Amiens and La Boisselle in July 1916, silhouetted against the setting sun. In its formal composition, the photograph has a stately, funereal air about it.

demanded the movement of 40,000 men every day. But sheer distance meant that a soldier from Ireland or Scotland might get home for just three days out of a week's leave; by contrast, men from London and the Southeast could be home in bed on the day they left France.

The selection of men to be sent on leave varied from unit to unit and sometimes involved urgent compassionate reasons – or some colourful variation of them. Lieutenant Bennett of the Leinster Regiment awarded leave to "the best liar in the section. It was apparent from his story that the entire fate of the British Army depended on his going home to see his father, who is, I believe, confined to bed with a slight chill." When leave was granted, the news usually came at short notice. Then men would rush from their trenches, take extraordinary risks hurrying to the rear and, having collected their passes and warrants, beg a lift to the nearest railhead, where special leave trains would be waiting.

At Boulogne or Le Havre new clothing and "vermin free" certificates would be issued. Then anxious men would finally realize that fear and hardship really were suspended, and pile aboard cross-Channel steamers for the voyage home and the fast train to London. By the time the Tommies walked out of Victoria Station – often to be accosted by the innumerable prostitutes – they became aware of (re-)entering a very different world, one that did not share their values.

The first thing most men did – after a good meal and perhaps trying to explain to a dubious family and neighbours just what life at the Front was really like – was sleep. Some men on leave found soft civilian beds uncomfortable and actually slept long hours on the floor. But others resented every moment asleep and used every waking hour to savour the comforts of home. Some men gorged on rich food; others spent far too much time in the pub.

One universal experience was a growing awareness by the soldier on leave of just how uncomprehending civilians were of what life was like at the Front. This was perhaps the most troubling aspect of leave and was commented upon by many. One King's Royal Rifle Corps soldier wrote: "I became increasingly uncertain of the value of returning to England for periods of leave ... Not being able to discourse about the things at the forefront of one's feelings. Such was England's attitudes I ought to have known". Some men even felt that their modest leave was too long. As bad as life at the Front was, at least one's pals there could *empathize*.

The sense of alienation was increased by many civilians' conversation and behaviour. During the last two years of the war men on leave heard endless complaints about shortages, having to queue, lack of fuel, rising prices and the other hardships that civilians were enduring. One thing that particularly irked the soldier on leave in England's Southeast was to be told by civilians that they were sharing his dangers, especially if an anecdote about a Zeppelin or Gotha air raid could be invoked. It all baffled soldiers, who could find no vocabulary to explain the yawning gulf between the real terrors of the trenches and the worries of civilians back home. Most men chose not to do so. There was no comparison.

Insult could be added to injury by civilians in public. In 1914–15, there were numerous incidents of self-righteous women thrusting a white feather into the hand of a hapless young man on leave in civilian dress, with the stern exhortation that he should join up and do his bit. Yet when in uniform, soldiers on buses and trams could sometime find themselves shunned.

One area of resentment was the realization that many folks back home were doing very nicely out of the war. A soldier on leave would contrast his pay – which could be as low as a shilling a day – with the £3 and 10 shillings per week paid to some skilled munitions workers. Others noticed that profiteering was rampant. Pre-war interest rates on war-related equity shares such as steel, oil, shipping and motor vehicles had rocketed, and some investors were getting very rich indeed while the average soldier risked his life abroad. Such anomalies troubled thoughtful soldiers.

The putting of so many young men into uniform, who then struggled to square their frontline experiences and home life, could bring social disruption. A sizeable minority of men on leave took their frustrations out on their countrymen by going on the rampage. Drunken soldiers were a common experience, and the military on leave figure strongly in contemporary reports from the magistrates' courts. Indeed, what with drunk and disorderly behaviour, sexual misconduct, petty theft and assaults on other citizens – even on policemen – soldiers on leave seem to have cut a minor swathe through the God-fearing communities of Britain.

Civilians, other than the nearest and dearest, were often glad to see the back of soldiers when they headed to the Front again. And the feeling could be mutual. But while a spell of leave might, for some, fuel a desire to get back to chums in the trenches, many found the moment of return deeply depressing. A not insignificant number of soldiers on leave took the chance to desert – but many were caught and returned, under guard, to France to face court-martial. Drunken soldiers at Victoria Station were commonplace and even hard-headed Military Police found the scenes heartrending as weeping sweethearts and newly married young wives saw their men off, often for the last time. It was thus with very mixed emotions that men waved from the windows as the train pulled out, taking them away from a peaceful, but alien, civilian world back to the well-understood dangers of the trenches.

Members of the BEF on leave, still in their full trench kit and carrying rifles. They queue to change their hard-earned French francs into pounds sterling at London's Victoria Station. Railway stations, and Victoria in particular, were the scenes of high emotion for civilians and soldiers alike. All knew that the return trip to France or Flanders could be the final one.

The stakes were high, for both sides. Winston Churchill summed it up in his later description of the Grand Fleet's commander, Admiral Sir John Jellicoe, as "the only man who could have lost the war in an afternoon". For the British, destruction of the Royal Navy's superiority could open the way to Germany once again having a true "high seas" fleet, able to circumvent the British blockade – the ramifications for Britain, her empire and the Allied cause would be enormous. For the Germans, it was a probably unrepeatable gamble that could seal the fate of the High Seas Fleet for good.

Unfortunately for Scheer, the British were, with their access to German codes (*see* Chapter 16), able to read his "secret" signals. On 30 May, the Grand Fleet put to sea, prepared to meet the German sortie. The next day, off the Skagerrak waters between Norway and the Danish Jutland coast, 20 years of Anglo-German naval rivalry reached a head as 151 British warships converged upon 99 German vessels.

Shortly after 15.45, Admiral Beatty's six battlecruisers – the target the Germans were hoping to draw out and isolate – made contact with Hipper's leading Scouting Group of battlecruisers. The Germans promptly turned tail and ran hard to the south, intent on drawing the pursuing British onto the advancing guns of Scheer's battleships. Beatty was happy to do this, for his objective was to locate the main High Seas Fleet and draw it, in turn, back towards the Grand Fleet. But, as battle began, and Beatty pursued the German battlecruisers, disaster befell the British ships. They were struck time and again by accurate German gunnery. HMS *Indefatigable* and HMS *Queen Mary* were both sunk by plunging shellfire followed by massive magazine explosions. The best witness to the destruction was Commander Georg von Hase, the First Gunnery Officer aboard the German battlecruiser *Derfflinger*:

> The enemy was shooting superbly. Twice the *Derfflinger* came under their infernal hail and each time she was hit. But the *Queen Mary* was having a bad time; engaged by the *Seydlitz* as well as the *Derfflinger*, she met her doom at 16.26. A vivid red flame shot up from her forepart; then came an explosion forward, followed by a much heavier explosion amidships. Immediately afterwards, she blew up with a terrific explosion, the masts collapsing inwards and the smoke hiding everything.

Beatty's own, memorable, observation was: "There seems to be something wrong with our bloody ships today!" He was right. The Royal Navy had got into the habit of leaving the metal doors open in its turrets, in order to speed up the supply of shells from the magazines down below, even leaving extra shells and volatile explosive in silk bags in the area beneath the turrets to increase the rate of fire: British pre-war doctrine had been to "smother" enemy ships with shells. The results were disastrous in practice, because when a British turret was hit the explosion started a flash fire that went straight through the open doors to the magazines, blowing the ship apart. It was a danger that the Germans had narrowly avoided at Dogger Bank, and they had adapted accordingly: afterwards, German warships closed all internal doors and kept minimum propellant charges safely out of the way.

Despite the losses, Beatty's ships had done their job. Having closed to within 20,000 yards of the main High Seas Fleet, his remaining battlecruisers now turned and ran back north shortly after 16.30, to lead the Germans onto the guns of the Grand Fleet. But here another British failing was revealed. Beatty was still relying on

Two young seamen aboard
HMS Chester attempt to clear
and repair some of the damage
inflicted on their ship after the
ravages of the Battle of Jutland.
Damage from shell bursts is
visible behind them. It was
a close call for Chester; she
escaped thanks to the skills of
her captain, but it would take
more than a broom to get her
fully operational.

hoisted flag signals to communicate his orders. Across 5 miles of sea, thick with
funnel smoke, signals often went unread. As a result, when Beatty turned, his
supporting squadron of fast battleships – the most modern ships in the world – were
slow to realize and fell behind, coming under heavy fire from the guns of Scheer's
battleships as they came within range. Now, as the High Seas Fleet chased Beatty
north and the Grand Fleet progressed from the other direction, 250 ships of the two
fleets were converging.

Admiral Hood's 3rd Battlecruiser Squadron was steaming southeast, ahead
of Jellicoe's battleships, to try and locate the Germans, with the light cruiser HMS
Chester scouting ahead. Suddenly, at 17.40, four German light cruisers emerged from
the murk and subjected Chester to crippling fire, hitting her 17 times in three minutes.
Three of her ten guns were disabled and one-fifth of her crew were either killed or
wounded, including the entire crew of the forward 5.5-inch Quick-Firing Gun turret
where 16-year-old Jack Cornwell was stationed as sight-setter. The protective gun
shields did not reach down to the deck, and a storm of steel splinters swept
underneath, slicing legs and cutting down men. Shells bursting behind sprayed red
hot metal into the gun crews.

62

A U-BOAT'S WIRELESS RECEIVER
SUBMARINE WARFARE AFTER JUTLAND

1916 TO 1918

The Battle of Jutland (*see* Chapter 61) had confirmed a basic truth by June 1916: that the German High Seas Fleet was only safe in port. It was not quite the end of the story as regards the fleet's forays into the North Sea, but German strategic thoughts were turning back to what seemed the only way of breaking the Royal Navy's deadlock and imposing their own counter-blockade on Britain: the resumption of unrestricted submarine warfare against merchant shipping. It was a potent threat, for there seemed little that could be done to counter the predations of the underwater killers. But during 1917 the British, despite Admiralty conservatism and faulty analysis of the problem, found tactics and technology that, while not eliminating the threat, could at least reduce it to manageable proportions.

In 1914, the Royal Navy had no answer to the U-boat threat, and over the next two years only 46 U-boats were destroyed by British countermeasures, mostly mines. Gradually the Royal Navy's armoury developed, so that by mid-1917 effective depth charges were allowing British warships to hit back hard. The next 18 months saw a ruthless campaign against U-boats in the waters around Britain, and one of its victims was *UB-110*, which entered service in March 1918 and undertook two patrols along Britain's east coast. Her second patrol began on 5 July. For ten days, *UB-110* was depth-charged daily by British warships. She still managed to attack an oil tanker, which did not sink, and a steamer carrying iron ore, which did. On 19 July, *UB-110*'s periscope was sighted as she approached another coastal convoy, and the submarine was saturated with depth charges. With her hydroplane damaged, inhibiting control of diving, she was forced to the surface where she was rammed by the destroyer HMS *Garry*. Badly damaged, *UB-110* sank. The following October, the wreck was raised by the Royal Navy and towed back to Newcastle for evaluation. Several valuable items, including code-books were found, and some of the salvaged objects were passed to the Imperial War Museum in January 1919, including this high-frequency wireless radio receiver. Plain and technical it may appear, but it provides a tantalizing glimpse into the claustrophobic world of the bitter war fought beneath the waves.

After Jutland, Admiral Scheer initially tried to raise morale among his fleet with another sortie in August 1916. But the signals intelligence analysts at Room 40 warned the Grand Fleet. The British submarine *E23* put a torpedo into the battleship *Westfalen*, and a Zeppelin misreported approaching ships as being the Grand Fleet; Scheer fled back to safety. In October, he tried again, only to lose the cruiser *München*

> **"COMMANDERS OF GERMAN UNDERSEA VESSELS HAVE ATTACKED MERCHANT SHIPS WITH GREATER AND GREATER ACTIVITY... NOT ONLY UPON THE HIGH SEAS SURROUNDING GREAT BRITAIN AND IRELAND, BUT WHEREVER THEY COULD ENCOUNTER THEM, IN A WAY THAT HAS GROWN MORE AND MORE RUTHLESS, MORE AND MORE INDISCRIMINATE"**
>
> *President Woodrow Wilson, Address to US Congress, 19 April 1916*

to another British submarine; again the German ships turned tail, and later nearly lost the battleships *Grosser Kürfurst* and *Kronprinz* to British torpedoes.

Scheer had better luck raiding off Dover with his light forces. On 28 October 1916, his torpedo boats sank a destroyer and six fishing vessels, and a month later he bombarded Margate in broad daylight. But increasingly the weight of German naval action was being borne by the U-boats. Events prompted a post-Jutland shake-up at the Admiralty, with Jellicoe moved to become First Sea Lord in London, leaving Beatty as Commander-in-Chief of the Grand Fleet in Scapa Flow.

There was a taking stock in the German navy, too. Ever since Jutland, German naval staff had been pressing for a resumption of unrestricted submarine warfare, and the numbers of U-boats in service had been rising. Admiral Henning von Holtzendorff now played his trump card. He prepared a statistical analysis that showed that if Germany could sink 600,000 tons of shipping for four months, and thereafter a monthly total of 400,000 tons, it would bring Britain to the brink of starvation within less than six months. The Kaiser accepted that only by wrecking Britain's economic existence could Germany now hope to win the war; an Imperial War Council on 9 January 1917 ordered the resumption of unrestricted submarine warfare from the beginning of February. Chancellor von Bethmann Hollweg opposed the plan, pointing out the dangers of alienating the United States, but was overruled.

With over 100 U-boats operational, sinkings of merchant vessels now rose alarmingly, from 520,000 tons in February to over 860,000 tons in April. If sinkings continued at this rate, by the end of the summer Britain would no longer be able to sustain the war; supplies of coal to French war industries would dry up; and Britain's reserves of food might dip below their current low of just six weeks' supply. The Grand Fleet's exercises even had to be cut back because of shortage of fuel. Despite the looming danger, the Admiralty – and Jellicoe in particular – solemnly advised an anxious War Cabinet that there was absolutely nothing the Royal Navy could do.

A helping hand came from a quite different direction, as predicted by the German chancellor. The United States, after strong protests to Berlin, severed diplomatic relations with Germany. On 26 February, President Wilson asked Congress for authority to arm American merchant ships: no country could permit attacks on her shipping on the high seas, and in addition Wilson had learned of the explosive contents of the "Zimmermann telegram" (*see* Chapter 66). Berlin was taken aback by the peaceable Wilson's reaction, but continued with its attacks, sinking three US-flagged vessels on 15 March. On 2 April, Wilson alerted Congressmen that the German unrestricted submarine campaign was "a war against all nations" and advised them that "the status of a belligerent had been thrust upon us" by Germany. Within days came the US declaration of war.

Once settled in at the Admiralty, a tired and overworked Jellicoe could think of little to beat off the U-boat menace. In spring 1917, there was no real means of detecting a submerged U-boat, and no very effective weapons with which to attack them. There was also no coordinated response to their attacks. Jellicoe's first move was to set up an Anti-Submarine Division of the naval staff under the bright Rear Admiral Alexander Duff. Despite his efforts, the Admiralty continued to insist that all it could do was step up the anti-submarine patrols, and that looking for submarines in the broad oceans was like looking for a needle in a haystack. Sinkings continued to rise. In fact, the solution lay right under the Admiralty's nose but it refused to accept it: convoys (*see* Chapter 83).

Two crew members of a U-boat in the torpedo room of their vessel; the cramped conditions on board are evident. Jutland forced the German navy back towards a naval policy based on U-boats, reigniting British fears of the underwater killers.

Ever since 1914 troop transports had sailed in convoys, with minimum losses, and in February 1917 coalers to France began adopting convoys, too. But until the late spring of 1917 Jellicoe and the navy's commanders at sea rejected the wider implementation of convoying. But when it did become policy, it came with a bonus, because convoys brought the attacking U-boats directly into contact with the escorts, now armed with their better depth charges. U-boat losses, which had only been 14 in the first three months of the campaign, began to climb to 10 a month, a loss ratio that could not be replaced by new builds. The U-boat campaign was effectively over by the end of the year – as was a war-weary Jellicoe, dismissed on 24 December 1917 by Lloyd George to be replaced by the more aggressive Admiral Sir Rosslyn Wemyss. The initiative in the naval war was back with the Allies. Although Scheer's cruisers made two sallies from port in late 1917, destroying two Scandinavian convoys, they fled back to port as soon as British dreadnoughts closed in. It merely confirmed that the fleet war had already run its course.

The naval war finally petered out in the autumn of 1918 when Berlin realized that Germany was doomed while submarine attacks persisted. On 21 October 1918, Germany – already putting out peace feelers – finally abandoned U-boat attacks on passenger ships, at the insistence of the country whose entry into the war had been forced, to a large degree, by unrestricted submarine warfare: the United States.

63

EDWARD THOMAS'S LAST WORDS
A "LOST GENERATION"?

1914 TO 1918

After the war, the expatriate American writer Gertrude Stein was watching a particularly ham-fisted French garage mechanic at work. She asked the owner, sarcastically, where his employee had been trained. He replied that apprentices were easy to train, but men in their mid-twenties to thirties who had gone into the war were *une génération perdue* – "a lost generation". It was a phrase – and an idea – that took hold. Ernest Hemingway took inspiration from it: to him the lost generation were rootless, disorientated postwar survivors. In Britain, however, the phrase has more literally been applied to the idea of a generation swept away between 1914 and 1918.

The war was not fussy. It cut down men regardless. But the loss was perceived to be greater where it seemed disproportionately high. Justifiably could the mothers of Barnsley or Accrington feel that their sons, dying together in the Pals battalions (*see* Chapter 9), were not only their own personal tragedies but also represented a chasm in their communities. In the wider culture, an idea of talent and potential cut short exerted a powerful influence, creating an impression of so many future artists and scientists, poets and painters, thinkers and leaders, prematurely felled by war.

At 07.36 on the morning of 9 April 1917, Edward Thomas's pocket watch stopped dead. The Battle of Arras had been raging for two hours and Thomas was an officer on its southern flank, directing the heavy guns of the 244th Siege Battery, Royal Garrison Artillery. A German shell passed so close to him that the shock wave sucked all the air from his lungs, which collapsed. It froze the hands on his watch and creased the pages of this, his diary, hidden deep inside his greatcoat pocket. But it left no mark on his body. Thomas's death robbed English literature of one of its most lyrical poets. Although a professional writer for over ten years, it was only in November 1914, at the encouragement of his friend the American poet Robert Frost, that Thomas began writing verse. Between then and his departure from Britain in January 1917, he wrote 144 poems, though none of them in France. Mostly his poetry considered the fragile transience of life in contrast to the reassuring permanence of the countryside. Such was his connection to the land that when, as a 37-year-old family man, he enlisted in 1915 and was asked by a friend what he was fighting for, he picked up a handful of soil and said: "Literally for this." People might come and go, but the English hills, trees and fields would always be there. His final poem, "The Sorrow of True Love", is shown here: it was written two days after saying goodbye to his wife and children for the last time.

"THERE SEEMED TO BE NOTHING LEFT IN THE WORLD, FOR I FELT THAT ROLAND HAD TAKEN WITH HIM ALL MY FUTURE AND EDWARD ALL MY PAST."

Vera Brittain, describing her dead fiancé (Roland) and her brother in her memoir Testament of Youth, *1933*

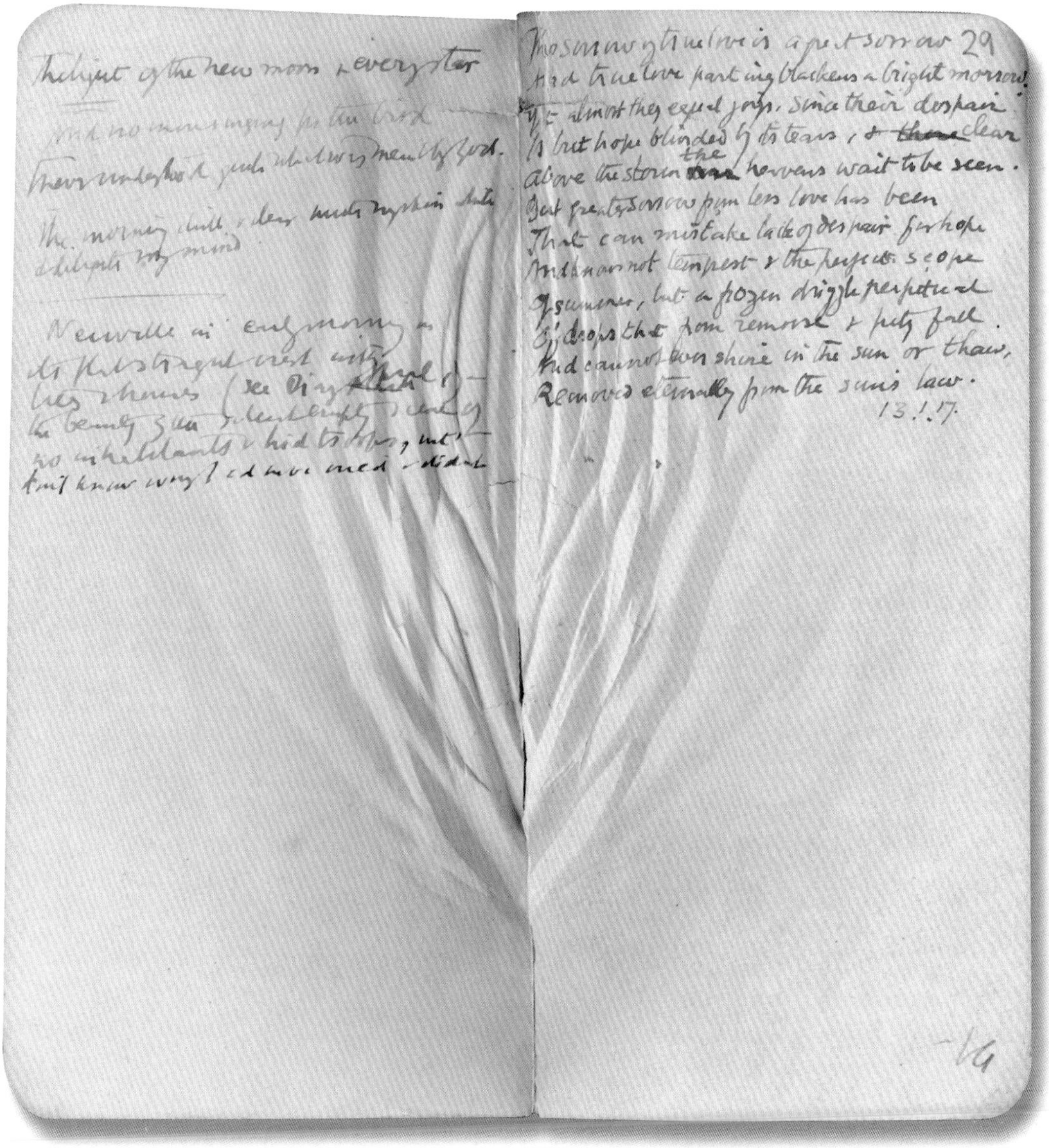

The light of the new moon & every star

_____ no ___ _____ for the bird

Their undertook ___ which was meant by God.

The morning ___ & dew ___ ___ ___
___ ___ my mind

Neuville in ___ morning _
its first straight ___ with
lies & ___ (see ___ ___)—
the beauty ___ & ___ ___ ___ of
no inhabitants & hid to ___, but
don't know ___ I ___ ___ ___

The sorrow of true love is a great sorrow 29
And true love part ing blackens a bright morrow.
___ almost they expect joys, since their despair
Is but hope blinded by its tears, & ~~there~~ clear
Above the storm ~~the~~ the heavens wait to be seen.
But greater sorrow from less love has been
That can mistake lack of despair for hope
And know not tempest & the perfect scope
Of summer, but a frozen drizzle perpetual
Of drops that from remorse & pity fall,
And cannot even shine in the sun or thaw,
Removed eternally from the sun's law.
                                        13.1.17.

—VG

Did Europe lose so many young men that it threw society out of kilter? In the words of historian Hew Strachan, "in the crude statistics of the rates of marriage and reproduction there was no 'lost generation'". Of the 6 million men from the British Isles who served in the war, one in eight died. As a proportion of the total population this figure is much smaller than that of France or Germany. It is hard to maintain a literal claim for a lost generation due to the war. But that has never been the point. It has always been about perceptions and concentrations, about loss not statistics.

The memorials at institutions of learning, from schools to universities, bearing the names of the dead, created just such impressions of loss concentrated in groups and communities. For the elite public schools particularly, supplying so many of the officer class, this is the case. Eton College, that bastion of privilege and wealth, records a hefty 1,157 of its sons who lost their lives between 1914 and 1918, and the melancholy tributes at Oxford and Cambridge colleges tell a similar story. Other schools lost as many former pupils as there were attending the school at any one time: a sobering numerical equivalence.

Privileged, wealthier young men tended to volunteer early and proportionately in greater numbers than other groups in society. They often had no job or dependants to maintain, and so were freer to volunteer. More than that, by the standards of their time, as fit, public-school-educated young men over 18, they were automatically deemed officer material. By volunteering, they had sentenced themselves to becoming platoon commanders on the frontline – the most dangerous position in the British Army. Educated by a regime of muscular Christianity that stressed

Proud, pre-war members of Eton College's Officer Training Corps stand to attention as they are inspected by Edward, Prince of Wales (the future Edward VIII), in June 1914. A sizeable proportion of the sons of the top public schools would go on to fight, and die, in the war, contributing to the impression of a generation's fallen elite.

team games and cold baths, and which concentrated on history and the Classics, they were imbued with Sir Henry Newbolt's famous poetic line: "Play up! Play up! And play the game!" and, like Billie Nevill on the Somme (*see* Chapter 52), genuinely believed that it was their duty to set an example to inspire their men.

The conditions of the Western Front meant that proportionately more of this particular social class was killed by the war than any other. The heavy casualties among young army subalterns in the trenches are no myth. Estimates for the *mortality* rates among these officers (below the rank of captain) range from 55 per cent to 81 per cent, depending on the battle. This – even at its lowest estimate – is double the rate for non-commissioned ranks. This statistic is true across all the warring nations. The Germans had higher mortality rates for officers and lost over 50 per cent of the males aged 20–24 in their officer class. The sense of a layer of society being sliced off was encapsulated in historian A.J.P. Taylor's verdict: "The slaughter of the subalterns in World War I destroyed the flower of the English gentry."

Such statistics fuelled the idea that the conflict had deprived society of the brightest and best – a generation of luminaries in their fields. The handsome young poet Rupert Brooke, who died in Greece from blood-poisoning in 1915, is often cited as epitomizing this concept of some lost *jeunesse d'orée*. Hugh Dalton, who was later Chancellor of the Exchequer in the 1945 Labour government, had known Brooke at Cambridge and wrote: "with his passing, a bright light seemed to go out of my life, and a bright hope out of the future". Churchill's own eulogy to Brooke summed up a certain ideal of intellectual and physical prowess joined together: "Joyous, fearless, versatile, deeply instructed, with classic symmetry of mind and body, he was all that one would wish England's noblest sons to be."

Brooke stands alongside Edward Thomas, Isaac Rosenberg and Wilfred Owen as fallen poets, while the war also took away the composer George Butterworth, the brilliant scientist Henry Moseley, and many others. In France, the politician and writer Maurice Barrès calculated that of the 161 students of the elite *École Nationale Supérieure* in 1911–13, half (81) were dead or missing and 64 wounded by 1918 – a 90 per cent casualty rate. We can, of course, never know what outstanding leaders, what great inventions or what great literature and art perished in the trenches – we cannot know what might have been. Writers such as Owen and Rosenberg never got to be just "poets" – their early deaths forever defined them and fixed their reputations as war poets. Arguably, that narrow legacy explains their potency.

That sense of a generation fixed in sepia is not limited to the "brightest and best". The playwright Alan Bennett wrote of his late uncle, Clarence, who died in Flanders: "He was always twenty all through my childhood, because of the photograph on the piano at my grandmother's house in Leeds. He was her only son ... When Uncle Clarence's name comes up it is generally in connection with the undisputed nobility of his character." Bennett wryly identifies the very human wish to make some sense of a young man's death by investing the individual with the finest of humanity's qualities. The belief that a dead comrade or relative was a good person gives comfort to the bereaved and makes it seem less of a waste. And, away from the public figures and the elites, Bennett returns us to the ordinary but much more pervasive sense of loss, affecting households everywhere. However much they came to grip the postwar imagination, the "brightest and the best" and the sons of Eton remain but a small part of the lost generation compared to the widespread loss among ordinary families. For every Brooke, there were thousands of photographs on pianos after 1918.

64

THE EASTER REBELS' SURRENDER
IRELAND'S EASTER RISING

24 TO 29 APRIL 1916

In August 1914, Ireland appeared to be on the verge of civil war (*see* Chapter 2). However, the outbreak of European war had the effect of suspending partisan strife among most groups in the face of a greater common enemy. The British government put implementation of the much-disputed Third Home Rule Bill on hold for the duration, and Ulster Unionists and the Irish National Party, the latter led by John Redmond, agreed to suspend their differences. Irishmen of all political hues volunteered for the armed forces. However, for the more radical Nationalists – such as the revolutionary Irish Republican Brotherhood (IRB) – the struggle with Britain remained paramount. For the IRB, its policy by 1914–15 was that "England's troubles are now Ireland's opportunity". And it seized its moment on Easter Monday 1916.

The Irish insurrection at Easter 1916 remains arguably the most important event in modern Irish history. But at the time it lacked popular support. Many moderate Irish men and women felt the rebels were mad. What eventually swayed public opinion and kick-started a wider movement towards an independent Irish nation was the brutal treatment of the rebels by the British authorities, and the executions of its leaders. Padraig Pearse, James Connolly and Tomas MacDonagh had surrendered, after six days of resistance, by signing this document. Pearse signed first, at 3.45 p.m. on 29 April, with Connolly following suit on the same day. MacDonagh was some distance from Dublin's city centre and did not sign until 3.15 p.m. on 30 April. Pearse and MacDonagh were among the first to be shot on 3 May. Connolly, who had been badly hurt in the fighting, was too sick to stand and was executed in a chair: his treatment, above all, inflamed public opinion, in exactly the way the leaders of the insurrection had hoped. Moderate Irish opinion quickly began to lose faith with constitutional efforts to achieve Home Rule and turned increasingly to the newly formed Sinn Fein to voice political frustration. The roots of the popular republicanism that followed lay not in the act of rebellion, but in the inept response of the British authorities to the rebel leaders' surrender.

If the IRB's idealistic but determined leaders, including Padraig Pearse, were clear on their political aim – "to control Ireland's destiny" – they were never really clear on how this was to be achieved. However, in 1915 the IRB established a military council charged with planning a general uprising. Leaders of the paramilitary Irish Volunteers, who had men scattered throughout the island, were co-opted into it – as was James Connolly's underground Irish Citizen Army, consisting of about

"THE TREE OF LIBERTY MUST BE REFRESHED FROM TIME TO TIME WITH THE BLOOD OF PATRIOTS AND TYRANTS"

Thomas Jefferson, letter to William Stephens Smith, 13 November 1787

In order to prevent the further slaughter of Dublin
citizens, and in the hope of saving the lives of our
followers now surrounded and hopelessly outnumbered, the
members of the Provisional Government present at Head-
Quarters have agreed to an unconditional surrender, and the
Commandants of the various districts in the City and Country
will order their commands to lay down arms.

P. H. Pearse
29th April 1916
3.45 p. m.

I agree to these conditions for the men only
under my own Command in the Moore
Street District and for the men in
the Stephen's Green Command.

James Connolly
April 29/16

On consultation with Commandant Ceannt
and other officers I have decided to
agree to unconditional surrender also.

Thomas MacDonagh
30.IV.1916
3.15 p.m.

250 armed men, and the Socialist Women's group, plus a group of boys to act as messengers. The conspirators were helped with money from the Irish-American organization *Clan na Gael*, which shared their aims and provided the secret communication channel between the rebels and Germany, from whom they hoped to receive military backing.

Intelligence sources in the Royal Irish Constabulary and in Dublin Castle (the British GHQ) were well aware that the IRB was planning an uprising. London was tracking the movements of the pro-Nationalist Sir Roger Casement, who had travelled secretly to Germany specifically to bring arms to Ireland. As Casement landed from a U-boat in County Kerry on Good Friday 1916, he was promptly arrested; the next day the German ship carrying the arms was captured.

This setback split the rebels. Eoin MacNeill, leader of the Volunteers, warned that without the rifles any uprising was off. But Pearse and others were determined to go ahead, even though it was obviously now a hopeless – if not suicidal – venture. Tempers flared and orders, counter-orders and confusion reigned, with personal recriminations flying. British intelligence seems to have been aware of this dispute and of the messenger boys bicycling around Ireland telling Volunteers on Easter Sunday that the rising was off and to "stand down". It may account for GHQ's surprise when, at noon on Easter Monday, 24 April, dumbfounded Bank Holiday crowds in Dublin were suddenly joined by 1,200 armed men. They were marching to seize five important locations – the General Post Office; the Law Courts (where they used heavy law books as sandbags); the South Dublin Union (workhouses); St Stephen's Green; and Boland's Flour Mill – and to proclaim a "Provisional Government of the Irish Republic". An attempt to seize Dublin Castle was chased off.

The battle was on. As the rebels barricaded themselves in and prepared for defence, the British cautiously tried to find out exactly what was going on. Martial Law was declared. A troop of Lancers reconnoitring in the crowded streets was shot down. Most of Tuesday was spent throwing cordons around the rebel strongholds and bringing in reinforcements; some Dubliners, aggrieved at the rebels' actions, got into violent confrontations with them – while others took cover as firing broke out.

Wednesday, 26 April brought serious fighting. The rebels, outnumbered by twenty to one, came under fire as the British brought the *Helga*, a small gunboat, up the River Liffey and bombarded Connolly's regular HQ, Liberty Hall, which the rebels had prudently vacated. Fires were started in the city and, with no food coming in from the countryside, large-scale looting was reported, exacerbated by the removal of the police from the streets. British reinforcements marching in from the coast were ambushed at Boland's Mill by men led by an Irish Volunteer, Eamon de Valera. Despite casualties, the soldiers fought their way through to clear St Stephen's Green. The rebels retreated and set up a new strongpoint in the College of Surgeons.

On Thursday, 27 April, the army closed in on Boland's Mill and the South Dublin Union, and artillery firing over open sights set the General Post Office on fire. Connolly was badly wounded in the foot but kept going on morphine. Much of Dublin was now also alight, and any male in civilian clothes seen in the streets risked being shot by trigger-happy soldiers, as barricades were thrown up and the army prepared for the final assault.

By Friday it was clear that the end was in sight. Connolly ordered the women who had fought in the General Post Office to leave the building, which was now in danger

"IRISHMEN AND IRISHWOMEN: IN THE NAME OF GOD AND OF THE DEAD GENERATIONS FROM WHICH SHE RECEIVES HER OLD TRADITION OF NATIONHOOD, IRELAND, THROUGH US, SUMMONS HER CHILDREN TO HER FLAG AND STRIKES FOR HER FREEDOM"

Padraig Pearse, from the Proclamation of the "Irish Republic", 24 April 1916

A British officer and two privates stand guard near some of the worst damage in Dublin, in the aftermath of the Easter Rising (April 1916). The British use of artillery to try and dislodge the rebels proved a blunt, though effective, weapon. This shattered pub boasts the now-unlikely prospect of "select bar upstairs".

of collapse. Later he and Pearse fled as the red-hot bricks crashed down around them. The survivors took cover nearby, but it was now only a matter of time. A last battle was fought for King's Street, where the South Staffords finally stormed the remaining rebel stronghold – and bayoneted any male they found hiding in the cellar. On Saturday morning, Pearse and the survivors surrendered. The rising in Dublin was over – and smaller uprisings in Ashbourne, Wexford and Galway had also been extinguished. But much of the city was battered, and while the dead included 64 rebels and 132 British soldiers, over 250 were civilians.

As the surviving rebels were marched away they were hissed at, pelted with refuse and denounced as "murderers" by angry Dubliners; only their soldier guards saved them from being manhandled by the crowds. Under government orders, and following a wave of arrests, the commander-in-chief, General Sir John Maxwell, swiftly court-martialled around 200 rebels. Fifteen were executed immediately, including all seven signatories to the Proclamation. The wounded Connolly, who was unable to stand, was shot strapped to a chair. De Valera was spared: for one thing, he could claim US nationality.

A wave of revulsion swept Ireland and the United States at such draconian punishment. How could Englishmen denounce the shooting of Edith Cavell and yet justify summary executions of Irishmen? Anti-British sentiment ran high in America and the executions were universally denounced as "tyrannical". The *New York American* wrote: "Thank God for freedom's martyrs in every age and land." Suddenly, thanks to Britain's maladroit response, instead of the foolish and suicidal gesture it was, the Easter Rising became a martyr's cause. It shifted public support away from the moderate stance of Redmond, and radicalized and broadened Nationalist feeling.

Pearse, Connolly and their comrades had not died in vain. Their sacrifice bore fruit. In the short term, it focused attention on the London government's failure to secure universal backing for the war effort throughout the British Isles. Unsurprisingly, conscription was never introduced in Ireland. In the longer term, the roots of the demise of the British Empire can be traced back to London's clumsy response to the Easter Rising. And one of the Easter Rising's surviving participants, de Valera, would go on to become leader of an independent Irish state.

65

MODEL PRIME MINISTERS
A CHANGE OF LEADERSHIP

DECEMBER 1916

With hindsight, it is clear that 1916 was in many ways the pivotal point of the war. The onslaughts and massive losses of Verdun and the Somme, the clash at Jutland, Brusilov's Russian offensive, the British evacuation of Gallipoli and surrender at Kut, the collapse of Romania and Zeppelin raids over England – all these brought home the totality and scale of the war. The warring nations were in too deep, their politics, economies and societies configured to fuel the war effort. By the end of the year any chance of a negotiated peace was off the table and both sides were resigned to a war to the death.

This hardening of attitudes had a major impact on the existing political leadership in both Germany and Great Britain. In the former, Hindenburg and Ludendorff – the "Duo" – took over military leadership of the Western Front, and were soon beginning to exert their commanding political voice in both Germany and her increasingly enfeebled ally, Austro-Hungaria. In Britain, the year ended with political intrigues culminating in what was a form of palace coup, which toppled Asquith and brought in a very different sort of Liberal as prime minister: Lloyd George.

First-World-War Britain saw two very different prime ministers. In 1914, the urbane and intellectual Herbert Asquith had already been in charge for six years. But his style of government proved too indecisive for a nation at war and in December 1916 he was replaced by the dynamic and charismatic David Lloyd George. As Chancellor of the Exchequer, Lloyd George had been one of the most radical members of Asquith's pre-war Cabinet. In May 1915, he became the first Minister of Munitions and demonstrated an energy and ruthlessness lacking in Asquith. Made Secretary of State for War after Kitchener's death in June 1916, Lloyd George went on to engineer Asquith's downfall within months, leaving himself the only credible candidate to take over. These contrasting personalities are clearly reflected in two wooden figures bought by the new War Museum in 1917 from the Lord Roberts Memorial Workshops. The workshops were established after the Anglo-Boer War to provide vocational training and employment for men disabled in the fighting. They expanded rapidly in 1915 with new branches across the country, each specializing in different practical skills. In London, the men made wooden toys including dolls, houses, vehicles and figures like these. In a style developed by the sculptor Edward Carter Preston, Asquith is shown (left) in majestic elegance as "The Last of the Romans". Utterly different, the sharp and modern Lloyd George carries two heavy shells, one under each of his movable arms.

> **"THE ONE PREDOMINANT TASK BEFORE THE GOVERNMENT IS THE VIGOROUS PROSECUTION OF THE WAR TO A TRIUMPHANT CONCLUSION."**
>
> *David Lloyd George, written message to the House of Commons after being appointed prime minister, 11 December 1916*

Crowds gather outside Parliament, hoping to catch a glimpse of their new prime minister, David Lloyd George (20 December 1916). The "Welsh Wizard's" populist and pragmatic streak meant that he always had a sharp sense of the political impact of decisions. His charismatic appeal was a far cry from the quiet, reserved Asquith.

For much of 1916 it seemed unlikely that there was any alternative to the wartime Coalition government presided over by the dignified and distant figure of Asquith, and it was generally assumed that there could be no general election in the middle of a major war. However, the political crisis of December 1916 changed things.

The roots of the crisis can be traced to the death of national icon Lord Kitchener, Secretary of State for War, on 5 June 1916, when his ship struck a mine on the way to talks with the Russians. He had already become sidelined in the Cabinet; now there was the question of who would succeed him. The choices were limited, and Asquith's consideration of Lord Derby was blocked by Lloyd George and Conservative leader Andrew Bonar Law. One other figure stood out – Lloyd George himself.

Lloyd George was a highly controversial figure. A gifted and natural demagogue in the Welsh Chapel tradition, he was also a successful social reformer and a Machiavellian political intriguer. His string of sexual conquests earned him the well-deserved nickname of "The Goat", and this anti-Establishment former solicitor was trusted by few; but – and it was a huge "but" – he got things done. His restless energy and sharp mind had transformed Munitions and helped marginalize Kitchener.

Asquith's character was entirely different. He was a cautious, consensual politician, without passion, much admired for his calm, steady reliability. By 1916 he had overseen nine years of revolutionary reform in Britain's domestic politics and he was tired. A barrister by background, he had dedicated his life to Parliament and a Liberal Party memorably described in 1935, by historian George Dangerfield, as an "irrational mixture of Whig aristocracy, industrialists, dissenters, trades unionists, quacks and Mr. Lloyd George". Discernible here is Asquith's dilemma. Giving Kitchener's job to the big beast Lloyd George would inevitably make a serious rival even more powerful. Nevertheless, and reluctantly, Asquith did so. His perceptive wife noted in her diary: "We are out: it can only be a question of time now when we will have to leave Downing Street."

In July 1916, with Britain embarked on the Somme offensive, Parliament, the great newspaper magnates and even his own Cabinet noted Asquith's lack of urgency and vim. By contrast, Lloyd George took to his new task with characteristic energy and drive. He initially backed the generals, and in September was confidently predicting "a knock-out blow" before winter. But by November, as the promised gains were not delivered, he was expressing serious doubts about political decisiveness and military strategy. Concerns were reflected in the press: "Unless the Coalition shows more grip than it latterly has," wrote the *Daily Chronicle*, 'it seems to us in serious danger of coming to grief... Its arch defect is its inability to make up its mind." This was a shrewd thrust at Asquith. Crushed by the recent death of his son on the Somme and unwilling to give up the hallowed procedures of peacetime, the prime minister was losing his authority.

Unbelievably, Asquith had no real Cabinet secretariat. Its methods were those of another age with no agenda, no order of business and no formal minutes, except for the prime minister's hand-written reports to the king. Lloyd George described Cabinet meetings as a "daily disastrous essay in the dilatory". He was now determined to seize control of the political process by means of a new cabal within government. In this project he found powerful allies – first and foremost Bonar Law, who disliked Lloyd George but recognized the need for change, and Sir Edward Carson, leader of the Ulster Unionists. They were supported outside the Cabinet by both Lord Northcliffe and Max Aitken (soon to become Lord Beaverbrook), controllers of the *Times*, the *Daily Mail* and the *Daily Express*.

Thus, on 25 November, the three politicians presented to Asquith an announcement for the formation of a new body with executive powers, described as a new "Civilian General Staff", to oversee the strategic conduct of the war, and asked for Asquith's signature. Lloyd George would be its chairman, with the prime minister as merely its figurehead. After (the usual) delay, Asquith turned the scheme down flat. A week of political infighting followed. While Bonar Law's Conservative colleagues wanted nothing to do with the "*parvenu* Welsh lawyer", all sides recognized that a Lloyd George resignation could bring down the Coalition government. So did Lloyd George, and on 1 December 1916 he fired an ultimatum at Asquith demanding that he "withdraw from the Presidency of the War Council in favour of another".

The press agreed. Northcliffe considered Lloyd George the lesser of two evils. On 3 December, a worried Asquith promised to negotiate with Lloyd George, after meeting Bonar Law and seeing Unionist support slipping away. He announced that he was advising the king to "consent to a reconstruction of the government".

Conservatives and Liberals alike then rounded on Asquith for giving in to Lloyd George's blackmail. Asquith was trapped. He wrongly concluded that a devastating attack on his premiership in the *Times* was the work of Lloyd George and Northcliffe, and he now informed Lloyd George in frosty terms that, while he did propose to form a new government, Lloyd George should not automatically expect to be part of it.

Lloyd George struck. He reproached Asquith for going back on his word and, on 5 December, resigned as Secretary of State for War. It was too much. Believing that neither Lloyd George nor Bonar Law would be able to form a government, Asquith resigned the same day. But his bluff failed. When Bonar Law was summoned to the Palace, he advised the king that only Lloyd George could unite the people, Parliament and the squabbling politicians.

Two days later, after Lloyd George had secured sufficient support, Britain had a new prime minister and – at last – a war leader.

66

THE STARS & STRIPES
AMERICA ENTERS THE WAR

JANUARY TO APRIL 1917

In 1914, the prospect of Europeans gearing up "to cut each other's throats" (*see* Chapter 36) was an enormous blessing to the economy of the United States. Industrial production, and stocks and shares that had been in the doldrums during the summer, soared in the autumn of 1914 as the British and French placed massive orders for weapons with American companies. The war was distant – confirmed by President Woodrow Wilson's declaration of strict neutrality on 19 August – and profitable.

But the New World found it much harder, in practice, to put the Old World out of mind. As reports of German atrocities in Belgium became worldwide news, attitudes began to harden. Many Americans were genuinely shocked, and there were some open calls for war. But over a quarter of Americans were either German immigrants or of German descent, and there were many vociferously anti-English Irish-Americans, too. Although most Americans did genuinely regard the Kaiser's Germany as an anti-democratic, militaristic power, the US Congress supported a strongly isolationist foreign policy and, with one eye firmly on the melting pot of US voters, saw itself as no more than championing the rights of neutral nations. The prevailing view was that it was not in the US interest to get involved in the "Europeans' War". But in 1917 two German blunders completely alienated American sentiments. And with that radical swing of popular opinion, the scales of war tipped decisively.

It would have been almost impossible for France and Britain to win the war without the United States. During the years of US neutrality, both France and Britain received huge material support from the government and individuals across the United States, spending around $7 billion on American goods. To sustain this level of support, it was vital that France and Britain were well favoured by American public opinion, and both countries fared well in the propaganda war – in contrast to the Germans. But French and British statesmen knew that, in the end, the war would only be resolved when the United States finally committed herself to the Allied cause, even if eventually this was not as a full member of the alliance but only an "Associated Power". The US entry into the war on 6 April 1917 was greeted with relief and muted celebration by the two leading Allied nations. In Paris, they marked the day by hoisting this American "Stars and Stripes" over the Hôtel de Ville, headquarters of the city's civil administration. This was seen as so significant an act of respect and welcome that within only a few weeks the flag was heading the list of acquisitions destined for the new War Museum in London.

"IT IS A FEARFUL THING TO LEAD THIS GREAT PEACEFUL PEOPLE INTO WAR, INTO THE MOST TERRIBLE AND DISASTROUS OF ALL WARS, CIVILIZATION ITSELF SEEMING TO BE IN THE BALANCE. BUT THE RIGHT IS MORE PRECIOUS THAN PEACE."

President Woodrow Wilson, Address to Extraordinary Session of US Congress, 2 April 1917

67

A BOLSHEVIK BANNER
RUSSIA IN TURMOIL

1916 TO 1917

By the autumn of 1916 there were many signs that a major crisis was looming for Russia. The ultimate failure of the summer's Brusilov offensive (*see* Chapter 51) had left both the army and the country dispirited, and the prospect of another winter in the trenches lowered morale still further. However, Russia's greatest problems were behind the lines. The combination of mass migration of peasants into the cities, rising costs, inflation and shortages of food led to growing public anger. The massive industrial complex around the capital Petrograd (now renamed from the Germanic-sounding "St Petersburg"), whose population had soared to run the wartime industries, became a natural hotbed of industrial action and demonstrations calling for bread and fuel to withstand the Baltic winter. But the Russian railway system was breaking down under its own inefficiencies and the demands of the army. Before the war, Petrograd received 90 grain wagons a day; by early 1917, it was receiving only 50.

It was these basic shortages of food and fuel that provided the principal catalyst for a political storm. In 1917, Russia witnessed not one, but two, revolutions – or more precisely a revolution and a *coup d'état* – and the rise of the anti-war Bolshevik Party would suddenly fragment the war's Allies.

The Allies knew that any Russian exit from the war would allow the Germans to move large numbers of troops to France and Belgium. They were also worried that weapons and other resources previously sent to Russia might fall into either Bolshevik or German hands. In the months after the October Bolshevik Revolution, pressure grew for Allied intervention, and Britain and France sent troops to the northern Russians ports of Murmansk and Archangel. They included Sergeant Leslie Clarke, who had spent much of the war since 1915 training men to use Lewis and Hotchkiss machine guns, and was now on his first overseas posting. By July 1918 he was in the isolated Russian town of Kemi Karelia, where British troops were forced to break up massed protest meetings, firing into the crowds and even killing locals. Clarke explained: "These Bolshevik agitators had brought with them 3 or 4 Socialistic-Revolutionary Banners which had been used in Petrograd during the first upheaval. The Banners were of red bunting, painted in white Russian lettering, with the translated manifesto: 'Workmen of all nations come together! By fighting you will obtain your rights!'" Somehow Clarke managed to keep one and brought it back when he returned, sick, to Britain the following spring. Coarse and home-made, it still exudes the raw power of revolutionary zeal.

"IN THE DAYS OF THE GREAT STRUGGLE AGAINST THE FOREIGN ENEMIES ... THE LORD GOD HAS BEEN PLEASED TO SEND DOWN ON RUSSIA A NEW HEAVY TRIAL. INTERNAL POPULAR DISTURBANCES THREATEN TO HAVE A DISASTROUS EFFECT ON THE FUTURE CONDUCT OF THIS PERSISTENT WAR."

Tsar Nicholas II, Abdication Proclamation, 2 March 1917 (Old Style date)

ПРОЛЕТАРІИ ВСЕХ СТРАН СОЕДИНЯЙТЕС"! В БОР'БЕ ОБРЕТЕШ ТЫ ПРАВО СВОЕ!

Once Tsar Nicholas had assumed overall command of the Russian armies in 1915, he became absorbed by military matters at the Russian headquarters in Mogilev. He devolved much domestic government of his autocratic state to his wife, Tsarina Alexandra, but her German lineage and dependence on a coterie of advisors – including, until his assassination in December 1916, the notorious "mystic" Rasputin – made her extremely unpopular with the Russian aristocracy and wider populace. She did little to counteract the growing suspicion that the Germans, capitalist profiteers and "speculators" were bringing the country to her knees. Popular opinion was that treachery started at the top. As early as October 1916, the Tsar's secret police

68

CULLEY'S SOPWITH CAMEL
THE BATTLE FOR THE SKIES

1915 TO 1917

With the importance of aerial reconnaissance established (*see* Chapter 37) – as a way to observe enemy positions, help plan battles and direct and vary artillery fire – aircraft were soon changing the way battles were fought. A junior officer in the air now had the responsibility to select and prioritize targets for a whole corps' artillery. This very success meant it was essential to remove the enemy's eyes in the sky – that aircraft needed to attack and drive off the enemy's aircraft. The war would see a host of new machines, new technologies and new tactics as the constituents of an "air war" – so familiar in the next world war – were born.

> Aviation developed with astonishing speed under the urgency of the war. In only three years, the slow, underpowered machines of 1914 had grown into fast, robust modern aircraft. Perhaps the best remembered British aeroplane is the Sopwith Camel, which entered service in the summer of 1917, helping to transform the Royal Flying Corps' fortunes. It was a quirky machine, driven by a rotary engine that turned so powerfully that if not fully controlled it could throw the aircraft to the right so quickly it would spin out of control. But skilful pilots used this unique characteristic to whip around faster than other aircraft and move them into a dominating position behind their opponents, turning the Camel into a superb fighting aircraft. This one, serial number N6812, was part of the newly formed Royal Air Force in 1918, though it was actually in naval service, towed on a floating launch ramp behind a destroyer. On 11 August 1918, it was patrolling the North Sea. Previous patrols had been threatened by Zeppelins flying overhead, and when one was spotted in the distance, Canadian-born Lieutenant Stuart Culley was ordered to take off from his precarious platform and shoot it down. For over an hour, Culley climbed at full throttle towards the distant airship. Once in position, he turned to attack with his two Lewis guns fixed on the upper wing. One jammed, but Culley still poured all the bullets from the other into the airship. As he pulled away, the Zeppelin ignited and plunged 18,000 feet towards the waves – the last ever to be shot down. Culley's famous aircraft has been on display at the Imperial War Museum since 1935.

By August 1915 the innovative forward-firing Fokker Eindecker was taking its toll of Allied reconnaissance planes – and aircraft equipped to drop bombs. The French were already fielding what can be defined as the world's first bomber force, which was raiding railway junctions in the Saar valley, dropping converted 155mm shells with considerable effect. On 25 August 1915, a formation of 62 bombers

attacked the steelworks at Dillingen, and another raid the following day against an aircraft factory prompted its relocation further east. However, the French pilots began to encounter serious opposition from the German "attack" machines and began to insist on having an escort of the new "fighters", such as the diminutive but highly effective Nieuport 11, known as the *Bébé*, which appeared in January 1916.

In early 1916, two developments moved the aerial war on further. Under the influence of successful "aces" Oswald Boelcke and Max Immelmann, the Germans began to improve fighter tactics and group their fighters in teams. In their turn, the British began to escort their reconnaissance missions with fighters. These included planes of the "pusher" type (with rear-mounted propellers), such as the new FE2,

DH2 and the Vickers FB5 "Gunbus", a light, manoeuvrable aircraft with a forward-firing machine gun and more than a match for the Fokker Eindecker.

The first great aerial clash of the war was the struggle for air supremacy over Verdun in 1916. The Germans mounted "barrage patrols" to protect their build-up of troops and *matériel* from the prying eyes of French reconnaissance planes. The French were outclassed by the newer German machines like the two-seater Roland C-III, and forced out of the sky. In response, special *escadrilles de chasse* (including the famous volunteer American Lafayette squadron) were hastily formed with orders to "seek out the enemy, fight him, and destroy him". At Verdun, by engaging the German aircraft in this intensive way, the French launched the first independent air campaign in history. They redressed the balance of power in the air, albeit at heavy cost; Georges Guynemer, one of the first aces, was shot down, wounded, as were many others.

Further north, the Royal Flying Corps (RFC) was preparing for the Somme. The first British single-seater fighter squadrons reached France by spring 1916, and from July onwards the pusher fighters and "tractor"-type Sopwith 1½ Strutters (with propeller at the front) ended the so-called "Fokker scourge" as the RFC gained air supremacy over the battlefield. One German soldier wrote: "During the day one hardly dares to be seen in the trench owing to the English aeroplanes." The British had also developed their own effective "interrupter" mechanism, which used the turning of the propeller to fire the machine gun through the rotating blades. And the British were now even able to boast their own *bona fide* fighter ace and national celebrity in the shape of Albert Ball, whose tally of "kills" was 17 by the end of August.

However, by autumn 1916 the air war began to swing back again as the first of the fast, streamlined Albatros D1 fighters appeared in new hunting groups (*Jagdstaffeln*), organized under the influence of Boelcke, who was emerging as Germany's leading air-war tactician and theorist – and its pre-eminent ace, especially after Immelmann was killed in June 1916. In two months Boelcke shot down 20 RFC and French aircraft. The British doggedly tried to maintain air superiority, but were completely outclassed. The single-minded strategy of Major General Hugh Trenchard, the RFC's commander, remained resolutely offensive, so patrols were maintained at all times over German lines; this brought the inevitable result that damaged planes could rarely get home and the prevailing westerly wind meant air battles drifted deep behind German lines, which is exactly what the Germans wanted. Air casualties mounted as the ground offensive petered out. By November 1916 the RFC had lost 782 planes, and – with 499 airmen killed – there had effectively been a 100 per cent casualty rate since 1 July.

British reaction was confused. The government's Royal Aircraft Factory was castigated for turning out slow and inefficient designs. In Parliament, MPs accused the government-designed and obsolete BE2 aircraft of "murdering our pilots". Fortunately, the civil aircraft industry was responding and innovative new designs were slowly coming into production. In France, the new Spads were a match for any German fighter.

For spring 1917 it was, however, too little, too late. The first four months of the year rammed home the hard truth: in the air, numerical advantage was no answer to technical superiority. Obsolete aeroplanes, poor training and slow delivery now brought the RFC into real crisis. In just five days before the Battle of Arras opened at Easter (*see* Chapter 69) the RFC lost 75 aircraft and 105 aircrew. Another 56 aircraft were lost through crashes. During "Bloody April" of that year, some new pilots arrived

"THE BLAST OF WIND FROM THE PROPELLER DISTURBED ME ENORMOUSLY. IT WAS IMPOSSIBLE TO COMMUNICATE ... MY CRASH HELMET KEPT SLIPPING, MY SCARF LOOSENED, MY JACKET WAS NOT BUTTONED SECURELY. IN SHORT, IT WAS MISERABLE"

Future German ace Manfred von Richthofen, remembering his first flight, May 1915

on the squadrons with just ten hours flying experience and thought themselves lucky to survive for three weeks. The German combination of better aircraft, better organization and superior training – plus, of course, an abundance of slow and vulnerable targets – made them formidable and dangerous opponents.

The air war escalated into a series of epic battles. On 23 April 1917, 68 RFC fighters came to the rescue of vulnerable artillery observation aircraft circling over their German targets. At the same time, aircraft of the fighter squadron (*Jagdstaffel 1*) directed by Germany's latest ace, Manfred von Richthofen, tried to shoot them down. The RFC suffered heavy losses after an hour-long dogfight with Richthofen's "Flying Circus" – so called because of the brightly coloured way their aircraft were painted (Richthofen's own plane was red) and the regular movement of their canvas hangers like circus tents. The new two-seater Bristol Fighters, of which much was expected, suffered 60 per cent casualties on their first sortie due to faulty tactics. The overall statistics were devastating: between March and May 1917, 1,270 British aircraft were lost.

Fortunately, by mid-May the worst was over. The arrival of 56 Squadron with its new Royal Aircraft Factory SE5s began to tilt the balance. Within the next two months, new machines capable of outfighting the German fighters would at last begin to pour in from England and, along with them, better-trained pilots. Together with Sopwith's extraordinarily manoeuvrable Camel (credited with shooting down 1,294 enemy aircraft, more than any other Allied fighter of the war), the SE5s and the reorganized Bristol Fighters would wrest aerial superiority from the Germans by the end of 1917.

The Sopwith Camel proved an adept and versatile, if quirky, addition to the Royal Flying Corps' repertoire of aircraft, and helped tilt the air advantage away from the Germans. This particular one had an unfortunate end, although the fact that it is still in one piece suggests it did not fall from too great a height.

69

A TRENCH MORTAR FROM VIMY
THE BATTLE OF ARRAS & NIVELLE'S OFFENSIVE

APRIL TO MAY 1917

The year 1916 left the armies on the Western Front battered and exhausted. Huge amounts of ammunition, weapons and lives had been consumed on the Somme and at Verdun. Both campaigns had degenerated into protracted battles of attrition with no breakthrough, and had left the combatants reeling. The question was: what now? The early months of 1917 would see a strategic retreat of the German armies, but also a renewed Franco-British offensive. Spring 1917 would bring disaster for the French and a rather limited success for the British – yet for the Canadian divisions of the British Army, it produced one of their finest moments of the war.

On 9 April 1917, fighting side by side for the first time, the four Canadian divisions in the BEF captured Vimy Ridge. In 1915, the Germans had defeated repeated French attempts to take the ridge and regarded the position as impregnable. The meticulously planned operation was covered by a massive artillery bombardment. At 05.30, 15,000 Canadian soldiers surged over the ridge. Four hours later, fresh troops crashed through the fortified villages on the far side. By the end of the second day, the entire ridge was in Canadian hands: it had been a complete triumph. In freezing rain and sleet, the 31st Battalion from Alberta had overrun the village of Thélus and, among its shattered ruins, they found this 25cm heavy trench mortar, or *Minenwerfer*, which the Germans had used for bombarding enemy trenches too close to be shelled by field guns. Within weeks it had been passed to the new War Museum in London as a symbol of Canadian victory. The capture of Vimy Ridge showed the world the skill and strength of Canada's soldiers. The French press hailed their success in snatching the positions that had thwarted their own soldiers and portrayed Vimy Ridge as an Easter gift from Canada to the people of France. It is fitting that today, in a reciprocal act of gratitude, Canada's national memorial to its dead of the First World War stands astride Vimy Ridge, on land freely given by France.

First, however, there was a change of personnel. By December 1916, Joffre's star as French Chief of the General Staff was waning, as criticism of his handling of the war arose on every side. Despite his steady leadership and legendary sang-froid he was increasingly seen as a man devoid of ideas. French Premier Briand, under intense pressure from the Chamber of Deputies, faced a choice: either his government fell or Joffre went. Unsurprisingly, the politician ditched the general, appointing him "Military Technical Advisor to the Government", with a small office in Paris.

"BUILDINGS WERE DEMOLISHED, TRENCHES OBLITERATED AND WIRE SMASHED TO ATOMS. THERE WAS HARDLY AN INCH OF GROUND THAT DID NOT BEAR WITNESS TO THE TREMENDOUS EFFECT OF OUR GUNS"

Battle report of the 31st (Alberta) Battalion, regarding the capture of Thélus, 9 April 1917

His replacement was General Robert Nivelle, who had risen remarkably quickly from a mere colonel of artillery in 1914. At the Aisne in 1914, and at Verdun in 1916, he had handled his guns with great skill, and he was responsible for the successful counterattacks that retook the Verdun forts of Vaux and Douaumont. According to the British Liaison Officer at French GHQ, he was "good-looking, smart, plausible and cool"; he had two other advantages: he spoke fluent English, thus commending him to his British allies; and, as a Protestant and a Republican, he was not deemed a threat in the snakepit of French politics.

Nivelle proposed a double offensive for spring 1917. The British would mount an attack around Arras, in Artois; and, once the German reserves had been committed, the French would then attack further south in the Champagne. Unfortunately, Nivelle overplayed his hand, announcing that he had a confident plan to "rupture the enemy's front line in such a manner that the rupture can be immediately exploited". These claims excited war-weary politicians, especially as Nivelle claimed that he now had his "method". This consisted of a two-day bombardment against a selected area, which would turn into a creeping barrage as the infantry closed up to attack. Enemy artillery would be swamped by brisk counter-battery fire once it had revealed its position. Many of his military contemporaries had doubts, arguing that what may have worked on a small scale at Verdun could not be guaranteed on the 23-mile frontage now proposed.

Unfortunately, Nivelle soon fell out with the recently promoted Field Marshal Haig over how much of the Front the British were prepared to take over from the French. Nivelle wanted to hand over another 20 miles south of the Somme. Haig would only accept 8 miles. Nivelle then embarked on an intrigue with Britain's new prime minister, Lloyd George, which damaged relations between the Allies and – worse – left Lloyd George and Haig distrusting each other for the rest of the war. At Calais on 26 February, Lloyd George unveiled a surprise proposal to place Haig under Nivelle's command, without having consulted the Cabinet, Haig or the astonished Chief of the Imperial General Staff. After a furious exchange the idea was whittled down to a temporary subordination for the spring offensives; relations between Haig and the slippery Lloyd George were damaged irreparably.

Events now reared their head. Having suffered heavy losses on the Somme and at Verdun in 1916, the Germans had decided to withdraw to a better defensive position. The result was the building of a shorter, heavily fortified line between Verdun and Loos, incorporating deep and mutually supporting defences: the *Siegfried Stellung*, or "Hindenburg Line" as the British called it. In late February 1917, the Germans began a large-scale strategic withdrawal to this new position, and over two months this retreat, codenamed Operation Alberich, dissolved the "vulnerable" salient that the Germans had been defending at high cost – and took away many of the very positions that Nivelle had proposed attacking. France now had more of her sacred soil back, but it threw Allied planning into disarray.

Political turmoil was also wracking the Allies: there was a revolution in Russia as the Tsar abdicated (*see* Chapter 67); and during March, Briand's government fell in Paris. A number of politicians and senior military figures began to express doubts about the forthcoming attack. But Nivelle insisted and threatened to resign. A special Presidential Council of War was formed and only when Nivelle had received a unanimous – and mendacious – assurance that the new government backed his plans did he agree to continue. As it was, he was forced to postpone his attack for a month.

Canadian troops in the remains of a battered trench at Vimy Ridge (1917). The shell-torn landscape beyond, denuded of any sort of vegetation, is a testament to the ferocity of battle.

When it did get underway, at Easter 1917, it began in the north with the British "diversionary" attack, a week ahead of the main French offensive. The aim was to pin down German forces, draw in reserves and act as the anvil for Nivelle's hammer when he broke through further south. Unfortunately, German withdrawal to the Hindenburg Line meant that the British had been forced to replan their whole attack. Nevertheless, it became clear that the Germans had committed a number of errors in their redeployment. The main German reserves were being held about 30 miles to the rear and the local reserves had been pushed well forward – well within range of any British bombardment.

To the north of Arras the primary objective was the long slope of Vimy Ridge, which climbed gently up to a crest before falling sharply away to give a spectacular view of the Douai plain as far as German-occupied Lille. Drawing away to the southeast was Arras, with both positions undercut by an ancient network of caves and quarries that had been used to provide the stone to build the city, and which now provided well-lit, well-ventilated, but above all safe shelters for up to 30,000 soldiers.

Lieutenant General Sir Edmund Allenby's Third Army was to launch the main thrust of the battle out of Arras itself, flanked by the First and Fifth armies to the north and south. Allenby had a bold plan. Eight infantry divisions would emerge from the ground on the Germans' doorstep, to attack with the support of 70 tanks to crunch through the wire. The assault would be ushered in by a meticulous artillery fire plan using 2,000 guns, of which 700 were heavies. The main thrust was only 7,000 yards wide, but was supported by subsidiary attacks on the flanks, of which General Sir Henry Horne's First Army assault on Vimy Ridge was the most important. Once through, Allenby genuinely believed he would be able to release cavalry onto the Douai plain and exploit his breakthrough.

Bad weather postponed the attack for 24 hours, but on Easter Monday, 9 April 1917, it went in covered by sleet and snow showers. The infantry erupted from their warm tunnels and bunkers and rushed the dazed and frozen German frontlines. But for the

73

A SIMPLEX TRENCH LOCOMOTIVE
LOGISTICS IN THE WAR

1914 TO 1918

"Logistics" – supplying troops with everything they need, from food to ammunition – has always been the lifeblood of war. The First World War was no exception to the iron rule that "armchair generals talk strategy and tactics – professionals talk logistics and intelligence".

More technically, military logistics means "supply, transport and re-supply". Transport had been revolutionized by the coming of the railway, which offered the ability to move vast numbers of men and *matériel* quickly over long distances. Throughout the First World War, railway networks remained the arterial system for most armies, enabling that lifeblood to flow – albeit at different levels of efficiency. As the war developed, temporary rail lines also sprang up, to service the frontlines.

In the First World War, moving anything around in quantity depended, in the first instance, on railways. But standard-gauge trains could not move men and supplies all the way to the trenches. From distant railheads, men and stores had to move forward by road and on foot, and as the fighting became more intense this system became harder to sustain. From late 1916, a network of narrow-gauge railways was laid down to transport men and shells to the frontlines, and eventually it extended to over 600 miles of track along the Western Front. A rugged petrol locomotive was developed to pull trains in the dangerous battle zones. Built by the Motor Rail and Tramcar Company of Bedford, the Simplex 40-horsepower "rail tractor" came in three variants. One was completely armoured; another was "protected" front and back, with a solid roof and sliding doors but open windows; and the simplest kind had protection only at the ends with canvas doors on the sides. The "protected" Simplex was the most common, with over 220 built for use mostly on the Western Front but also in Italy, Salonika and Palestine. After the war, this particular example was used by Newall's Insulation and Chemical Company at its works in Renfrew. It was restored to working order by Newall's apprentices and later displayed, first at Beamish North of England Open Air Museum and, more recently, at the Imperial War Museum's Duxford site. Despite looking a little like an armour-plated garden shed on wheels, this rather strange vehicle was a vital cog in the machinery that kept the Western Front working.

The problem confronted in 1914 was that once the fixed rail lines stopped, the armies were not that much more mobile than in Napoleon's day. They still relied on horses, hundreds of thousands of them (*see* Chapter 45), and increasing numbers of motor vehicles – with the war seeing the use of London buses to ferry many

> ### "AN ARMY MARCHES ON ITS STOMACH"
>
> *Napoleon's famous dictum of military success*

of the BEF (*see* Chapter 15). And the armies still had to march, carrying whatever they could.

These logistical limitations were starkly revealed in the miscalculations of the Schlieffen plan, the Germans' opening gambit to knock out France (*see* Chapter 11). The sheer distance of the lengthening supply chain as the German armies moved across Belgium, complicated by Belgian resistance, destroyed bridges and wrecked railway lines, contributed significantly to the plan's failure. Most of the fodder to feed the horses was being consumed by the *other* horses further back in the chain, and the further the Germans advanced the worse it got, until the frontline horses were having to survive on green corn from French fields or dying of disease and malnutrition.

Once the war solidified into the trench lines of siege warfare, the supply problem changed. Although the frontlines were now largely static, they consumed unheard of quantities of *matériel*. "Trench stores" needed wood, corrugated iron, sandbags and barbed wire, sometimes even concrete, especially for the Germans who were consolidating territory won. Ammunition expenditure rocketed with the variety of static targets available to shoot at. Casualties had to be moved; food and water had somehow to be got to the frontline – usually by soldiers in carrying parties. The problems were compounded by the French and British imperative to attack and try to eject the invaders, which required massive logistical build-ups. By mid-1916, for example, the British stockpiled – and fired – a million shells on the Somme, more than they had used in the entire war to date. Such quantities had to be transported, and now everywhere behind the lines, especially on the Western Front, the narrow-gauge trench railways grew up, snaking forward as far as they dared to feed the men, horses and guns in the combat zones.

The biggest supply problem in the first years of the war was ammunition. Before the war the French had planned for 10,000 shells a day: in fact, by the end of 1915 they had to manufacture and move 200,000 per day. The Germans at Verdun (*see* Chapter 50) laid new railway lines direct from the factory to bring up shells. The French only survived the first month of Verdun by their own logistical lifeline, the road dubbed *La Voie Sacrée*, which delivered almost 80 per cent of the 48,000 tons of French ammunition used. When it came to ammunition, the British were initially even worse off, because British industry was unprepared. By 1915 the "great shell scandal"

A column of British lorries and horse-drawn wagons threads its way along the Menin Road, in the Ypres Salient, between emaciated trees (November 1917). In conditions like these, to slip off the road into the water-filled shell holes could spell disaster.

erupted (*see* Chapter 30), forcing the government to issue compulsory contracts to manufacturers and introduce a programme of emergency war industrialization, as well as the new Ministry of Munitions.

Britain also had a unique transport problem: everything from a bullet to a bandage had to be sent by sea. The solution was a huge new military port at Richborough on the North Kent coast. As Southampton was used primarily to recover casualties and Folkestone to ferry drafts across the Channel, Richborough, with its excellent railway lines, sidings and loading docks, supplied the British Army on the Western Front. The port was run by the Royal Engineers (RE) and the Army Service Corps, and even had a "roll-on, roll-off" ferry for complete railway trains. The biggest commodity was fodder: it amounted to 25 per cent of all the stores that passed through the port. The British Army had almost 370,000 horses and 82,000 mules on the Western Front by 1917. The cavalry, now much reduced, accounted for only a tiny percentage, but all the beasts had to be fed.

Another particular logistical problem for the British was the Grand Fleet in its northern base at Scapa. Most of its ships were coal-burning ones and literally millions of tons of coal were produced, which then had to be transported from the coalfields of England and Wales by trains called "Jellicoe Specials". It is no exaggeration to say that the Royal Navy depended on the railways for its wartime operations, as did the army in France. Royal Engineer Railway Companies were used behind the lines, laying miles of track, with spurs to take shells straight to the guns, ambulance and tank-train sidings, and even bridges. The aim was always to take standard-gauge railways as close to the Front as possible, and only then to use narrow-gauge systems, horsed transport and manpower. By 1918 there were no less than 45 RE Train Companies, including in theatres such as Egypt and Salonika. In 1916, the problem of managing this vast logistical and transport network, including canals, was given to a civilian railway manager, Sir Eric Geddes, one of the businessmen brought in by Lloyd George when Minister of Munitions to energize government: he was even made an honorary major general at Haig's HQ.

Beyond the Western Front, the other theatres of war raised their own logistical difficulties. In Sinai and Palestine water was a perennial problem, as it was in Mesopotamia, and it directly influenced the fighting. Indeed, in Sinai the British advance depended on the laying of a waterpipe, along with a railway and a wire-netting "road". In Mesopotamia the absence of road or railway meant the rivers were vitally important: the Tigris and Euphrates became the main supply routes, used with great success. And across the desert environments, the stamina of camels played an important role.

Whatever other criticisms may be thrown at them, British generals and their hard-pressed staffs proved themselves to be thoroughly professional in their administration as they dealt with the British Army's global supply problems. The horses were watered, and the men were fed – no mean feat for the unprecedented demands of the First World War. This logistical competence – plus the combined effort of British industry – truly supplied the "sinews of victory". It is telling that German infantrymen were astonished at the well-stocked BEF food and ammunition dumps they captured in 1918 during their last attempts to snatch victory. It is no wonder they paused, to Ludendorff's ire, in order to sample the bully beef, biscuits, warm clothing, whisky and service rum left by the retreating British. It was a far cry from what they, or their hungry compatriots back home, could get.

"THE DECAUVILLE LIGHT RAILWAY, WHEN IT HAD BEEN LAID UP TO THE BATTERY, WAS A GREAT SAVING TO THE WAGON LINES ... THE TRACK WAS LAID UP OUR SHALLOW VALLEY WHICH WAS SUBJECT TO HEAVY GERMAN FIRE. THE DRIVER OF THE ENGINE DID NOT ALWAYS LIKE THIS, AND UNCOUPLED HIS ENGINE AND WENT BACK."

Major Roderick Macleod, 241st Brigade, Royal Field Artillery, 27 August 1917

74

THE "C TYPE" AERIAL CAMERA
BRITISH INTELLIGENCE DURING THE WAR

1914 TO 1918

In the first decade of the 20th century, a sense of growing threat from Germany gave rise to "spy fever" in Britain. When added to fears of Germany's blatantly anti-British naval programme and German commercial penetration of British markets, the idea that Germany was one day planning to invade the British Isles seemed only too believable. The lead-up to war saw new dedicated intelligence organizations emerge in Britain, and the war itself saw the latest technology and techniques ingeniously harnessed for information gathering and intelligence purposes.

In the troglodytic world of the trenches, possibly the most valuable intelligence either side could possess was knowledge of what was happening beyond the opposing frontline. Direct observation on the ground was almost impossible. Accurate and methodical reconnaissance from the air was needed to fill this gap, and soon cameras were in use in the skies. Basic cameras were first used by the British as early as September 1914, but it was not until the formation of an experimental photographic section in January 1915 that aerial photography began to develop. A hand-held wooden camera, the "A Type", took images on glass plates, but it was complicated to operate. One observer remembered: "You had to take your slide out of the box – with your glove off of course – get it into the camera, take your photograph, close up the plate, take the slide out of the camera, back into your box. By that time your hand was so cold that over and over again I've lost the plate as I took it out of the camera. I've cried with numbness and the pain in my hand." The "C Type", shown here, was introduced in summer 1915. Fixed to the aircraft's fuselage, it produced a more consistent quality of photo. In addition, after each exposure, a semi-automatic mechanism changed the plates within the camera frame. The "C Type" facilitated a widespread expansion of aerial photography, allowing it to keep pace with the Royal Flying Corps' rapid growth. New cameras appeared – lighter, stronger and with better focal lengths. By 1918 no-one could fight a battle without taking pictures from the skies.

In 1909, a worried Committee of Imperial Defence set up a Secret Service Bureau, with a Home Section under Army Captain Vernon Kell, and a Foreign Section under a passed-over naval officer, Commander Mansfield Cumming. These were the forerunners of today's Security Service (better known as MI5) and Secret Intelligence Service (MI6). At the outbreak of war, Kell vindicated his appointment: he ordered police throughout the country to lift 21 of the known 22 German agents he had identified – the 22nd was in Germany on leave – and thus Britain disabled the

> **"THERE WAS MORE IN THOSE EYES THAN ANY COMMON TRIUMPH. THEY HAD BEEN HOODED LIKE A BIRD OF PREY, AND NOW THEY FLAMED WITH A HAWK'S PRIDE ... THIS MAN WAS MORE THAN A SPY; IN HIS FOUL WAY HE HAD BEEN A PATRIOT."**
>
> *Richard Hannay's verdict on a captured German spymaster, in John Buchan's 1915 novel of pre-war espionage,* The Thirty-Nine Steps

German spy network in Britain for the rest of the war – with one notable exception (*see below*). Kell's organization was renamed MI5 ("Military Intelligence 5") in 1916.

As war began, the War Office had no troops trained in intelligence matters. It quickly identified a number of army officers, Metropolitan Police officers and qualified civilians and invited them to join the newly formed Intelligence Corps to go to France with the BEF. They were divided into the Intelligence Police, responsible for security, and an Intelligence Branch, working for the General Staff. The new corps was soon in action providing field intelligence on the advancing Germans and interrogating refugees and prisoners of war. Behind the frontlines the former police officers of the Field Security Police ensured that the rear areas and lines of communications remained free from the threat of subversion, espionage and sabotage, and identified enemy agents.

One new area for intelligence lay in interception of cable traffic and wireless signals. Signals intelligence – "Sigint" – soon became invaluable. In the first month of the war the French used the Eiffel Tower to listen in to signals of German units at the Marne. And early on, the British severing of Germany's transatlantic cable forced the Germans to depend on neutral Sweden's cable – conveniently routed through Britain. In fact, Sigint had, unknown to the Allies, already scored its first victory in August 1914: the outcome of the Battle of Tannenberg owed a great deal to radio intercepts informing the Germans exactly where their Russian enemies were and what they were going to do next (*see* Chapter 18).

Much Sigint was simple direction-finding to locate enemy units. British Sigint was helped enormously by the acquisition of three German maritime and diplomatic codebooks. Despite this, in May 1916 Sigint was blamed for a significant intelligence lapse when the Director of Naval Operations, Captain Thomas Jackson, asked the specialists of "Room 40" (*see* Chapter 16) where German Admiral Scheer's call-sign "DK" was. Room 40 replied truthfully: "still in port" at Wilhelmshaven, which Jackson duly passed on; in fact, Scheer and the High Seas Fleet had already set off into the North Sea. The trouble was that Scheer always left his call-sign in port, and used a different one for sorties. Jackson had asked the wrong question. As a result, for a while Jellicoe and the Grand Fleet were wrong-footed in the lead-up to the Battle of Jutland, unaware that the Germans were out.

By contrast, Room 40's greatest success was to change the balance of the war. The interception and decoding of the "Zimmermann telegram" (*see* Chapter 66) by British Sigint revealed that Germany was a genuine threat to the United States and finally brought America into the war.

Telephone lines were vulnerable to interception, too. German monitors quickly developed a system of exploiting the vulnerability of British battlefield telephones (*see* Chapter 41). The Allies only became aware of the German eavesdropping equipment in early 1916 and swiftly ordered new security measures, while copying the technology. By the end of the war the Signals Service of the Royal Engineers could monitor German signals from a buried landline 3,000 yards away.

Aerial photography was also becoming increasingly important. Photographs revealed enemy trenches, defences, artillery locations and railheads, and the Royal Flying Corps' aerial reconnaissance and artillery target-spotting role expanded quickly. By 1916 some cameras were even able to produce stereoscopic imagery. And by 1918 the British had processed over half a million aerial photographs. Beyond the Western Front, aerial photography's mapping role was even more important.

An official Ministry of Information photograph shows a British intelligence officer scrutinizing some captured German correspondence for valuable nuggets of information. By the First World War, intelligence gathering was already acquiring its modern breadth of means and techniques, from good old-fashioned spying to radio intercepts.

Ostensibly trackless wastes in Palestine and Mesopotamia could be plotted and maps issued to everyone who needed one. As generals of all eras have agreed, good intelligence in the first instance is an accurate map.

To coordinate Allied intelligence, in 1917 an Inter-Allied Intelligence Bureau was created at Folkestone, Kent. This brought together reports from German-occupied territory on defensive works, shipping movements, technical details of artillery and aviation developments, as well as economic intelligence on German purchases abroad. Its main contribution, though, was in sifting reports from spies.

As in any war, by far the most difficult area for intelligence was what is nowadays called "human intelligence" or "Humint". Running sources and agents, especially behind enemy lines, was always difficult and chancy. The key Allied task was watching trains in occupied territory to identify the movements of German units: essential information for drawing up an accurate enemy order of battle. In 1918, the French landed a Lieutenant Baschwitz-Meau in Germany. There he set up a train-watching service that was able to observe the movement of German troops across the Continent and provide timely and accurate indications of German intentions on the Western and Eastern fronts.

Perhaps the most famous spy was the Dutch exotic dancer "Mata Hari". As a neutral, Margaretha Zelle (to give her real name) was able to cross national borders freely. In 1916, she was arrested and interrogated at length by Scotland Yard and she admitted to working for French intelligence. However, in February 1917 the French arrested her and tried her as a double agent working for the Germans. Despite flimsy evidence she was found guilty and executed. A more discreet and successful agent was the German Jules Silber, who had served with the British in the Anglo-Boer War and passed for an Englishman; in 1914, he came to London and was able to get a job as a British postal censor. Using his access to "Cleared by the Censor" stamps, he posted intelligence gleaned from reading the mail back to Germany via neutral capitals. Silber survived the war, even receiving a glowing testimonial letter from the Director of Military Intelligence, before returning home to Germany.

By the end of the war intelligence had proved its worth as the ultimate "force multiplier". But in the euphoria of victory and peace, MI5 almost disappeared and the Intelligence Corps was disbanded. In the absence of war, it was time to save money – and Britain's superb intelligence organization was dismantled.

75

PRIVATE HIGHGATE'S CHARGE SHEET
MILITARY DISCIPLINE & DESERTERS

1914 TO 1918

All armies throughout history have had some code of military discipline, because an army without law is just an armed mob. Discipline is the glue that binds an army together. British Army discipline in 1914 was strict and reflected the values of its day. For the British, it was outlined in the 1913 *Manual of Military Law* and its companion, *King's Regulations for the Army* as approved by parliamentary statute. Both are clear on military law as it stood at the time and how it was to be administered. Even in the best-behaved military forces there are exceptions to the law-abiding rule, but military discipline in the BEF of 1914, on active service, was uncompromising.

On 8 September 1914, Private Thomas Highgate of the 1st Battalion, Royal West Kent Regiment, became the first of 266 British soldiers to be shot for desertion during the war. Judged by modern standards it seems a callous punishment, particularly in the speed with which it was carried out. As a regular soldier, Highgate had arrived in France on 15 August and withstood the ferocity of the German assault at Mons. After retreating for two weeks, on 6 September he left his battalion, took off his uniform and put on civilian clothes. He was found in a barn by the British gamekeeper of Baron Edouard de Rothschild. A former soldier, the gamekeeper claimed that Highgate said: "I have lost my army and I mean to get out of it." A Field General Court Martial was immediately convened and, as noted in this formal record, Highgate was found guilty and sentenced to death. The sentence was confirmed first by the commander of II Corps, General Sir Horace Smith-Dorrien, and then the commander-in-chief, Field Marshal Sir John French. At 7.07 a.m. on 8 September, only 36 hours later, Highgate was shot by a firing squad and buried. Ever since, the execution of British soldiers has remained a controversial subject and has been constantly debated. In 2007, this led to the issuing of a blanket pardon by the British government. Yet it is vital to remember the historical context in which these punishments took place. However severe they were, many at the time considered them essential to maintain the fighting spirit of the BEF.

Most petty military offences were dealt with summarily by company commanders, who could award extra parades and "CB" (Confined to Barracks) to rein in petty malefactors for such crimes as drunkenness, being late on parade or having a dirty rifle. More serious charges were dealt with by commanding officers, who could strip junior NCOs of their rank and impose sentences of up to 28 days in the guardroom, with loss of pay. On active service in the field a soldier could instead be sentenced

"I COULD NOT LOOK ON DEATH, WHICH BEING KNOWN, / MEN LED ME TO HIM, BLINDFOLD AND ALONE"

Rudyard Kipling, "The Coward", one of his Epitaphs of the War, *1922*

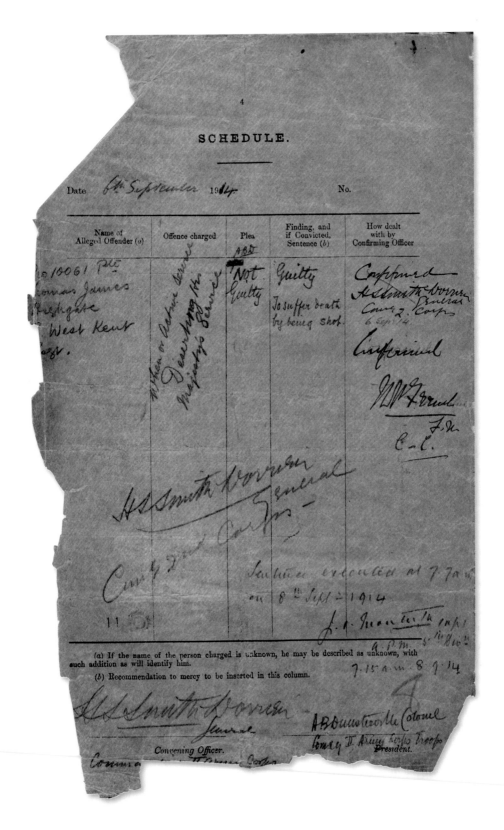

4

SCHEDULE.

Date _6th September_ 1914   No.

Name of Alleged Offender (a)	Offence charged	Plea	Finding, and if Convicted, Sentence (b)	How dealt with by Confirming Officer
No 10061 Pte Thomas James Highgate 1 West Kent Regt.	When on Active Service Deserting His Majesty's Service	Not Guilty	Guilty. To suffer death by being shot.	Confirmed. H. L. Smith-Dorrien General Comdg. 2. Corps 6 Sep/14. Confirmed. D.W. French F.M. C-C.
	H. L. Smith Dorrien General Comdg 2nd Corps –		Sentence executed at 7.7a.m on 8th Sept. 1914. J. A. Monteith Captn A.P.M. 2nd Div. 7.15 a.m. 8.9.14	

(a) If the name of the person charged is unknown, he may be described as unknown, with such addition as will identify him.

(b) Recommendation to mercy to be inserted in this column.

H. L. Smith-Dorrien
General
Convening Officer.
Commandg 2 Army Corps

A.B. Dunsterville Colonel
Comdg II Army Corps Troops
President.

and then, instead of signalling for reinforcements, sitting down to read a volume of poems. Most did not take their love of words that far.

Among the poets, principally remembered are Sassoon, Graves and Edmund Blunden, together with those that did not survive, like Rupert Brooke, Wilfred Owen, Edward Thomas and Isaac Rosenberg, whose "Break of Day in the Trenches" is arguably one of the most profound literary pieces of the war. But how to account for the enduring power of the poetry? In part, the answer lies in the traumatic shock to the young authors of the murderous realities of industrial warfare: trenches, gas, indiscriminate slaughter from artillery barrages, maimed and mangled casualties in unbelievable quantities. Wilfred Owen, who wrote the excoriating "Dulce et Decorum Est" (1917–18), evoked the terror of a gas attack in language that was a world away from the pre-war optimism of the so-called Georgian poets:

> If you could hear, at every jolt, the blood
> Come gargling from the froth-corrupted lungs,
> Obscene as cancer, bitter as the cud
> Of vile, incurable sores on innocent tongues

He succeeded in crystallizing both a sense of modern war's horror, and then laying it at the door of the generation that sent the young men out:

> My friend, you would not tell with such high zest
> To children ardent for some desperate glory,
> The old Lie: *Dulce et Decorum est*
> *Pro patria mori.*

Owen was killed in the very last week of the war. His disillusion is surprisingly echoed by Rudyard Kipling, to whom the loss of his only son at Loos was a shattering, guilt-inducing blow. In *Epitaphs* he wrote very much in the bitter vein of an Owen or Sassoon: "If any question why we died, / Tell them, because our fathers lied." (*See also* Chapter 99.)

Owen and Sassoon's work represents the war weariness and loss of hope after 1916 and stands in stark contrast to the fervour embodied in Rupert Brooke, who in his sonnets *1914* could proclaim: "Now, God be thanked Who has matched us with His hour, / And caught our youth, and wakened us from sleeping". Brooke's lines reflect the mood of the early months of the war. The death of this handsome young man *en route* to the Dardanelles transformed him into a national hero, thanks to strong support from influential friends. However, unlike Brooke, few people had heard of Owen until his mentor, Sassoon, edited (with Edith Sitwell) his poems in 1920. With Blunden's fuller, better known edition of 1931, Owen matched the zeitgeist of the "no more war" appeasement movement of the 1930s.

Although poetry is regarded in Britain as the major literary genre, the war provided grist for the prose mill too. Graves wrote his memoir, *Goodbye to All That*; Ernest Hemingway reflected his personal experience driving ambulances on the Italian Front in *A Farewell to Arms*; and the dark horror of J.R.R. Tolkein's Mordor in *The Lord of the Rings* was influenced by his experiences on the Western Front. For many well-known writers too old to fight, propaganda was a natural way of using their talent (*see* Chapter 31). Enduring prose legacies include Frederic Manning's *Her*

"THREE HOURS AGO, HE STUMBLED UP THE TRENCH; / NOW HE WILL NEVER WALK THAT ROAD AGAIN: / HE MUST BE CARRIED BACK, A JOLTING LUMP / BEYOND ALL NEEDS OF TENDERNESS AND CARE."

Siegfried Sassoon, from "A Working Party", published 1918

Privates We (1929), a novel of the Somme, and two memoirs: Captain J.C. Dunn's astonishing *The War the Infantry Knew* (1938), which gives some soldierly insights into Graves and Sassoon, and Frank Richards' down-to-earth *Old Soldiers Never Die* (1933). C.S. Forester's fictional *The General* (1938) remains perhaps the subtlest critique of the BEF's High Command. A less nuanced critic was George Bernard Shaw, whose Fabian views and Irish contempt for the English upper classes led him to openly oppose the war and attack the government in his pamphlet "Commonsense About the War". An infuriated Asquith privately averred that he should be shot.

Other nations produced their own classics – in France, Henri Barbusse's novel *Le Feu* (1916) or Guillaume Apollinaire's poetic evocations of the gas, fear, darkness and blood made a deep impression on the public consciousness of the war. In Germany, the message of Ernst Jünger's postwar memoir of frontline life, *Storm of Steel* (1920), is equally as powerful. Jünger frequently survives the jaws of death, and the work becomes a search for something noble and truly heroic amid the horror. It is very different to Erich Remarque's *All Quiet on the Western Front*. Significantly, this was published later – in 1929 – and was the first of a flood of books critical of the war, with its lines: "I am young, I am twenty years old; yet I know nothing of life but despair, death, fear, and fatuous superficiality cast over an abyss of sorrow. I see how peoples are set against one another, and in silence, unknowingly, foolishly, obediently, innocently slay one another."

But not every young man could afford despair when they somehow had to carry on. For a perhaps representative view, the troops' own newspapers tell a different story to that of the anguished poets. The classic is the *Wipers Times*, first published by the Sherwood Foresters in 1916, which went on to be distributed across the BEF. Never officially sanctioned by Authority, it was nevertheless popular among all ranks with its gallows humour (such as a bogus advertisement for a new film: *Over the Top! – A screaming Farce*) and irreverence about the war and army life. Interestingly, much of the copy submitted was poetry. Some was excellent and some was doggerel – but the quantity was such that the journal had to announce: "An insidious disease is affecting the Division, and the result is a hurricane of poetry".

A British soldier takes the opportunity of a quiet moment and a conveniently unused stretcher to catch up on the news, somewhere amid the blasted landscape of the Somme. A hunger for the written word was ubiquitous among men at the Front.

77

JOHN SINGER SARGENT'S *GASSED*
ARTISTS' RESPONSES TO THE WAR

1914 TO 1918

Although the British art of the First World War did not inform later generations' sense of what the war *was* to quite the same extent as its poetry, it nevertheless left a large and varied body of work, and a core of undoubted masterpieces. At one level there was the popular, graphic art of the day, from cartoons in *Punch* to magazine illustrations and posters, much of it inspired by a propaganda or morale-boosting purpose. Those genres generated the single best-known war-related image: the Kitchener recruiting poster (*see* Chapter 8). In fine art, this new industrial war of mass production and mass killing resulted in experimentation with styles to match the unprecedented scenes and experiences that unfolded. The result was many powerful and moving works of art, undertaken both by artists who experienced the war in the frontline as well as established figures who were too old to fight.

John Singer Sargent was one of the best-known painters of the Edwardian era, famous for his society portraits. In March 1918, he was commissioned by the British War Memorials Committee to paint an epic work that would form the centrepiece of a planned Hall of Remembrance. So in July Sargent journeyed to France to find a suitable subject. Late on 21 August, he and fellow artist, Henry Tonks, drove past a dressing station between Arras and Doullens, which was overrun by men temporarily blinded in a mustard gas attack. Both were stunned by what they saw. Tonks later explained: "Gassed cases kept coming in. They sat or lay down on the grass, there must have been several hundred, evidently suffering a great deal." Sargent captured the scene in possibly the best-known painting of the entire war. Using his gift for subtle composition within a monumental frame, he bathed the agony of the wounded men in languidly beautiful light from the evening sun, while offering hope beyond their present suffering through the sight of healthy men playing football in the distance. In *Gassed*, Sargent delivered the grand subject he had been asked to find and, in a way that is possible only through art, he encapsulated the essence of the war in a work that still deeply affects people a hundred years on.

At the outbreak of war, artistic responses were mainly in the field of ephemeral, graphic art: patriotic drawings and political cartoons in satirical magazines like *Punch* in Britain, *Simplicissimus* in Germany or, from 1915, *Le Canard Enchaîné* in France. One of the earliest exponents was Britain's Bernard Partridge, who trained as an architect before joining *Punch* in 1891 as a cartoonist. His mixture of the realistic

The dashing Captain Bruce Bairnsfather, as depicted on a 1916 postcard. His wryly humorous cartoons, compiled in book form in Fragments from France, captured the soldiering zeitgeist and turned him into something of a celebrity.

and the allegorical is seen at its most powerful in drawings such as *Danse Macabre*, where the Kaiser dances with the Angel of Death. His colleague Frederick Henry Townsend's *Bravo Belgium* was one of the best-known drawings in this vein, showing a sausage-laden Teuton armed with a club advancing on a little Belgian boy standing before a gate marked "No Thoroughfare". In their use of stereotype and stark, simple contrasts, they encapsulated the indignant British mood of the time.

Another graphic artist whose work remains popular is Bruce Bairnsfather (*see also* Chapter 60). Relatively unsuccessful before the war (he could only get work in advertising), once in the field in the Royal Warwickshire Regiment, from 1914, he drew scenes of trench life, which were published from 1915 in the *Bystander*. That year, he was wounded and deemed no longer fit for active service; but in 1916 he was appointed an official cartoonist for the Allies. He is chiefly remembered for the humorous cartoon series based on "Old Bill", a grumpy Regular old soldier with a walrus moustache, which achieved huge popularity at home and – as a mark of the way the cartoons captured the essence of things – among the troops.

The first *official* British War Artist was the Scotsman Muirhead Bone, who specialized in black and white drawings. He was recruited in May 1916 by Charles Masterman's War Propaganda Bureau (*see* Chapter 31), and his drawings of the war had the advantage of being easily reproduced in newspapers and magazines. After the Somme campaign, he returned home to record Britons at work on the Home Front, and Glasgow School of Art-trained Francis Dodd was sent to France in his place. Dodd worked in a variety of materials, producing drawings and portraits of commanders and informal glimpses of ordinary sailors at sea

After that, Dodd was followed to the Western Front by a further clutch of officially appointed artists, including the established portrait painters William Orpen and John Singer Sargent, and William Rothenstein. They were joined in this capacity by men who had previously served at the Front, or behind the lines, and whose talents had come to the attention of Masterman's department. This group included Christopher R.W. Nevinson (*see* Chapter 80) and (Percy) Wyndham Lewis of the contemporary "Vorticist" school, and Eric Kennington and Paul Nash.

Orpen in fact had offered his services in 1915, but had ended up doing routine office work until his friend, the Quartermaster General Sir John Cowans (whose portrait he was painting), commissioned him to paint military portraits of generals, privates and politicians, including a surprisingly amiable Sir Douglas Haig. After experiencing the Front at first hand, he produced one of the war's starkest works, the bluntly named *Dead Germans in a Trench* (1918), an eerie form of still-life. He would go on to be appointed the official portrait artist at the Paris Peace Conference in 1919, for a fee of £3,000. He painted *The Signing of the Peace*, a subtly critical work that came to seem a premonition of the days to come. It contrasts the fragmented world as literally shown in Versailles' Hall of Mirrors with the rather diminutive delegates in the foreground, believing they have secured Europe's future (*see* Chapter 93).

Paul Nash has been regarded as a "soldier artist", but he was a Slade School-trained professional artist before joining up with the Artists Rifles – the 28th Battalion, London Regiment – in 1914. (His younger brother, John Nash, followed a very similar trajectory from the Artists Rifles to official War Artist later on.) At the Slade, Paul had shown little talent for life drawing and had sensibly gravitated towards landscapes. He favoured the new dynamic style of Vorticism, an offspring of international Futurism, which rejected Victorian and Edwardian aesthetics in favour of bold lines and bright colours to draw the eye towards the centre of a dynamic world. In the words of Wyndham Lewis, the movement's godfather, Vorticism was "a whirlpool. At the heart of the whirlpool is a great silent place where all the energy is concentrated." It launched itself onto the world a few months before war broke out, via the movement's magazine *Blast*.

Nash served in the Ypres sector, where he sketched, but in 1917 he was invalided home. An exhibition led to his appointment as an official War Artist in 1917 with a roving commission. Now he could flex his talent properly and unite it with his deep experience of trench life to produce his great war paintings such as *The Ypres Salient*

"I AM NO LONGER AN ARTIST INTERESTED AND CURIOUS, I AM A MESSENGER WHO WILL BRING BACK WORD FROM THE MEN WHO ARE FIGHTING TO THOSE WHO WANT THE WAR TO GO ON FOR EVER."

Paul Nash, letter, 1918

LAWRENCE OF ARABIA'S RIFLE
T.E. LAWRENCE & THE ARAB REVOLT

1916 TO 1918

British withdrawal from Gallipoli in January 1916 changed the war in the Middle East. The Ottomans were now able to redeploy and reinforce their three main theatres of operations: fighting the Russians in the Caucasus, and the British in Sinai/Palestine and Mesopotamia (*see* Chapters 23 and 78). General Falkenhayn, arriving in Aleppo in early 1917 to direct Ottoman forces, knew that any British advance through Palestine into Syria risked severing the Ottomans' already fragile communications with the Mesopotamian Front 500 miles to the southeast.

At the same time, corruption and shortages were weakening the Ottoman Empire, and poor communications and lack of supplies were eroding the army's efficiency. Worse, the burden of Ottoman casualties was falling on ethnic Turks; other nationalities in the empire were openly hostile, and army desertions were up to 300,000 by December 1916. German influence and personnel were increasingly resented, too. Into this deteriorating situation came the Arab Revolt, beginning in summer 1916, and with it an extraordinary Englishman, who combined charisma, guile, diplomacy and guerrilla warfare in a cocktail that would create a legend.

> "I GAVE HIM A FREE HAND … HE WAS THE MAINSPRING OF THE ARAB MOVEMENT AND KNEW THEIR LANGUAGE, THEIR MANNERS AND THEIR MENTALITY."
>
> *General Sir Edmund Allenby, commanding the Egyptian Expeditionary Force on the Palestine Front*

The real T.E. Lawrence is often confused with the simpler romanticized character from David Lean's epic 1962 film *Lawrence of Arabia*. But Lawrence himself was a complex, mercurial individual – deeply committed to Arab independence, yet also intensely loyal to his own country, producing contradictions that in the end almost overwhelmed him. He was a visionary, understanding that Arab self-determination would only be possible if they moved north from the Hejaz desert to Syria itself; he understood guerrilla warfare, too, using a handful of men to pin down and intimidate much larger numbers of regular troops. He also appreciated that the Arabs had to protect the open flank of the Allied armies as they advanced through Palestine. From late 1916 until 1918, Lawrence served alongside Sherif Feisal, son of the Grand Sherif of Mecca. Feisal gave Lawrence this British rifle, which had been captured at Gallipoli and presented to him by the Ottoman authorities. Lawrence used it constantly and carved his initials and five notches on the stock to record the Turks he killed with it. After the war, Lawrence considered giving the gun to the Imperial War Museum, but in the end presented it to King George V. It was only after the king's death in 1936 that it arrived at the Museum, along with other royal wartime souvenirs. This well-used weapon, with its intriguing history, evokes both the complex, many-sided war in the Middle East and the continually fascinating personality of Lawrence of Arabia himself.

Although the Ottoman Empire had long claimed overlordship of the entire Arabian Peninsula, to all intents and purposes the central desert region (the "Nejd") was under the control of local Bedouins, who were largely neutral in the war. In the western Hejaz region, however, encompassing Medina and Mecca, the powerful Hashemite dynasty had ambitions to throw off the Ottomans and establish an Arab state centred on Damascus. Promoting these aspirations was Sir Henry McMahon, Egypt's High Commissioner. He had encouraged Hussein ibn Ali, the Sherif

(overlord) of Mecca, to start a revolt against Ottoman rule by promising that Britain would guarantee an independent Arab kingdom after the war. On 10 June 1916, the Sherif called for a full rebellion. GHQ's special "Arab Bureau", based in Cairo, immediately offered Britain's support.

At the time, GHQ's staff in Cairo included a polyglot scholar and archaeologist working as a junior intelligence officer: T.E. Lawrence. In January 1916, he had analysed any Arab revolt as: "beneficial to us, because it marches with our immediate aims, the break up of the Islamic 'bloc' and the defeat and disruption of the Ottoman Empire, and because the states ... set up to succeed the Turks would be ... harmless to ourselves". In October 1916, Lawrence, with his local expertise and excellent Arabic, began his historic task with the British Military Mission, working with Hussein's forces. He was a good choice to act as liaison officer. He had already been an intermediary in Mesopotamia in spring 1916, trying to use a £1 million bribe to rescue the besieged British at Kut: an unusual responsibility for such a junior officer. When Lawrence met Emir Feisal, Hussein's third son (and warlord), the two men got on: it was Lawrence's initial job to identify which of the king's sons would make the best leader. The calculating and ambitious Lawrence reported that Feisal could be trusted to lead the Arab Revolt, urging Cairo not to send troops to the Arabs but rather advisors, weapons and money instead, with, naturally, himself in a leading role.

GHQ agreed and in January 1917 established a military mission to the Hejaz under Lieutenant Colonel S.F. Newcombe. He ordered Lawrence to attach himself to Feisal's ragged army of 7,000 Bedouins and encourage them to cut the Hejaz Railway, the vital Ottoman lifeline through Damascus and down to Medina. This strategy tied down large numbers of Ottoman troops defending and repairing the railway, while Feisal's roaming warriors could strike anywhere. For the next year, Lawrence fought a guerrilla war alongside Feisal and made him the principal beneficiary of British aid.

In July 1917, Lawrence persuaded the Arabs to make a surprise overland attack on Aqaba, the Ottomans' sole remaining port on the Red Sea. Its capture opened new supply lines from Egypt to the Arabs massing in the Sinai, allowing them to extend their operations northwards towards Palestine. When Lawrence reported to General Allenby, who was now commanding the Palestine Front, the general recognized the value of Lawrence's rag-tag guerrilla army harassing Ottoman supply lines and protecting his right flank; he quickly spotted Lawrence's Achilles' heel, too: vanity. Lawrence was promoted to major on Allenby's orders. With the commander-in-chief's personal backing, Lawrence was now in a much more powerful position. Through Aqaba he was able to funnel thousands of rifles and camels as well as artillery and armoured cars, but above all hundreds of thousands of gold sovereigns, to buy Feisal's Arabs.

On 24 October 1917, Lawrence and Feisal led the Arab forces on a 350-mile trek around the Turkish left flank to attack the Yarmuk Gorge, north of Jerusalem, in support of Allenby's renewed assault on Beersheba and Gaza. But this venture failed. Depressed and guilty over his failure, Lawrence made an ill-advised personal reconnaissance of the key Turkish railway junction at Der'aa and was captured. Although Lawrence's true identity was never discovered, he claimed he was sexually assaulted and beaten by his captors before escaping. Recovering in Palestine, he was invited to accompany Allenby's triumphal entry into Jerusalem on 11 December 1917.

"I WAS TIRED TO DEATH OF THESE ARABS; PETTY INCARNATE SEMITES WHO ATTAINED HEIGHTS AND DEPTHS BEYOND OUR REACH, THOUGH NOT BEYOND OUR SIGHT. THEY REALISED OUR ABSOLUTE IN THEIR UNRESTRAINED CAPACITY FOR GOOD OR EVIL; AND FOR TWO YEARS I HAD PROFITABLY SHAMMED TO BE THEIR COMPANION!"

T. E. Lawrence, in his autobiographical Seven Pillars of Wisdom, *1922*

At Tafilah, southeast of Amman, in January 1918 there was greater success when Lawrence's Arab forces routed a Turkish brigade sent to recapture the town, an action described in the *Official History* of the war as a "brilliant feat of arms". Lawrence was awarded the DSO and promoted lieutenant colonel. The Ottomans recognized his value, too, putting a price of £15,000 on his head, but still he evaded them. His Arab raiding campaign continued throughout the summer, in support of Allenby's continued advance northwards into Syria (*see* Chapter 89). On 1 October, Damascus fell and Lawrence helped to set up a provisional Arab government as the war drew to its close.

What happened next has remained in dispute ever since. A conference took place at Damascus between Allenby and Feisal, with Lawrence and the Australian General Chauvel present. Afterwards Allenby recorded that he merely emphasized his need to keep his victorious cavalry advancing north to push the fleeing Ottomans back. Chauvel, however, records a bitter dispute when Allenby told Feisal that he would have to accept French overlordship of the region under the terms of the Sykes–Picot agreement (*see* Chapter 89). Appalled at Britain's double dealing, Lawrence refused to work with the French after Feisal's humiliation and asked for long overdue leave. So ended the Arab Revolt. Lawrence returned to England a disillusioned man, tired of war, but determined to continue pressing the Arab cause in London.

The classic image of T.E. Lawrence during his time as guerrilla leader with the Arab Revolt. Here he is at Aqaba. Despite the Bedouin trappings, Lawrence was caught between conflicting loyalties to his British superiors and the aspirations of the Hashemite Arabs of the Hejaz.

Much of Lawrence's heroic image is due to an American war correspondent, Lowell Thomas, who filmed him in the desert for two weeks in 1918. After the war, Thomas began a series of illustrated lectures, supported by dramatic pictures – of Lawrence in his Arab robes, of charging camels and of Bedouin warriors. Lawrence cooperated happily and Thomas's film, *With Allenby in Palestine and Lawrence in Arabia*, was shown around the world, making Lawrence a household name and Thomas rich. When Lawrence tried to distance himself from his growing celebrity, Thomas dryly observed that he "had a genius for backing into the limelight".

Lawrence's extraordinary postwar career reflected his complex and conflicted character. He attended the Paris Peace Conference in 1919 as an interpreter to the Arab delegation, only to see his promises to the Arabs betrayed. Election to All Souls College in Oxford, a literary autobiography of variable veracity (*Seven Pillars of Wisdom*), mysterious episodes of sado-masochism and service – under pseudonyms – as a ranker with the RAF and the Tank Corps all followed, before his death in a motorcycle accident in 1935. His legend was immortalized by the film biopic *Lawrence of Arabia* in the 1960s. Perhaps Lloyd George best summed up this strange and brilliant man: "a most elusive and un-assessable personality".

5

FROM NEAR-DEFEAT TO VICTORY

84

FIELD MARSHAL HAIG'S SPECIAL ORDER
THE GERMAN SPRING OFFENSIVES –
KAISERSCHLACHT

21 MARCH TO 18 JULY 1918

By the autumn of 1917 General Ludendorff – now, with Hindenburg, wielding effective political control in Germany – knew he had to force a decision in the war before US divisions had a chance to make a decisive impact on the battlefield. Bolshevik Russia's unilateral truce in November gave Germany the opportunity to swing 40 divisions from the Eastern Front across to France: it happened at a rate of two divisions per week, from the end of 1917. But this fillip was balanced by growing internal problems on the German Home Front. Events emphasized what the German "Duo" of Hindenburg and Ludendorff knew too well: that time was running out. In 1918, Germany must either win or lose the war.

In the event, Germany made one last, massive attempt to win it. And it nearly succeeded, bringing Paris within artillery range and inspiring Field Marshal Haig to ask his men to "fight on to the end" whatever might come.

The powerful offensive launched by the Germans east of the Somme on 21 March 1918 inflicted a serious defeat on the BEF. Sir Douglas Haig quickly concluded that its underlying purpose was to destroy the BEF and divide it from the French. Over the following days, Haig became deeply concerned, feeling that the French were not reacting fast enough and with sufficient urgency to the plight of their British allies. For the first time since becoming commander-in-chief in 1915, he appeared rattled. By early April Haig had recovered his equilibrium. But almost immediately his resolve was severely tested again when the Germans began another push against the British line in Flanders on 9 April. Possibly because he was facing a challenge to the integrity and cohesion of his army for the second time in less than a month, Haig issued this remarkable personal appeal to his troops. Reserved and taciturn, he generally avoided emotional expression. But on 11 April, he urged his men to remain firm and resolute: "With our backs to the wall and believing in the justice of our cause each one of us must fight on to the end." His words became famous among the troops, possibly because they were so uncharacteristic. This copy was posted up somewhere, as shown by its pin hole, and Haig later signed it in person. For a man usually lost for words, Haig's message encapsulated the anxiety but unbroken resolve that was felt by every man under his command.

The fateful decision was taken by Ludendorff at Mons on 11 November 1917, ironically a year to the day before the war's final Armistice. If Germany could divide and defeat France and Britain before the American armies arrived, Germany could

"WE CHOP A HOLE. THE REST FOLLOWS."

General Erich Ludendorff, to Crown Prince Rupprecht, March 1918

SPECIAL ORDER OF THE DAY
By FIELD-MARSHAL SIR DOUGLAS HAIG
K.T., G.C.B., G.C.V.O., K.C.I.E
Commander-in-Chief, British Armies in France.

D. Haig. F.M.

To ALL RANKS OF THE BRITISH ARMY IN FRANCE AND FLANDERS.

Three weeks ago to-day the enemy began his terrific attacks against us on a fifty-mile front. His objects are to separate us from the French, to take the Channel Ports and destroy the British Army.

In spite of throwing already 106 Divisions into the battle and enduring the most reckless sacrifice of human life, he has as yet made little progress towards his goals.

We owe this to the determined fighting and self-sacrifice of our troops. Words fail me to express the admiration which I feel for the splendid resistance offered by all ranks of our Army under the most trying circumstances.

Many amongst us now are tired. To those I would say that Victory will belong to the side which holds out the longest. The French Army is moving rapidly and in great force to our support.

There is no other course open to us but to fight it out. Every position must be held to the last man: there must be no retirement. With our backs to the wall and believing in the justice of our cause each one of us must fight on to the end. The safety of our homes and the Freedom of mankind alike depend upon the conduct of each one of us at this critical moment.

D. Haig. F.M.

Commander-in-Chief,
British Armies in France.

General Headquarters,
Thursday, April 11th, 1918.

PRINTED IN FRANCE BY ARMY PRINTING AND STATIONERY SERVICES.

PRESS A—4/18.

At Doullens on 26 March a momentous decision was taken by politicians and generals. Lloyd George had been trying to establish political control over Haig, and now he got his way, although not quite in the manner he intended. An Allied Supreme Command would now be formed to coordinate the Western Front. General Ferdinand Foch was appointed effectively as the Allied *generalissimo*, with the power to issue orders to both armies.

Foch promptly insisted that Gough was sacked, and the imperturbable Rawlinson became the new commander of the Fifth Army. Better luck was about to attend the Allied defence now. Byng's forces around Arras stood firm, repelling a concerted attack by Below's Seventeenth Army on 28 March. On 4 April, Operation Michael finally ran out of steam, when an Australian-led counterattack at Villers-Bretonneux foiled the German thrust 10 miles short of the strategically important British railhead at Amiens. Although the Germans had advanced about 40 miles, captured 1,300 guns, and reduced the British Fifth Army from 14 divisions to a jumble of dispirited and confused soldiers, the failure to take Amiens was a serious one. The French were now pushing divisions into the Somme valley to reinforce their stricken ally, too. In addition, the Germans had outreached their supplies and their artillery – and, more worryingly, had lost around a quarter of a million men, many of them their irreplaceable stormtroopers.

Nevertheless, as a shaken BEF tried to catch its breath, Ludendorff struck again on 9 April, this time further north on a 12-mile front between La Bassée canal and Armentières, and then north of Armentières the next day. "Operation Georgette" was specifically aimed at cutting off the Ypres Salient from the south and capturing Hazebrouck, another important railway junction. Facing the Germans were primarily Horne's First Army in the south of the sector, with Plumer's Second Army north around Ypres. Part of the line heavily hit was held by two weak Portuguese

German stormtroopers practise infiltration techniques prior to the Kaiserschlacht. *The photograph captures the dynamism of the new tactics. Unfortunately for Ludendorff and his armies, the British and French soon adapted to the German methods and devised their own responses.*

divisions near Armentières. When Bruchmüller's hurricane bombardment struck, they broke and ran; the Germans penetrated about 3.5 miles west following the River Lys, recapturing Messines Ridge and reaching the commanding Mount Kemmel as the end of the month neared.

At the crisis of this Battle of the Lys, Haig made his only dramatic gesture of the war, publishing his Special Order of the Day appealing for his men to do their utmost. He need not have worried. The hard-pressed defenders fought the Germans to a standstill, and the furthest extent of the German advance was reached by 29 April. So far the offensives had cost the BEF about 235,000 casualties, many of them prisoners, and the French about 90,000, but the Germans had suffered as many as 350,000. For the attackers it was attrition in reverse.

Towards the River Aisne, in "Operation Blücher" on 27 May, Ludendorff struck again, between Soissons and Rheims, lured by the proximity of Paris. During the spring Krupp's monster long-range Paris Gun had been dropping shells on the city. The French commander, General Denis Auguste Duchêne, foolishly disregarded Foch and GQG's advice and packed his forward trenches, with the inevitable result that his soldiers were butchered by Bruchmüller's 5,000-odd guns. Stormtroopers – although not so many this time – surged through a 25-mile gap in the Allied lines and within six hours had crossed the Chemin des Dames Ridge and reached the Aisne. The Germans captured another 50,000 Allied soldiers and over 800 guns. By 3 June they were once again on the River Marne, only 35 miles from Paris. Only well-organized counterattacks by Pétain and the recently arrived Americans stopped them. Both sides had lost another 130,000 men, but there was one big difference as regards casualties: the Germans could not sustain such numbers; with the American Expeditionary Force (AEF) flooding into France at 250,000 men a month, the Allies could. Germany had lost nearly 800,000 men since the start of the year, while now having to man a frontline that had increased from 245 miles to 320.

At German High Command in Spa, Belgium, the Kaiser and his warlords reviewed their situation on 3 July. It was one of contrasts. Battlefield gains and the *coup de théâtre* of landing shells on Paris could not hide the increasingly severe shortages and unrest at home. The German leadership, however, confirmed that its terms for peace would remain annexation of Luxembourg and retention of the French iron and coal fields in Lorraine. And the attack would continue. So, on 15 July, Ludendorff launched his last offensive with 40 German divisions on either side of Rheims. He hoped to split the French, but this time he walked into an ambush. The tactical novelty of the German methods had worn thin. East of Rheims, General Henri Gouraud had pulled back nearly 3 miles. The attackers wasted their bombardment on empty space and were cut down when they advanced. To the west the German assault bridged the Marne and established a small bridgehead, but American and French counterattacks with strong air support stopped them within two days.

Pétain then launched his masterstroke. At Villers-Cotterêts on 18 July a major counterattack with 24 divisions, including two American divisions, supported by 300 tanks and aircraft, and led by the uncompromisingly aggressive General Charles Mangin cut into and overwhelmed the German right flank, inflicting severe casualties. The Germans retreated, a battered army.

The *Kaiserschlacht* that began on 21 March had burnt out. Ludendorff's gamble had failed, and a sense of impending crisis now began to grip him. There would inevitably be an Allied riposte, and the only question was: when?

85

A TOBY JUG FOR THE FIELD MARSHAL
GENERALSHIP IN THE WAR

1914 TO 1918

By and large the British generals of the First World War have received a bad press. Thanks to such bitter lines as Siegfried Sassoon's poem "The General" ("He's a cheery old card, grunted Harry to Jack, / As they slogged up to Arras with rifle and pack, / But he did for them both with his plan of attack"), they have been portrayed as murderous buffoons, or at least – along with their staffs – as hopelessly inefficient or mule-headedly stupid. It is true that in 1915–17 the gulf between frontline units and the General Staff was profound. Some of the criticisms are well-founded, some less so. But generalizations about generals can be misleading.

For a start, the war lasted four years. At the outset, few could properly envisage what this "total war" would entail – as the tactical and logistical failures in 1914 showed. By 1918 things were very different. The generals, just like the rank and file, were learning their trade, adapting to new technologies, experimenting tactically, adjusting to changing politics and personalities. The general of 1914 was, by and large, not the same as the general of 1918.

To modern sensibilities, Field Marshal Sir Douglas Haig, the BEF's commander-in-chief, embodies the idea of British generalship in the war and is a controversial figure. He is inextricably linked to the worst excesses of leadership – callous attrition, heavy casualties and unimaginative thinking. Much of this view originates in the sharp criticism of his command published after Haig's death by Lloyd George and Churchill, and it was a view that fed popular culture. From the 1960s' satirical revue (and film) *Oh, What a Lovely War!* to the television comedy series *Blackadder Goes Forth* (1989), Haig has regularly been portrayed as an incompetent, indifferent buffoon. But recently, scholars have unpicked this one-sided image, and many historians now recognize a calm, measured commander of vision and determination, who led the largest army Britain has ever placed in the field to its greatest series of victories in 1918. Nowadays, the wider perception of Haig probably lies somewhere between the two extremes. Perhaps the best clues, though, are found in evidence of how he was viewed at the time. In December 1917, London's new War Museum bought this Royal Staffordshire Pottery "toby jug" for its Children's Section. Resolute and imperturbable, Haig sits on the great new weapon of the war: the tank. A year later, a popular postcard showed a stolid-looking photograph of Haig on one side, with an explanation of who he was on the other. "He is at once trusted and loved by his own officers and men. His name will be handed down in History as one of the great leaders in the Great War for Freedom."

"IT SEEMS QUITE STRANGE TO ME, THAT I SIT HERE AT MY DESK AND MAP TABLE WHILE MY TROOPS FIGHT BETWEEN THE WARTHE AND THE VISTULA. SUCH, HOWEVER, IS THE CONDUCT OF MODERN WARFARE."

General August von Mackensen, 14 November 1914

Before the war, the great Prussian strategist Schlieffen had envisaged the generalship of the future: "There, in a comfortable chair before a wide table, the modern Alexander has before him the entire battlefield on a map." Herein, though, lies the essence of the complaints about wartime relationships between staff officers and the frontline: that staff officers were rarely seen in the trenches; that plans of attack frequently took no notice of realities on the frontline; and, as in every war, those who had to sleep in wet, dangerous holes in the ground found it hard not to resent those who enjoyed warm, dry beds. It all fed the idea of "château generals", well back from any danger or true understanding of the reality of the war.

It is perhaps surprising, therefore, that more British generals were killed in the First World War than in any other. No less than 78 British and Dominion generals died on active service, most as a result of shellfire and sniper fire, while 146 were wounded: a casualty rate of about 18 per cent. At the Battle of Loos in 1915, three of the nine commanders were killed in the frontlines, and the situation reached such an extent in 1916 that Haig had to issue a stern warning to his divisional commanders to stay at their desks. If generals were expected to devise strategies to win their battles, that was incompatible with exposing them to the same dangers as their frontline troops

But effective command and control was hampered by the inadequate communications with the frontlines (*see* Chapter 41). Many generals, particularly divisional commanders, chafed at the difficulties of commanding from positions far back while their men were in the line. Imbued with the regimental ideal of sharing their soldiers' discomforts, many were deeply uncomfortable at the feeling of impotence of having to command their units by telephone while their men risked their lives. Yet a visit to the frontline by a divisional major general, to see what things were like for himself, generally involved a trek of several miles through muddy trenches – with the knowledge that he then might be out of touch with his own headquarters in the case of any emergency. It must have been an intensely frustrating experience, and one that could certainly not be risked in the middle of a major battle.

A lingering criticism has been that generals stuck to a kind of bovine inflexibility and acclimatized themselves too much to the high casualty figures that the war unleashed. It is true that many of the old school felt that their duty lay in driving their men onwards, whatever the cost. One unnamed corps commander on the Somme supposedly said: "The men are much too keen on saving their own skins. They need to be taught that they are out here to do their job. Whether they survive or not is a matter of complete indifference."

The other great criticism was of generals' poor planning, particularly in the early years of the war. The problem was that all the regular generals had been trained on pre-war Napoleonic maxims – "the artillery blasts a hole, the infantry assaults and the cavalry exploits". The reality of trench warfare, the potency of modern artillery and machine guns, the novelty of gas and aircraft, and a host of other factors created a gulf between those maxims and what the generals actually had to deal with. It is hard to deny the historian Gary Sheffield's long-held assertion that for the BEF – as others – the First World War was "a long learning curve". But learning there was, and by 1918 the importance of the element of surprise, new infiltration tactics, the emergence of combined all-arms warfare, the discovery of how best to use tanks and much else showed it. Some lessons of both success and failure took long to sink in. But General Rawlinson's army that failed on the Somme in 1916 was a very different body to the Rawlinson army that defeated and drove the Germans back in 1918.

"IT MIGHT HAVE BEEN … MORE ADVANTAGEOUS FOR ENGLAND IF THE BRITISH ARMY HAD NOT BEEN SO FULL OF MEN OF HIGH RANK WHO WERE SO READY FOR RESPONSIBILITY, SO UNFLINCHINGLY DEVOTED TO THEIR DUTY, SO UNMOVED IN THE FACE OF DIFFICULTIES, OF SUCH UNFALTERING COURAGE."

C.S. Forester, in his novel The General, *1936*

When it came to the standard staff work involved in procedures for fire plans, tactics and systems, the BEF also learned steadily. For example, the first day of the Somme took staff officers 115 days to plan and mount; by August 1918, the Battle of Amiens was mounted in just 26 days; and in the final days of the war, the BEF attack at Cambrai on 8 October 1918 took just 3 days. Senior officers understood better what they needed to do, and how to do it with the means available.

At the operational level, it is hard to see exactly what more the generals on the Western Front in the early years of the war could have done. A line of trenches and fortifications from the English Channel to Switzerland presented a wholly new sort of challenge. When Foch complained in 1914 that without flanks he could not manoeuvre, he was merely stating the truth. The generals on both sides were reduced to siege engineers. The years 1915–17 provided some tantalizing glimpses of potentially effective new tactics, but appreciation of them was easier in hindsight. Only after March 1918 did the Front break open and mobile warfare become a real possibility. Elsewhere, where generals had space to manoeuvre, they could demonstrate their skill: Hindenburg, Ludendorff and Brusilov on the Eastern Front, or Allenby's masterly swinging of his attacks from flank to flank in Palestine, for example.

Most of the First World War generals were far from stupid. On the Western Front, generals of *all* nations were faced by what seemed an insoluble problem: how to break what was effectively one long siege. They learned the hard way, albeit at terrible cost for those under their charge. German and French attacks ended with even longer casualty lists than the BEF's. But most who fought recognized the dreadful truth: there was no easy solution. At Haig's funeral in 1928 thousands of his old soldiers turned out to watch his cortège. Whatever the judgements of posterity, those who served with the stubborn Scot recognized Haig's achievement as "the general who won the war".

A visit to the trenches. Major General Gerald Cuthbert (foreground, left) and Brigadier General George Armytage, with staff officers, see things for themselves in a trench near Thiepval, on the Somme, 1916. But increasingly generals had to keep away from forward lines and trust to their often unreliable communications to keep abreast of events.

86

THE RED BARON'S BROKEN ENGINE
FIGHTER ACES & THE LATER AIR WAR

1917 TO 1918

From the summer of 1917, new and more effective aircraft were pouring from the factories to be committed in increasing numbers in the burgeoning air war. There was still room for a few of the older types; James McCudden, who took over Albert Ball VC's place in the elite 56 Squadron after Ball was killed in May 1917, sometimes flew his outdated Sopwith Pup in mid-1917. With its rotary engine and flimsy airframe it should have been mincemeat for the roving Albatrosses of the German air service. But the calculating, highly professional McCudden had worked out that with its light wing loading, at 17,000 feet his Pup could out-turn any aircraft in the German inventory; and he did, shooting down 57 enemy aircraft before his accidental death in July 1918, latterly flying the new SE5a.

McCudden was the first real British flying ace after Ball. But the whole culture of flying aces had really begun in Germany with the likes of Boelcke and Immelmann (*see* Chapter 68). Above the squalor of the trenches, the knights of the air achieved a fame granted to few soldiers on the ground. Fêted in their home countries, the aces and their exploits captured the public's imagination.

> Fighter aces like Albert Ball VC or France's Georges Guynemer became household names, and their deaths were widely mourned. But chief among them, the most enduring name, was German ace Baron (*Freiherr*) Manfred von Richthofen, or the "Red Baron". By mid-April 1918 he had been credited with 80 "kills". Richthofen had been promoted to command *Jagdgeschwader 1* (literally "Hunting Wing 1"), known as the "Flying Circus" because of the varied colours disguising its aircrafts' outlines as well as its peripatetic nature. He was piloting a red Fokker Dr.1 Triplane when, on 21 April 1918, he pursued a novice British pilot in a Sopwith Camel. A more experienced Canadian pilot, Roy Brown, swooped down and fired a burst that raked Richthofen's machine. Close to the ground, Richthofen was also hit by Australian machine gun fire. Whoever delivered the fatal bullets, he was mortally wounded and his plane then crashed. He was so famous that people clamoured for souvenirs. Pieces of canvas were cut from his aircraft, and his flying boots went to Australia. His Oberursel UR2 rotary engine from the crash-site, shown here, came to Britain as a trophy for the Royal Air Force, which passed it on to the new War Museum the following year. It remains a symbol of the man and machine that epitomized the era of the fighter ace.

After McCudden's death, his place within the RAF as the most highly respected combat pilot was taken by Major Edward "Mick" Mannock, who entered service over

"FIND THE ENEMY AND SHOOT HIM DOWN! ALL ELSE IS NONSENSE!"

Baron Manfred von Richthofen, German flying ace

the Western Front in 1917. From a shaky start – he was even suspected of cowardice – he screwed himself up for an extraordinary string of sorties, earning the Military Cross (and Bar), and then in May 1918 the DSO and two Bars (in other words, the DSO three times) for achieving 20 kills that month alone. He went on to become the highest-scoring British ace of the war, claiming 73 kills – the exact number is hard to verify.

But for the aces, as for all pilots, previous success was no guarantee as to future survival. Life expectancy was shockingly short for serving airmen. They inhabited a (literally) "live fast, die young" culture. Mannock lasted longer than most, but his end came on 26 July 1918, not from an enemy fighter but from ground fire as he crossed the lines at a low level. He was posthumously awarded the Victoria Cross, in 1919.

The days of the individual duel and the roving knight of the air were being challenged in other ways. The last 18 months of the war saw new and more powerful "in-line" engines, more professional operational techniques, better-trained pilots, new tactics and more experienced aircrew make their impact. If any one moment symbolizes the beginning of this shift it was the shooting down of Baron von Richthofen on 6 July 1917 by slow, cumbersome two-seater FE2s, whose defensive formation of flying in a circle like a wagon train, to cover each other's tails, paid off. Richthofen charged at this "merry go round" only to fall victim, as a British bullet grazed his skull. The unconscious ace's plane fell out of the sky, and he came round just in time to crash-land. It was a narrow escape.

The Richthofen who returned to the fray in October 1917 found a new and more challenging situation awaiting him. The Royal Flying Corps (RFC) was still taking casualties, but the combination of good fighting aircraft such as the new high-level Sopwith Dolphins, plus the increasingly numerous SE5s, Camels and Bristol fighters, as well as the fast, well-armed DH4 light bombers, were proving more than a match for the German air arm's increasingly outdated Albatrosses and Pfalzes.

In Britain, air power was now important enough to merit a completely new service, the Royal Air Force. The catalyst for the new service had been alarm about the seeming inability to prevent Gotha raids over Britain (*see* Chapter 28). Lloyd George ordered a wider inquiry into aerial warfare. A committee under Lieutenant General Jan Christian Smuts, in the War Cabinet from June 1917, recommended a single air service combining the RFC and the Royal Navy Air Service, under a new Air Ministry and Chief of the Air Staff, to undertake home defence, field operations and strategic bombing. The War Cabinet agreed, and there was a Parliamentary Bill in October 1917. But Lord Rothermere, the new Air Minister, and Sir Hugh Trenchard, the new Chief of the Air Staff, did not get on; Trenchard resigned, but remained in post until the foundation of the RAF on 1 April 1918; Rothermere fell soon after.

While these political battles were fought, on the real battlefront the German spring offensives of 1918 never achieved anything like air superiority. The large numbers of ground-attack planes assembled to bolster the offensive made little difference as the RAF fought back hard. British, French and growing numbers of American squadrons made life difficult for the advancing Germans by artillery spotting, reconnaissance and, increasingly, their own ground attack. The RFC/RAF's only real problem in spring 1918 was being forced to retreat from its frontline airfields before the advancing Germans. But in the air, large numbers of capable aircraft were fighting the Germans to a standstill.

As the German offensive pushed up the valley of the Somme, in April it claimed the life of the Red Baron himself. His Fokker half spun, stalled and crash-landed in

> "FEELING NERVY AND ILL DURING THE LAST WEEK. AFRAID I'M BREAKING UP."

Edward Mannock, British fighter ace, in his diary, 1917

a field, ending up on its nose near Corbie. A bullet had entered his right side and exited via his heart. No-one knows who fired the fatal shot. Germany's idol was gone, to be given a very public hero's funeral by the British – a good propaganda coup. Many British pilots noted Richthofen's death with respect and some sadness. But Mannock had a different view: "I hope he roasted the whole way down."

Richthofen's death symbolized the waning of German air power. The RFC took delivery of no less than 2,500 new aircraft in March 1918 alone, while Germany was suffering shortages of everything from oil to new pilots. Air supremacy was moving irrevocably to the Allies. Even the arrival of the superlative, dangerous Fokker D-VII fighter in June could not turn the tide. New aces like the Canadians' Billy Bishop and the Royal Navy's Raymond Collishaw began to rack up impressive scores of kills.

As the summer of 1918 wore on, the whole pattern of aerial warfare changed. Over the frontlines older fighters such as the Sopwith Camel were now used extensively for ground attack, shooting up and bombing the retreating Germans' positions. Above them, the artillery-observation two-seaters, now equipped with reliable and longer range radios, controlled artillery bombardments. Higher still were the massed fighters, including the new Sopwith Snipe: although, as the last of the rotary engine fighters, not a fast aircraft by the standards of its time, it was more than a good match for contemporary German fighters. Deep behind German lines, light bombers such as the excellent DH4 roamed day after day to attack railheads, headquarters and airfields, secure in the knowledge that the speedy (140mph) aircraft could outrun all its opponents, even the Fokker D-VII.

In June 1918, Trenchard became commander of the new Independent Air Force in France, and it began bombing military targets deep inside Germany. Bigger aircraft, carrying bigger bombloads, were rolling off the production lines. Even as news of the Armistice came through, the first of the four-engined Handley Page V/1500 aircraft were preparing to undertake bombing raids on Berlin. They didn't need to complete their flights. But if the First World War proved anything, it was that air power had come of age and that no future war could be successfully fought without it.

Oberleutnant Manfred von Richthofen poses (centre) *with fellow pilots of his* Jagdstaffel *in April 1917. Their self-confidence perhaps reflects that this was the Royal Flying Corp's "Bloody April" of losses, many inflicted by Richthofen and his friends. The pilots here include Richthofen's brother,* Leutnant Lothar von Richthofen (second from right).

87

A BRITISH MARK V TANK
THE BLACK DAY OF THE GERMAN ARMY

8 AUGUST 1918

The *Kaiserschlacht* (*see* Chapter 84) had been a calculated gamble by the German High Command. By July 1918, its failure now spelled disaster. It had cost Germany 800,000 men, and within weeks its consequences would cost Ludendorff a nervous breakdown – and eventually his job. On 20 July, Crown Prince Rupprecht gloomily noted of the fighting at Villers-Cotterêts: "we stand at the turning point of the war ... the necessity to go over to the defensive is now upon us, and in addition all the gains which we have made in the spring ... have been lost again". Summer 1918 saw the pendulum swing: now it would be the Allies' turn to strike back.

On 8 August 1918, the hammer blow came, spearheaded by Australians and Canadians – and using every operational tank the British had.

On 8 August, British, Australian and Canadian forces delivered a mortal blow against the Germans, in a well-planned attack east of Amiens. It incorporated many of the tactics and technologies developed over the previous years: a devastating, surprise bombardment that evolved into a creeping barrage; ground-attack aircraft; and all 552 vehicles of the Tank Corps, including nearly 350 Mark V fighting tanks. The new Mark V, like this one preserved at the Imperial War Museum, was the most effective tank yet. Previous machines had required four crewmen just to drive them. But, with a new 150-horsepower Ricardo engine linked to an improved transmission system, the Mark V could be driven by just one man. The blueprint for Amiens had been tested in a sharp action on 4 July, when the village of Hamel was captured quickly by the Australian Corps using every element of the new all-arms battle, including Mark V tanks for the first time. The Australian commander, Lieutenant General John Monash, showed that he fully understood the nature of what war had become: "A perfect modern battle plan is like nothing so much as a score for an orchestral composition, where the various arms and units are the instruments, and the tasks they perform are their respective musical phrases." The modern general's role was to conduct the orchestra, and bring in all the sections at the correct time to deliver the symphony of battle.

Foch, as supreme commander, had concluded that the best strategy for retaliation was for the individual Allied armies to mount their own offensives – but, crucially, limited in space and time, and against achievable objectives. There was to be no single great breakthrough. The aim was to pull the German reserve divisions hither and thither, keeping their dwindling reserves always on the move.

"WITH HOPE FOR MANKIND AND WITH VISIONS OF A NEW
WORLD A BLOW WILL BE STRUCK TOMORROW WHICH WILL
DEFINITELY MARK THE TURN OF THE TIDE."

Lieutenant Hedley Goodyear MC, 102nd Canadian Battalion, letter to his mother, 7 August 1918. He was killed in action, 22 August.

A clutch of German PoWs, now in the hands of Canadian troops (9 August 1918), testify to the fact that, with the severe setback of the Battle of Amiens, the tide was turning irrevocably against the Germans. From now on, German soldiers surrendering – or even deserting – became an increasingly common phenomenon.

Subsequently described by Ludendorff as the "Black Day of the German army", a surprise attack combining artillery, tanks, aircraft and new assault troops near Amiens revealed just how low German morale had sunk. The keys were speed, surprise and deception. Rawlinson, the very same general who had commanded on the disastrous first day on the Somme two years before, now planned and launched the first major *Blitzkrieg*-type all-arms operation in history. His Fourth Army (as the Fifth Army was now renamed), embracing the Canadians and Australians, smashed the German lines on a 15-mile front and advanced 8 miles in a day. It was a triumph for the BEF and its new methods.

Planning had started weeks before. Haig had accurately forecast the risks to Germany of any massive final attack as far back as January 1918, when he had agreed with his intelligence staff that "if Germany attacks and fails she will be ruined". The stalling of the German offensive short of Amiens in April 1918 not only dashed hopes of a German breakthrough on the Somme, but the new line gave Haig an ideal spot to counterattack across open ground. By 21 July Rawlinson had sold his battle plan to Haig with the enthusiastic support of his corps commanders – Monash for the Australians, Lieutenant General Sir Arthur Currie for the Canadians – plus the BEF's III Corps and the Cavalry Corps, backed by the senior artillery, air force and tank officers. When Foch was briefed a few days later he not only endorsed Rawlinson's plan strongly but placed the French First Army under Haig's command to join the fight.

One of the reasons for the confidence was that the plan was based on evidence. At Hamel, south of the Somme overlooking the road east from Amiens, on 4 July the Australians (with some Americans under their command) had demonstrated that combined all-arms tactics could not only break an enemy trench line but do so quickly and with minimum casualties. The attack had taken all its objectives in under two hours, using the combination of a surprise creeping barrage, supported by 60 tanks, and aircraft. The infantry effectively mopped up the shocked German survivors. The victory owed much to Monash's detailed staff planning, thorough preparation and the novel use of 12 supply tanks to bring forward vital stores such as ammunition, each tank ferrying as much ammunition and stores as 1,000 men could carry. Aircraft were used to para-drop medical supplies and ammunition to advanced troops, too. This successful employment of new tactics, combined with the battle-tested experience among the staff of the Fourth Army, now made the BEF a strong attacking machine.

Rawlinson's mission was to clear the Germans away from the railway link between Amiens and Paris. To do this he had four corps, plus the support of the French on his right. The Australian and the Canadian Corps were particularly formidable assault troops. The Dominion divisions were numerically stronger than the British divisions and, concentrated in their national armies, they had strong cohesiveness, too.

The attack would prove the model for the BEF's victorious advances for the rest of the war. Rawlinson's secret weapon was surprise. He went to great lengths to ensure security: the attack was called "The Raid"; soldiers' pay books had a slip pasted in with "Keep Your Mouth Shut"; all unusual movement was at night; *pavé* roads were sanded to reduce noise; and aircraft flew daily missions to check that nothing was visible from the air. Canadian signal units were sent to Ypres to broadcast a false Canadian presence there. The 550-odd British and French tanks that were to spearhead the assault, supported by over 2,000 guns, moved forward only when covered by the noise of aircraft engines. Crucially, there would be no preparatory bombardment.

Rawlinson struck at 04.20 on 8 August. The British tanks rolled forward accompanied by a hurricane bombardment modelled on Bruchmüller's "Fire Waltz" (*see* Chapter 84). Led by the Canadians and Australians, the Allied onslaught overwhelmed seven German divisions. On the right flank, the French started later but pushed the Germans back; and on the left, the British III Corps fought hard to evict the Germans from the wooded slopes north of the Somme. In the centre, five German divisions were swept away. By 11.00 the attackers had broken through along a 10-mile front and cavalry and light Whippet tanks were running amok, causing havoc in the German rear areas. Overhead the Royal Air Force bombed and strafed targets of opportunity. By the end of the day the attackers had punched a hole 8 miles deep, at its furthest, in the German lines and the new frontline was out of range even of the heavy guns. German sources admit to the loss of 28,000 men and 400 guns for the first day. Significantly, around 12,000 of the German losses had surrendered.

Two days later German reserves of troops and aircraft rushed to plug the gap. With the British objectives gained, and despite pressure from Foch to continue, Haig ordered the offensive stopped. With 13 infantry and 3 cavalry divisions, Rawlinson had routed 25 German divisions. German losses by the end were 70,000, almost 30,000 of them surrendering, and 1,300 guns. The battle had been a crushing riposte to Ludendorff's army, as he acknowledged.

"The Black Day of the German army" had a profound effect on the victors, too. Confidence and morale were restored to the BEF after the horrors of the March retreat. Haig and the BEF had made a key realization: strike hard, regroup, plan and then strike again at areas of weakness, rather than batter away relentlessly against stiffening resistance as German reserves arrived. British war correspondent Philip Gibbs detected a change "in the enemy's mind": "They no longer have even a dim hope of victory on this western front. All they hope for now is to defend themselves long enough to gain peace by negotiation."

He was right. Ludendorff and the Germans were now on the run.

> "ON OUR SIDE THE ARMY SEEMS TO BE BUOYED UP WITH THE ENORMOUS HOPE OF GETTING ON WITH THIS BUSINESS QUICKLY"
>
> *Philip Gibbs, official British war correspondent, 27 August 1918*

88

CAPTURED GERMAN SHOULDER STRAPS
THE LAST HUNDRED DAYS

JULY TO NOVEMBER 1918

With the British strike at Amiens on 8 August 1918 (*see* Chapter 87), what would later be called "The Last Hundred Days" was well and truly underway: a series of Allied attacks that kept the defeated German army on the run in the closing phase of the war. It is the story of the collapse of the German army on the Western Front, to the accompaniment of the psychological collapse of its master, General Erich Ludendorff.

In 1918, the war once again became one of dramatic movement. As August flowed into September, the Allies gained the ascendancy and began to drive the Germans relentlessly back. Influenced by Haig's incisive understanding of how events were unfolding, the Allied armies launched a series of attacks up and down the line. Instead of getting bogged down in protracted fighting, when the momentum of one attack waned the focus switched to another part of the line. The Germans were bewildered and unable to re-establish the kind of strong defensive positions they had held for four years. "It is very interesting in the front line just now," wrote Lieutenant Colonel Walter Vignoles, commanding the 9th Battalion, Northumberland Fusiliers, "continually chasing the Boche, moving forward every day, no billets, no shelters, everyone just sleeping under hedges or in shell holes. There is no doubt Fritz is in a great mess." German morale plummeted; masses of prisoners were taken. Between 21 August and the Armistice in November, V Corps (part of the British Third Army) moved steadily eastwards from the old 1916 Somme battlefields until on 11 November it was positioned around 8 miles south of Maubeuge, where the BEF had started the war in August 1914. V Corps captured thousands of prisoners, and as a record the shoulder straps of one man from each German regiment it encountered were mounted on three display boards at Corps HQ. These insignia provided intelligence as to the units being encountered, but more than that, the astonishing number and variety of them added up to a picture of a defeated army.

General Mangin's highly successful counterattack at Villers-Cotterêts on 18 July had already shaken the surprised Germans, who retreated almost as quickly as they had advanced. It also shook Ludendorff's nerve. Hindenburg suggested a counterattack north of Soissons, to which Ludendorff exploded: "Madness!" Even the core relationship of Germany's "Duo" was falling apart. By 20 July the defence expert Colonel Friedrich von Lossberg was calling for a complete withdrawal and defence behind the Hindenburg Line, to be dismissed by "a really agitated and nervous" Ludendorff. There was clearly no chance of going ahead with his next

"IT IS NOW THE ENEMY WHO IS ON THE DEFENSIVE, DREADING THE HAMMER BLOWS THAT FALL UPON HIM DAY AFTER DAY, AND THE INITIATIVE OF ATTACK IS SO COMPLETELY IN OUR HANDS THAT WE ARE ABLE TO STRIKE HIM AT MANY DIFFERENT PLACES."

Philip Gibbs, official British war correspondent, 27 August 1918

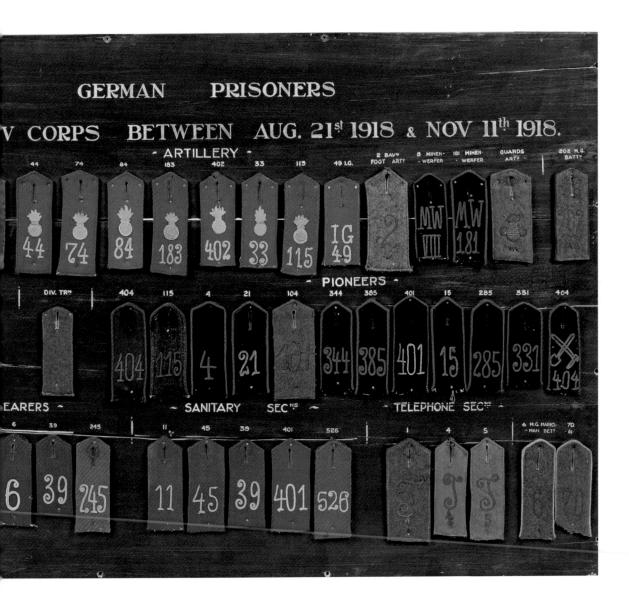

planned offensive, Operation Hagen, against the British at Ypres. To do so would mean ignoring the French and Americans, who were now cutting deep into the south of the great German salient in the Champagne. The truth was that Germany, its great gamble of the *Kaiserschlacht* having failed (*see* Chapter 84), had run out of reserves, ideas and military options.

Sensing his adversary's weakness and indecision, on 24 July Foch, as Allied *generalissimo*, called a strategic conference of Allied commanders. They agreed on a strategic masterstroke against their weakened but still dangerous enemy: limited individual national offensives, which, crucially, would stop when each had achieved its objective. In effect, Foch planned to unleash a coordinated series of limited counterattacks, but switching from front to front as each one suceeded and ran out of steam. There was to be no single breakthrough, no surge to the Rhine; instead, the focus of attack would always move to another sector and divert the German reserves yet again.

The BEF's triumph at Amiens on 8 August conformed to this strategy. It also confirmed German weakness. So began a relentless pursuit of the whole German army as it withdrew under a succession of hammer blows. "The Hundred Days Offensive" would actually consist of no fewer that ten major Allied offensives, one after the other, all separated by space and time.

By now even Ludendorff could see the writing on the wall and offered to resign his responsibilities, only to be told by both Hindenburg and the Kaiser to stay at his post. At the German High Command, on 10 August, Ludendorff briefed the Kaiser in sombre terms, pointing out that "the war must be ended". The Kaiser's reaction to this apocalyptic analysis was, according to his personal liaison officer, one of surprise, well masked. After all, this was the general who only a month before had been briefing him that the war was as good as won.

A few days later, at the general conference at Spa on 13–14 August – the so-called *Kaiserkonferenz* – Ludendorff, despite fighting talk, admitted that Germany now had no alternative but to call for peace talks, with the Dutch acting as intermediaries. The political and social unrest back in Germany, combined with the disintegrating morale at the Front, left little alternative. Unrest in the German army on the Western Front was now widespread. Fresh drafts coming to the Front were being met by cries of "strike breakers, blacklegs" and accusations that they were "only prolonging the war for the capitalists and bosses". However, it was not surrender that Ludendorff was contemplating in August, but negotiation from Germany's current position: occupation of Belgium and parts of France.

Ludendorff's view was reinforced by the prospect of having to fight the American army in France, now moving into the line in the French sector west of Verdun; he realized it would be beyond the weakened German army's capabilities. He knew that his mistrustful, exhausted battalions, wracked by influenza, war weariness and a desire to go home, would be unlikely to stand up to the massive 28,000-strong divisions and the 1.5 million fresh troops of the oncoming steamroller that was the American Expeditionary Force – despite its inexperience.

A month later, on 12–16 September, Ludendorff's fears were realized. With the Americans now united under General Pershing, the US First Army launched its own offensive on the German salient at St Mihiel, southeast of Verdun. Twelve divisions, including two French, 2,900 guns, 1,100 aircraft and 273 tanks launched two deep strikes on converging axes into the salient to encircle the Germans. Although the defenders had been planning to abandon the sector, the American assault came as

"OCTOBER 1918 ... AT EXACTLY 4 O'CLOCK, ONE GUN FIRED – AND THEN ALL THE GUNS OPENED UP ALL THE WAY ALONG THE LINE, AND THERE WAS A CURTAIN OF FIRE FROM HORIZON TO HORIZON AS FAR AS THE EYE COULD SEE. IT REALLY WAS A MAGNIFICENT SIGHT."

Private W.G. Brown, 2/3rd Field Ambulance

In St Mihiel, in Lorraine, children enthusiastically swarm over a French officer's car, waving the Tricolore *in celebration of their liberation after four years of German occupation (13 September 1918). So rapid was the Allied advance in some areas during the "Hundred Days" that the only way of getting supplies to forward troops was by air-drop.*

a nasty shock. Taken by surprise in the middle of their withdrawal, the Germans surrendered in droves. By the end of the day Pershing's men had pinched out the whole salient, capturing 16,000 prisoners and over 440 guns, and shortening the Front by 16 miles. However, American courage and enthusiasm did not compensate for their lack of battle experience. The unskilled, half-trained "Doughboys" fought with a disregard for danger not seen since the opening campaigns of 1914.

This success augmented the other Allied actions of late August, which clearly exemplified Foch's strategy. By now, Haig was one of the few Allied commanders who could sniff victory, briefing a disbelieving Churchill (back in the Cabinet as Minister of Munitions since July 1917) that "we ought to do our utmost to get a decision this autumn". That same day, 21 August, the British Third Army attacked south of Arras; on 22 August, the British Fourth Army recaptured Albert; the next day, across a 33-mile front on the Somme, both armies attacked, supported by the US II Corps; and on 26 August, the British First Army launched itself out of Arras. All the old Somme positions of 1916 were won back; everywhere the German Front was breaking down.

On 31 August, the Australians of the Fourth Army added to Ludendorff's woes by beginning a masterly assault-crossing of the Somme, tearing apart the German lines between St Quentin and Péronne and pushing deeper into occupied territory: it was an action described by General Rawlinson as the greatest military achievement of the war. Three days later the Canadians struck to the north against the strong German defences between Drocourt and Quéant, to the east of Arras, driving the Germans back from this advance position of the Hindenburg Line on a 30-mile front. By mid-September, the BEF's advance in the Somme region was at least 25 miles, along a front of around 40 miles.

As the French closed in to the south, Ludendorff had no option but to pull his troops back to the apparent safety of the Hindenburg Line. It negated all the gains of the spring offensives. He ordered yet another withdrawal, this time to the Canal du Nord. German resistance remained strong, in places, but elsewhere morale was plummeting; increasingly, the withdrawing troops were relying on well-sited and determined teams of machine gunners to cover their backs.

Although American strength had not yet peaked on the Continent, Foch now realized that the Germans really were on the run and ordered a number of

The fog of war made manifest in this famous smoky battle scene, as machine gunners of the US 2nd Infantry Division blast away with their 37mm guns. It probably depicts the wasted woods of the Argonne, and shows the difficult terrain that American troops had to contend with in this, their most intensive contribution to the war.

simultaneous attacks, sometimes referred to as the "Final Grand Offensive", designed to cut into German communications from the flanks. It was a case of all hands on deck, or, in Foch's memorable phrase "*Tout le monde à la bataille*" – "Everyone to the battle!" And everyone came.

It unfolded in four steps. On 26 September, to the west of Verdun the Americans and French unleashed what would prove to be their final offensive, as over 25 divisions attacked the Germans in the forested Argonne region and up the Meuse in the greatest and bloodiest American battle of the war. In six weeks the Americans advanced 60 miles and lost over 26,000 killed and 95,000 wounded, but Pershing's men inflicted 130,000 casualties on the Germans as well as capturing 26,000 prisoners and over 870 guns.

No sooner had German reserves been ordered south to deal with this onslaught, when, at dawn on 27 September, four BEF divisions of the First and Third Armies attacked north and south of Cambrai before dawn, crossing the supposedly impassable Canal du Nord to approach the Hindenburg Line. The very next day, far to the north, the Flanders Army Group under the command of the King of the Belgians with 12 Belgian, 10 British and 6 French divisions, quickly penetrated the German defences beyond Ypres. They advanced up to 6 miles on the first day and only stopped 18 miles into the German lines when logistic support was unable to get any further forward across the all too numerous water obstacles.

On 29 September, the British Fourth Army north of St Quentin finally assaulted the Hindenburg Line itself along a 12-mile front, inaugurated the previous day by an extraordinarily ferocious bombardment. American and Australian divisions had heavy going against the defences, but the British 46th (North Midland) Division crossed the St Quentin canal in a brilliant *coup de main*, slicing through the Hindenburg's defences and capturing four-fifths of the enemy in the area.

Finally, Ludendorff's nerve snapped. On 28 September, he broke down in what was described as "a paranoid rage", blaming the Kaiser, the German people, the navy and civilian politicians in the *Reichstag* – anyone but himself – for Germany's impending defeat. That day, far from the Western Front, Bulgaria had broken ranks with the Central Powers and called for an armistice. So many shocks and reversals could not be withstood. The broken, frantic general went to see Hindenburg and told him that they now had no alternative but to seek a negotiated peace. The next day, as the Bulgarian Armistice was agreed, the Kaiser visited High Command at Spa to be told by the General Staff that the war could not be won.

But in the days and weeks to come, the Western Front Allies pushed on relentlessly, advancing and capturing. In the north, after a 10-mile advance in three days, bad weather caused a two-week delay, but by the third week of October a string of major towns and cities had been retaken – back in Allied hands for the first time since 1914, including Lille, Ostend, Douai and Zeebrugge. And they kept on.

In the centre, on 3 October, more of the Hindenburg Line was breached, and on 8 October, the British Third and Fourth armies, along with the French First Army, stormed the Hindenburg Line defences over a 17-mile front around Cambrai. The town itself fell on 9 October. A week later, and 4 miles further on, the retreating Germans were attacked along the River Selle.

To the south, the French and Americans were grinding their way through the difficult terrain of the Argonne Forest, but in mid-October they breached their section of the Hindenburg Line; once out of the Argonne, by the end of the month, they pushed on as far as Sedan.

The Germans were attempting a controlled retreat, and despite depleted numbers could still offer stiff resistance. But determined rearguards could only mask the completeness of defeat. The final offensive on the Western Front commenced on 4 November along a 30-mile front in the direction of Mauberge and Mons. The BEF was back where it had started the war. Haig threw his First, Third and Fourth armies at the German defenders, who lay behind a canalized stretch of the River Sambre and in the Forest of Mormal. The fighting was often intense, but the canal was bridged. To the south, the French First Army attacked, capturing Guise. Between them, the Allies broke through on a 40-mile front.

On 9 November, Foch prepared to administer the *coup de grâce*. He signalled each of the Allied armies:

> The enemy, disorganized by our repeated attacks, retreats along the entire front. It is important to coordinate and expedite our movements. I appeal to the energy and the initiative of the commanders-in-chief and of their armies to make decisive the results obtained.

In the end, his orders didn't need to be carried out. Within two days, the war was over.

These Hundred Days, for all their gains, were far from cheap. The victorious final advance had been as expensive as any other campaign of a very bloody war. The BEF lost over 350,000 men – at least as many as at Passchendaele on the Somme in 1916. However, the difference was that this time the BEF had advanced nearly 100 miles. Of course the victory was an *Allied* one, a coalition effort, but the figures show clearly that the BEF's contribution was both the costliest and the most decisive. Despite numbering less than a third of the Allied forces, the BEF suffered more casualties but also captured almost half the number of German prisoners taken (189,000) and around 40 per cent of the enemy guns. Haig's BEF had won Britain's greatest ever victory.

And all the time, as soldiers of all nationalities died in their thousands, a parallel series of events were shaping the final result. Germany was attempting to negotiate as advantageous as possible an armistice; but the Central Powers – and the German state itself – were imploding.

89

A WREATH FOR SALADIN
THE END OF THE PALESTINE CAMPAIGN

SEPTEMBER TO OCTOBER 1918

Following the success of the Egyptian Expeditionary Force (EEF) in capturing Jerusalem in December 1917 (*see* Chapter 78), General Allenby's Palestine campaign slowed as winter weather set in; before spring, troops were transferred to the Western Front to help resist the German offensives. After two EEF raids across the River Jordan were beaten back, Allenby then went on the defensive during the summer heat, while he incorporated his new Indian Army units and replacements. By late summer 1918, "The Bull" was ready to move again. In September, the EEF began its final offensive, this time against the strong defence lines of the Ottoman "Yilderim Army Group" with its 100,000 men, including 15,600 Germans and 500 guns. It would take Allenby – and T.E. Lawrence and the irregulars of Sherif Feisal – to Damascus, the symbolic heart of Arab aspirations, and beyond.

> On 23 October 1916, in a cool, shaded house at Wadi Safra in the Hejaz, T.E. Lawrence had his momentous first meeting with Sherif Feisal, whom he would go on to serve for the next two years. He deliberately invoked Damascus, noting that they were "far from" it: both men were already conscious of the need for the Arabs to liberate this historic city in distant Syria. Some weeks later, Feisal told his gathered tribesmen that when they arrived in Damascus they should "clean up the tomb" of Saladin, the renowned 12th-century Muslim warrior. To Feisal and many Arabs, Saladin's tomb had been defiled by Kaiser Wilhelm II when, following his state visit in 1898, he sent this ornate bronze wreath to be placed on it as a symbol of German–Ottoman friendship. On 1 October 1918, when the Arabs finally arrived in Damascus, Lawrence and a small group went to the tomb and cleansed it as Feisal had ordered. It was a highly symbolic act of political ascendancy, stripping away European influence from this venerated Islamic site. The wreath was given to Lawrence who, within days, returned to Britain to fight the Arab cause in London. On 8 November, he took it to the Imperial War Museum to hand it over for preservation, since, as he put it, "Saladin no longer required it."

Beginning on 19 September, Allenby smashed through the Ottoman defences in one of the war's most successful British and Imperial campaigns, dubbed the Battle of Megiddo (the Biblical Armageddon). Unlike his fellow generals on the Western Front, Allenby was able to use his infantry to break through the enemy lines and then send in his cavalry to exploit and attack the enemy rear.

He began by pretending to repeat his tactics at Gaza, by attacking on the right flank in the desert with the Camel Corps and cavalry, plus Arab irregulars, against

"I REMINDED THE AMIR FEISAL THAT THE ALLIES WERE IN HONOUR BOUND TO ENDEAVOUR TO REACH A SETTLEMENT IN ACCORDANCE WITH THE WISHES OF THE PEOPLES CONCERNED AND URGED HIM TO PLACE HIS TRUST WHOLE-HEARTEDLY IN THEIR GOOD FAITH."

General Sir Edmund Allenby, report to London, 18 October 1918

the Hejaz Railway. Rail communications between Damascus and the main Ottoman army were broken for a crucial week. The RAF gave close air support, strafing enemy columns and, more importantly, locating Ottoman positions. The Arab forces then continued their advance north up the railway towards Damascus. Meanwhile, Allenby switched his mobile cavalry across to his left flank and three days later launched an all-arms offensive against the Ottoman Seventh and Eighth armies dug in on the line from the Dead Sea to Jaffa on the coast. By mid-morning the infantry had broken through and Allenby's cavalry was pouring north up the coast road. The next day they had even reached the Ottoman GHQ at Nazareth, nearly capturing the German commander-in-chief himself, General Liman von Sanders, the man who had masterminded the Ottoman defence at Gallipoli.

The Ottoman forces were streaming back across the Front, and by 24 September the Seventh and Eighth armies had effectively ceased to exist. Thousands surrendered. On 25 September, Australians stormed the vital railway junction at Samakh, 50 miles to the north, and took it after hand-to-hand street fighting. The vital Ottoman railway, on which all their supplies depended, was lost for good.

While his main forces were pushing up the coast towards Haifa and Acre, Allenby now planned the final advance of his campaign, inland along the Jordan Valley. He switched his assault to a narrow thrust past the Sea of Galilee and Golan Heights towards Quneitra and then the road to Damascus, 70 miles to the northeast. By 28 September the leading elements were at Quneitra and, after a delay caused by German machine guns at Sa'sa the next day, pushed on to just 10 miles south of Damascus on the 30th.

Three cavalry divisions were now converging on the city. In ten days they had covered 150 miles, in a country with no food and little water, and destroyed two Ottoman armies. In Damascus, ammunition, petrol and military dumps were set ablaze, and the wireless mast for communication with Constantinople and Berlin was blown up. The Ottoman forces were on the run, many killed as an Australian brigade brought machine guns into action on the narrow road running west to Beirut, literally blocking a gorge with the dead bodies of transport animals and hundreds of men.

On 1 October 1918, the advance elements of General Chauvel's Desert Mounted Corps – the 10th Australian Light Horse – were the first Allied forces to enter Damascus, to a hero's welcome. But they moved on quickly having been ordered to avoid the limelight. The honour had to be seen to fall to Lawrence and the Arab irregulars, who, for political reasons, had to enter before the main part of Chauvel's force. The streets became alive with Arabs on horseback, firing in the air.

It remained for the last Ottoman resistance to be put down. On 8 October, the Indian contingents reached Beirut, and on 20 October Chauvel ordered his Desert Mounted Corps to halt their advance. Six days later, Aleppo fell to Major General H.J. MacAndrew. For the Ottomans in Palestine the war was over. In 38 days Allenby's EEF had advanced 350 miles and taken 75,000 prisoners, including 4,000 Germans, and 400 guns. It was a triumph for Allenby, and for his masterly handling of his forces. Using deception, concentration of force, surprise and the cavalry's mobility, he had shown himself to be one of the outstanding generals of the war.

Unfortunately, the clarity of the military triumph would give way to a muddied, bitter political legacy. British promises had been dangled in 1915–16 promising Arab independence as the reward for an Arab revolt against the Ottomans. But in May 1916, speaking for their respective governments, Sir Mark Sykes, an MP with knowledge

"WHEN A SOLDIER APPEARED IN THE STREETS OF DAMASCUS HE WAS SURROUNDED BY THE EXCITED AND DELIGHTED THRONG. THEY THREW OFF THEIR STOLID EXTERIOR, AND RECEIVED US WITH ECSTATIC JOY ... AND ACCLAIMED THE DAY AS THE GREATEST IN THE 4,000 YEARS OF THE HISTORY OF DAMASCUS."

Eyewitness to the liberation of Damascus, 1 October 1918

In October 1918, amid the celebrations of throwing off the Ottoman yoke, Damascus officially came under the control of an Arab administration, which now had to keep law and order. Here, members of the Hejaz Camel Corps impose discipline on Bedouin looters.

of the political problems of Mesopotamia and Syria, and François Georges-Picot, a former French consul in Beirut, came to an agreement: that after the war Britain would occupy Palestine, and France would occupy Syria (including modern Lebanon); they added some qualified statements about Arab self-rule. In May 1917, an uneasy Foreign Office warned: "French intentions in Syria are surely incompatible with the war aims of the Allies as defined ... utterly incompatible with our ideas of liberating the Arab nation and of establishing a free and independent Arab State." To compound the problem, in a series of communications, culminating in Foreign Secretary Arthur Balfour's "declaration" – a letter to Lord Rothschild, leader of the British Jewish community – Britain appeared to be offering Jews a homeland in Palestine. In effect, there were now three conflicting promises for Arab land.

Lawrence communicated the gist of the Sykes–Picot discussions (if not all the details) to Feisal, but to Feisal there still appeared sufficient hope for Arab aspirations. If the Arabs could be seen as the liberators of Damascus, along with Homs, Hama and Aleppo, the agreement offered them some degree of independence. So, as soon as Ottoman forces evacuated Damascus, the Arabs proclaimed an Arab government over Syria and the surrounding region under King Hussein, Feisal's father. Thus, when Allenby entered Damascus, on 3 October, an Arab administration was already in being and the Arab flag was flying from government buildings. This was as Allenby had expected, and was consistent with the earlier British assurances. Feisal also arrived on 3 October, but it soon became clear to him and to Lawrence (*see* Chapter 79) just how unreliable any British assurances were, despite Allenby's continuing efforts to plead British good faith.

Allenby's victory left a hollow legacy, as the region was subsequently carved up between Britain and France (*see* Chapter 93). After Versailles, Syria was given to France, whose heavy-handed rule was, within two years, putting down Arab rebellion. There were consolation prizes: Feisal became the British client king of the new state of Iraq, while his brother Abdullah established the (continuing) royal dynasty of Trans-Jordan (now Jordan). Their father Sherif Hussein, though, remained in the Hejaz, his own kingdom taken over by the neighbouring Saudi dynasty in 1924. The victories of 1918 would bear bitter fruit and the politics of the Middle East have never recovered.

90

AN *ERSATZ* NIGHTDRESS
THE COLLAPSE OF THE CENTRAL POWERS

It was inevitable, after the failure of the last German throw of the dice in the 1918 spring offensives (*see* Chapter 84), and the beginning of the Allied counteroffensives (*see* Chapters 87 and 88), that a disintegration of German morale at the Fighting Front would feed, and be fed by, the demoralization and confusion on the Home Front. In Germany, economic privations, social disruption and political agitation from all quarters were eating away the will to fight on. That so many German troops on the Western Front were surrendering was not only a testament to the Allies' overwhelming force and new tactics, but also the German rank and file, increasingly, had had enough.

In 1917–18, Germans had endured a severe winter of coal scarcities and a failed potato harvest. More generally, the country was plagued by lack of food, labour shortages, rising inflation and political radicalization. Resentment that the available supplies were still being prioritized for a war that clearly could not now be won was turning many Germans, whether in uniform or not, against the war and against the leadership and institutions behind the war effort. There was more than a whiff of revolution in the air.

Throughout the war, the Central Powers lacked the economic depth of Britain and France, which were able to fall back on the abundance of their empires and the considerable material support of the United States. By 1916 both Germany and Austria-Hungary had started to run short of many key resources. Over the next two years, the situation deteriorated rapidly. The British blockade successfully prevented the import of vital goods, ranging from chemicals to food, both directly into German ports and via the neutral northern European countries. To compensate, the Germans looked for substitute, or *Ersatz*, products. Never quite the same as the originals they were intended to replace, coffee was produced from roasted barley, tea from raspberry leaves and a variety of strange substances were billed as "meat". Textile staples such as cotton and wool were also hard to come by. Military uniforms took priority, and civilians had to find other ways of producing "cloth". Both paper and wood fibre were used to make clothes. Many were quite effective, but clearly they could not be washed or worn in the rain. This full-length white nightdress, complete with "lace" cuffs and collar, was made from lengths of woven paper string. It is one of several items obtained by the Imperial War Museum to show the extraordinary means by which German and Austro-Hungarian civilians kept themselves going during the war. But, despite this immense effort and all the ingenuity, by 1918 most citizens of both countries were tired, hungry, poorly clothed and fed up.

"THERE IS PRACTICALLY NO COAL TO BE HAD, AND I LIVE IN THE HOUSE IN MY OLD FUR COAT. THE GAS BURNS FROM 11 TO 1 IN THE MIDDLE OF THE DAY, FOR COOKING, AND FROM 4 TO 12 AT NIGHT – OTHERWISE IT IS CUT OFF."

A German resident, relating the privations of war

If Germany was beginning to disintegrate, her allies were even further along that road. On the Italian Front, whole Czech and Croat units of the Austro-Hungarian army were deserting and going over to the Allies, while the empire was crippled by strikes and shortages. The Habsburg Emperor Karl warned the Kaiser that Vienna could no longer fight on and had to seek peace if the dynasty were to survive. His foreign minister, Baron István (Stephen) von Burian, had proposed a joint proclamation calling on all sides to negotiate. This was too much for the Germans, whose officials at that time still believed Hindenburg and Ludendorff's assurances that the military position was strong. But on 1 September the Austro-Hungarian General Staff warned that "the army can no longer sustain the battle against the enemy" and any military collapse would lead to an internal revolution, Bolshevik-style. On 14th September, Vienna unilaterally called for peace talks in a neutral country, adding – much to Berlin's annoyance – that it was speaking on behalf of the other Central Powers: but the call was rebuffed anyway. To make things worse, Bulgaria was soon reeling under Franchet d'Espèrey's offensive out of Salonika (*see* Chapter 26). The Balkan front collapsed as his victorious forces flooded north into Bulgaria and Romania, even threatening Hungary. This was a direct blow to Germany too, threatening her vital supplies of grain and oil from Romania and the Ukraine, on which her tottering food supply and fuel for vehicles so much depended.

On the Western Front, thousands of German soldiers were deserting or not returning from leave that autumn and there were so many deserters hiding in the cellars and attics in Brussels that the German Military Police gave up making raids to arrest them. The military conference at High Command headquarters in Spa, on 28–29 September, confirmed Germany's, and the remaining Central Powers', need to seek an end to the fighting. In Ludendorff's own words, the capitulation of Bulgaria on 29 September "sealed the destiny of the Quadruple Alliance".

Despite this, and despite his own sudden breakdown at the end of September, Ludendorff, backed by Hindenburg, still planned for a fighting withdrawal from the German-occupied territories and proposed to "take up the battle on the German Frontier". The Duo thought that unilaterally they could better negotiate favourable peace terms with President Wilson, based on his Fourteen Points, from a position of relative strength. But they needed to demonstrate Germany's democratic credentials. Ludendorff reluctantly approved a visit by the recently appointed German Foreign Minister Paul von Hintze to Spa to hammer out a crucial deal between the military in the West and the politicians in Berlin. With the agreement of the Kaiser, a new chancellor would be appointed – the third since Bethmann Hollweg's resignation in July 1917 – replacing the elderly Count Georg Hertling. The new incumbent would then form a broadly based democratic government containing Social Democrats. This government would bring in political reforms and approach the United States, calling for peace on the basis of the Fourteen Points.

The new chancellor, officially appointed on 3 October, was Prince Max von Baden – a known liberal, despite his aristocratic breeding, and no admirer of Ludendorff. He formed a government of politicians from all parties and, to strengthen his hand, obtained a statement from the military that "there was no further chance of forcing a peace on the enemy", though this did allow the army to then distance itself from any subsequent peace moves. Prince Max, fully sensible of the potential catastrophe of an abject military surrender and defeat, and wary that an armistice request might sharpen the Allies teeth, nevertheless requested exactly that and asked to negotiate

A groundswell of protest. By autumn 1918, mass demonstrations, such as this one on Berlin's Zimmerstrasse, were common on the streets of the capital and other large German cities, as people reacted angrily to shortages and demanded political change. They would continue in 1919, reflecting factionalism, radicalism and German anger at the Treaty of Versailles.

on the basis of the Fourteen Points. But through October, in three separate formal replies, Wilson's tone increasingly stiffened in the light of his Allies' feelings, and he demanded as conditions the evacuation of all occupied territories and the cessation of all submarine attacks; he also insisted that the Allies could only negotiate with the government of a properly democratic state – that is, one without the Kaiser, or at the very least a constitutional monarchy. Among the Allies, Lloyd George was pressing the view that conditions for an armistice could not be fixed "until after consultation with the military experts", and a hardline Clemenceau played for time.

The last five weeks of war and haggling were agonizing: for the Germans; for the Allied politicians; but, above all for the troops who were still being wounded and killed, on all sides. Berlin begged the US president not to impose conditions "irreconcilable with the honour of the German people and the establishment of a just peace". But by the last week of October Wilson's hands were tied. The Allies had to speak with one voice and as their conditions hardened, so opposition grew in Germany to their proposals.

Ludendorff, back from his personal nadir, was feeling more bullish, suggesting Germany could still defend herself, that winter would slow the Allies and that holding out longer would bring better terms. But, having recovered his nerve if not his sense, he then made a fatal mistake. He attempted to rally the troops once more to fight on and ignore the civilian government's peace negotiations. On 24 October, he drafted a personal proclamation to the army saying that the politicians' plans for peace were "unacceptable to us as soldiers. [They] can thus be nothing ... but a challenge to continue our resistance with all our strength".

Two members of the Austrian delegation outside the Villa Giusti, near Padua, on the day they agreed an armistice to end the war with Italy (3 November 1918). Although the phrase "shackled to a corpse" came to describe Germany's relationship with her weaker partner, Austria-Hungary's surrender was still a psychological blow.

The new chancellor was furious, as was the Kaiser. A draft copy of Ludendorff's (unissued) challenge to the political authority of Berlin was seen by a member of the Independent Socialist Party. The *Reichstag* erupted in rage and insisted that this "overmighty and insubordinate" general must go; and so, on 26 October Germany's "First Quartermaster General" was forced to submit his resignation personally to the Kaiser and dismissed without thanks, to be replaced by the more moderate, and more politically aware, General Wilhelm Groener. Prince Max of Baden reluctantly accepted all the Allied conditions. He had little choice. Germany was falling apart.

The game was already up for Austria-Hungary. Imperial authority collapsed on 16 October, when the emperor proclaimed a federation of nations. But it was already too late for many – Poles, Czechs and the Serbs and Croats were all busy forming provisional independent governments. Hungary was preparing to declare independence too. On 24 October, the rejuvenated Italians, with British and French help, stormed across the River Piave at Vittorio Veneto and put to flight those troops who had not deserted or come over to the Allies. Far off in the Aegean, on 30 October, the defeated Ottoman Empire signed an armistice at Mudros harbour, on the island of Lemnos. And by 1 November Vienna was anxiously suing for peace.

Germany was alone. The Kaiser had removed himself from Berlin to the High Command at Spa on 29 October. His beloved High Seas Fleet, idle in port for so long, was ordered by Admiral Scheer to steam out into the North Sea for one final confrontation with the Grand Fleet in order to go out in a blaze of glory and salvage Germany's honour – and, it was hoped, undermine the politicians' peace negotiations. The disgruntled, radicalized sailors were much less keen on what seemed a blatantly suicidal mission and, on 30 October, mutinied at Wilhelmshaven and Kiel. Sailors' soviets were proclaimed. At Kiel on 3 November the sailors joined striking workers in a mass revolt and raised the Red Flag. The German Revolution had begun, as insurrection spread to the streets of Berlin and half a dozen other major cities. Germany in 1918 was beginning to resemble Russia in 1917, with competing poles of power, and competing armed factions.

By now, after a series of military-political conferences, Marshal Foch had outlined his military terms for a ceasefire. The wording was harsh, harsher than Wilson anticipated, reflecting continued debate about interpretations of the Fourteen Points. Foch called for the liberation of all occupied territory including Alsace-Lorraine; reparations for all damage caused to France; and the occupation of the German Rhineland (which Lloyd George had contested). Haig demanded rolling stock, and Pershing surprised everyone by insisting on the immediate relinquishing of all U-boats – the freedom of the seas had always been an important issue for the United States. The final list also demanded the surrender of 5,000 heavy guns, 3,000 trench mortars, 36,000 machine guns, 2,000 aeroplanes (including the entire fleet of the latest Fokker D-VII fighter) and a big chunk of the High Seas Fleet in addition to the U-boats. This formidable list worried the Americans, and on 31 October "Colonel" House, on Wilson's behalf, asked Foch whether he believed that the war should continue or the Allies should seek an armistice? Foch replied: "I do not make war simply to make war ... the aim being achieved through an armistice ... no-one has the right to spill another drop of blood."

On 5 November, Wilson told the Germans that he was prepared to discuss an armistice, but that Foch would present the Allied terms. By then Germany was collapsing into anarchy. The Social Democratic Majority was warning two days later that they might pull out of the government, and that nationwide revolution threatened, unless the Kaiser went. On 9 November, Prince Max was forced to try and pacify popular opinion by announcing the Kaiser's abdication – slightly ahead of schedule.

On that day, as Foch was rallying Allied commanders for a possible final hammer blow, at Spa the Kaiser confronted his fate. Facing his generals, his belief that loyal troops would be despatched to quell the revolutionaries back home was rebuffed by Groener. German would fire on German: it could mean a civil war. But the generals were not even sure whether their weary and disgruntled army could be relied on. Groener told his master the unpalatable truth: he must abdicate. The incredulous "All Highest" stammered out: "but what about the soldiers' Blood Oath of loyalty?" Groener replied coldly: "The army no longer stands behind Your Majesty. The Blood Oath is only a form of words." Wilhelm II duly abdicated, fleeing the next day to Holland as Imperial Germany collapsed into a leaderless vacuum of competing states, politicians, soldiers, revolutionaries and starving citizens.

As revolutionaries across Germany tried to seize power, and in Munich the Independent Socialists under Kurt Eisner proclaimed a Bavarian Workers' Republic, the King of Bavaria abdicated, too. Prince Max stood down as chancellor to be replaced by the Majority Leader of the *Reichstag*, Friedrich Ebert, leader of the Social Democrats. To forestall a Bolshevik-style revolution, his colleague, Philipp Scheidemann, announced on the *Reichstag*'s steps the creation of a new workers' republic. Imperial Germany was no more.

One of Prince Max's last acts had been to choose the leader of the Centre Party, the Catholic Matthias Erzberger, to meet the Allies and get an immediate ceasefire. Erzberger was shocked by the General Staff now telling him to hurry with his mission, "as the Front could be broken from one minute to the next". By 7 November he was on his way to meet Foch face to face.

He travelled with Hindenburg's injunction ringing in his ears: "Go with God's blessing and try and obtain as much as you can for our homeland."

91

QUEEN MARY'S UNION JACK
THE ARMISTICE

11 NOVEMBER 1918

On 7 November 1918, a cavalcade of cars from German High Command headquarters at Spa, in eastern Belgium, rumbled through the night straight towards the enemy. As they neared the lines, a French bugler on the running board of the leading vehicle sounded a warning call to alert sentries not to shoot at the strange procession. It was carrying the German envoy Matthias Erzberger and his delegation, charged with procuring a ceasefire at all costs. It would take another four days, but an armistice there was. On 11 November the war ended, and the Allies had won a great victory.

> As news of the Armistice spread across London, people went wild. Big Ben chimed for the first time in years, having been silent during the war. Air-raid warning rockets burst overhead and Boy Scouts raced through the streets shouting out the news. Everywhere crowds thronged the streets. One woman officer worker in Kingsway remembered how "we tore out of the building. And we tore down the Strand. And the extraordinary thing was, before you could sneeze, there were thousands and thousands of tiny little Union Jacks everybody was holding. And we were carried right up to Oxford Circus in that crowd. It was quite terrifying." A mass of excited people gathered in front of Buckingham Palace, cheering for the king and the queen. It was, Queen Mary noted in her diary, "the greatest day in the world's history ... at 11 we went on to the balcony to greet the large crowd which had formed outside. At 12.30 we went out again & the massed bands of the Guards played the National Anthem." In the evening, after dinner, the royal couple went out for a third time and witnessed "another wonderful scene". During one of these appearances, the normally restrained queen waved this Union Jack at the crowd. For her and the king, as for all their peoples, the war had been a terrible ordeal. Now it was over, brought to an end by, in Queen Mary's words, "a day full of emotion & thankfulness – tinged with regret at the many lives who have fallen in this ghastly war".

Any notion that there was going to be much room for negotiation would soon evaporate. By 8 November the German delegation arrived at Tergnier, in Picardy, to be housed in a special train. The next day it moved to the Forest of Compiègne to arrive alongside Foch's command train hiding under the trees: Foch had deliberately chosen not to meet the Germans at his HQ at Senlis, because he felt it might be a target for a last-ditch bombing raid to scupper the talks. The Allied delegation of Foch and Admiral Sir Rosslyn Wemyss for Britain (there was no US representative) received the Germans coldly. Foch began by asking why they were present. After

"HISTORY HAS NO MORE GLORIOUS DAY THAN YESTERDAY, WHICH SAW THE END OF THE GREAT WORLD WAR AND THE TRIUMPH OF GREAT BRITAIN AND HER ALLIES. GERMANY, BEATEN IN THE FIELD, MENACED BY CERTAIN INVASION AND OVERWHELMED BY INTERNAL REVOLUTION, CAPITULATED TO THE ALLIES"

Daily Mirror, *12 November 1918*

some embarrassed cross-questioning, the Germans admitted that they sought an armistice. Foch brightened and told them that if they were here to "*ask for*" a ceasefire, then here were the Allies' conditions, take them or leave them. He was perfectly prepared to continue the war. Faced with this threat, a shocked Erzberger backed down. Germany could not carry on fighting.

Over the next 36 hours of wrangling he tried hard to obtain better terms, to little avail. An envoy was sent back to Spa (Foch refused to accept radio messages) with the final list of Allied demands. The German High Command argued hard for softer terms, stressing the dangers of a Bolshevik-style revolution throughout Europe, their need to retain some weapons to maintain order at home and the impossibility of feeding the German population in the face of the continuing Allied blockade, claiming that it was "unfair". Admiral Wemyss pointed out that Germany had engaged in her own "unfair" blockade using U-boats. Erzberger did, however, get an undertaking that the Allies would see that Germany was not reduced to famine. At 5 a.m. on the morning of 11 November an exhausted Erzberger signed for Germany. The final page was signed three hours later.

At 11 a.m. on the 11th day of the 11th month the guns fell silent. Despite some scattered last-minute fighting, this did indeed prove to be the end of the First World War. The BEF stopped its furthest advance at Mons – the very town where it had fought its first battle in August 1914. By a supreme irony two plaques now stand less than 100 yards apart near the Casteau crossroads there: the first commemorates the very first shot fired by the BEF in 1914; the second honours the very last member of the BEF to be killed in action (a Canadian) at 10.58 on 11 November 1918. Fittingly, Private George Lawrence Price is buried in the nearby St Symphorien cemetery alongside "old man" John Parr, the very first BEF soldier to be killed in far-off 1914.

News of the Armistice travelled fast. Foch immediately took the signed copy back to Paris for Clemenceau, to be read out in the Parliament at 16.00. The BEF sent flash signals to all units ordering "HOSTILITIES WILL CEASE AT 11.00". In the trenches the impact was immediate. British guns fired their last salvoes and stopped. Many batteries fired off all their ammunition to get rid of it. Men on both sides died in the last few hours. Many German machine guns, the scourge of the advancing BEF, kept firing until 11.00 on the dot. There are numerous reports of machine gunners firing one long last burst, standing up and just walking away. One group even walked over and shook hands with their former enemies. Another German was seen to stand up and make a theatrical bow, before disappearing over the hill.

As the artillery finally fell silent many soldiers could not take in the news. While behind the BEF lines celebrations and wild parties took place, for many others the news was greeted with stunned disbelief. The day was often remembered as a strangely quiet one. Soldiers in the trenches mostly sat quietly around campfires talking and remembering, or sleeping. Sentries were still posted. Officers still did their rounds, although they walked around in the open. For units in reserve there were rousing speeches by commanding officers, church services, impromptu football matches and a double issue of rum. The national anthem was sung. Further back, leave trains blew their whistles and soldiers cheered out of the windows as they rattled across northern France to the sound of church bells. At Folkestone leave boats sounded their sirens and foghorns, prompting puzzled soldiers to ask what all the noise was about.

Back in London news of the Armistice was greeted with rapture. Londoners exploded in a spontaneous celebration with drinking and dancing, and a happy

"TO ME THE MOST REMARKABLE FEATURE OF THAT DAY AND NIGHT WAS THE UNCANNY SILENCE THAT PREVAILED. NO RUMBLING OF GUNS, NO STACCATO OF MACHINE-GUNS, NOR DID THE ROAR OF EXPLODING DUMPS BREAK INTO THE NIGHT AS IT HAD SO OFTEN DONE."

Lieutenant Evans, Royal Welsh Fusiliers, diary entry for 11 November 1918

excitable crowd cheered the royal family as they drove through the West End and the City. Later, thousands surged to Buckingham Palace to roar out "God Save the King". In Paris similar celebrations took place. The church bells of Notre Dame boomed out; France had suffered grievously, and her citizens were relieved that their long nightmare appeared to be over. Americans, because of the time difference, awoke to victory at breakfast time. In Times Square, New York, huge emotional crowds rushed onto the street to sing, dance and cheer.

For many Germans, as for all the populations of the defeated Central Powers, the Armistice inevitably generated complex feelings. On the one hand there was relief. If the war really was ending, the nations' economies would no longer be enslaved to a war effort, the young men no longer dying for increasingly hollow-sounding reasons. But the Armistice raised new and disturbing questions for the vanquished. There would be no quick end to existing miseries and instabilities, especially with winter coming on and 1918's devastating influenza pandemic now entering a more deadly phase.

Of course, the Armistice was just a ceasefire – in theory, war could break out again at any moment. But as the peace held over the days and weeks to come, for the first time in many years the men in uniform could contemplate the future, now they actually *had* a future. The realization that they were going to live came as a surprise to many. For the tired and war-weary soldiers of all nations, from Scotland to Sarajevo where it all began, thoughts began to crystallize around one idea: demobilization. For the Allies, not everyone could be released – for example, 32,000 men of the BEF would be needed to occupy the Rhineland, and demobilization turned out to be slow. And the whole question of re-entry of millions of men back into a civilian society that had, itself, been irrevocably changed by war created new questions, new tensions.

But that was for the future. At least, on 11 November 1918, the Allied Home Fronts and Fighting Fronts could savour the moment.

Armistice Day witnessed explosions of a very different kind to those that typified the war – outpourings of joy, relief, celebration, patriotism, victory. Here, civilians occupy every possible surface on a London bus to cheer the news, and to entertain the passers-by. Some of the occupants of the buildings have also put out flags.

93

SIR WILLIAM ORPEN'S *UNKNOWN BRITISH SOLDIER*
THE PARIS PEACE CONFERENCE

JANUARY TO JUNE 1919

The Armistice brought the ending of hostilities and a panoply of interim arrangements to move Europe from a climate of war to a climate of peace. But more was needed to move the Armistice on to the next stage – actual peace treaties. The years 1919 and 1920 saw the emergence of five separate treaties, dealing with all the defeated powers. Their fates were decided at the Paris Peace Conference, in the Palace of Versailles.

Thus, for the first six months of 1919 the leaders of the great powers descended on the French capital to hammer out an agreement to reshape their world and mould it in a new image. Empires were broken up and horse-traded over tea and biscuits in the Quai d'Orsay; new countries were debated and confirmed – or not. Royalty, politicians, journalists, economists, bankers, political advisors, not to mention the inevitable prostitutes and hangers on, poured into the "City of Light" to make their own unique contributions to building a new world order. Most of them had one overriding aim: to make sure that there could be no more wars on the calamitous scale of what they knew as "The Great War". But noble visions contrasted, as ever, with national interests and personal agendas.

The Imperial War Museum commissioned Sir William Orpen to paint three collective portraits of the proceedings at the Paris Peace Conference as an artistic record for the nation. Orpen had spent considerable time in France during the war, being particularly struck by the stoic resilience of the ordinary soldiers. As the negotiations continued, he became increasingly disenchanted by the politicians. He completed two works, portraying the leading figures in the architectural magnificence of Versailles. But when it came to the third, he found he could not continue. In his memoir he reflected: "The 'frocks' had won the war. The 'frocks' had signed the Peace! The Army was forgotten." From this painting, *To the Unknown British Soldier in France*, which shows the entrance to the Hall of Mirrors, he removed all the famous personalities he had already inserted and replaced them with the flag-draped coffin of the Unknown Warrior, flanked by two emaciated, half-dressed soldiers standing beneath a pair of hovering cherubs. Displayed at the Royal Academy in 1923, the painting was a popular success but a critical disaster. Perplexed, the Museum refused to accept it. Five years later, Orpen wrote to the Director General and offered to rework the image, removing the soldiers and the cherubs to leave behind only the image that exists today. The painting would be a gift, he explained, in memory of Earl (Sir Douglas) Haig who had died only a few weeks earlier, "one of the best friends I ever had".

"WE WERE JOURNEYING TO PARIS, NOT MERELY TO LIQUIDATE THE WAR, BUT TO FOUND A NEW ORDER IN EUROPE ... FOR WE WERE BENT ON DOING GREAT PERMANENT AND NOBLE THINGS."

Harold Nicolson, a junior official at the Peace Conference, in his Peacemaking 1919, *published in 1935*

Meanwhile, the peacemakers turned their attention to creating a new and supposedly more peaceful Europe. New countries sprang up in the Balkans – where the war had been sparked – from the now defunct Austro-Hungarian Empire: not only a separate Austria and Hungary, but a new Czechoslovakia and a "Kingdom of the Serbs, Croats and Slovenes" – Yugoslavia. Greece won the defeated Bulgaria's Thracian coast along the Aegean, and Bulgaria lost western border lands to the new Yugoslavia, too. Romania absorbed Transylvania.

An independent Poland was created and given a slice of Germany to provide it with a curious corridor to the Baltic, thus splitting the old Prussian states and isolating East Prussia – to create a serious international hostage to fortune. Danzig (modern Gdansk, in Poland) became an independent Free City, under the auspices of the new League of Nations. The Baltic states of Lithuania, Latvia and Estonia reappeared on the map, along with Finland. Italy was rewarded by northeastern frontiers now expanded to take in the Trentino, South Tyrol and Istria, from Austria.

At the edge of Europe, the Ottoman Empire was broken up, reduced to Anatolian Turkey, though retaining its small strip of mainland Europe beyond Constantinople. She lost control of the sea route from the Straits to the Black Sea to an international regime. The problem of the former Ottoman territories of the Middle East was solved by the device of "mandates", a legal method for transferring control of one country to another under a cloak of League of Nations' responsibility. (Many of these were agreed during Wilson's absence from the conference.) As a method of parcelling out the spoils of victory, mandates seemed to have much to recommend them. After a bitter squabble, the British failed to back the Arab claims for an independent kingdom with Damascus as its capital (*see* Chapter 89), so France came to acquire Syria (including modern Lebanon), while Britain got territory to the east ("Trans-Jordan"), much of Mesopotamia (to be renamed Iraq) and Palestine.

Five treaties emerged from the Paris Peace Conference during 1919–20, including the Treaty of St Germain (with Austria), Neuilly (with Bulgaria), Trianon (with Hungary) and Sèvres (with Ottoman Turkey – later superseded). But the main Treaty of Versailles was with Germany. When the details of the proposed terms were passed to Germany on 7 May, the immediate response was outrage at the nature of this "*diktat*" (as it was called) and a lengthy list of written complaints, most of which were simply ignored.

The final terms of the Treaty of Versailles were judged as harsh. The blame for the war was placed firmly on Germany. The "War Guilt Clause" (Article 231) in particular rankled. How could Germany be the only country to blame for the war, when it was sparked by a Serbian hothead assassinating an Austro-Hungarian archduke? Germans believed that they were being made the scapegoats for everything that had happened since. The detailed articles of the treaty deprived Germany of just over 13 per cent of her 1914 territory and 10 per cent of her population, around 7 million people. Part of East Prussia was handed over to Lithuania, and the ethnic German Sudetenland to Czechoslovakia; even Belgium and neutral Denmark got some of Germany. Germany's former colonies in Africa became mandates, passing to Britain, France and South Africa, while Australia, New Zealand and Japan retained the former German Pacific islands.

Germany was also ordered to pay reparations of around 226 billion gold marks by the Inter-Allied Reparations Commission – equivalent to about £284 billion in today's prices. The German army was reduced to a paltry 100,000 men; the navy

Georges Clemenceau (left), Woodrow Wilson (centre) and David Lloyd George (right) attend the Peace Conference at Versailles. Italy's prime minister, Vittorio Emanuele Orlando, was the fourth major Allied leader present, but in practice it was the other three who dominated proceedings.

to six warships and no submarines; and all military aircraft were to be destroyed. Heavy artillery, gas, tanks and military aircraft were banned. In addition there were to be no German soldiers or military equipment within 30 miles of the east bank of the Rhine. The former Kaiser and some German army officers were held guilty for "war-crimes" – although only about a dozen of them were later tried by the German courts and given light punishments, unlike the Kaiser who got to live out his retirement in the Netherlands.

The Allies also imposed a new form of government on Germany based on proportional representation. It was meant to prevent Germany from being taken over by a dictatorship; instead it would lead to more than 30 competing political parties, none of them big enough to form a government on its own, which did not help to stabilize the fragile new country.

The final act of Versailles was overshadowed by German refusals to sign. The government of Chancellor Philipp Scheidemann resigned: no politician was prepared to put his signature to what was seen as a dishonourable capitulation. Without a government there could be no treaty. The Allies refused to compromise, threatening to start Foch's armies marching again. But Germany's army was now, in Hindenburg's view, too weak to defend the country – renewed war was simply not an option – and Germany was still being blockaded. A new German coalition government was formed, and Germany was given just three weeks to accept the terms of the treaty, take it or leave it. With no alternative, republican Germany's National Assembly voted it through, and two German ministers headed to Versailles,

On 28 June 1919, in a glittering ceremony in the Hall of Mirrors at Versailles, the Treaty of Versailles was finally signed to end the First World War. The next day, the circus broke up as world leaders went home to sell their labours to dubious electorates. Paris rejoiced, *en fête*; in Germany the flags were at half-mast.

Some problems were solved at Versailles. A later generation would have to deal with those that remained – and with those that were *created* on 28 June 1919.

94

A GUN TO SHOOT SEAGULLS
THE END OF THE HIGH SEAS FLEET

NOVEMBER 1918 TO JUNE 1919

When it came to thrashing out the terms of the Versailles Treaty, one issue mattered to Britain above all else: the fate of the German High Seas Fleet. Prior to the war, Anglo-German tensions had revolved around an intense naval rivalry (*see* Chapter 4) and a naval arms race to rival anything seen later in the Cold War. But, despite the dreadnoughts, the war at sea eventually came down to a prolonged attempt by both navies to blockade and strangle the other's economy. By the time admirals of the Allied Armistice Commission and the German navy faced each other across the wardroom table on HMS *Hercules*, on 4 December 1918, the Royal Navy was merely putting the seal on what amounted to the greatest naval victory in its 500-year existence.

The Armistice of 11 November 1918 ordered the surrender of all German U-boats and, under Article XXIII, called for the internment in Allied or neutral ports of 74 named warships, their future to be determined at Versailles. The unvanquished German fleet might have expected better treatment than it received: to be turned over to its principal enemy, and to stagnate for seven months, while its restless, mutinous and hungry crews eked out an existence as virtual floating prisoners.

Only a fortnight after the signing of the Armistice, the 74 warships from the once proud and mighty High Seas Fleet sailed into their enemy's heartland and dropped anchor for the last time. Among the bleak surroundings of Scapa Flow, they resigned themselves to weeks of enervating internment. Technically, they had not surrendered, but few sailors could feel the difference. Slowly the bulk of the 20,000 men who had sailed the ships across the North Sea were returned to Germany until by early December fewer than 4,500 remained. Throughout the winter they remained on board their ships, bored and listless. The terms of the internment barred them from going ashore. Post from home was irregular and censored, even though they were not formal prisoners. But worst of all was the food. All rations came from Germany, which was still locked in the British blockade and enduring another wretched winter of extreme shortages. Supplies were sent twice a month. But the food was of poor quality and very monotonous. To supplement their diet, the men caught fish when they could and killed seagulls for meat. The crew of the destroyer *V125* improvised this gun to shoot at the gulls. A compressed spring inside the metal tube fired a sharp, solid bolt attached to a line that could then be hauled back in, with luck with a bird attached. Ingenious though this may have been, it showed how low the men had sunk, grubbing off the sea to solve their hunger and boredom.

"IT IS UNTHINKABLE TO SURRENDER DEFENCELESS SHIPS
TO THE ENEMY. WE OFFICERS ARE BOUND BY OUR OATH
AND DECISION OF THE ALL HIGHEST TO DESTROY THEM"

Rear Admiral Ludwig von Reuter

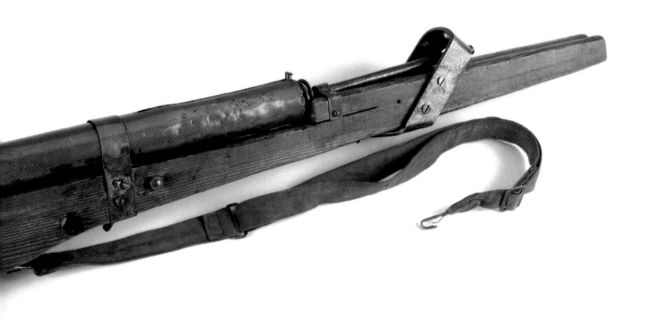

The designated warships – 50 destroyers, along with 8 light cruisers, 11 battleships and 5 battlecruisers – arrived off the Firth of Forth on 21 November, to be met by the massed ranks of the Grand Fleet under Admiral Beatty plus representatives of other navies. Led by the cruiser HMS *Cardiff*, two great lines of 44 battleships turned inwards to escort their prisoners north to internment at Scapa Flow. The massive British encirclement was not just a warning. It was also a victory parade at sea, intended to overawe the Germans with an overwhelming demonstration of naval power. At 03.57, Beatty ordered the German flag to be hauled down and not to be hoisted again.

Within days, the German fleet was in internment at Scapa Flow. For the next seven months the German ships rotted at anchor, their crew numbers reduced in December to around 4,500. Rear Admiral Ludwig von Reuter aboard the flagship *Friedrich der Grosse* had major problems. Despite his attempts to preserve the honour of the German navy he found his task humiliating. His sailors were angry at the internment, and at being confined on board their ships. Unlike the British, who lived on board when in port, the Germans had spent most of the war in comfortable naval barracks ashore. Instead, their food and drink was now curtailed and their conditions spartan. They also felt, with some justification, that they should have been interned in a neutral port and allowed ashore. The sailors made their point to their superiors by marching up and down all night on the deck above their admiral's cabin. A sleepless Reuter transferred his flag to the cruiser *Emden*, and had some troublemakers sent back to Germany. But officers increasingly found it difficult to maintain discipline. Many of the sailors had been involved in the Kiel mutinies of early November and were Bolshevik sympathizers. Sailors' councils were formed to be consulted and agree any orders from officers. Only the hope that the fleet would be allowed home after the peace talks kept the once proud German navy together.

As spring turned to summer, the talking at Versailles dragged on, and tensions rose. The fate of the German fleet was a potentially explosive issue. The British wanted to keep as many of the German ships as possible. The French, Italians and Americans wanted as many as they could get, too, but the British were notably wary of bolstering French naval power to potentially competitive levels. The Germans, however, were determined that the Allies would not get their hands on any of their ships. Meanwhile at Scapa, in June 1919, the ships' manpower was reduced further to mere skeleton crews: 75 per battlecruiser, 60 per battleship, 30 per cruiser and the bare minimum for the destroyers.

The crucial moment came when the news arrived that the German government was unwilling to sign the Versailles Treaty by the advertised deadline of 21 June: should the peace talks not succeed, then a state of war would break out again. What Rear Admiral Reuter did not know was that Germany had been granted an extension, and the signing was postponed to 28 June. Believing a crisis beckoned, Reuter resolved to scuttle his entire fleet rather than let the British seize it.

On the morning of 21 June, the British guardships of the 1st Battle Squadron left for exercises. Reuter, believing Germany's shame was imminent, signalled: "Paragraph eleven. Confirm" – the code for immediate scuttle. Below decks the Germans opened seacocks, cooling inlets and condensers. Bulkheads were torn down; watertight doors were jammed open. Crucial damage control equipment was sabotaged. Sea water flooded in, the ships began to settle and the skeleton crews took to the boats.

"AT DUSK AS THE SKY REDDENED OVER THE SCOTTISH HILLS, THE BUGLERS OF THE BRITISH FLEET SOUNDED THE CALL 'SUNSET', THE ENSIGNS OF THE IMPERIAL GERMAN NAVY FLUTTERED SLOWLY DOWN FOR THE LAST TIME. AND DARKNESS CLOSED LIKE A CURTAIN ON THE FINAL ACT OF THIS MIGHTY DRAMA AT SEA."

Rear Admiral W.S. Chalmers, on the German fleet steaming into captivity.

The principal witnesses to this extraordinary, unforgettable event were schoolchildren from Stromness on a boat trip. One of them, James Taylor, later wrote how "Suddenly without any warning and almost simultaneously these huge vessels began to list over to port or starboard." Another recalled "the marvellous display as the German ships sank all around us. In a way it was a very sad sight to see all these men getting into their boats, you really wondered what would happen to them. They had lost all their possessions ... The whole thing was done in such a peaceful way."

The only way to stop the ships from sinking was to tow them ashore. However, the only British warships present were the destroyers *Vespa* and *Vega* plus some auxiliary trawlers. They frantically signalled the 1st Battle Squadron to return at full speed. But, even as they watched, *Friedrich der Grösse* sank at noon, followed by the *Bayern*. Boatloads of German sailors could be seen landing on the islands around Scapa.

By 2 p.m. the British 1st Battle Squadron had arrived, in a desperate attempt to stop the débâcle. Armed Marines boarded the German ships, and nine Germans were shot dead, the last deaths of the war. The British managed to beach the *Baden* and the cruisers *Nürnberg*, *Emden* and *Frankfurt*. At 5 p.m. the last ship, the *Hindenburg,* went under. Over 400,000 tons of modern warships went beneath the waves, the largest ever loss of shipping in a single day.

Fifty-two German ships were sunk that day – out of sight until an intrepid scrap-metal dealer, Ernest Cox, salvaged most of them during the next decade and made himself rich. The few beached survivors, including destroyer *V125*, were later distributed among the Allied navies. In public the British professed themselves outraged by what they claimed was an act of war and a flagrant breach of the Armistice. The German crews were rounded up and thrown into PoW camps. However, a political problem had also gone away. Admiral Wemyss wrote: "I look upon this as a real blessing. It disposes of the thorny question of the distribution of the German ships."

The First World War at sea was finally over.

A deceptively tranquil scene shows the interned German High Seas Fleet, moored in the Orkney Islands setting of Scapa Flow. The quiet was rudely interrupted by Admiral von Reuter's decision to scuttle his ships en masse *to prevent them falling into enemy hands.*

95

A NEW STAMP FOR A NEW COUNTRY
THE BIRTH OF THE LEAGUE OF NATIONS

Poland has had a long and chequered history. From a medieval commonwealth with Lithuania, to being carved up between Imperial Russia, Prussia and finally the Austrian Habsburgs in 1795, Poland's fortunes, and identity, have ebbed and flowed. After centuries of rule by her neighbours, a new independent Poland was just one of the countries brought into existence from the dismantled German, Austrian, Ottoman (and Russian) empires by the Paris Peace Conference (*see* Chapter 93). For their security they looked to another invention from the Paris deliberations and embraced in the Treaty of Versailles: the League of Nations.

Postage stamps are a symbol of national identity. Only *real* countries need stamps. A few weeks into the Arab Revolt, while still in Egypt, T.E. Lawrence designed a set of stamps for Sherif Hussein to confirm and declare the independence of the Hejaz. Lawrence was determined that the look and appearance of the stamps would show they were "an entirely new and independent national issue which had not moulded itself on that of any other Government". They were a statement of arrival, a new badge for a new nation. This "20 marka" postage stamp is from the issue of 1921, which performed the same role for Poland. Before the war, the territory of modern Poland had been split, with part being German, most Russian and the rest Austro-Hungarian. The border between the Central Powers and Russia ran down the middle. For three years, fighting swept over these territories, with ethnic Poles serving on both sides. By 1917, a distinct Polish nation had begun to emerge, strengthened by a specific reference to an independent Poland in President Wilson's Fourteen Points. Fighting between Poland and her neighbours continued long after the war, and it was not until 1921 that the country's borders achieved some stability. It had been a long, tiring struggle to bring Poland back to life. In a neat, understated way, the intensity of this effort was reflected in this stamp. A man, who has cast off his sword, sows the seeds of peace under a rainbow that offers the promise of calm after the storm.

The last of Wilson's Fourteen Points (*see* Chapter 82) had called for the establishment of "a general association of nations" to be formed "for the purpose of affording mutual guarantees of political independence and territorial integrity to great and small states alike". The League had two basic aims: the first was to prevent war by collective action, disarmament and settling international disputes through negotiation and arbitration by the League's Council, and if that failed, to impose economic, then military, sanctions. The second was to promote international

> "IT [A LEAGUE OF NATIONS] WILL ONLY RESULT IN FAILURE … IT WILL PUT A VERY STRONG LEVER INTO THE HANDS OF THE WELL-MEANING IDEALISTS WHO ARE TO BE FOUND IN ALMOST EVERY GOVERNMENT, WHO DEPRECATE EXPENDITURE ON ARMAMENTS"

Sir Maurice Hankey, Secretary to the Cabinet, 1919

cooperation in economic, social and legal affairs such as labour conditions, arms trading, global health and protection of minorities.

It was all easier said than done. These typically ambitious Wilsonian objectives depended on the Great Powers acting as enforcement agents because, crucially, the League lacked any hard power – no armed forces or police to serve in its name and impose its will. Not for nothing had the 17th-century philosopher Thomas Hobbes pointed out that "covenants without swords are but words and of no strength to secure a man at all". Nevertheless, ever since Immanuel Kant's *Perpetual Peace* of 1795, calling for a "league of nations" that would control conflict and establish a peaceful world community, the idea had attracted many. In 1919, the founders of the League of Nations were determined to build a better world and desperate to avoid a repetition of the horrors of the Great War – a goal reflected in the League's Covenant, which referred to "open, just and honourable relations between nations, by the firm establishment of the understandings of international law as the actual rule of conduct among Governments, and by the maintenance of justice and a scrupulous respect for all treaty obligations in the dealings of organised peoples with one another".

The League originally consisted of 42 countries, 26 of which were non-European. At its largest, 57 countries were members. But there were three major absentees at the start: Germany, which was at first not allowed to join; Bolshevik Russia, which refused to join; and the country whose president had actually proposed the birth of the League – the United States. Germany's absence, as a defeated power, was initially no problem for the organization, and Russia was absorbed in her post-revolutionary civil war. Both countries were later admitted. But the American absence was a serious setback.

The US failure to join the League was part politics, part bad luck and partly reflective of how Americans viewed themselves. Many Americans now wanted to extricate themselves from Europe. They were only too conscious of the war's casualties, small though they were compared with Europe's dreadful losses. Isolationism was resurgent, and there was fear that a League would embroil the country in future conflicts. There were worries that the League would interfere with the ability to pursue trade and commerce freely, as well as a lingering suspicion of kow-towing to the Old World empires of Britain and France. Wilson strenuously sought to counter these views, but (literally) a stroke of bad luck intervened. While travelling by train on his hectic nationwide tour to sell the Treaty of Versailles and the League, he suffered a stroke on 2 October 1919. He was then unable to influence the national debate.

In Washington, the politics typified the perpetual struggle between the White House and Congress over the control of foreign policy. Republican opposition to the terms of the treaty and the Covenant's Articles, which defined the League, was led by the powerful Henry Cabot Lodge, Republican Senate Leader and Chairman of the Foreign Relations Committee. Over summer and autumn 1919 Wilson refused to compromise, urging Congressional Democrats to vote down Republican changes. In November 1919, the Senate rejected both Lodge's amended treaty and the full treaty. In March 1920, the now bedridden president tried to get it through again – and met another Senate defeat, by 49 votes to 35.

The nail in the coffin was the looming presidential election in 1920, on the back of an economy that was beginning to slide into recession. Wilson was too ill to stand, and while his Democratic replacement backed the League, the Republican candidate, Warren G. Harding, espoused an anti-League "return to normalcy" – and was elected

"THE MEMBERS OF THE LEAGUE UNDERTAKE TO RESPECT AND PRESERVE AS AGAINST EXTERNAL AGGRESSION THE TERRITORIAL INTEGRITY AND EXISTING POLITICAL INDEPENDENCE OF ALL MEMBERS OF THE LEAGUE."

From Article X, Covenant of the League of Nations, 1919

in a landslide. It effectively killed the issue. The United States went into her own version of "splendid isolation".

Thus, even before its first meeting of delegates in November 1920, the League of Nations had suffered what turned out to be a crippling handicap. Without US membership and with Britain and France too impoverished by the war – militarily, economically and spiritually – to provide firm leadership, the organization was compromised from the start. There were successes, such as the plebiscite that divided Silesia between Poland and Germany, and the arbitrations – between Sweden and Finland over the Aaland Islands in 1921, with Turkey over her claim to Iraqi Mosul in 1924, and in the 1934 war between Colombia and Peru. And the League used the power of moral condemnation in 1925 to stop the Greeks invading Bulgaria.

But the League could not stop wars and grabs by determined belligerents, especially if they were large states. It was ineffective regarding Poland's invasion of western Russia in 1920 or Greece's ill-fated attempt to seize Western Anatolia the same year, which ended with the sack of Smyrna (Izmir) in 1922 and the birth of Atatürk's new Turkey. And in German eyes, since the League was created by the Treaty of Versailles, and in turn was supposed to uphold the treaty, the body remained suspect.

In 1933, the weakness of the League in an era of resurgent nationalism and arms races was clearly demonstrated when, faced with comprehensive condemnation of her invasion of Manchuria, Japan simply walked out, followed by Germany. By 1935 Mussolini's invasion of Abyssinia could only provoke toothless sanctions, and in 1937 Italy left, in the wake of Germany and Spain's departure. Hitler's final seizure of Czechoslovakia and onslaught on Poland in 1939, along with the Soviet Union's invasion of Finland, finally exposed the League's impotence in the face of unabashed aggression.

The League was founded as a response to a world war. It closed its doors for ever in 1946 having failed in its primary purpose: to prevent another one.

Delegates at the inaugural session of the League of Nations, in Geneva, turn to the camera for a photo opportunity (15 November 1920). At this stage, 42 nations had ratified their membership, with the notable – and permanent – exception of the United States. Deeply flawed though the international body was, it provided lessons for the future.

96

THE OLD KAISER'S CROWN
GERMANY IN TURMOIL

NOVEMBER 1918 TO MARCH 1919

The Armistice saved the German army from having to fight a last-ditch battle on Germany's borders to defend the homeland. But while a hostile invasion from the Allies was averted, that did not mean that there would be no foreign soldiers on German soil. It was a condition of the Armistice that the German military should vacate miles of German land not only west of the Rhine, but also east of it, so that Allied contingents could enter and established occupation zones. Cold and hungry Rhinelanders watched with astonishment as the glossy horses and gleaming guns of the BEF's 29th Division clattered across the Cologne Bridge in the first week of December 1918 to set up the "British Army of the Rhine".

> British troops were to remain in possession of Cologne for over ten years. It was, and remains, one of Germany's most important cities. A century-old centre for commerce and trade, goods flowed through it, via its major river port but also on the railway. By the 1890s, Cologne's original central station was bursting at the seams and a new *Hauptbahnhof* was built, fronted by a grand new facade and imposing ticket hall. Kaiser Wilhelm II even had his own separate waiting room, adorned with the symbols of Hohenzollern majesty, including a throne. Being a significant link in Cologne's chain of communications, the station was controlled by the British occupying forces, one of whom, Captain A.H. Cooper, was involved in overseeing its administration. He set up his office in the former Royal Waiting Room. Conscious of the revolutionary tides that were sweeping over Germany, Cooper, as he later explained, carefully removed this large, imposing mahogany crown from the canopy over Wilhelm's throne only just in time: hours later, a German gang arrived to strip the room of "all emblems of the old Imperial regime". It was all change in the new Germany.

The British occupied an area roughly between Düsseldorf and Siegburg; to the south, around Koblenz, was the American zone, and to their south the French were based around Mainz. While everyday administration was still in the hands of local authorities, the Allied presence imposed an overarching order. Elsewhere in Germany, things were taking a very different course.

In the febrile atmosphere leading up to the Armistice, the Social Democratic Party (*Sozialdemokratische Partei Deutschlands*, or SPD), which led the *Reichstag*, and the revolutionaries outside it both manoeuvred for advantage. Gustav Noske, a Social Democrat, headed for Kiel to try and harness the sailors' revolt to the Social Democrat cause. But as mass protests and strikes swept the country, mutinous sailors

"ONLY ONE WEEK AGO, THERE WAS STILL A MILITARY AND CIVIL ADMINISTRATION SO DEEPLY ROOTED THAT IT SEEMED TO HAVE SECURED ITS DOMINION BEYOND THE CHANGE OF TIMES ... YESTERDAY AFTERNOON IT WAS ALL GONE."

Berliner Tageblatt (*newspaper*), *10 November 1918*

were heading home, spreading revolution as they scattered. Around 3,000 went to Berlin to join the Bolshevik-inspired revolutionaries, taking over the Imperial Palace and Stables, and calling themselves "the People's Naval Division". As the Kaiser and his last chancellor fell on 9 November, the SPD in the *Reichstag* tried to head off the radical Left by immediately announcing the foundation of a new German republic, before rapturous crowds.

Friedrich Ebert, the SPD leader, now faced the unenviable task of securing the Armistice, keeping order on the streets and trying to keep the country running as the soldiers came home in their millions. The SPD were mostly moderate socialists, committed to Parliamentary rule. To their left were the Independent Socialists

(USPD), many of whom began to capitalize on the unrest on the streets; some even seized the Berlin police HQ, their leader making himself police chief. In Bavaria, Independent Socialists under Kurt Eisner had effected a coup (though were later to hold elections). Even further to the left were the revolutionary Marxists of the Spartacist League, who drew their support from the slums of Berlin's eastern quarters and demanded nothing less than a full-blown Bolshevik revolution.

The army's generals had stood back from propping up the Kaiser with force. But now, with the streets in ferment, the army intervened. Troops loyal to the government surrounded the Chancellery and arrested prominent Independent Socialists and revolutionaries. Shots were fired and soldiers opened fire on a Spartacist demonstration, killing 16. By 11 December 1918 no fewer than nine army divisions had returned to Berlin, and a civil war appeared inevitable – except that most of the soldiers voted with their feet and deserted to get home for Christmas.

The revolutionary People's Naval Division now flexed its muscle by demanding money to disband and marched to the Chancellery to blockade the building. Ebert begged the army's High Command for loyal troops, and a regiment of Guards entered Berlin, blocked the sailors' retreat and an armed standoff ensued. Ebert now panicked and asked the army leadership to withdraw. But General Groener refused: "[We] are determined to hold to the plan of liquidation of the Naval Division, and we shall see to it that it is carried out."

At 7.40 a.m. on Christmas Eve 1918 the army opened fire, blasting the naval mutineers and seized the Imperial Palace and Stables. The sailors raised a white flag. The army then made a fatal mistake by agreeing to the truce, and thousands of protesters sympathetic to the rebels poured onto the streets. Surrounded by civilians, the troops held their fire and army commanders ordered a retreat. Ebert and the SPD government were appalled at the loss of control; conversely, the Spartacists now saw their chance for outright revolution before new elections (to be held in January could

Pro-government forces on the streets of Berlin, the day after the Kaiser abdicated (10 November 1918), anticipating trouble. A fragile power-sharing Cabinet of the SPD and USPD soon fractured, and by December the revolutionary Spartacists and their allies were strong enough to mount a challenge on the streets. Brute force would play a large role in determining events.

give Ebert a democratic mandate. At the end of 1918, the extreme Left formed the German Communist Party (*Kommunistische Partei Deutschlands*, or KPD) and prepared for revolution.

Matters came to a head when the militants and trade unions called a general strike, for 5 January 1919. However, they had not reckoned on the SPD's new enforcers, the *Freikorps*. These were military veterans, hand-picked for their reliability, many of whom had served as stormtroopers on the Western Front but who were now estranged from civilian life and smarting from Germany's defeat. The *Freikorps* phenomenon, with its deep historical roots as a volunteer militia, came to the fore as ex-soldiers banded together, with the army's tacit support, to take the law into their own hands. They were well armed and determined to restore order.

By 6 January 1919, following government attempts to dislodge the USPD police chief, the political situation was spiralling out of control in Berlin with huge protests and a growing expectancy of full-scale revolution. But now the *Freikorps* mobilized. On 11 January, Major Franz von Stephani of the Potsdam *Freikorps* called on the Spartacists to surrender. They refused and opened fire. The superior firepower of the ex-regulars then battered the rebels with artillery, mortars and machine guns. Spartacists who surrendered were executed.

The next day – led by Noske himself, now Defence Minister – other *Freikorps* units moved in to assault the rebel stronghold in the police headquarters. No quarter was given as the *Freikorps* stormed the building. On 13 January, the government unleashed its full repertoire of measures: massive searches, roadblocks, the breaking up of protest meetings by force, a civilian curfew, street shootings and the arrest of suspected revolutionaries. The two Spartacist leaders Karl Liebknecht and Rosa Luxemburg were captured and executed out of hand, achieving lasting fame as revolutionary martyrs. By 15 January the general strike was called off and the Bolshevik-Spartacist revolution collapsed.

The promised elections went ahead, on 19 January, and the SPD won with 40 per cent of the vote. A new National Assembly gathered at Weimar, well away from the revolutionary ferment of Berlin. But uprisings continued to flare up across the country, though the *Freikorps* was there to crush each insurgency.

In March 1919, the Spartacists once again tried to seize control, calling for another general strike. *Freikorps* units entered Berlin on 4 March, along with infantry and even a tank, and for a week Berlin was rocked by civil war. The People's Naval Division joined the demonstrators, to be chased into the suburb of Lichtenberg, where 10,000 armed revolutionaries barricaded themselves in for the final showdown. The government issued the notorious order: "Any individual bearing arms against government troops will be summarily shot", and for the next four days the *Freikorps* ran riot in the barricaded slum tenements of East Berlin, with atrocities all round. The Spartacists and rebel sailors were crushed. The casualties were high, but one-sided: up to 1,500 revolutionaries and civilians were dead and roughly 12,000 wounded. The *Freikorps*' losses were negligible. But the results were profound.

The general picture of Germany's politics for the "Weimar Era" was emerging. In the middle stood a fragile democracy, with a myriad of competing parties, whose leaders were unable to prevent the humiliation of the Treaty of Versailles later that year; to the left stood the determined KPD, with which the USPD merged in 1920; to the right stood equally determined ultra-nationalists, the *Freikorps* – and the new German Workers' Party. It would become better known by a later, shorthand name: the Nazi Party.

97

AUGUSTUS AGAR'S BOAT
THE ALLIES VERSUS THE BOLSHEVIKS

1918 TO 1920

The Bolsheviks' unilateral ceasefire in winter 1917, followed by the humiliating Treaty of Brest-Litovsk to which the Germans subjected Russia in March 1918 (*see* Chapters 67 and 82), threw the Western Allies into confusion. Their instincts, mostly, were to help topple the upstart Bolshevik regime and aid the Tsarist ("White Russian") and other local "Green" counter-revolutionary peasant forces, with the aim of restoring Russia as a fighting ally; at the very least, they wanted to secure the war supplies they had sent for the Tsar's army. After the Armistice, they were more interested in destabilizing a regime whose revolutionary ideology was proving too attractive to the discontented across Europe, and already causing havoc in the defeated Central Powers, notably Germany (*see* Chapter 96). In the end, 14 Allied nations sent troops into Russia, including Britain.

Late in 1918, Lieutenant Augustus Agar RN was asked by "C", the head of Britain's Secret Intelligence Service, to undertake a dangerous and clandestine mission in the Baltic as part of the Allied intervention in the Russian Civil War. Secretly, Agar was to take two fast, shallow draught Coastal Motor Boats (CMBs) and from a covert base in newly independent Finland, only 13 miles from Petrograd, he was to land and recover British agents working deep under cover inside Bolshevik Russia. Agar was a career naval officer who had learned independent thought and initiative. He became deeply concerned at the sight of defenceless White Russian soldiers inside the fortress of Krasnya Gorka being shelled by Red Russian warships. Agar decided to act. Armed with an unofficially obtained torpedo, on the night of 17 June 1919 he took this boat, *Coastal Motor Boat 4*, and under cover of darkness penetrated the Bolshevik destroyer screen surrounding the Russian cruiser *Oleg*. Throwing caution to the wind, Agar launched his strike, then raced away as fast as possible. All the Russians guns immediately leapt into action. But it was too late. The torpedo hit home and the *Oleg* exploded. Turning and twisting, Agar escaped unscathed and returned in triumph to his secret headquarters. It had been an intrepid and audacious act, in keeping with the finest traditions of the Royal Navy. But it was part of a secret war. Agar's deeds could not at first be publicly acknowledged. Instead, he simply became known as "the mystery VC".

Murmansk, on the Barents Sea, had been built as an ice-free port to accept (mainly British) supplies during the war, and an 800-mile railway connected it with the interior. Over 160,000 tons of war stores lay on the docks by mid-1918 and the British naval squadron based there could do little to prevent the Bolsheviks removing the *matériel*, without payment, to Moscow, which Lenin had proclaimed as Russia's new capital. In June 1918, British, French and US forces – along with Canadians, Italians and Serbs – landed at Murmansk, and in August at Archangel, on the White Sea inlet. Apart from trying to secure the *matériel*, a rather more strategic goal was to send forces south to try and link up with elements of the Czech Legion, considered the most powerful Allied asset in the country (*see below*). The British force headed south by rail to check the line and encountered a train-load of Red Guards heading north. Fighting broke out and soon British, American and French contingents were digging in to protect the ports, with the cooperation of local anti-Bolshevik groups, against the encircling Reds. An American-led advance south along the River Dvina ran into heavy fighting until the winter of 1918–19 forced both sides into a series of isolated skirmishes in sub-zero temperatures. With the spring of 1919 came the decision to withdraw, and by October 1919 the last of the Allied forces left Archangel, to be followed by the evacuation of Murmansk.

Meanwhile, the Royal Navy attempted to support the firmly anti-Bolshevik forces of the soon to be independent Baltic states of Latvia, Lithuania and Estonia, by way of a Baltic blockade that encompassed the Russian naval base at Kronstadt, near Petrograd. It was conducted by the British Baltic squadron (1st Light Cruiser Squadron), commanded by Rear Admiral Sir Walter Cowan, and used Coastal Motor Boats (CMBs) – some weeks after Lieutenant Agar's unofficial action had shown the way – to torpedo several Russian warships in Kronstadt's harbour, sinking a cruiser and damaging two battleships.

The first act of Allied intervention was, however, in the Far East, when in December 1917 Japanese troops landed, sensing an opportunity to move into eastern Russia and control Vladivostok – to the initial alarm of the United States. There were at least half a million tons of Allied war supplies lying on the dockside and – initially – no Bolsheviks in sight. Also heading towards Vladivostok from the west, by May 1918, were as many as 60,000 men of the so-called "Czech Legion" – Czech and Slovak nationalists, who had been fighting with the Russian Imperial Army. When Red Guards attempted to disarm them, at the behest of the Germans in the aftermath of Brest-Litovsk, a battle ensued, and the legion began an extraordinary fighting trek eastwards along the Trans-Siberian Railway, which it eventually controlled east of the Volga.

With the aim of evacuating the legion, along with Austro-Hungarian PoWs in Siberia whose nationalist tendencies made them potential Allied recruits, a multinational force including 7,000 Americans landed at Vladivostok in August 1918. By September 1918 the Czechs, strung out along the railway corridor, had steamrollered in their armoured trains as far as Lake Baikal, pausing to fight ad-hoc naval actions there against Bolshevik patrol boats, and even capturing a hoard of imperial gold. They reached Vladivostok, but after the Armistice, Czechoslovakia's president ordered those remaining Czechs to support (with the British and French) the White Russian campaign led by Admiral Alexander Kolchak in Siberia.

American forces were more cautious, though they helped the Czechs guard the Trans-Siberian Railway, which they did for much of 1919. The British contingent

"EVERYBODY THEN OPENED FIRE ON ME. WE WERE GOING FULL SPEED (25 KNOTS). 2 BIG SHELLS MISSED OUR STERN BY 5 TO 10 YARDS. SPRAY AND SEA COMING OVER, DRENCHING US TO THE SKIN BUT WE WERE MERRY AND BRIGHT AND GAVE 3 CHEERS THOUGH WE COULD HARDLY HEAR EACH OTHER."

Lieutenant Augustus Agar VC RN, diary entry for 17 June 1919

in Siberia, after an initial battle with Red Guards, moved west to Omsk for the winter of 1918–19. There they supported Kolchak, who had taken over the "Supreme Leadership" of the anti-Bolsheviks and had set up a White Russian government in Irkutsk. All civil wars tend to be merciless, but Kolchak's rule specialized in a brutal oppression, one of his orders reading: "Those villages whose population meets troops with arms, burn down the villages and shoot the adult males without exception. If hostages are taken in cases of resistance to government troops, shoot the hostages without mercy." Not surprisingly, his methods drove the infuriated peasantry of Siberia into the Bolsheviks' camp.

In December 1918, the British and French began to back the equally unsavoury White General Anton Denikin in southern Russia and the Crimea, despite his series of pogroms based on a conviction that the Bolsheviks were "the evil force which lives in the hearts of Jew-Communists". British and French ships supported actions by Denikin and General Peter Wrangel along the Black Sea coast from 1919, but in 1920 were having to evacuate defeated White Russians from the region.

The Western Allies, and even the Germans postwar, continued to try and undermine the Bolshevik regime. Germans left in Finland helped defend that country, while the French supported newly independent Poland in her 1919–21 war with Russia. But Allied policy regarding the Bolsheviks, as shown during the Paris Peace Conference, was inconsistent, and their forces in Russia were never big enough to sway the outcome; their main support was supplying arms and ammunition to Kolchak

A young Bolshevik volunteer, pictured c.1919, is armed for action with hand grenades and a bolt-action rifle. A mixture of idealism, terror, superior organization and sheer numbers came together to create, in the Red Army, a force coherent enough to see off the challenges of White Russian armies, Allied intervention forces and other opponents.

and the other Whites. But the White forces were vastly outnumbered by the millions of soldiers in Trotsky's new and potent Red Army, who advanced, picking off and defeating their rivals piecemeal, from the invading Poles at the gates of Petrograd to the Don Cossacks of the south.

By the end of 1919 the Bolsheviks were even advancing east against Vladivostok, and their opponents were falling apart from desertion, lack of food, typhus and a general collapse of hope and morale. By 1920 most of the Allies in Siberia had left, including the last of the Czech Legion, having swapped its gold for a truce with the Bolsheviks. On 25 October 1922, Vladivostok fell to the Red Army – and the last anti-Bolshevik government was extinguished.

The Russian Civil War had been a bloody affair. But it did have a clear result: Communist Russia – the Soviet Union. The Allies' failure to strangle it at birth would have dramatic consequences for the course of the 20th century.

98

THE FAMOUS NÉRY GUN
THE CREATION OF THE IMPERIAL
WAR MUSEUM

1917 TO 1920

In 1914, the widespread recruitment of "Kitchener volunteers" and the Pals battalions in particular (*see* Chapters 8 and 9) created direct connections between many British villages, towns and cities and the events of the war. The legacy of that connection continues to this day. That early flood of volunteers reflected the widespread civic pride felt by communities large and small, as their men marched off to war. Come 1916, as the casualties among these volunteers on the Somme sank in, individual communities became increasingly conscious of the sacrifices that were being made.

The breadth and depth of this feeling could not be compared to Britain's colonial wars, even one as large as the Anglo-Boer War. It was like no event that people had experienced before. Its scale and its nature needed to be made sense of. A widespread desire built up to make sure that the men of this unprecedented war, and the dead in particular, be remembered, and that their actions be recorded and understood for generations to come.

The direct result was the establishment of the Imperial War Museum in London.

As a mist-filled dawn broke on 1 September 1914, from positions beyond the French village of Néry, the British 1st Cavalry Brigade suddenly came under intense and accurate German fire. Three 13-pounder field guns of "L" Battery, Royal Horse Artillery, turned to engage the invisible enemy, but two were instantly knocked out. The third continued to fire. Its officer, Captain Bradbury, was mortally wounded, but Sergeant Nelson carried on working the gun. Soon Battery Sergeant Major Dorrell arrived, and between them they kept shooting until all the shells had gone. As the mist cleared, an infantry counterattack brought the action to an end. "The Affair at Néry" became one of the most celebrated episodes of the opening months of the war. The British were outnumbered and overwhelmed, but pluck and tenacity won out. The Germans were beaten, and three men received the Victoria Cross. Out of the battery's six guns, only this one was fit to be driven away. It was returned to Britain, and in 1919 the famous "Néry gun" was among the first artillery pieces to arrive at the Imperial War Museum. It became one of the focal points of the displays in the Museum's first exhibition at the Crystal Palace. Every year on 1 September a large laurel wreath was reverently placed on the gun to commemorate the battery's gallant stand and heavy losses, a practice that continued until the 1950s. Battle-scarred and broken, the gun's physical presence provides a tangible, evocative link with the terror of that day. A hundred years on, it remains one of most powerful objects in the Museum's collection.

"TO US IT STANDS, NOT FOR A GROUP OF TROPHIES WON FROM A BEATEN ENEMY, NOT FOR THE SYMBOL OF THE PRIDE OF VICTORY, BUT AS AN EMBODIMENT AND A LASTING MEMORIAL OF COMMON EFFORT AND COMMON SACRIFICE"

King George V, at the opening of the first Imperial War Museum at the Crystal Palace, South London, 9 June 1920

A full-size model of an 18-inch naval gun is carefully hoisted into position in the Naval Gallery of the Imperial War Museum's first venue, the Crystal Palace, prior to its opening in 1920. That a national museum was felt necessary even before the war concluded says much about the contemporary sense of the Great War's unprecedented nature.

In March 1917, Sir Alfred Mond MP outlined to the Cabinet an ambitious plan to establish a National War Museum. The museum would be broad-based and reflect all levels of society. It would not just be about leading figures, or political or military events, but would cut across class boundaries to ensure the widest possible experience was recorded. It would be about everyone's war.

For Lloyd George, this was an attractive proposition. Heavy casualties, air raids, food shortages and conscription were all straining the nation. The cost of the war seemed high; the return felt low. The new prime minister saw an opportunity to lift morale. The sacrifices of ordinary people would be more tolerable if they were publicly recognized. This new national institution could ensure that future generations understood what the men and women had gone through on their behalf, and reassure contemporaries that their efforts would not be overlooked or forgotten.

Events moved quickly. A steering committee, chaired by Mond, was soon established, with the curator of the Tower Armouries, Charles ffoulkes, appointed Museum Secretary and the Slade Professor of Art at Cambridge, Sir Martin Conway, as Director General. A series of sub-committees were formed to record the work being undertaken by women (*see* Chapters 29 and 30), and the role of the Dominions and of the air services. Charles ffoulkes appealed directly to fighting units for trophies (*see* Chapter 26) and was keen to ensure there would be much in the Museum's eventual displays that old soldiers would recognize. To highlight the efforts of individuals, he appealed in newspapers like the *Daily Mail* for details of soldiers' services to be sent to the Museum together with photographs. A steady stream of responses began to flow in.

A Canadian officer, Major Henry Beckles Willson, was appointed the Museum's field agent. Beckles Willson believed that the collections should reflect the detail of battle and the involvement of ordinary soldiers at ground level. From late spring 1917, he set about his task with great enthusiasm and energy, meeting both soldiers and French civilians, and observing and collecting wherever he could (*see* Chapter 66).

Inevitably, much of the first material he acquired related to the Somme, including the steel helmet worn by Private William Short VC (*see* Chapter 48).

While these initiatives were underway, ffoulkes, Conway and Mond also began to think in more detail about what role the new Museum should fulfil. All wanted to see the Museum take on a more overt role as a national memorial. But the Cabinet was not impressed, remaining sceptical about the suitability of a museum to act as a memorial. They agreed only to establish a ministerial committee under Lord Crawford to examine the proposals in greater depth.

The following month another important development took place. The Dominions sub-committee suggested that, as so many soldiers from Canada, Australia, New Zealand and South Africa were fighting with the British armies, it should not be a National War Museum, but an Imperial War Museum. This apparently small change, adopted in January 1918, ultimately amounted to a fundamental recasting of the Museum's purpose, giving it a very special status. Instead of being concerned solely with Britain and Ireland, the new Imperial War Museum would concern itself equally with the wider contribution of the other nations of the British Empire (*see* Chapter 69), embracing a wider common wealth (in the literal sense) of history.

A week before the great crisis of the German spring offensives began in March 1918, Lord Crawford's committee finally delivered its verdict. It did not agree with the idea that the Museum should also be a national memorial, which naturally disappointed the Museum. But Conway clung to the hope that the Cabinet might still come round. As it was, soon the people themselves made their voices heard and answered the questions of how, and where, the nation should remember its dead: a temporary Cenotaph in Whitehall soon gave way to a permanent structure and the Tomb of the Unknown Warrior allowed over a million pilgrims to pay their respects within a week and lay their ghosts to rest (*see* Chapter 100).

So quickly and firmly were the Cenotaph and the Unknown Warrior established as the rightful symbols for the national memory of the "Great War", that no possibility remained of this function being carried out by the Imperial War Museum. Instead, the Museum turned to fulfilling the two key tasks that only it could undertake: creating a place of learning and scholarship, where the war could be studied and more closely understood; and, above all, providing a living exhibition, constantly reconfigured to record and interpret for changing generations the events and experiences that had made the First World War a unique global event.

Early in 1920 it was agreed that the Museum's first galleries would open in the Crystal Palace, Sir Joseph Paxton's celebrated glass and cast-iron exhibition hall then in Sydenham, South London, though originally adorning Hyde Park for the Great Exhibition of 1851. Displays were put together in just six weeks; over 400 tons of material were installed, from a collection already estimated at more than 136,000 items. Prominent among them was "Mother", the first 9.2-inch howitzer (*see* Chapter 35), and the naval gun that fired the first British shell of the war (*see* Chapter 10).

Initial visitor numbers were high – 2.5 million in the first year. But what did the future hold? What role would the Museum continue to play as the generation of 1914–18 faded away? King George V gave some insight, when he opened the Museum on 9 June 1920. He explained that the museum was not about "trophies won from a beaten enemy", nor about "the pride of victory", but rather "a lasting memorial of common effort and common sacrifice" and a record of the impact of war upon ordinary people's lives. And so it continues to be.

99

GUNNER MILLER'S CROSS
WAR GRAVES & REMEMBRANCE

FROM 1918

After the First World War, something like a collective case of Post-Traumatic Stress Disorder set in. The realization that something enormous had happened overwhelmed the combatant countries. The sheer magnitude of loss sank in as millions of individual deaths combined to become huge, almost incomprehensible, numbers. Individual families grieved over their sons, brothers, husbands and fathers; factories, schools, colleges, villages, towns – all kinds of communities – tallied up their losses. The results were unprecedented manifestations of commemoration – indeed, the creation of the modern concept of war remembrance – expressed in everything from the names carved in a school's roll of lost alumni to the grand monuments on the Western Front. But first there was the urgent matter of burying the dead.

Reginald Miller was a 19-year-old gunner in "B" Battery, 190th Brigade, Royal Field Artillery. In March 1918, the brigade arrived back on the Western Front after four months in Italy, going straight into the line with the rest of the 41st Division, northeast of the old 1916 Somme battlefields. But on 21 March the Germans struck, and everyone retreated. Soon the British were back where they had been in February 1917. The exhausted 41st was ordered north to Flanders to recover. On 2 April, its infantry boarded buses at Bienvillers, but the gunners stayed behind. It made no difference to Reginald Miller: on that day, he was killed and buried nearby. Bienvillers Military Cemetery was first used from September 1915 to March 1917. In March 1918, it was reopened and used again for six months. It was here that Reginald Miller came to rest, 200 miles from his home in South London. This, his original grave marker, was apparently made from fence posts. In the middle of the hand-painted details, the Graves Registration Unit placed one of its regular zinc strips to confirm his name and details. After the war the Imperial (now Commonwealth) War Graves Commission rebuilt the cemetery at Bienvillers and replaced the original crosses with headstones. As with many grieving families, Miller's parents had his wooden cross sent back so that it could act, as it still does, as a poignant reminder of just one of the hundreds of thousands of British and Commonwealth soldiers who were killed on the Western Front.

Between 1914 and 1918 Britain lost over three-quarters of a million dead; France 1.4 million; Germany 2 million; Canada 65,000 and Australia 62,000; even little New Zealand lost 18,000 men, a proportion comparable to Britain's. Russia's losses have never been accurately assessed but are accounted as at least 5 million. Overall, the war had cost over 16 million dead, of whom about 10 million were military and the

> "THESE MEN, BE THEY OFFICERS OR RANK AND FILE, WHO FELL, DIED WITH THE SAME COURAGE AND THE SAME DEVOTION AND FOR THE SAME CAUSE, AND THEY SHOULD HAVE THEIR NAMES AND THEIR SERVICES PERPETUATED BY THE SAME MEMORIAL."

Herbert Asquith, debating in Parliament whether war graves should have a uniform design, 4 May 1920. As Asquith noted, "There are some of us, of whom I am one, who have a direct and personal interest in this matter": his own son was a war casualty.

rest civilians. Another 20 million men had been wounded. The horrific "butcher's bill" was the worst in recorded history – up to that time.

So much death, meted out on chaotic battlefields, made for an immediate problem in the days after the Armistice. Hundreds of thousands of bodies remained unburied, while others lay in temporary or shallow graves. Among the debris of war, skeletons and rotting body parts had to be buried – and quickly. In the chaos of the Eastern Front, mass graves were dug, although many of the dead just lay where they had fallen. However, on the Western Front a huge effort was made to observe the decencies.

Germany had left many of her sons in the earth of France and Flanders. But after the war reluctant French and Belgian farmers gave up the smallest plots of land they could get away with and shovelled German corpses into mass graves as quickly as possible. The German War Graves Commission (*Volksbund Deutsche Kriegsgräberfürsorge*), founded under the Treaty of Versailles, became responsible for the discovery and upkeep of the German war dead, and by 1925 began consolidating remains from the thousands of scattered Flanders graves into 128 cemeteries. In 1954, these were concentrated into just three large cemeteries – at Langemarck-Nord, Vladslo and Menin – along with 25,000 unnamed dead reburied under the huge concrete slab of the "Comrades Grave" (*Kameradengrab*) at Langemarck. Vladslo contains 25,662 bodies, plus a mother's powerful tribute to her dead son in the shape of Käthe Kollwitz's world-famous statues *The Parents*, showing two kneeling figures wracked by grief. But the largest German military cemetery on the old Western Front is in France at Neuville Saint Vaast, near Arras. Like the others it is a "concentration cemetery", with many soldiers buried four to a grave, and contains the remains of 44,833 German soldiers, 8,040 of them unidentified and buried in a common grave.

France also has some very large cemeteries and, in the French tradition, a number of ossuaries, of which Verdun's is the biggest. Perched high on the ridge overlooking Fort Douaumont, Verdun's Monument contains the bones of 130,000 unknown French and German soldiers who fell on the battlefields there. Bleached skulls stare out, sightlessly, over this French National Cemetery with its 15,000 graves of French soldiers, "*mort pour la patrie*". As in other French cemeteries each grave is marked by a simple white cross with a name plate. French Muslim soldiers from North Africa are buried beneath a suitable gravestone facing towards Mecca.

Further north in Artois is the largest French National Cemetery and Memorial anywhere, covering wars from 1914 to the Algerian War. Its imposing chapel and monument of Notre Dame de Lorette, with its basilica and the remains of 39,985 French soldiers, commemorates the sacrifices made to seize Vimy Ridge in 1915 and the attack on Notre Dame de Lorette itself. Four mass graves contain the unidentified remains of thousands more. Yet, even those buried here represent only 2.5 per cent of the French war dead of 1914–18. At its dedication in 1922, the Bishop of Arras used words that embrace the loss of all the nations: "she must become the voice which weeps for her youth cut down in its flower, the voice which prays for the eternal rest of their souls, the voice which talks of hope to the widows, fiancées, parents".

The United States suffered under 117,000 casualties, but made sure the dead were laid to rest with fine monuments. The largest war cemetery appropriately enough is at Meuse-Argonne, with its 14,246 graves in over 130 acres of ground. Unexpected nationalities are represented elsewhere. There is a Russian war cemetery at St Hilaire le Grand, on the Marne, with 1,000 graves of the Imperial Russian Special

"THE SACRIFICE OF THE INDIVIDUAL IS A GREAT IDEA AND WORTHY OF COMMEMORATION; BUT THE COMMUNITY OF SACRIFICE, THE SERVICE OF A COMMON CAUSE ... THESE ARE GREATER IDEAS, WHICH SHOULD BE COMMEMORATED IN THOSE CEMETERIES WHERE THEY LIE TOGETHER"

Lieutenant Colonel Sir Frederick Kenyon, War Graves, *report for the Imperial War Graves Commission on the design and purpose of military cemeteries, November 1918*

Edward, Prince of Wales, leads 11,000 British Legion "War Pilgrims" on a march to the Menin Gate (8 August 1928), in Ypres, for a ceremony of remembrance. The very large number of "missing" servicemen – one of the truly shocking aspects of the war – created a need for major communal monuments to honour their collective contribution.

Force, which fought – and then mutinied – on the Western Front from 1917. There is even a cemetery for Czech and Polish volunteers, who fought with the French Foreign Legion, in Artois.

In previous wars, British soldiers who died on campaign were usually buried anonymously in mass graves. Occasionally, individual monuments were erected to officers. By early 1915 it was becoming clear that – as with so much else in this unparalleled war – something different was required. But the BEF was simply not prepared for the scale of its losses and had no effective organization for dealing with them. In October 1914, a British Red Cross Mobile Ambulance Unit under the leadership of a volunteer called Fabian Ware began to plot the known burial sites (*see also* Chapter 59). This was difficult, because individual units buried their own dead, and his unit was soon overwhelmed by the work. The BEF eventually formalized the unit as the Graves Registration Commission in March 1915, and it became the Directorate of Graves Registration & Enquiries (DGR&E) in February 1916. Its Military Graves Registration Units became responsible for recording the burial of the dead and plotting the location of military cemeteries. The ground for permanent graves was confirmed by a French law in December 1915, which granted land to be maintained as a *sépulture perpétuelle* for British war dead.

The actual work of burying the bodies was often given to battalions "resting" out of the line. It was not a popular task. The 1/19th Battalion, London Regiment, cleared the battlefield after the successful assault on High Wood on 15 September 1916. The divisional chaplain noted: "Many men who have stood it all, cannot stand this clearing of the battlefield ... no words can tell you all I feel, nor can words tell you of the horrors of clearing a battlefield ... several men went off with shell-shock ... caused not just by the explosion of a shell nearby, but by the sights and smell and horror of the battlefield in general."

The BEF worried about the strain this work put on morale. In early 1917 the Adjutant-General noted: "the necessity of provision of some special organisation to

undertake burials". He also pointed out: "It is doubtful policy, from the point of view of morale, to use as burial parties troops as may be called upon to fight later."

Ware, by now promoted an acting temporary major general, was also concerned about the problems of military morale and, more important, public perception, writing in June 1917: "We are on the verge over here of serious trouble about the number of bodies lying out still unburied on the Somme battlefields. The soldiers returning wounded or in leave to England are complaining bitterly about it and the War Office has already received letters on the matter." In response to what was a growing problem, the Imperial War Graves Commission (IWGC) came into being by Royal Charter in May 1917, with Ware as its leader, tasked with identifying and interring all the British Empire's war dead.

At the end of the war it was plain that clearing the battlefields of equipment, ammunition, debris and bodies was going to be a major task. Over 160,000 individual graves had to be concentrated and over half a million missing men had to be located and identified. By early 1919, with 587,000 graves identified, a political row blew up over the problem of how to treat the dead. For logistical reasons, repatriation was impossible, but there was heated debate on whether the planned cemeteries abroad should reflect individual families' wishes, with different kinds of memorials and headstones, or whether there should be uniformity. The previous year, a report for the IWGC made the case for uniform designs to prevent any discrimination over rank or class. It also made a distinction between the private family memorial in local parishes, reflecting individual loss, and the sense of communal sacrifice on the battlefields. Eventually, the report's principles won through, and leading architects were engaged for the new cemeteries.

The exhumation of the bodies was a major undertaking. Volunteers were recruited with extra pay of 2 shillings and sixpence per day, with Chinese Labour Corps workers and PoWs drafted in to help. By mid-1919 there were 20,000 men working on the old Western Front. Exhumation Companies had squads of 32 men, who gathered up what they found and carried them away on stretchers soaked with creosol, a coal-tar-based disinfectant.

Not all the work was so grisly: one exhumer reported that: "It's jolly hard work. But it 'as its better side. Some fellers the other day came on a dug-out with three officers in it, and they picked up five thousand francs between 'em." Identification was the most important task. Relatives needed the truth. The workers had to search pockets, the neck, wrists and braces for "dog tags" or any other means of identification. Many of the earlier fibreboard ones had rotted: hence today's metal tags. Most of the corpses were

Remembrance, French style. An early photograph of the ossuary (in the background) and cemetery at Douaumont, Verdun. The cloister, containing the bones of 130,000 French and German dead, and the tower, offering panoramic views, were designed by Léon Azéma, Max Edrei and Jacques Hardy. Opened in 1932, they provided a fitting memorial to what both sides called the "hell of Verdun".

identified by identity discs; about 30 per cent by other methods, such as a name on a cigarette case, or half-rotted letters; and about a quarter were unidentifiable.

By 1921 the first IWGC cemeteries were being built. They had uniform headstones of Portland stone engraved with the man's name, rank, dates, his regimental badge and a maximum number of characters of text chosen by the family. VCs, uniquely, had the medal carved into their headstone. The model chosen was the tranquil cemetery at Forceville, where designer Gertrude Jekyll had created a walled English rose garden. Depending on the size of the cemetery, a Cross of Sacrifice with a bronze crusader's cross of varying sizes, as designed by Sir Reginald Blomfield, stood as a marker; in the bigger cemeteries there was an altar-like stone of remembrance, designed by Sir Edwin Lutyens, engraved with words from the Book of Leviticus chosen by Rudyard Kipling: "their name liveth for evermore". Over the next ten years hundreds of cemeteries were constructed in France, Belgium, Italy, Egypt, Palestine, Macedonia, Mesopotamia and at Gallipoli.

The known, identified dead were one thing, but the war generated millions of "missing" (*see also* Chapter 59), whose last remains were lost or unidentified. The IWGC took a policy decision that they, too, should have permanent places of remembrance, and large memorials were built up and down the Western Front to give recognition to them. Grandest among them were Lutyens' imposing arch at Thiepval, on the Somme, which was unveiled in 1932; and Blomfield's Menin Gate at Ypres, at whose dedication in 1927 General Lord Plumer memorably said: "they are not missing – they are here". At Thiepval, over 72,000 men from Britain, Ireland and South Africa are remembered, while at the Menin Gate almost 55,000 Commonwealth names are recorded.

The imposing cemeteries and memorials in Flanders and France were echoed, in miniature, across the home nations, in thousands of local war memorials – expressions of grief and loss, but also of local and civic pride, which act as reminders of how the war's tendrils crept into all corners of Britain and her empire. It remains a sobering experience to chance upon a small village's war memorial and register the unlikely number of names etched into it. Remembrance seeped into the culture in other ways, too. The London Brighton and South Coast Railway even named one of its tank engines "Remembrance" and the London North Western Railway built a Claughton express engine with the number "1914" in memory of its dead employees.

Inevitably, not all the spirit of remembrance was reverential or uncritical. Perhaps the complexity of it all is best summed up in Kipling, poet of empire, patriot and a stalwart of the war effort, whose chosen inscriptions adorn the Menin Gate, yet also the father who helped his medically unfit son "Jack" get a commission that led to Jack's death at the Battle of Loos, and who afterwards wrote so unsparingly of his own generation's shortcomings. In one of his *Epitaphs* (1919), "A Dead Statesman" goes to meet his maker:

Now all my lies are proved untrue
And I must face the men I slew.
What tale shall serve me here among
Mine angry and defrauded young?

As demonstrated by the discovery in 2007 of the remains of hundreds more bodies (mainly Australian) near Fromelles, the "young" continue to be found.

"TWO PAIRS OF RUBBER GLOVES, TWO SHOVELS, STAKES TO MARK THE LOCATION OF GRAVES FOUND, CANVAS AND ROPE TO TIE UP REMAINS, STRETCHERS, CREOSOL AND WIRE CUTTERS."

The typical equipment of a British Exhumation Company after the war

100

A SKETCH FOR THE CENOTAPH
ENDURING SYMBOLS OF THE GREAT WAR

1919 AND BEYOND

When the war was over, a new set of pressing problems and concerns presented themselves. Life went on. For Germans, it was everything that went with defeat and a revolution: *vae victis* (*see* Chapter 96). For returning soldiers of all nations, it was coming to terms with civilians and family life again, followed by the imperative to find work to replace soldiering. In Britain, and elsewhere, generals were concerned with the welfare of their ex-soldiers. Politicians and leaders in all spheres of life had to reshape their countries from a war footing back to "regular life", while internationally they tried to carve a new world order that – they hoped – would ensure that the Great War remained a unique, unrepeatable, phenomenon.

The war had touched nearly everyone. Beatrice Webb wrote after the Armistice: "Every day one meets saddened women with haggard faces ... and one dare not ask after husband or son." There was, accordingly, a universal need to find some meaning for what soldiers and civilians alike had endured and to try and comfort those who had lost loved ones. The public mood demanded an immediate recognition of this huge national trauma. The result was the creation of some enduring rituals and symbols that, in time, came to memorialize not only the First World War but every conflict since.

"Cenotaph." Today it is such a familiar word that it is hard to remember that in 1919 few would have known what one was. Early in July 1919 the British government learned that the French were planning to place a catafalque, or symbolic grave, at the heart of France's parade to mark the signing of the Treaty at Versailles. The Cabinet felt Britain should have one, too, for its own parade the following week. The architect Sir Edwin Lutyens had already been informally asked to design something, and now he proposed to Lloyd George not a catafalque but a "cenotaph", or empty tomb, a quieter, more elegiac structure. This is one of Lutyens' first drawings, dated 4 June, already showing the clean, straight lines and freedom from religious or nationalistic adornment that would invest the memorial with such universal power and meaning. It was simply about remembering "The Glorious Dead". Quickly approved, the first Cenotaph was built in five days from plaster and wood for the Peace Parade of 19 July. It brilliantly captured the public mood and a campaign immediately began to retain it where it stood in Whitehall. The Cabinet agreed. A new stone structure was built and unveiled on 11 November 1920, as part of the funeral of the Unknown Warrior. Its simplicity and elegance allowed each grieving relative – mother, widow, father, son – to invest it with their own emotions. Within a week, more than a million people had filed past and a carpet of flowers covered its base, 10 feet deep.

> "ALL THAT THEY HAD THEY GAVE – THEY GAVE; AND THEY SHALL NOT RETURN, / FOR THESE ARE THOSE THAT HAVE NO GRAVE WHERE ANY HEART MAY MOURN."

Rudyard Kipling, from "The King's Pilgrimage", 1922

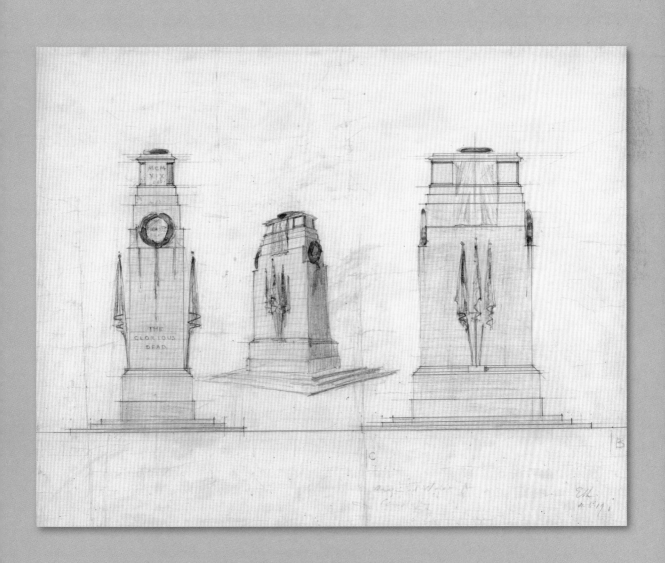

It was King George V who suggested that on the first anniversary of the Armistice, 11 November 1919, the nation should remember the fallen. That first two-minute silence was described by the Manchester *Guardian*:

> The first stroke of eleven produced a magical effect. The tram cars glided into stillness ... Someone took off his hat ... An elderly woman, not far away, wiped her eyes ... Everyone stood very still ... the hush deepened. It had spread over the whole city ... It was a silence which was almost pain ... And the spirit of memory brooded over it all.

Armistice Day has become one of the enduring symbols of the war, its powerful *tableau vivant* in Whitehall matched by similar ceremonies across the world. In the United States and the old Dominions, even still in Chinese Hong Kong, the ceremony lives on. In France the anniversary of the Armistice remains one the most important national days, remembered with blue cornflowers. After the war, memorials to the dead sprang up everywhere, their symbolism ranging from the Christian cross to iron crosses in Germany, while in France weeping Madonnas, triumphant *poilus* and many a proud cockerel can be seen in every French town and village as its memorial dedicated to those who fell in the conflict – a situation paralleled in Britain.

Some permanent, physical focal point – a national memorial – was clearly needed and for Armistice Day November 1920 Sir Edwin Lutyens' permanent version of his Cenotaph was unveiled by the king. The Whitehall Cenotaph was followed by other permanent and imposing memorials elsewhere: in Flanders, the Menin Gate (*see* Chapter 99), where since 1928 "The Last Post" is played every evening; the Australian War Memorial at Villers-Bretonneux and the towering Canadian memorial atop Vimy Ridge. In 1960, Turkey completed a striking memorial, the Çanakkale Martyrs' Memorial, to "253,000 immortals" at Gallipoli. Long after the Armistice, the Memorial Park to the Heroes of the First World War was finally dedicated in Moscow in 2005.

The 1920 ceremonies surrounding the Cenotaph included the burial of Britain's "Unknown Warrior" at Westminster Abbey. The idea to inter an anonymous soldier with national honours came from an army chaplain, who remembered seeing a rough grave with a pencilled inscription: "An Unknown Soldier of the Black Watch". The Dean of Westminster Abbey approached the government, which backed the idea. Six unidentified bodies were disinterred, one each from the battlefields of the Marne, Aisne, Ypres, Somme, Arras and Cambrai. They were placed on stretchers in the Chapel of St Pol and a brigadier, blindfolded, touched one of the flag-covered bodies, which was sent by ambulance to Boulogne. There it was transferred to a coffin, made of wood from Hampton Court, with a cast of a crusader's sword from the Tower of London, and guarded by French soldiers for its last night on French soil. The next morning the sealed coffin set sail, along with barrels of soil from Ypres, aboard the destroyer HMS *Verdun* for Dover.

On 11 November, at the Cenotaph the king laid his wreath on the coffin, then followed the gun carriage to Westminster Abbey, where the coffin passed through two rows of Victoria Cross holders. At the end of the service King George sprinkled earth from the battlefields into the grave and buglers sounded "The Last Post" and "The Rouse". By 27 November as many as 1.5 million people had filed past the grave.

**"FOR KING AND COUNTRY /
FOR LOVED ONES
HOME AND EMPIRE /
FOR THE SACRED
CAUSE OF
JUSTICE AND /
THE FREEDOM OF
THE WORLD"**

From the inscription on the grave of the Unknown Warrior, Westminster Abbey, London

Recognition of Field Marshal Haig himself eventually came in the form of an earldom, and, from Parliament in March 1919, a vote of thanks and £100,000. Haig was very conscious that while the dead needed remembering, the living needed help, and he called for government aid for demobilized soldiers. By the early 1920s the big cities were awash with unemployed ex-soldiers. Even former officers were begging or selling matches in the street. For the rest of his life Haig – the man whose unenviable job it had been to send men to face death – devoted himself to raising money for ex-servicemen in need, irrespective of rank. It is in the context of helping the living while simultaneously remembering the dead that the potent symbol of the poppy emerged.

Poppies grow quickly on disturbed earth. In 1915, at the dressing station at Essex Farm, near Ypres, after a long day's surgery, the Canadian doctor John McCrae came and found poppies and other wild flowers covering the broken soil. They inspired his famous lines of verse beginning: "In Flanders' fields the poppies grow, / Between the crosses, row on row". The poem rapidly became synonymous with the soldiers who died. Nevertheless, it was the American Legion that first used the poppy as a symbol of remembrance, in 1919. One American teacher, Moina Bell Michael, was so moved by McCrae's poem that she sold poppies to raise funds for US ex-servicemen. Anna Guérin, a Frenchwoman present at the American Legion's convention in September 1920, took up the idea and popularized the selling of artificial poppies as a way to raise funds for ex-servicemen. In 1921, millions were sold throughout the United States.

A Remembrance Day poster from 1923 urges people to wear a poppy on 11 November and support Earl Haig's charitable fund and the British Legion. Along with the Imperial (Commonwealth) War Graves Commission, the Royal British Legion, as it is now called, has proved a permanent legacy of the war.

As part of Guérin's efforts, she persuaded Haig to adopt the poppy. Thus, for Remembrance Day in 1921, he set up the Earl Haig Poppy Fund with the first Poppy Appeal, in order to raise money for the newly established British Legion – which brought together the previously disparate veterans' organizations – so that it could help disabled and needy ex-servicemen. In Britain, the factory to make and sell poppies was set up in 1922 by Major George Howson, founder of the Disabled Society, with five ex-servicemen. He suggested to the British Legion that the artificial flowers should be designed so that someone who had lost the use of a hand could assemble them. Within a few months the factory was providing work and an income for 50 disabled veterans. To this day, it still makes millions of poppies – the most visible, most portable, most ubiquitous and enduring reminder of the calamitous First World War.

To say that the conflict still affects us today is no exaggeration: the shadow of that grim conflict between 1914–18 has shaped our modern world. The millions who died or were maimed a century ago stand as grim testimony to political failure and the horrors of modern war… "lest we forget".

EUROPE IN 1914 & WARTIME ALLIES

Allied Powers
Central Powers
Neutral countries

NORWAY

Christiana (Oslo)

SWE

NORTH SEA

DENMARK

Copenhage

BRITISH
ISLES

Dublin

NETHERLANDS

The Hague

Berlin

Potsdam

GERMAN

London

Brussels

BELGIUM

LUX.

LORRAINE

Paris

ALSACE

FRANCE

Berne

TYROL

SWITZERLAND

TRENTINO

ITALY

Rome

PORTUGAL

Madrid

SPAIN

M E D I T E R

Lisbon

Tunis

Gibraltar

Algiers

TUNISIA
(France)

ATLANTIC
OCEAN

Casablanca

ALGERIA
(France)

Tripoli

MOROCCO
(France)

FINLAND

khoïm

St Petersburg (Petrograd)

ESTONIA

BALTIC SEA

LIVONIA

LATVIA

COURLAND

Moscow

LITHUANIA

RUSSIA

RUSSIA

Warsaw

POLAND

Kiev

Kharkov

GALICIA

U K R A I N E

Vienna

Budapest

Odessa

AUSTRIA-
HUNGARY

CRIMEA

Sebastopol

BOSNIA-
Sarajevo

ROMANIA

RZEGOVINA

Belgrade

Bucharest

BLACK SEA

SERBIA

MONTENEGRO

Sofia

BULGARIA

ALBANIA

Constantinople

GREECE

O T T O M A N

E M P I R E

Athens

PERSIA

A N E A N S E A

CYPRUS
(Britain)

PALESTINE

Baghdad

Jerusalem

LIBYA
(Italy)

EGYPT (Britain)

CENTRAL ARABIA
(NEJD)

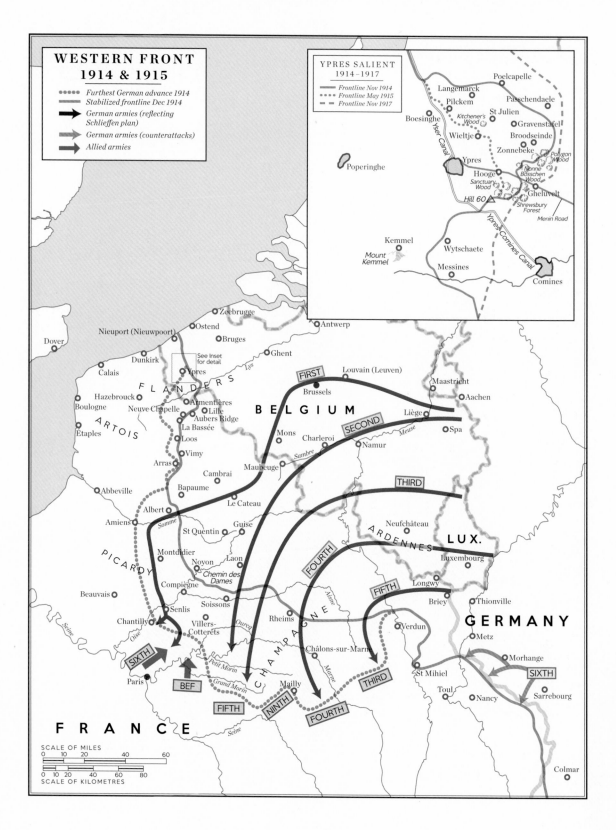

WESTERN FRONT 1914 & 1915

- **······** Furthest German advance 1914
- **▬▬▬** Stabilized frontline Dec 1914
- **➡** German armies (reflecting Schlieffen plan)
- **➡** German armies (counterattacks)
- **➡** Allied armies

YPRES SALIENT 1914–1917

- **▬▬▬** Frontline Nov 1914
- **······** Frontline May 1915
- **- - -** Frontline Nov 1917

Poelcapelle
Langemarck
Pilckem
Passchendaele
St Julien
Boesinghe
Kitchener's Wood
Wieltje
Gravenstafel
Broodseinde
Zonnebeke
Ypres
Polygon Wood
Poperinghe
Nonne Bösschen Wood
Hooge
Sanctuary Wood
Gheluvelt
Hill 60
Shrewsbury Forest
Menin Road
Kemmel
Wytschaete
Mount Kemmel
Messines
Comines

Yser Canal
Ypres-Comines Canal

Dover
Zeebrugge
Ostend
Bruges
Antwerp
Nieuport (Nieuwpoort)
Dunkirk
Ghent
Calais
Ypres
See Inset for detail
FLANDERS
Lys
Louvain (Leuven)
FIRST
Maastricht
Hazebrouck
Armentières
Brussels
Aachen
Boulogne
Neuve Chapelle
Lille
BELGIUM
Liège
Étaples
ARTOIS
Aubers Ridge
La Bassée
Mons
Charleroi
SECOND
Namur
Spa
Loos
Maubeuge
Meuse
Vimy
Sambre
Arras
Cambrai
Le Cateau
THIRD
Abbeville
Bapaume
Albert
Guise
Neufchâteau
ARDENNES
LUX.
Amiens
Somme
St Quentin
Montdidier
Laon
Luxembourg
Noyon
Chemin des Dames
FOURTH
Beauvais
Compiègne
Aisne
FIFTH
Longwy
Soissons
Rheims
Briey
Thionville
Chantilly
Villers-Cotterêts
Ourcq
Verdun
GERMANY
Senlis
Oise
SIXTH
Petit Morin
Châlons-sur-Marne
St Mihiel
Metz
Paris
BEF
Grand Morin
Mailly
Marne
THIRD
Morhange
Toul
SIXTH
FIFTH
Seine
NINTH
FOURTH
Nancy
Sarrebourg
Rheims
CHAMPAGNE
PICARDY
Seine

FRANCE

Colmar

SCALE OF MILES
0 10 20 40 60

SCALE OF KILOMETRES
0 10 20 40 60 80

EASTERN FRONT
1914–1918

Frontline end Sept 1914
Frontline Armistice 1917
Brest-Litovsk Treaty Line

SCALE OF MILES
0   50   100 150 200

SCALE OF KILOMETRES
0 50 100 150 250

St Petersburg (Petrograd)
Tsarskoe Selo

ESTONIA

LATVIA

Pskov

RUSSIA

Riga
COURLAND
Dvina
Dvinsk

BALTIC SEA

Moscow

LITHUANIA
Memel
Kovno
(Kaunas)
Lake Naroch
Neris (Vilija)
Vilna (Vilnius)

Smolensk

Königsberg
Gumbinnen
EAST
PRUSSIA
Danzig
*Masurian
Lakes*
Tannenberg
Thorn

Grodno
Neman

Minsk

Mogilev

Bialystock

GERMANY

Posen

Vistula
Warsaw
Lodz

POLAND

Bug
Brest-Litovsk

Lublin

Breslau
SILESIA
Oder

Krasnik
Komarov

Kovel
Lutsk

Kiev

Vistula
Cracow
Tarnow
Jaroslav
Lvov (Lemberg)
Przemysl
Limanova-Lipanov
Gorlice
San

Ternopil

Dnieper

AUSTRIA-HUNGARY

CARPATHIAN MOUNTAINS

Rostov

UKRAINE

Vienna
Danube
Budapest

Theiss

Dniester

Odessa

ROMANIA

BLACK SEA

BOSNIA-
HERZ.

SERBIA
MONTENEGRO

BULGARIA

ALBANIA

GREECE

Constantinople

OTTOMAN
EMPIRE

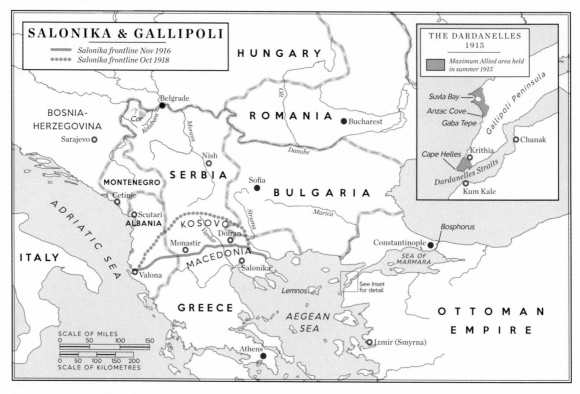

SALONIKA & GALLIPOLI

——— Salonika frontline Nov 1916
········ Salonika frontline Oct 1918

HUNGARY

ROMANIA

Bucharest

BOSNIA-
HERZEGOVINA

Sarajevo

Belgrade

Cor

Kolubard

Morava

Olt

Danube

Nish

SERBIA

MONTENEGRO

Cetinje

Scutari

ALBANIA

KOSOVO

Monastir

Doiran

Vardar

Sofia

BULGARIA

Struma

Marica

MACEDONIA

Salonika

ITALY

ADRIATIC SEA

Valona

GREECE

Lemnos

AEGEAN SEA

Athens

SEA OF MARMARA

Constantinople

Bosphorus

OTTOMAN EMPIRE

Izmir (Smyrna)

See Inset for detail

THE DARDANELLES 1915

Maximum Allied area held in summer 1915

Suvla Bay
Anzac Cove
Gaba Tepe
Cape Helles
Krithia
Dardanelles Straits
Kum Kale
Gallipoli Peninsula
Chanak

SCALE OF MILES
0 50 100 150

0 50 100 150 200
SCALE OF KILOMETRES

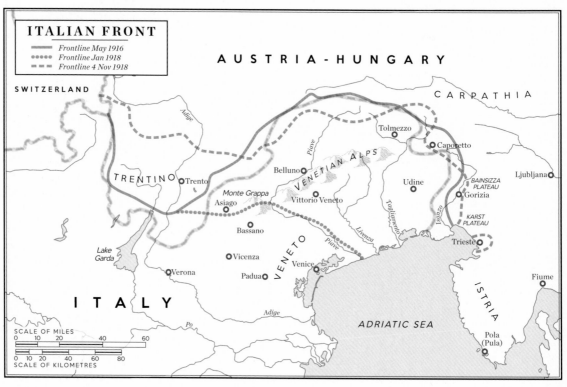

ITALIAN FRONT

——— Frontline May 1916
········ Frontline Jan 1918
– – – Frontline 4 Nov 1918

AUSTRIA-HUNGARY

SWITZERLAND

CARPATHIA

Adige

Tolmezzo

Caporetto

Piave

TRENTINO

Trento

Belluno

VENETIAN ALPS

Udine

Ljubljana

BAINSIZZA PLATEAU

Gorizia

Monte Grappa

Asiago

Vittorio Veneto

Tagliamento

Isonzo

KARST PLATEAU

Bassano

Livenza

Piave

Trieste

Lake Garda

Vicenza

VENETO

Venice

Fiume

Verona

Padua

Adige

Po

ADRIATIC SEA

ISTRIA

Pola (Pula)

ITALY

SCALE OF MILES
0 10 20 40 60

0 10 20 40 60 80
SCALE OF KILOMETRES

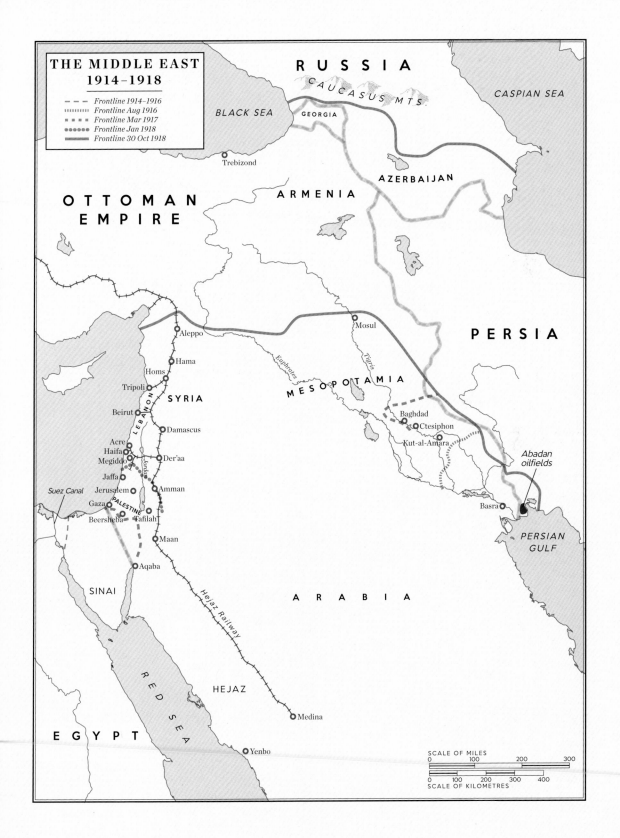

THE MIDDLE EAST
1914–1918

- – – – Frontline 1914–1916
- Frontline Aug 1916
- Frontline Mar 1917
- Frontline Jan 1918
- Frontline 30 Oct 1918

RUSSIA

CAUCASUS MTS.

BLACK SEA

CASPIAN SEA

Trebizond

GEORGIA

AZERBAIJAN

ARMENIA

OTTOMAN
EMPIRE

PERSIA

Aleppo

Hama

Homs

Tripoli

SYRIA

Beirut

Damascus

Acre

Haifa

Megiddo

Der'aa

Jaffa

Amman

Jerusalem

Suez Canal

Gaza

PALESTINE

Beersheba

Tafilah

Maan

Aqaba

SINAI

Mosul

Euphrates

Tigris

MESOPOTAMIA

Baghdad

Ctesiphon

Kut-al-Amara

Abadan
oilfields

Basra

PERSIAN
GULF

LEBANON

Jordan

ARABIA

Hejaz Railway

RED SEA

HEJAZ

EGYPT

Medina

Yenbo

SCALE OF MILES

0   100   200   300

SCALE OF KILOMETRES

0   100   200   300   400

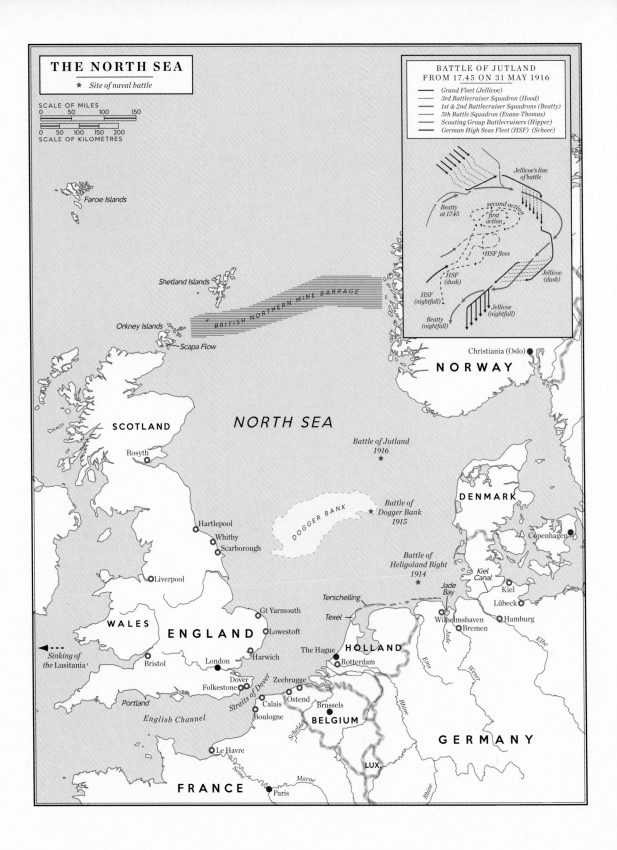

THE NORTH SEA

★ *Site of naval battle*

SCALE OF MILES
0   50   100   150

SCALE OF KILOMETRES
0   50   100   150   200

BATTLE OF JUTLAND
FROM 17.45 ON 31 MAY 1916

—— *Grand Fleet (Jellicoe)*
—— *3rd Battlecruiser Squadron (Hood)*
—— *1st & 2nd Battlecruiser Squadrons (Beatty)*
—— *5th Battle Squadron (Evans-Thomas)*
—— *Scouting Group Battlecruisers (Hipper)*
—— *German High Seas Fleet (HSF) (Scheer)*

Jellicoe's line of battle

Beatty at 1745

second action
first action

HSF flees

HSF (dusk)

Jellicoe (dusk)

HSF (nightfall)

Beatty (nightfall)

Jellicoe (nightfall)

Faroe Islands

Shetland Islands

BRITISH NORTHERN MINE BARRAGE

Orkney Islands

Scapa Flow

Christiania (Oslo) ●

NORWAY

SCOTLAND

Rosyth ◉

NORTH SEA

Battle of Jutland 1916
★

DENMARK

DOGGER BANK

Battle of Dogger Bank 1915
★

Copenhagen ●

Hartlepool ◉
Whitby ◉
Scarborough ◉

Liverpool ◉

Battle of Heligoland Bight 1914
★

Kiel Canal

Jade Bay

Kiel ◉
Lübeck ◉

Terschelling

Texel

Wilhelmshaven ◉
Bremen

Hamburg ◉

WALES

ENGLAND

Gt Yarmouth ◉

Lowestoft

Harwich ◉

The Hague
HOLLAND

Rotterdam ●

Jade

Ems

Weser

Elbe

◀--- *Sinking of the Lusitania*

Bristol ◉

London ●

Dover ◉
Folkestone ◉

Straits of Dover

Zeebrugge ◉
Ostend ◉

Calais ◉
Boulogne ◉

Brussels ●
BELGIUM

Portland

English Channel

Le Havre ◉

Seine

Marne

FRANCE

Paris ●

Schelde

Rhine

LUX

Rhine

GERMANY

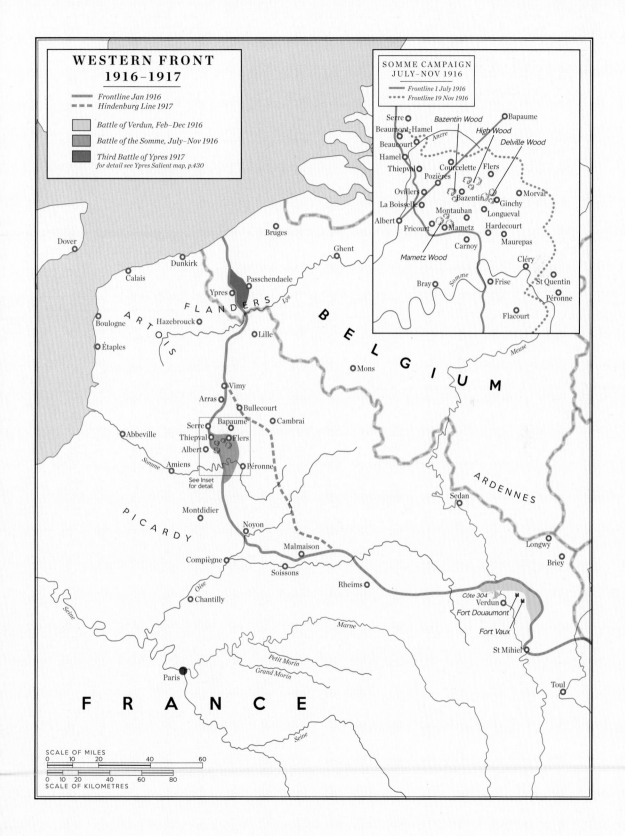

WESTERN FRONT
1916–1917

Frontline Jan 1916
Hindenburg Line 1917

Battle of Verdun, Feb–Dec 1916

Battle of the Somme, July–Nov 1916

Third Battle of Ypres 1917
for detail see Ypres Salient map, p.430

SOMME CAMPAIGN
JULY–NOV 1916

Frontline 1 July 1916
Frontline 19 Nov 1916

Serre
Beaumont-Hamel
Beaucourt
Hamel
Thiepval
Pozières
Ovillers
La Boisselle
Albert
Fricourt
Mametz Wood
Bray
Frise
Bazentin Wood
High Wood
Delville Wood
Courcelette
Flers
Bazentin
Longueval
Montauban
Mametz
Hardecourt
Carnoy
Maurepas
Bapaume
Morval
Ginchy
Cléry
St Quentin
Péronne
Flacourt
Ancre
Somme

Dover
Calais
Dunkirk
Bruges
Ghent
Boulogne
ARTOIS
Hazebrouck
Étaples
FLANDERS
Ypres
Passchendaele
Lys
Lille
BELGIUM
Mons
Vimy
Arras
Bullecourt
Cambrai
Serre
Bapaume
Thiepval
Flers
Albert
Péronne
See Inset
for detail
Abbeville
Somme
Amiens
PICARDY
Montdidier
Noyon
Malmaison
Compiègne
Soissons
Rheims
Oise
Chantilly
ARDENNES
Sedan
Longwy
Briey
Côte 304
Verdun
Fort Douaumont
Fort Vaux
St Mihiel
Toul
Meuse
Marne
Petit Morin
Grand Morin
Seine
Paris
Seine

FRANCE

SCALE OF MILES
0 10 20 40 60

0 10 20 40 60 80
SCALE OF KILOMETRES

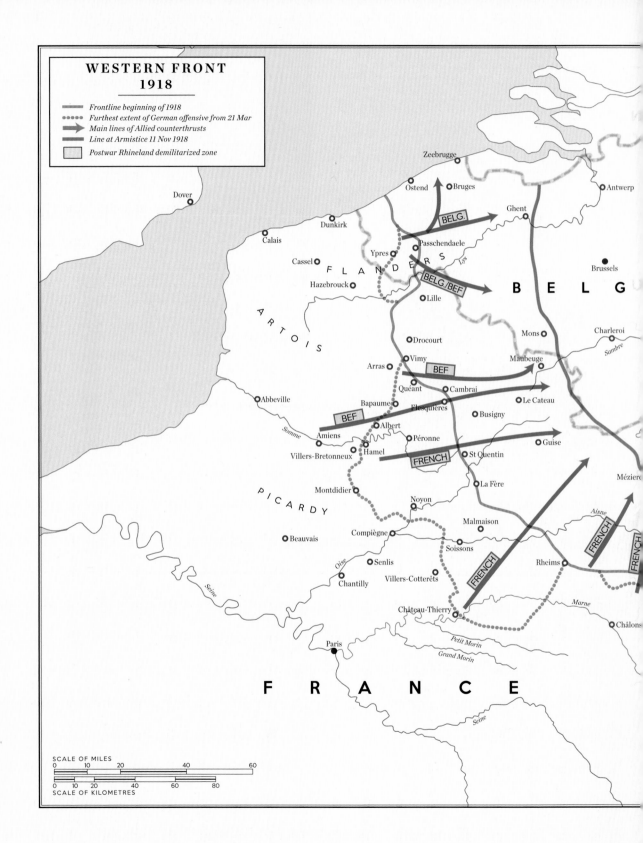

WESTERN FRONT
1918

▬ ▬ Frontline beginning of 1918
• • • • Furthest extent of German offensive from 21 Mar
➤➤➤ Main lines of Allied counterthrusts
▬▬▬ Line at Armistice 11 Nov 1918
▨ Postwar Rhineland demilitarized zone

Zeebrugge

Dover

Ostend   Bruges   Antwerp

Dunkirk   Ghent

Calais   Ypres   Passchendaele   BELG.

Cassel   F L A N D E R S   Brussels

Hazebrouck   Lille   BELG./BEF   B E L G

A R T O I S   Charleroi

Drocourt   Mons   Sambre

Arras   Vimy   BEF   Maubeuge

Abbeville   Quéant   Cambrai

Bapaume   Flesquières   Busigny   Le Cateau

BEF   Albert

Somme   Amiens   Péronne   Guise

Villers-Bretonneux   Hamel   FRENCH   St Quentin   Mézier

P I C A R D Y   Montdidier   La Fère

Noyon   Malmaison   Aisne   FRENCH

Beauvais   Compiègne   Soissons   FRENCH

Oise   Senlis   FRENCH   Rheims   FRENCH

Chantilly   Villers-Cotterêts

Château-Thierry   Marne   Châlons

Petit Morin

Seine   Grand Morin

Paris

F R A N C E

Seine

SCALE OF MILES
0   10   20   40   60

0 10 20   40   60   80
SCALE OF KILOMETRES

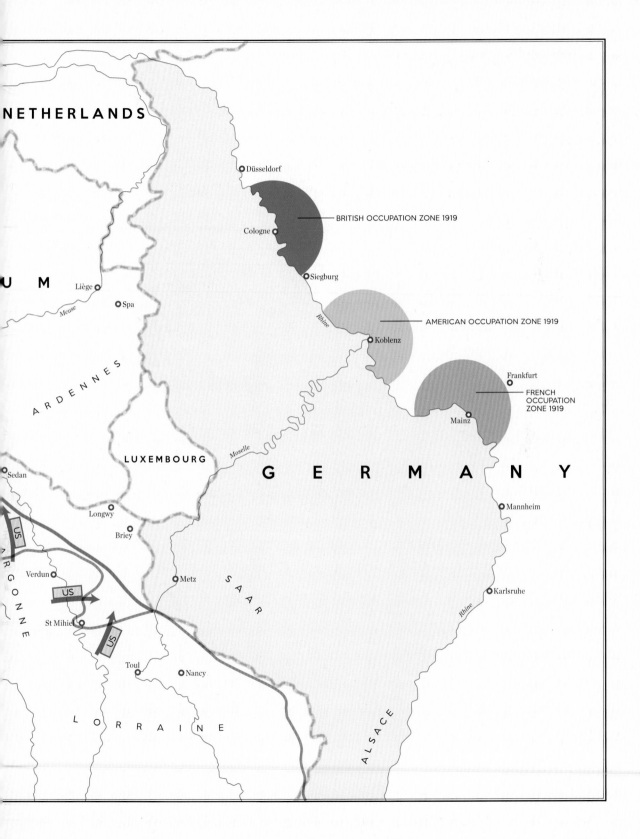

NETHERLANDS

Düsseldorf

BRITISH OCCUPATION ZONE 1919

Cologne

Siegburg

Liège

AMERICAN OCCUPATION ZONE 1919

Meuse

Spa

Rhine

Koblenz

U M

Frankfurt

FRENCH OCCUPATION ZONE 1919

ARDENNES

Mainz

Moselle

LUXEMBOURG

G E R M A N Y

Sedan

Mannheim

Longwy

Briey

S
A
A
R

Verdun

US

Metz

Karlsruhe

St Mihiel

US

Rhine

A
R
G
O
N
N
E

US

Toul

Nancy

L O R R A I N E

A
L
S
A
C
E

EUROPE AFTER
THE PEACE TREATIES
1919–1925

Areas of dispute or League of Nations control

NORWAY

Christiana (Oslo)

SWEDE

NORTH SEA

DENMARK

Copenhagen

GREAT
BRITAIN

Dublin

IRISH FREE STATE (1922)

London

NETHERLANDS

Berlin

Rhineland occupied /
demilitarized zone

GERMAN

BELGIUM

Weimar

LUX.

Saar, to Germany
in plebiscite 1935

Prag

Paris

LORRAINE

ALSACE

FRANCE

Berne

SWITZERLAND

AUSTR

ATLANTIC
OCEAN

Klagenfurt,
to Austria
in plebiscite
1921

STRIA

Fiume Free Sta
1920–24

ITALY

Corsica (Fr.)

Rome

PORTUGAL

Madrid

SPAIN

Sardinia (It.)

Lisbon

M E D I T E R

Tunis

Algiers

Casablanca

MOROCCO
(France)

ALGERIA
(France)

TUNISIA
(France)

Tripoli

FINLAND

Helsinki

Leningrad (Petrograd)

Tallinn

ESTONIA

Stockholm

BALTIC SEA

Riga

LATVIA

Occupied by Lithuania,
1923

Memel

LITHUANIA

Free City of Danzig

Vilna (Vilnius)

Kovno

EAST
PRUSSIA

Moscow

POLISH
CORRIDOR

Central
Lithuanian Republic,
1920–22

retained by Germany
in plebiscite 1920

Warsaw

RUSSIA/
SOVIET UNION

POLAND

Kiev

Upper Silesia to
Germany and Poland
in plebiscite 1921

GALICIA

CZECHOSLOVAKIA

Vienna

BESSARABIA

Budapest

TRANSYLVANIA

HUNGARY

ROMANIA

YUGOSLAVIA

Belgrade

BOSNIA-
HERZEGOVINA

SERBIA

Bucharest

DOBRUDJA

BLACK SEA

Sofia

BULGARIA

ALBANIA

THRACE

Constantinople (Istanbul)

GREECE

Ankara (capital from 1923)

Athens

TURKEY

PERSIA

CYPRUS
(Britain)

SYRIA
(France)

ANEAN SEA

Beirut

Damascus

IRAQ
(MESOPOTAMIA)
(Britain)

Baghdad

PALESTINE
(Br.)

Amman

TRANS-JORDAN
(Br.)

Jerusalem

LIBYA
(Italy)

EGYPT (Britain)

ARABIA

FURTHER READING

Asprey, Robert, *The German High Command at War: Hindenburg and Ludendorff and the First World War* (New York, 1991)

Bainton, Roy, *A Brief History of 1917: Russia's Year of Revolution* (London, 2005)

Banks, Arthur, *A Military Atlas of the First World War* (London, 2001)

Barker, Ralph, *A Brief History of the Royal Flying Corps in World War I* (London, 2002)

Barnett, Correlli, *The Swordbearers: Supreme Command in the First World War* (London, 1963)

Bennett, Geoffrey, *Naval Battles of the First World War* (London, 1968)

Blaxland, Gregory, *Amiens, 1918* (London, 1968)

Brook-Shepherd, Gordon, *November 1918: The Last Act of the Great War* (London, 1981)

Brown, Malcolm, *Tommy Goes to War* (London, 1978)

Brown, Malcolm, *The Imperial War Museum Book of the Western Front* (London, 1993)

Cecil, Hugh and Peter Liddle, *Facing Armageddon: The First World War Experience* (London, 1996)

Churchill, Winston, *The World Crisis 1911–1918* (London, 1923; new edition 2005)

Clayton, Anthony, *Paths of Glory: The French Army 1914–18* (London, 2003)

Coogan, Tim Pat, *1916: The Easter Rising* (London, 2001)

Cooksey, Jon, *The Barnsley Pals: The 13th and 14th Battalions, York & Lancaster Regiment* (Barnsley, 2008)

Cooper, Bryan, *The Ironclads of Cambrai* (London, 1970)

Cooper, Jilly, *Animals in War* (London, 1984)

Corns, Cathryn and John Hughes-Wilson, *Blindfold and Alone: British Military Executions in the Great War* (London, 2001)

Corrigan, Gordon, *Mud, Blood and Poppycock* (London, 2003)

Creveld, Martin van, *Supplying War: Logistics from Wallenstein to Patton* (Cambridge, 1977)

Creveld, Martin van, *Command in War* (Cambridge, MA, 1987)

De Leeuw, Adele, *Edith Cavell: Nurse, Spy, Heroine* (London, 1968)

Dunn, J.C., *The War the Infantry Knew, 1914–1919: A Chronicle of Service in France and Belgium* (London, 1938; reprinted 1989)

Fromkin, David, *A Peace to End All Peace: The Fall of the Ottoman Empire and the Creation of the Modern Middle East* (New York, 2001)

Fromkin, David, *Europe's Last Summer: Who Started the Great War in 1914?* (New York, 2004)

Fussell, Paul, *The Great War and Modern Memory* (Oxford, 1975)

Gordon, Andrew, *The Rules of the Game: Jutland and British Naval Command* (London, 1996)

Griffith, Paddy, *British Fighting Methods in the Great War* (London, 1998)

Hay, Ian, *The First Hundred Thousand* (London, 1916)

Haythornthwaite, Philip J., *The World War One Source Book* (London, 1992)

Hayward, James, *Myths and Legends of the First World War* (London, 2002)

Holmes, Richard, *The Western Front* (London, 1999)

Holmes, Richard, *Tommy: The British Soldier on the Western Front 1914–1918* (London, 2004)

Horne, Alistair, *The Price of Glory: Verdun 1916* (New York, 1994)

Horne, John and Alan Kramer, *German Atrocities, 1914: A History of Denial* (London, 2001)

Hough, Richard, *The Great War at Sea: 1914–18* (Oxford, 1986)

Hughes-Wilson, John, *The Puppet Masters: Spies, Traitors and the Real Forces Behind World Events* (London, 2002)

Keegan, John, *The First World War* (London, 1998)

Kennedy, Ross A., *The Will to Believe: Woodrow Wilson, World War I, and America's Strategy for Peace and Security* (Kent, OH, 2009)

MacDonald, Lyn, *1914: The Days of Hope* (London, 1987)

MacDonald, Lyn, *1915: The Death of Innocence* (London, 1993)

Macmillan, Margaret, *Peacemakers: The Paris Conference of 1919 and Its Attempt to End War* (London, 2002)

Marwick, Arthur, *The Deluge: British Society and the First World War* (London, 1965)

Massie, Robert K., *Castles of Steel: Britain, Germany and the Winning of the Great War at Sea* (New York, 2003)

Middlebrook, Martin, *The Kaiser's Battle* (Barnsley, 2007)

Millar, Ronald, *Kut: The Death of an Army* (London, 1969)

Morris, Captain Joseph, *The German Air Raids on Great Britain, 1914–1918* (London, 1925; reprinted 2001)

Mosley, Leonard, *Duel for Kilimanjaro: An Account of the East African Campaign, 1914–1918* (London, 1963)

Murphy, David, *The Arab Revolt 1916–18: Lawrence Sets Arabia Ablaze* (Oxford, 2008)

Nutting, Anthony, *Lawrence of Arabia: The Man and the Motive* (London, 1966)

Palmer, Alan, *The Gardeners of Salonika: An Account of the Campaign in Macedonia, 1915–1918* (London, 1965)

Philpott, William, *Bloody Victory: The Sacrifice on the Somme and the Making of the Twentieth Century* (London, 2009)

Pipes, Richard, *The Russian Revolution* (New York, 1990)

Prior, Robin and Trevor Wilson, *Passchendaele: The Untold Story* (New Haven, CT, 1996)

Purnell (publishers), *History of the First World War*, partwork series of 128 issues in 8 vols (London, 1969–71)

Ramsay, David, *Lusitania: Saga and Myth* (London, 2001)

Richards, Frank, *Old Soldiers Never Die* (London, 1933)

Ritter, Gerhard, *The Schlieffen Plan: Critique of a Myth*, translated by A. Wilson and E. Wilson (London, 1958)

Ritter, Gerhard, *The Sword and the Sceptre: The Problem of Militarism in Germany*, translated by Heinz Norden, 4 vols (London, 1971–3)

Salandra, Antonio, *Italy and the Great War: From Neutrality to Intervention* (London, 1932)

Sheffield, Gary, *Forgotten Victory: The First World War – Myths and Realities* (London, 2001)

Showalter, Dennis E., *Tannenberg: Clash of Empires, 1914* (Hamden, CT, 1991)

Simpson, Andy, *Hot Blood and Cold Steel: Life and Death in the Trenches of the First World War* (London, 1993)

Steel, Nigel and Peter Hart, *Defeat at Gallipoli* (London, 1994)

Stevenson, David, *1914–1918: The History of the First World War* (London, 2004)

Stone, Norman, *The Eastern Front 1914–17* (London, 1975)

Stone, Norman, *World War One: A Short History* (London, 2007)

Strachan, Hew, *The First World War: A New Illustrated History* (London, 2003; paperback edition, without subtitle, 2006)

Taylor, A.J.P., *The Struggle for Mastery in Europe: 1848–1918* (Oxford, 1954)

Terraine, John, *White Heat: The New Warfare 1914–18* (London, 1982)

Tolson, Roger, *Art from the First World War* (London, 2008)

Travers, Tim, *The Killing Ground: The British Army, the Western Front and the Emergence of Modern Warfare, 1900–1918* (London, 1987)

Tuchman, Barbara W., *The Zimmermann Telegram* (London, 1958)

Tuchman, Barbara W., *The Guns of August* (London, 1962)

Warner, Philip, *The Battle of Loos* (London, 1976)

Wheeler-Bennett, John W., *Brest-Litovsk: The Forgotten Peace – March 1918* (London, 1938)

Wilson, Trevor, *The Myriad Faces of War: Britain and the Great War, 1914–1918* (Cambridge, 1986)

Winter, Denis, *Death's Men: Soldiers of the Great War* (London, 1978)

Woodward, E.L., *Great Britain and the German Navy* (London, 1964)

Woollacott, Angela, *On Her Their Lives Depend: Munitions Workers in the Great War* (Berkeley, CA, 1994)

INDEX

Page numbers in *italic* refer to the illustrations

A

Admiralty: opposition to convoys 348–9; Room 40 74–6; *see also* Royal Navy
Adrian pattern helmet 198, *199*, 200, 201
Africa 88–91, 396
Agadir Incident (1911) 27, 31
Agar, Lt Augustus *410–11*, 411, 412
air warfare: aerial reconnaissance 158–61, *159*, *161*, 176–7, 283, 308, *309*, 310–11; airships 126–9, *128*; bombers 129, 282–3, 362, 363; communications 176–7; fighter aces 360–3; fighters 282–5, *282–3*, 363; machine guns 161; Sopwith Camel *282–3*, 285, *285*, 363
Aisne, River 69, 70, 164, 355
alcohol 42, 233, 243, 251
Aleppo 376, 377
Alexander, King of Greece 121
Alexandra, Tsarina 279
Allen, Clifford 149
Allenby, General Sir Edmund 289, 300, 328–9, *329*, 332, 333, 359, 374–7
Alsace-Lorraine 28, 56, 58, 60–1, 344, 355, 383, 395
American Expeditionary Force (AEF) 157, 200, 355, 370–3, *372*
Amiens, Battle of (1918) 354, 359, 364, 366–7, *366*, 368, 370
ammunition *see* munitions
Ancre, Battle of (1916) *229*, 231
Anderson, Major Alexander 102, *102–3*
Anglo-Boer War 14, 31, 46, 66, 162, 190, 195, 414
animals 188–91; *see also* dogs, horses, *etc*
Anzac Cove 109, 110, 111
ANZACs *190*, 348; Battle of Amiens 367; Battle of the Somme 226–7; camels 191; capture Hamel 364, 366–7; casualties 418; Gallipoli campaign 106, *107*, 108–11, *109*, *111*, 162; "Hundred Days Offensive" 371, 372; mining 182; Palestine campaign 326, 328, 376; Third Battle of Ypres 298–9; war memorial 426
Apollinaire, Guillaume 319
Arabs/Arab Revolt 330–3, 374, 376–7, 396, 402
Ardennes 58, 60–1

Argonne 372, *372*, 373
Armentières 237, 354–5
Armistice (1918) 91, 177, 187, 380–1, 384–7, 388, 392, 398, 426
Army Service Corps 307
Armytage, Brigadier General George *359*
Arras 353, 354
Arras, Battle of (1917) 262, 284, 288, 289–91
artillery 150–3, *151*, *152*
artists 320–5
Asquith, Herbert 16, 18, 110, 136, *271*, 319; Calais conference 204; Khaki Election 389; Lloyd George takes over from 270–3; and recruitment 44, 146, 148, 149
atrocities, German 62–5, 74, 140, *141*, 274
Aubers Ridge 136, 172
Australian troops *see* ANZACs
Austria-Hungary: alliance with Germany 30; assassination of Franz Ferdinand 32–6; Brusilov offensive 218–19, *219*; campaigns against Italy 112–15, 116–17; casualties 85; collapse of 117, 380, 382; commemorative ribbons 80, *81*; Eastern Front 83–5; *Ersatz* products 378; outbreak of war 37; Paris Peace Conference 396

B

Baden, Prince Max von 380–2, 383
Baghdad 104, *104*, 105
Bairnsfather, Bruce 70, 79, 248, *249*, 322–3, *322*
Balfour, Arthur 377
Balkans 30, 32–6, 118–21, *121*, 396
Ball, Albert 284, 360
balloons 158
Baltic 411, 412
Bank of England 114
banknotes 40–2, *41*
Barbusse, Henri 319
Barnardiston, Brigadier General Nathaniel 86, *87*
Barrès, Maurice 265
Battenberg, Admiral Prince Louis of 50
Bazentin Ridge, Battle of (1916) 226
Beatty, Admiral Sir David 52, 76–7, 252, 254–5, 260, 400
Beaumont-Hamel 222, 227, 230–1
Beaverbrook, Lord 140, 273

Beckles Willson, Major Henry 416–17
Belgium: cemeteries 420, 423; Edith Cavell in 142; floods 70; German atrocities 62–5, 140, 274; Germany invades 57; outbreak of war 37; Paris Peace Conference 394, 395
Below, General Otto von 115, 226, 354
Bennett, Alan 265
Bérenger, Private 198, *199*
Berlin 363, *381*, 382, 407–9, *408*
Bethmann Hollweg, Theobald von 30, 37, 138, 260, 380
Bismarck, Prince Otto von 22, 23, 28–30, 31
Black Hand 34–5
Black Sea 95, 216
Bloem, Walter 198
Blücher, SMS 77, *77*
Blunden, Edmund 318
Board of Agriculture 338–9
Boelcke, Oswald 283, 284, 360
Bojna, Field Marshal Svetozar von 117
Bolsheviks 278–81, 342, 345, 395, 400, 407–9, 410–13, *413*
Bone, Muirhead 323, *325*
boots 54, *55*
Bosnia-Herzegovina 30, 32
Breguet, Louis 160
Breslau, SMS 92–5, 108
Brest-Litovsk, Treaty of (1918) 342, *345*, 395, 410
Briand, Aristide 203, 204, 286, 288
British Army/British Expeditionary Force (BEF) 66–9; Armistice 386; British Army of the Rhine 406; camouflage 178; casualties 73, 121, 150, 220; cemeteries 421–2; demobilization 387, 388; discipline 312–15, *315*; helmets 200–1, *201*, 202, *203*; horses 190; improvements in planning 358–9; logistics 304–7; medals 192–4; Pals battalions 48–9, *49*; recruitment 44–7, *45*, *47*, 48–9, 146–9; shortage of shells 136; transport 70–1, *71*, *73*; trench warfare 164, 206–7; uniforms 66, *67*, 178; weapons 150–3, *151*, *152*, 154–7, *155*; *see also individual battles*
British Empire 12–15, 269, 417
British Legion 427
British Summer Time (BST) 42
Brodie helmet 200–1, *201*, 202, *203*

Broodseinde 297, 298
Brooke, Rupert 265, 318
Brown, Roy 360
Bruchmüller, Lt Colonel Georg 352, 353, 355, 367
Brusilov, General Alexei 215, 216–19, 227, 359
Brusilov offensive (1916) 216–19, *219*, 270, 278
Brussels, SS 144
Buchan, John 138
Bulgaria 118, 120, 121, 372–3, 380, 396, 405
Bülow, General Karl von 64
buses 70–2, *71*, *73*, 304–6
Butte de Vauquois 183
Butterworth, George 265
Byng, General Sir Julian 291, 300, 302–3, 352, 353, 354

C

Cadorna, General Luigi 114–15, 116
Cambrai, Battle of (1917) 300–3, *303*, 352
Cambrai, Battle of (1918) 359
camels 191, 307
camouflage 178, *179*, 346, *346–7*, 349
Canadian troops 348; Battle of Amiens 367; capture Hamel 364; capture Vimy Ridge 183, 286, *289*, 291; casualties 418; gas attacks 168; "Hundred Days Offensive" 371; Third Battle of Ypres 299; war memorial 426
Canal du Nord 371, 372
Cape Helles 108–11
Cape Horn 100, 101
Caporetto, Battle of (1916) 115–16, 352
Carden, Vice-Admiral Sir Sackville 108
Carpathian Mountains 83, 84, 85, 219
Carson, Sir Edward 18, 273
Cartwright, Major M.C.C. 187
Casement, Sir Roger 268
casualties 244, *245*, 262–5, 418–20
cavalry *152*, 160, 190, 290–1, 307
Cavell, Edith 140, 142, *143*, 269
cemeteries 244, 418–21, *422*
Cenotaph 417, 424, *425*, 426
censorship 42, 311
Champagne, the 202, 288, 291
Chantilly conference (1915) 204–5, *204*, 216, 222
Chapman, Guy 150, 153
Chauvel, General Sir Henry 328, 333, 376

Chavasse, Captain Noël 195
Chemin des Dames 291, 355
Chester, HMS 255–6, *255*
Chile 100
China 86, 87, 141
Chisholm, Mairi 192, *193*, 194
Christmas Truce (1914) 78–9, *79*
Churchill, Winston 27, 76, 203;
    Battle of Jutland 254;
    communications 176; criticism
    of Haig 356; Gallipoli campaign
    106–8, 110, 111; helmet 198;
    "Hundred Days Offensive" 371;
    on Rupert Brooke 265; seizes
    Ottoman ships 94; tanks 228
Clarke, Sergeant Leslie 278
Clayton, Rev. Philip (Tubby) 240,
    241, 242
Clemenceau, Georges 194, 344,
    381, 386, 394–5, *397*
clothes, *Ersatz* products 378, *379*
Clydeside shipyards 43
coal 307, 336
Coastal Motor Boats *410–11*, 411,
    412
Cologne 406
Coltman, Sergeant William 246
commemorative ribbons 80, *80*
Committee of Imperial Defence
    159–60, 308
communications 358; aerial
    reconnaissance 160, 176–7,
    308, *309*, 310–11; carrier
    pigeons 177, 188, 191;
    messenger dogs 188, *189*, 191;
    telephones 174–6, *175*, *177*,
    310; wireless 176, 177, 258, *259*
Compiègne, Forest of 384
Connolly, James 266–9
Conrad von Hötzendorf, Franz
    83
conscientious objectors 146,
    148–9
conscription 43, 146–9, *147*, 269
Conservative Party 110, 146, 273
consolation 240–3
Constantine I, King of Greece
    120, 121
Constantinople 93, 94–5, 106–8,
    120, 121
convoys 260–1, 346–9, *348*
Cope, Harold 224, *225*
Cornwell, Jack 255–6
Coronel, Battle of (1914) 100
"Corpse Factory" hoax 141
courts martial 312, 314–15
Cradock, Rear Admiral Sir
    Christopher 100
Crawford, Colonel Fred *17*, 18
crowns *13*, 14–15, *15*, 406, *407*
Ctesiphon, Battle of (1915) 104
Culley, Lt Stuart 282
Cumming, Commander
    Mansfield 308
Cunard 122, 134
Curragh Mutiny (1914) 19, 44

Currie, General Sir Arthur 299,
    366
Cuthbert, Major General Gerald
    359

D
Daily Mail 138–40, 273, 416
Dalton, Hugh 265
Damascus 333, 374, 376, 377, *377*,
    396
Dann, Private 242–3
Dardanelles 94, 106–10, 326
Dartmoor Prison 149
"Dazzle Painting" 178, 346, *346–7*,
    349
de Gaulle, Charles 60–1
de Valera, Eamon 268, 269
Defence of the Realm Act (DORA,
    1914) 42–3
Deighton, Ernie 157
Delhi Durbar (1911) 12, 14–15, *15*
Delville Wood 224, 226, 230
demobilization 387, 388
Denikin, General Anton 413
Derby, Lord 48, 148, 272
Derby Scheme 148
deserters 251, 312, *313*, 314–15,
    330, 380
Deventer, Major General J.L. van
    91
Devonport, Lord 338
Diaz, General Armando 116–17
Dickson, Bertram 159–60
Dimitrijević, Colonel Dragutin
    (Apis) 34, 35
discipline 312–15, *315*
disease 247
Dobell, Lt General Sir Charles
    328
Dodd, Francis 323
Dogger Bank, Battle of (1915)
    76–7, *77*, 252, 254
dogs 176, 188, *189*, 191
Douaumont, Fort 213, 214, 215,
    420, *422*
Dreadnought, HMS 26, *27*
Dresden, SMS 98
Driant, Lt Colonel E.A.C. 212, 213
Dröscher, Captain Otto 124
drums, Pals battalions 48, *49*
Dubail, General Auguste 60
Dublin 266–9, *269*
Duff, Rear Admiral Alexander
    260, 349
Dunn, Captain J.C. 319
Dunsterville, Major General
    Lionel 105

E
eagle, German 88, *89*
East Africa 88–91
Easter Rising (1916) 266–9, *267*,
    269
Eastern Front 80–5, 160, 190,
    216–19, *219*, *431*
Ebert, Friedrich 383, 407, 408–9

Edmonds, Charles 242, 339
Edward, Prince of Wales *264*, *421*
Edward VII, King 24, *27*, 31
Egypt 102, 109, 205
Egyptian Expeditionary Force
    (EEF) 326–8, 374
Eisner, Kurt 383, 408
Elles, Brigadier General Hugh
    300
Emden, SMS 98–100, 348
English Channel 124, 307, 348
Entente Cordiale 26, 30–1
entertainment 234–7, *235*, *236*
Enver Pasha 94, 95, *95*
Ersatz products 378, *379*
Erzberger, Matthias 383, 384–6
Estienne, Colonel Jean Baptiste
    228
Eton College 264, *264*, 265
Evert, General Alexei 218
executions: Charles Fryatt 144–5;
    deserters 312, *313*, 314, 315;
    Easter Rising *266–7*, 269;
    Edith Cavell 142; French
    mutinies 293

F
Falkenhayn, General Erich von
    72, 84, 210–12, 215, 219, 227,
    329, 330
Falkland Islands 74, 101
Fayolle, General Marie Émile
    198, 223
Feisal, Emir 328, 331–3, 374, 377
films *223*, *226*, 227, 228, *229*, 333
Fisher, Admiral Lord "Jackie" 24,
    26, 101, 110, 122
flags 106, *107*, 274, *275*, 384, *385*
Flanders *see* Ypres, *etc*
Foch, Marshal Ferdinand 359;
    Armistice 383, 384–6; Battle
    of Amiens 364, 366, 367;
    "Hundred Days Offensive"
    370–3; and the *Kaiserschlacht*
    354, 355; Plan XVII 60; trench
    warfare 164
Fokker, Anthony 161
Folkestone 129, 307, 386
food: army rations 232–3, *233*;
    canteens 236–7; prisoners
    of war 186; rationing 43,
    338–9, *338*, 340, *341*; shortages
    336–9, *337*, 340–1, 378
football 220, *221*, 236
Forester, C.S. 319
France: 1917 spring offensive
    286–9; aerial reconnaissance
    160; aircraft 282–4; anti-
    German propaganda 140;
    Armistice 383, 384–7;
    camouflage 178; carrier
    pigeons 191; casualties 61, 418;
    cemeteries 420–1, *422*, 423;
    Chantilly conference 204–5,
    204; Entente Cordiale 26,
    30–1; field guns 152, 210, *211*;

gas warfare 168; helmets 200;
    literature 319; medals 194;
    military discipline 314;
    military mining 183; munitions
    306; outbreak of war 37;
    pantalons rouges 58, *59*, 61, *61*,
    178; Paris Peace Conference
    394–7; Plan XVII 60–1; *poilu*
    dolls 292, *293*; and the
    Schlieffen plan 54, 160;
    soldiers mutiny 291, 292–3;
    spies 311; and Syria 377, 396;
    trench warfare 164; *see also*
    individual battles
Franchet d'Espèrey, General
    Louis 121, 380
Franco-Prussian War (1870–71)
    28, 54, 56, 58, 62, 154, 162
Francois, General Hermann von
    82
Franz Ferdinand, Archduke 32–6,
    33
Franz Josef, Emperor 37
Freikorps 409
French, Field Marshal Sir John
    164, 312; Battle of Loos 173,
    204; Battle of Mons 158;
    Chantilly conference *204*,
    205; and the Marne 68–9;
    resignation 205; Second Battle
    of Ypres 169; shortage of shells
    136
Frontiers, Battle of the (1914)
    60–1, *61*, 178
Fryatt, Captain Charles 144–5,
    145
Fullerphone 174, *175*

G
Galicia *80–1*, 83, 218
Gallieni, Joseph 160, 203
Gallipoli campaign (1915-16) 47,
    106–11, *107*, *109*, *111*, 120, 136,
    162, 203, 205, 216, 270, *432*
Garros, Roland 160–1
gas warfare 166–9, *166–7*, *169*,
    172, 318, *320–1*, 321
Gaza 326, 328, 329, 332, 374
Geddes, Sir Eric 307
General Election (1918) 388–9,
    389
generalship 356–9
geophones 180, *181*, 182
George V, King 12, *13*, 14–15, *15*,
    40, 70, *195*, 273, 331, 384, 417,
    426
Georges-Picot, François 377
Germany: aerial bombing
    campaign 126–9, *128*; aerial
    reconnaissance 160; aircraft
    283–5; alliance with Austria-
    Hungary 30; Armistice 383,
    384–7, 406; atrocities 62–5, 74,
    140, *141*, 274; Brest-Litovsk
    peace talks 345; casualties 418;
    cemeteries 420; collapse of

morale 378–80; deserters 380; East African campaign 88–91; Eastern Front 80–5; *Ersatz* products 378, *379*; executions 142, 144–5; flying aces 360, 362–3, *363*; food shortages 378; gas warfare 166, 168–9; intelligence operations 308–11; jackboots 54, *55*; *Kaiserschlacht* 345, 350–5, 364, 370; "Last Hundred Days" 368–73, 380–3; literature 319; logistics 306; medals 194; military discipline 314; military mining 180, 183; outbreak of war 35–7, *36*; Paris Peace Conference 394–7, *394*; *Pickelhaube* (helmet) 20–1, 198, 201; prisoners of war 186–7; propaganda 138–41, *139*, *141*; reparations 388, 394, 396; Schlieffen plan 54–7, 160, 306; "tapping" devices 174; trench warfare 164, 206; turmoil after war 382, 383, 406–9; unification of 20, 22–3, 31; weapons 153, 154, 156, 157, 306; *see also* High Seas Fleet, U-boats *and individual battles*
Gheluvelt 72, 297, 298
glove, petrified 166, *167*
Gneisenau, SMS 86, 100–1
Godley, Private Sidney 68
Goeben, SMS 92–5, *95*, 108
Good Hope, HMS 100
Gorlice 85
Gotha bombers 129, 251, 362
Gough, General Sir Hubert 19, 226, 230, 296–8, 352–3, 354
Gouraud, General Henri 355
Grand Fleet *see* Royal Navy
Graves, Robert 240–1, 316, 318, 319
Graves Registration Commission 244, 246, 421
Great Yarmouth 74, 128
Greece 118–21, 396, 405
Grey, Sir Edward 37
Groener, General Wilhelm 382, 383, 408
Grosz, Georg 325
guns *see* weapons
Guynemer, Georges 284, 360
Gwyer, Margaret *122–3*

H
Hague Convention (1899) 74, 158, 168, 184, 186
Haig, Field Marshal Sir Douglas 234, 323, *357*; 1917 Flanders offensive 294–6; appeals to the troops 350, *351*, 355; attitudes to 356; Battle of Amiens 366, 367; Battle of Cambrai 301–3; Battle of Loos 172, 173; Battle of the Somme 176, 222–4, 226, 227,

230; ceasefire terms 383; death 359, 392; earldom 427; First Battle of Ypres 73; "Hundred Days Offensive" 368, 371, 373; and the *Kaiserschlacht* 352, 353–4; military discipline 314–15; relations with Lloyd George 288, 296, 352, 354; strategy for 1916 205; tanks 228, 230; Third Battle of Ypres 296–9
Hakkı Bey, İsmail 105
Haldane, Richard 66
Hamel 364, 366–7
Hamilton, General Sir Ian 109–10, 111, 162
Hanukkah lamp 326, *327*
Harden, Arthur 234, *235*
Harding, Warren G. 404–5
Hardinge, Lord 102
Harper, Major General Sir George 290, 302
Harrison, Captain H.A. 187
Harrison, William 146, *147*
Hartlepool 74–6, *75*
Hase, Commander Georg von 254
Hassell, Gordon 300, *301*, 302
Hawthorn Ridge 182–3, 222, 227
Heffer, Corporal Randall 299
Hejaz 332, 376, 402
Heligoland Bight, Battle of (1914) 52, *53*
helmets and headgear 20–1, 112, *113*, 130, *131*, 198–201, *199*, *201–3*
Hemingway, Ernest 262, 318
High Seas Fleet/Imperial German Navy 8–9, 23; attacks English coast 74–6; Battle of Dogger Bank 76–7, *77*; Battle of the Falkland Islands 101; Battle of Jutland 252–7, 258; defeats Japan 86–7; in Indian Ocean 98–100; mutinies 382, 400, 406–7; opening of hostilities 50–3, *53*; and the Ottoman Empire 92–5; Paris Peace Conference 394; rivalry with Royal Navy 24–7; scuttled at Scapa Flow 398–401, *401*
Highgate, Private Thomas 312, *313*, 314
Hindenburg, Field Marshal Paul von 270, 359; Armistice 383; Battle of the Somme 227; Battle of Tannenberg 82–3; and the Brusilov offensive 218–19; Eastern Front 84; German propaganda 141; *Kaiserschlacht* 350; "Last Hundred Days" 368, 370; Versailles Treaty 397
Hindenburg Line 231, 288, 289, 300–2, 371–3
Hipper, Admiral Franz von 74, 76–7, 252, 254, 256, 257

Hitler, Adolf 191, 405
Hoffmann, Colonel Max 82–3
Holtzendorff, Admiral Henning von 260
Holzminden camp 184, 187
Homondos 118
Hood, Admiral 255
Horne, General Sir Henry 289, 354
horses 72, 188–91, *190*, 304, *306*, 307
Hossack, Anthony R. 166
House, "Colonel" Edward M. 342–4, 383, 395
House of Lords 16, 18
howitzers 150, *151*, 152, 153
Hulse, Captain Sir Edward 78
"Hundred Days Offensive" (1918) 190, 368–73
Hussein, Sherif 331–2, 377, 402
Hutier, General Oskar von 352, 353

I
Immelmann, Max 283, 284, 360
Imperial Navy *see* High Seas Fleet
Imperial War Graves Commission 244, 418, 422–3
Imperial War Museum, London (foundation) 414–17, *416*
Indefatigable, HMS 252, *253*, 254
Independent Labour Party 339
Independent Socialist Party (Germany) 382, 407–8
India 102; Delhi Durbar (1911) 12, 14–15, *15*; troops 90, 102–5, 168, 180, 348, 374
Indian Ocean 98–100
industry 23; armaments 132–3, *133*, 134–7, *137*; women workers 130–3, *134*, 137, 149
influenza 387
intelligence 74–6, 82, 308–11, *311*
Inter-Allied Intelligence Bureau 311
Ireland 16–19, 62, *63*, 266–9, *267*, *269*
Irish National Party 266
Irish Republican Brotherhood (IRB) 266–9
Irish Sea 124
Irish Volunteers 18, 19
Iron Cross 74, *75*, 76, 92–3, 194
Islam 102, 326, 374
Isonzo offensives (1915–17) 114–16, *115*, *116*
Italy *432*; aerial bombing 126; campaigns against Austria-Hungary 112–15, 116–17; casualties 115, 117; Isonzo offensives 114–16, *115*, *116*; last days of war 382; and League of Nations 405; military discipline 314; Paris

Peace Conference 394, 396; trench helmets 112, *113*

J
Jackson, Conway 170, *171*
Jackson, Captain Thomas 310
Japan 86–7, *87*, 162, 405, 412
Jellicoe, Admiral Sir John 51–2, 76, 254–7, 260, 261, 296, 310, 349
Jerusalem 326, *327*, 329, 332
Jews 326, *327*, 377
Joffre, General Joseph 203–4; Battle of Loos 170–2; Battle of the Somme 224, 226; Battle of Verdun 212, 213, 215; Chantilly conference *204*, 205; and the Marne 68–9; Nivelle replaces 286; and the "Noyons Bulge" 202; Plan XVII 60, 61
Jünger, Ernst 153, 319
Jutland, Battle of (1916) 77, 252–7, *255*, *256*, 258, 270, 310

K
Kaiserkonferenz (1918) 370
Kaiserschlacht (1918) 345, 350–5, 364, 370
Karl, Emperor 380
Kell, Captain Vernon 308–10
Kemal, Mustafa (Atatürk) 109, 405
Kennington, Eric 323, 324–5
Kerensky, Alexander 281
Khaki election (1918) 388–9, *389*
Kiel 382, 400, 406
Kings African Rifles 90, *91*
Kipling, Rudyard 12, 138, 318, 423
Kitchener, Earl 68, 204, 205; appointment to Cabinet 44–5; iconic image 44, *45*; Battle of Loos 172; death 272; Gallipoli campaign 108, 110; in Khartoum 12; recruiting campaign 44–7, *45*, 48, 146, 148, 320
Kluck, General Alexander von 67, 68, 69, 160
Knocker, Elsie 192
Kolchak, Admiral Alexander 412–13
Kressenstein, General Friedrich Kress von 328, 329
Kut 102, 104–5, 186, 270, 332

L
La Bassée canal 172, 354
La Boisselle 183, 223
Labour Party 148
Lancashire and Yorkshire Railway (LYR) 130, *131*
Lance, HMS 50, *51*
language, French 238, *239*
Lanrezac, General Charles 60, 61, 67

Law, Andrew Bonar 272, 273
Lawrence, T.E. (Lawrence of
    Arabia) 328, 330–3, *330–1,*
    333, 374, 376, 377, 402
Le Cateau, Battle of (1914) 68,
    152–3
League of Nations 394, 395, 396,
    402–5, *405*
leave 248–51, *249, 250*
Lenin *280,* 281, 342, 345, 395,
    412
Leroux, Georges Paul *214*
letters and parcels 243, *243*
Lettow-Vorbeck, Lt Colonel Paul
    von 90–1
Lewis, Cecil 183
Lewis, Wyndham 323, 324
Lewis guns 156, *157*
Liberal Party 148, 273, 389
"Liberty Bonds" 141
Liebknecht, Karl 409
Liège 57, 64, 65, 126, 212
Liman von Sanders, General Otto
    109, 376
Lissauer, Ernst 141
listening devices 180, *181,* 182
literature 262, 265, 316–19, *319*
Liverpool 128–9, 134
Lloyd George, David 15, 37,
    261, 333; 1917 Flanders
    offensive 295–6; and air
    warfare 362; Battle of the
    Somme 231; becomes prime
    minister 270–3, *271, 272;*
    ceasefire terms 381, 383;
    and the Cenotaph 424; and
    convoys 348, 349; denounces
    Anglo-Boer War 14; food
    rationing 338; Imperial War
    Museum 416; and the
    Kaiserschlacht 352, 354; Khaki
    Election 389; Minister for
    Munitions 134, 136, 272;
    Palestine campaign 327, 329;
    Paris Peace Conference 394–5,
    397; relations with Haig 288,
    296, 352, 354, 356; Third
    Battle of Ypres 299; and
    Wilson's Fourteen Points
    344
Lochnagar crater 183
logistics 304–7
London 126, 128, 129, 384, 386–7,
    387
London, Treaty of (1915) 114
London Regiment ("London
    Scottish") 72–3, 421
Loos 288
Loos, Battle of (1915) 156, 169,
    170–3, *172,* 182, 204, 358
Loraine, Robert 159
Lord Roberts Memorial
    Workshops 270, *271*
Lorraine *see* Alsace-Lorraine
lost generation 262–5
Louvain *64,* 65, 140, 142

Ludendorff, Erich von 117, 141,
    270, 292, 307, 359; assault
    on Liège 65; Battle of Amiens
    364; Battle of Arras 290, 291;
    Battle of the Somme 227, 231;
    Battle of Tannenberg 82–3;
    "Black Day" 367; and the
    Brusilov offensive 218–19;
    Kaiserschlacht 350–5; "Last
    Hundred Days" 368, 370, 371,
    372; loses Messines Ridge 296;
    and peace negotiations 380–2;
    in Poland 84; Third Battle of
    Ypres 299
Lusitania, RMS 122, *123,* 124–5,
    140, 142, 276
Lutyens, Sir Edwin 423, 424, 426
Luxemburg, Rosa 409
Lys, Battle of (1918) 355

M
McCudden, James 360
MacDonagh, Tomas 266
McDowell, John 227
machine guns 154–7, *155, 157,*
    161
MacIntyre, Lt Robert 118
Mackensen, Field Marshal von
    85, 120
McMahon, Sir Henry 331–2
Macmillan, Harold 236
MacNeill, Eoin 268
"Madonnas of Pervyse" 192, 194
Maginot, André 215
Mahan, Captain Alfred 24–5
Malins, Geoffrey 227
Mangin, General Charles 355,
    368
Manning, Frederic 315, 318–19
Mannock, Major Edward "Mick"
    360–2, 363
maps 311; of casualties 244, *245*
Marconi, Guglielmo 176
Marne, Battle of the (1914) 158,
    159, 191, 203
Marne, River 68–9, 355
Marshall, Lt General Sir William
    105
Martin, Captain Albert 388, *389*
Marwitz, General Georg von der
    353
Mary, Queen *15,* 384, *385*
mask, tank 300, *301*
Masterman, Charles 138, 323
Masurian Lakes 83, 85, 160
Mata Hari 311
Matania, Fortunino 325
Mathy, *Kapitänleutnant* Heinrich
    126, 128, 129
Maude, Lt General Sir Stanley
    105
Maxim-Vickers machine guns
    154–6, *155*
medals 192–5, *193, 195*
medical treatment 192, 241,
    246–7, *247*

Mediterranean 92–5
Megiddo, Battle of (1918) 190, 374
Menin Gate 244, *421,* 423, 426
Menin Road 72, 73, 294, 297, 298
mental health problems 240–1
merchant shipping 144; convoys
    260–1, 346–9, *348;* "Dazzle
    Painting" 178, 346, *346–7,* 349;
    U-boat threat 122–5, 258,
    260–1
Mesopotamia 102–5, 307, 311,
    377, 396
message streamers 158, *159*
Messer, Lt Colonel Arthur 244
Messines, Battle of (1917) 157
Messines Ridge 72, 183, 294, 296,
    355
Meuse, River 212, 215
Mexico 276, 277
MI5 310, 311
Military Service Act (1916) 148
Miller, Sergeant Major John
    24–5
Miller, Reginald 418, *419*
Milne, Admiral Sir Archibald
    Berkeley 92–3
mining, military 180–3, *182,* 222
Ministry of Food 338–9
Ministry of Information 140
Ministry of Munitions 132, 134,
    136–7, 148, 272–3, 307
"Miracle of the Marne" (1914)
    160, 203
"the missing" 244, 247, 423
Moltke, Helmuth von 35, 57
Moltke, Helmuth von "the
    Younger" 35, 57, 82
Monash, Lt General John 364,
    366–7
Mond, Sir Alfred 416, 417
money, paper 40–2, *41*
Monmouth, HMS 100
Monro, General Sir Charles 110
"Monroe Doctrine" 395
Mons 386
Mons, Battle of (1914) 67–9, 158,
    160, 198, 312
Montauban 49, 223
Monte Nero *115*
Moore, Montague 294
Morgan, J.P. 276
Morocco 27
Morse Code 159, 160, 174, 176, 177
Moseley, Henry 265
"Mother" of guns 150, *151,* 417
mules 190, 191, 307
Müller, Karl Friedrich Max von
    98–100
munitions: artillery 150–3, *151,*
    152; ceasefire terms 383; gas
    warfare 166–9; gun to shoot
    seagulls 398, *399;* HMS *Lance's*
    gun 50, *51,* 417; logistics 306–7;
    machine guns 154–7, *155, 157,*
    161; Maxim guns 118, *119;*
    mines 182; Néry gun 414, *415;*

production of 132–3, *133,*
    134–7, *135, 137;* revolvers 316,
    317; rifles *330–1,* 331; shells 47,
    110, 134–6, *135, 137,* 150–3,
    306–7; *soixante-quinze* field
    guns 210, *211;* trench clubs
    206, *207;* trench mortars 286,
    287; Zeppelin ammunition box
    126, *127*
Munro, Dr Hector 192
Murmansk 412
Murray, General Sir Archibald
    326–8
Mussolini, Benito 117, 405
mutinies: in Britain 388, 389;
    Curragh Mutiny 19, 44; French
    army 291, 292–3; German navy
    382, 400, 406–7

N
Namur 57, 212
Nash, John 323
Nash, Paul 323–4
National Service League 146
naval warfare *see* High Seas Fleet;
    Royal Navy
Nazi Party 409
Néry gun 414, *415*
neutrality, American 274–6
Neuve Chapelle, Battle of (1915)
    136, 150, 168, 170, 173, 176
Nevill, Wilfred "Billie" 220, *221,*
    265
Nevinson, Christopher R.W. 323,
    324, 336, *337*
New Zealand 106, 108–9, 418; *see
    also* ANZACs
Newcastle-upon-Tyne 48, *49*
newspapers 42, 138–40, 319
Nicholas II, Tsar 85, 217–18, 219,
    279–80, 288, 395
Nivelle, General Robert 215, 288,
    291, 292
Nixon, Lt General Sir John 104–5
No-Conscription Fellowship
    (NCF) 146, *147,* 148
no-man's land 78, 164, 178, 192,
    206, 209
North Sea 124, 125, *434*
Northcliffe, Lord 140, 273
Norton-Griffiths, Major John 182
Noske, Gustav 406, 409
Notre Dame de Lorette, Battle of
    (1915) 176, 420
Number Seven Filling Factory,
    Hayes 132–3

O
"Old Bill" character 70, 323
Operation Alberich 288
Operation Blücher 355
Operation Georgette 354
Operation Hagen 370
Operation Michael 352–3, 354
Orlando, Vittorio Emanuele 394,
    397

Orpen, Sir William 323, 392, *393*
Ostend 296, 373
Ottoman Empire: Arab Revolt 330–3; Armistice 382; Balkan Wars 30; collapse of 396; enters war 92–5; in Fourteen Points 345; Gallipoli campaign 106–11; Mesopotamian campaign 102–5; Palestine campaign 326–9, 374–7; prisoners of war 186
Ovillers *157*, 222
Owen, Wilfred 166, 265, 318

P
pacifism 148–9, *149*
Paget, Lt General Sir Arthur 18–19
Palestine 190, 191, 238, 307, 311, 326–9, *329*, 345, 359, 374–7, 396, *433*
Pals battalions 48–9, *49*, 222, 223, 262, 414
Pankhurst, Emmeline 18, 130
pantalons rouges 58, *59*, 61, *61*
Paris 129, 160, 350, 355, 387
Paris Peace Conference (1919) 323, 333, 392–7, *397*, 402, 413
Parr, John 386
Partridge, Bernard 321–2
Passchendaele (Third Battle of Ypres, 1917) *177*, 244, 294–9, *297*, *298*
Pearse, Padraig 266–9
pen, Ulster Covenant *16–17*
Pershing, General John 276, 370–1, 372, 383
Persia 105
Pétain, Philippe 213–14, 215, 292–3, 296, 353, 355
Petrograd 278–81, *280*, 345
photography 160, 308, *309*, 310–11
Piave, Battle of the (1918) 117
Pickelhaube helmet *20–1*, 198, 201
pig (Tirpitz) 98, *99*, 101
pigeons 177, 188, 191
Plan XVII 60–1
Plumer, General Lord 183, 295–9, 354, 423
Plüschow, Günther 187
poetry 262, 265, 316–18
Poland 84, 344, 396, 402, *403*, 405, 413
Poperinghe 237, 238, 240, 242
poppies 427, *427*
postage stamps 402, *403*
postal service 234, 243
postcards 216, *217*, 234
posters 28–9, 44–5, 62, *63*, 64, 141, *141*, 320
Pozières 150, *202*, 222, 226–7
prayer book 170, *171*
Price, Private George Lawrence 386
Prinćip, Gavrilo 32, 34, *35*

prison, conscientious objectors 146, 149
prisoners of war (POWs) *83*, 184–7, *185*, *187*, *366*, 368, *368–9*
Prittwitz, General Maximilian von 80–2
propaganda 62, *63*, 65, 138–41, *139*, *141*, 142
Prussia 20, 28–30, 62, 80–2, 396; *see also* Germany
Przemysl 84, *84*, 85
Punch 16, *31*, 320, 321–2

Q
Q ships 349
Quakers 149

R
Rabagliati, Euan 158
"the race to the sea" 70
radio 158, 176, 177, 258, *259*
railways 56–7, 130, *131*, 304, *305*, 307
Rasputin, Grigoriy 279
rationing 43, 338–9, *338*, 340, *341*
Rawlinson, General Sir Henry 205; Battle of Amiens 366, 367; Battle of the Somme 176, 222, 224, 226–7, 230, 358; and the *Kaiserschlacht* 354, 358; "Hundred Days Offensive" 371; and the Pals battalions 48
reconnaissance, aerial 158, *159*, 160, *161*, 176–7, 283
recruitment 44–7, *45*, 47, 48–9, *62–3*, 141, *141*, 146, 414
Red Cross 186, 194
Redmond, John 266, 269
religion 240, *241*, 242
Remarque, Erich 319
Remembrance Day 426, 427, *427*
Rennenkampf, General Paul von 82, 93
reparations 394, 396
Repington, Lt Colonel Charles 136
Representation of the People Act (1918) 133, 388–9
Reuter, Rear Admiral Ludwig von 400
Rheims cathedral *62–3*, 140
Rhineland 383, 387, 406
Rhodes, Cecil 14
Rhodes, Ernie 232
Rhondda, Lord 338
ribbons, commemorative 80, *81*
Richards, Private Frank 78–9, 236, 242, 246, 319
Richardson, Major Edwin 188
Richborough 307
Richthofen, Manfred von (the "Red Baron") 194, 285, 360, *361*, 362–3, *363*
Robeck, Vice-Admiral John de 108

Roberts, Field Marshal Lord 146
Robertson, Sir William 204, 205
Robinson, Frederick 228
Robinson, Lt William Leefe 129
Rogers, Gilbert 324
Romania 120, 205, 219, 270, 380, 396
Rommel, Erwin 194
Room 40 74–6, 258, 310
Roosevelt, Theodore 276
Rosenberg, Isaac 265, 318
Rothenstein, William 323
Rothermere, Lord 362
Rothschild, Lord 377
Rowden, Eric 78, *79*
Royal Aircraft Factory 284, 285
Royal Arsenal, Woolwich *133*
Royal Artillery 153, 191
Royal Engineers (RE) 162, 174, 178, 182, 307, 310
Royal Field Artillery (RFA) 152, 153
Royal Flying Corps (RFC)/Royal Air Force (RAF): aerial reconnaissance 160, 177, 308, 310; fighter planes 282, *283*, 284–5, 360–3; formation of RAF 362; medals 194; weapons 156, 284; and the Zeppelin raids 128–9
Royal Garrison Artillery (RGA) *150*, 153, *177*
Royal Horse Artillery 68, 152
Royal Naval Air Service (RNAS) 128, 160
Royal Navy/Grand Fleet: Battle of Coronel 100; Battle of Dogger Bank 76–7; Battle of the Falkland Islands 101; Battle of Jutland 77, 252–7; blockades Germany 52–3, 74, 340; communications 176; convoys 349; logistics 307; medals 194; in the Mediterranean 92–4; mutinies 389; opening of hostilities 50–3, *53*; rivalry with Germany 24–7; and Russian civil war *410–11*, 411, 412; submarine warfare 258
Royal Warwickshire Regiment *73*
Royal Welsh Fusiliers 242
Ruprecht, Crown Prince 60, 141, 298, 352, 353, 364
Russell, Bertrand 43
Russia: Battle of Tannenberg 80, 82–3, 160; Brusilov offensive 216–19, 278; casualties 83, 85, 418; cemeteries 420–1; civil war 345, 410–13; and the Gallipoli campaign 108; German successes against 83–5; Mesopotamian campaign 105; outbreak of war 37; Paris Peace Conference 395; peace talks 342–5, 350, 410; prisoners of war 186, 187;

relationship with Britain 31; Revolution 219, 278–81, *279*, 288, 339
Russo-Japanese War (1904–5) 162

S
St Mihiel 370–1, *371*
St Quentin 371, 372
Saladin 94, 326, 374, *375*
Salandra, Antonio 112–14
Salonika Front 118–21, *121*, 204, 205, 380, *432*
Samsonov, General Alexander 82
Sarajevo 32–5, *35*
Sargent, John Singer 166, *320–1*, 321, 323
Sarrail, General Maurice 120
Sassoon, Siegfried 316, 317–18, *317*, 319, 356
Scapa Flow 50, 51–2, 53, 398–401, *401*
Scarborough 74–6, *75*
Scharnhorst, SMS 86, 100–1, *101*
Scheer, Admiral Reinhard 252–7, 258–60, 261, 310, 382
Scheidemann, Philipp 383, 397
Schlieffen, Count Alfred von 23, 54–7, 358
Schlieffen plan 23, 54–7, 160, 306
schools 264–5, *264*
Schrecklichkeit 62, 65, 74
Schwaben Redoubt 222
Schwieger, Captain Walther 124
Secret Service Bureau 308
Serbia 30, 32–7, 118, 120
Serre 48–9, 222, 230
Sharqut, Battle of (1918) 105
Shaw, George Bernard 319
Shaw, Captain Jack 184, *185*
"shell shock" 241, 315
shells 47, 110, 134–6, *135*, *137*, 150–3, 306–7
Sherriff, R.C. 242
shipping *see* merchant shipping; High Seas Fleet; Royal Navy
Short, Private William 202, *203*, 417
shovel, trench 162, *163*
shrapnel 198, 246
signals intelligence (Sigint) 310
Silber, Jules 311
Sinai 190, 191, 307, 326–8
Sinn Fein 266
Smith-Dorrien, General Sir Horace 68, 79, 168, 169, 312
Smuts, General Jan Christian 90–1, 362
Social Democratic Party (SPD) 380, 383, 406–9
social life 234–7, 238–9
Somme, Battle of the (1916) 173, 286, *325*, 358–9; air warfare 284; casualties 48–9, 61, 244, *245*, 270; communications 176;

continuation of 224–7; film of *223*, *226*, 227, 228, 333; first day of 220–3; helmets 200, 202; machine guns 157; mines 182–3; road to the Somme 202–5; tanks 228–31
Sopwith Camel *282–3*, 285, *285*, 363
Souchon, Admiral Wilhelm 92–5, *92–3*
South Africa 90
South America 100–1
Southampton 307
Spartacist League 408–9
Spee, Admiral Maximilian Graf von 86, 98, 100–1, *101*
spies 308–10, 311
spring offensives (German, 1918) *see Kaiserschlacht*
Stahlhelm helmet 201
Stalin, Joseph 150
Startin, Harold 206, *207*
Stein, Gertrude 262
Stickings, F.G. 216, *217*
streamers, message 158, *159*
strikes 17, *19*, 43, 137, 388, 389, 406–9; *see also* mutinies
Sturdee, Vice-Admiral Sir Doveton 100
submarines *see* U-boats
Suez Canal 102, 326
Suffragettes 18, 130
superstitions 242
Supreme Censorship Office 140
Suvla Bay 110, 111
Sweden 276–7, 310, 348, 395, 405
Swinton, Major Ernest 228
sword, samurai 86, *87*
Sykes, Sir Mark 376–7
Sykes-Picot Agreement (1916) 333, 377
Syria 333, 345, 374, 376–7, 396

T

Talaat Pasha 94
Talbot, Rev. Neville 240
Talbot House ("Toc H") 240, 242
tanks 228–31, *229*, *231*, 290, 300–3, *301*, *303*, 364, *365*
Tannenberg, Battle of (1914) 80, 82–3, *83*, 141, 160, 186, 190, 310
Tarnow 85
telegraph 174, 177
telephones 174–6, *175*, *177*, 310
Tempest, 2nd Lt Wulfstan 126
Thiepval 222, 224, 230, 244, 423
Thomas, Edward 262, *263*, 265, 318
Thomas, Lowell 333
Tirpitz, Admiral Alfred von 24–6
Tirpitz (pig) 98, *99*, 101
"Toc H" 240, 242
Togoland 88, *88*
toilet paper 138, *139*
Tolkien, J.R.R. 318

Tonks, Henry 321
Townsend, Major General Sir Charles 104–5
Townsend, Frederick Henry 322
toys 292, *293*
trade unions 43, 132, 137
Trades Union Congress 148, 344
Train, Charles William *195*
transport: cross-Channel 307; horses 304, *306*; London buses 70–2, *71*, *73*, 304–6; railways 56–7, 130, *131*, 304, *305*, 307; women workers 130
tree, camouflage 178, *179*
trench warfare 69, 162–5, *165*; aerial reconnaissance 160; casualties 208; communications 174–7, *175*, *177*; daily life 206–7, *209*; dressing stations 192; helmets 112, *113*, 198–201, *199*, 202, *203*; intelligence 308, *309*; logistics 306; mining 180–3, *181*, *182*; shovels 162, *163*; trench clubs 206, *207*; truces 78–9
Trenchard, Major General Sir Hugh 284, 362, 363
Trieste 112, 114, 117
Triple Entente 26
Trotsky, Leon 281, 342, 345, *345*, 413
truces 78–9
Tsingtao 86–7, *86*, 98
Tudor, Brigadier General Hugh 300–2
Tunnelling Companies 182–3
Turkey 405, 426
Turner, Captain Bill 124

U

U-boats 27, *125*, 252, *261*; and America's entry into war 260, 276–7; attack merchant shipping 122–5, 144–5; ceasefire terms 383; and convoys 348–9; and "Dazzle Painting" 347; and food shortages 336–8; Q ships and 349; sink *Lusitania* 122, 124–5; surrender of 398; threat to Scapa Flow 51–2; unrestricted campaign 258–61, 296; wireless receiver 258, *259*
Ukraine 345, 380
Ulster Covenant 17, 18–19
Ulster Unionists 266
Ulster Volunteer Force (UVF) 18, 19
uniforms: British 66, *67*, 224, *225*; camouflage 178; German caps 294, *295*; jackboots 54, *55*; *pantalons rouges* 58, *59*, 61, *61*
United States of America: Armistice 383, 387; cemeteries 420; and Easter Rising 269;

enters war 260, 261, 274–7, *275*; and League of Nations 404–5; Paris Peace Conference 394–6; propaganda 140, 141, *141*; sinking of the *Lusitania* 124–5, 276; uniforms 178; Wilson's Fourteen Points 342–5, *343*, 380, 381, 383, 394, 395, 402; *see also* American Expeditionary Force
Unknown Warrior 392, *393*, 417, 424, 426
US Congress 274, 277, 344, 404

V

Venizelos, Eleftherios 120, 121
Verdun 288, 420, *422*
Verdun, Battle of (1916) 140, 173, 201, 205, 210–15, *213*, *214*, 222, 270, 284, 286
Versailles Treaty (1919) 117, 323, 392–7, 400, 402, 405, 409, 424
Vickers machine gun 154–6, *155*, 157
Victor Emmanuel III, King of Italy 114
Victoria Cross (VC) 195
Villa, Francisco "Pancho" 276
Villa Giusti, Armistice of (1918) 117
Villers-Bretonneux 426
Villers-Cotterêts 355, 364, 368
Vimy Ridge 173, 176, 183, 286, *287*, 289, *289*, 291, 420
Vittorio Veneto, Battle of (1918) 117
Vladivostok 412, 413
Vorticism 323, 324
Vosges 165

W

walking stick 102, *102–3*
war memorials 423, 424, *425*, 426
War Propaganda Bureau *see* Wellington House
Ware, Fabian 244, *245*, 421, 422
Warneford, Sub-Lt Reginald 128
Warrender, Vice-Admiral Sir George 76
Warsaw 85
watch, Charles Fryatt's 144, *145*
water, logistics 307
Watson, General Sir David 299
weapons *see* munitions
weather 209
Webb, Beatrice 424
Wellington House (War Propaganda Bureau) 138, 140, 141, 323
Wells, H.G. 138
Wemyss, Admiral Sir Rosslyn 261, 384–6, 401
Westminster Abbey, London 426
Whitby 74, *75*
Wilhelm I, Kaiser 20, 22

Wilhelm II, Kaiser *22*, 322; abdication 383, 389, 397, 407; aerial bombing 128, 129; ambitions 23, 31; anti-German propaganda 138, *139*, 140; Armistice 381; Battle of Jutland 252, 257; Battle of Verdun 210; crown 406, *407*; and the Eastern Front 80; First Battle of Ypres 72; and Imperial Navy 24–7, 76, 77; and the *Kaiserschlacht* 353; last days of war 355, 370, 373, 382; and the Ottoman Empire 94, *95*, 102; outbreak of war 35–7; and Saladin's tomb 374, *375*; submarine warfare 122, 260; Wilhelmshaven 53, 122, 382
Wilkins, Sister Elizabeth 142
Wilkinson, Norman 347
Wilkinson, Lt Commander Ralph 106
Wilson, General Sir Henry 296
Wilson, Woodrow: America enters war 260, 274, 276–7, *277*; Armistice 177, 381, 383; Fourteen Points 342–5, *343*, 380, 381, 383, 394, 395, 402; and League of Nations 404; Paris Peace Conference 394–6, *397*; sinking of the *Lusitania* 124–5; stroke 404
Wipers Times 319
wireless communications 176, 177, 258, *259*
women: employment 130–3, *130–1*, 137, 149; sex 237; voting rights 388–9
Women's Army Auxiliary Corps 133, 194
Women's Land Army 133, 339
Woolwich Arsenal *19*
wounds 246–7
Wrexham, SS 144
Wynne Jones, Captain E. 170

Y

YMCA 194, 237
Young Turks 94
Ypres 238, 244
Ypres, First Battle of (1914) 70, 72–3, *73*
Ypres, Second Battle of (1915) 166, 168–9
Ypres, Third Battle of (Passchendaele, 1917) *177*, 244, 294–9, *297*, *298*
Yser, River 165

Z

Zeebrugge 296, 373
Zeppelins 126–9, *127*, *128*, 251, 252, 258, 270, 282
"Zimmermann telegram" 260, 276–7, 310
Zouaves *61*

OBJECT SOURCE REFERENCES

01 Imperial crown
(Royal Collection)

02 Ulster pen
(Ulster Museum)

03 *Pickelhaube*
(IWM UNI 12198)

04 Recruitment sign
(IWM FEQ 144)

05 European map
(IWM PST 6964)

06 Archduke's tunic
(Heeresgeschichtliches Museum,
Vienna)

07 Paper money
(IWM CUR 12700 and CUR 12701)

08 Kitchener artwork
(IWM PST 2735)

09 Newcastle Commercials' Drum
(IWM EPH 3122)

10 HMS *Lance* gun
(IWM ORD 114)

11 Marching boots
(IWM UNI 12643)

12 *Pantalons rouges*
(IWM UNI 12209)

13 Atrocity poster
(IWM PST 13606)

14 Web equipment
(IWM EQU 714)

15 London bus
(IWM 4017.5.1)

16 Mock Iron Cross
(IWM EPH 2171)

17 Christmas Truce button
(IWM DOCS E Rowden)

18 Commemorative ribbons
(IWM EPHEM 00488 and IWM
EPHEM 00505)

19 Barnardiston's sword
(IWM WEA 1272/1)

20 African eagle
(IWM EPH 9011)

21 Souchon's medals
(IWM OMD 6240-
6250)

22 Tirpitz the pig
(IWM EPH 9032)

23 Anderson's stick
(IWM UNI 12252)

24 Australian flag
(IWM FLA 2038)

25 Italian helmet
(IWM UNI 12281)

26 Bulgarian maxim
(IWM FIR 9205)

27 *Lusitania* passenger's camisole
(IWM UNI 11978)

28 Zeppelin ammunition box
(IWM FIR 11621)

29 Ticket collector's hat
(IWM UNI 9694)

30 First heavy shell
(IWM MUN 3281)

31 Kaiser Bill toilet roll
(IWM EPH 5245)

32 Cavell's diary
(IWM DOCS Edith Cavell)

33 Fryatt's watch
(IWM EPH 10292)

34 NCF membership card
(IWM DOCS W Harrison)

35 "Mother" 9.2" Howitzer
(IWM ORD 108)

36 Vickers machine gun
(IWM FIR 8100)

37 Message streamer
(IWM FLA 394)

38 Trench shovel
(IWM FEQ 5255)

39 Petrified glove
(IWM EPH 4377)

40 Jackson's prayer book
(IWM DOCS 2nd Lieutenant
E C Jackson)

41 Fullerphone
(IWM COM 176)

42 Deceptive tree
(IWM FEQ 854)

43 Geophone
(IWM FEQ 874)

44 Escape aids
(IWM EPH 810)

45 Dog collar
(IWM COM 1068)

46 Chisholm's decorations
(IWM OMD 2623–2629)

47 Bérenger's helmet
(IWM UNI 8199)

48 Short VC's helmet
(IWM UNI 11312)

49 Startin's cudgel
(WEA 2160)

50 French 75mm gun
(IWM ORD 125)

51 Eastern Front postcard
(IWM EPH 947)

52 Nevill's football
(Museum of the Queen's (RWS)
Regiment)

53 Cope's jacket
(IWM UNI 10830)

54 Film programme
(IWM K 93/1572)

55 Army rations (IWM EPH 4379
and EPH 7442)

56 Douglas the dummy
(IWM EPH 3863)

57 Phrase book
(IWM K 76194)

58 Clayton's chalice
(Toc H, Poperinghe)

59 Body Density Map
(IWM 57c edition 2 M.5/761)

60 Bairnsfather cartoon
(Nigel Steel)

61 Remnant of HMS *Indefatigable*
(IWM MAR 72)

62 U-boat wireless receiver
(IWM COM 78)

63 Thomas's last words
(National Library of Wales)

64 Surrender document
(IWM DOCS Special Misc X)

65 Model prime ministers
(IWM EPH 3255 and EPH 9361)

66 Stars and stripes
(IWM FLA 5468)

67 Bolshevik banner
(IWM FLA 2055)

68 Culley's Sopwith Camel
(IWM 2010.275.1)

69 Vimy trench mortar
(IWM ORD 52)

70 Toy *poilu*
(IWM 6282)

71 German officer's cap
(IWM UNI 9414)

72 Hassell's tank mask
(IWM EQU 1654)

73 Simplex locomotive
(IWM 4109.71.1)

74 Aerial camera
(IWM PHO 26)

75 Highgate's charge sheet
(The National Archives)

76 Sassoon's revolver
(IWM FIR 11852)

77 Singer Sargent's *Gassed*
(IWM ART 1460)

78 Hanukkah lamp
(IWM EPH 6879)

79 Lawrence's rifle
(IWM FIR 8255, loan from Royal
Collection)

80 Nevinson's *The Food Queue*
(IWM ART 840)

81 Egg ration card
(IWM K12/1278)

82 President's 14 Points (Library
of Congress, Washington DC)

83 Dazzle ship model
(IWM MOD 2474)

84 Haig's order
(IWM K11670/130 EPH. C. PERS
– Rare B)

85 Haig's toby jug
(IWM EPH 8727)

86 Richthofen's engine
(IWM 2020.165.1)

87 Mark V tank
(IWM 4100.90.1)

88 German shoulder straps
(IWM EPH 9319)

89 Saladin's wreath
(IWM EPH 4338)

90 *Ersatz* nightdress
(IWM UNI 11991)

91 Queen Mary's flag
(FLA 5409, loan from Royal
Collection)

92 Election poster
(IWM PST 12171)

93 Orpen's To the *Unknown
British Soldier*
(IWM ART 4438)

94 Seagull gun
(FIR 11624)

95 A new stamp
(Mark Hawkins-Dady)

96 Kaiser's crown
(IWM EPH 9457)

97 Agar's boat
(IWM MAR 563)

98 Néry gun
(IWM ORD 102)

99 Miller's cross
(IWM EPH 8612)

100 Lutyens' Cenotaph sketch
(IWM ART 3991 b)

PICTURE ACKNOWLEDGEMENTS

akg-images Erich Lessing 33.
Alamy The Print Collector 115.
By permission of **The National
Library of Wales** 263. **Corbis**
152, 165, 303, 345, 8; Bettmann
31, 35, 53, 281, 353; dpa/dpa 36;
Museum of Flight 285; STR/
Keystone 405. **Getty Images**
Alinari via Getty Images 381;
Apic 204; A. R. Coster/Topical
Press Agency/Hulton Archive
315; Bob Thomas/Popperfoto
427; Central Press/Hulton
Archive 47, 264; De Agostini
382; Fotosearch 101; Gamma-
Keystone via Getty Images 390;
General Photographic Agency/
Hulton Archive 290; Henry
Guttmann/Hulton Archive 22,
348; Hulton Archive 15, 27, 83,
128, 149, 329, 397, 408; John
Warwick Brooke 298; London
Expressa/Hulton Archive 43;
Mondadori via Getty Images
116, 277; Oesterreichsches
Volkshochschularchiv/Imagno
84; P. Otsup/Slava Katamidze
Collection 413; Popperfoto 269,
322, 401; Roger Viollet 422;
Three Lions 394; Time & Life
Pictures 2 background, 372;
Topical Press Agency 19, 38;
Topical Press Agency/Hulton

Archive 272, 338, 387; UIG via
Getty Images 371; Universal
History Archive 141. **Imperial
War Museums** 3 (UNI 11312),
10 (Q 81771), 21 (UNI 12198), 25
(FEQ 144), 29 (PST 6964), 41
above (CUR 12701), 41 below
(CUR 12700), 45 (PST 2735), 49
(EPH 3122), 51 (ORD 114), 55
(UNI 12643), 59 (UNI 12209),
63 (PST 13606), 64 (Q 53271),
67 (EQU 714), 69 (Q 51200), 71
(4107.5.1), 73 (Q 57328), 75 (EPH
2171), 77 (Q 22687), 79 (DOCS
E Rowden), 81 (EPHEM 00488
and EPHEM 00505), 87 (WEA
1272/1), 89 (EPH 9011), 91 (Q
67818), 93 (OMD 6240-6250),
95 (Q 23732), 96 (Q 13622), 99
(EPH 9032), 103 (UNI 12252),
104 (Q 24191), 107 (FLA 2038),
109 (HU 53360), 111 (Q 13622),
113 (UNI 12281), 118 (FIR
9205/3), 121 (Q 31865), 123 (UNI
11978), 125 (Q 20220), 126 (FIR
11621), 131 (UNI 9694), 133 (Q
27854), 135 (MUN 3281), 137
(Q 30011), 138 (EPH 5245), 143
(DOCS Edith Cavell), 145 (EPH
10292), 147 (DOCS W Harrison),
151 (ORD 108), 155 (FIR 8100),
157 (Q 3987), 159 (FLA 394),
161 (Q 67057), 163 (FEQ 5255),

167 (EPH 4377), 169 (Q 48951),
171 (DOCS 2ND LIEUTENANT E C
JACKSON), 172 (HU 63277B), 175
(COM 176), 177 (Q 2750), 179
(FEQ 854), 181 (FEQ 874), 182
(E(AUS) 1681), 185 (EPH 810),
187 (Q 1598), 189 (COM 1068),
190 (E(AUS) 668), 192 (OMD
2623-2629), 195 (Q 9221), 196
(Q 1071), 199 (UNI 8199), 201
(Q 1778), 203 (UNI 11312), 207
(WEA 2160), 211 (ORD 125), 213
(Q 23760), 214 (ART 4415), 217
(EPH 947), 223 (Q 79501), 225
(UNI 10830), 226 (Q 70164), 229
(K 93/1572), 231 (Q 5575), 233
LEFT (EPH 7442), 233 RIGHT
(EPH 4379), 235 (EPH 3863),
237 (CO 2013), 239 (K 76194),
243 (Q 1152), 245 (57C EDITION
2 M.5/761), 247 (Q 721), 250 (Q
30515), 253 (MAR 72), 255 (SP
1592), 256 (SP 1708), 259 (COM
78), 267 (DOCS Special Misc
X), 271 (left, EPH 9361; right,
EPH 3255), 275 (FLA 5468), 279
(FLA 2055), 283 (2010.275.1),
287 (ORD 52), 292 (EPH
6282), 295 (UNI 9414), 297 (Q
2901), 301 (EQU 1654), 305
(4109.71.1.3), 306 (E(AUS) 844),
309 (PHO 26), 311 (Q 26945),
317 (FIR 11852), 320 (ART

1460), 325 (Q 1464), 327 (EPH
6879), 330 (FIR 8255), 333 (Q
60212), 334 (Q 65857), 337 (ART
840), 341 (K12/1278), 346 (MOD
2474), 351 (K11670/130 EPH. C.
PERS - Rare B), 354 (Q 47997),
357 (EPH 8727), 359 (Q 1065),
361(2020.165.1), 363 (Q 42284),
365 (4100.90.1), 369 (EPH 9319),
375 (EPH 4338), 379 (UNI
11991), 385 (FLA 5409), 389
(PST 12171), 393 (ART 4438),
399 (FIR 11624), 405 (EPH
9457), 410 (MAR 563), 414 (ORD
102), 416 (Q 20539), 419 (EPH
8612), 421 (Q 47901), 425 (ART
3991b). **Library of Congress**
343. **Mark Hawkins-Dady**
403. **Mary Evans Picture
Library** Epic/Tallandier 56;
Pump Park Photography 209,
319; Robert Hunt Collection 61;
Robert Hunt Collection/Imperial
War Museum 366. **National
Museums Northern Ireland
Collection, Ulster Museum** 16.
Nick Pope 221. **Nigel Steel** 249.
Royal Collection Trust,
©**Her Majesty Queen Elizabeth
II** 2013 13. ©**Talbot House**
241. **The National Archives**
WO71/387/1 313. **TopFoto** 289,
377; ullsteinbild 219, 261.